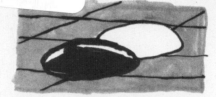

Takeshi Obata

I hear that expensive Go stones are made from carved shells. You get one stone from one shell. Stones are a simple round shape. But there must be a tremendous amount of labor involved in finishing the stones.
—Takeshi Obata

t all began when Yumi Hotta played a pick-up game of Go with her father-in-law. As she was learning how to play, Ms. Hotta thought it might be fun to create a story around the traditional board game. More confident in her storytelling abilities than her drawing skills, she submitted the beginnings of **Hikaru no Go** to **Weekly Shonen Jump**'s Story King Award. The Story King Award is an award that picks the best story, manga, character design and youth (under 15) manga submissions every year in Japan. As fate would have it, Ms. Hotta's story (originally named, "*Kokonotsu no Hoshi*"), was a runner-up in the "Story" category of the Story King Award. Many years earlier, Takeshi Obata was a runner-up for the Tezuka Award, another Japanese manga contest sponsored by **Weekly Shonen Jump** and **Monthly Shonen Jump**. An editor assigned to Mr. Obata's artwork came upon Ms. Hotta's story and paired the two for a full-fledged manga about Go. The rest is modern Go history.

HIKARU NO GO VOL. 4
SHONEN JUMP Manga Edition

This graphic novel contains material that was originally published in English from
SHONEN JUMP #25 to #29.

STORY BY YUMI HOTTA
ART BY TAKESHI OBATA
Supervised by YUKARI UMEZAWA (5 Dan)

Translation & English Adaptation/Andy Nakatani
English Script Consultant/Janice Kim (3 Dan)
Touch-Up Art & Lettering/Adam Symons
Cover & Interior Design/Courtney Utt
Editor/Livia Ching, Yuki Takagaki

Published by VIZ Media, LLC
P.O. Box 77010
San Francisco, CA 94107

10 9 8 7 6 5 4 3 2
First printing, May 2005
Second printing, June 2012

PARENTAL ADVISORY
HIKARU NO GO is rated A and is
suitable for readers of all ages.
ratings.viz.com

THE WORLD'S
MOST POPULAR MANGA

www.viz.com

www.shonenjump.com

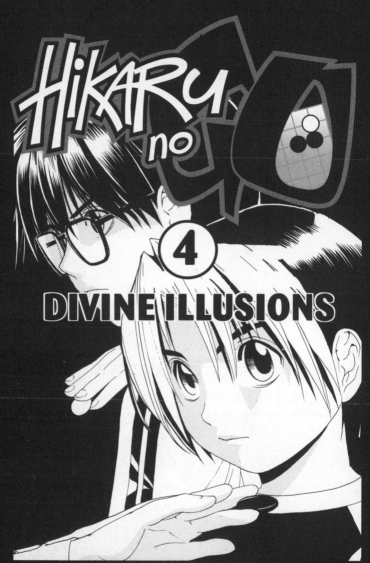

Hikaru no Go

no

4

DIVINE ILLUSIONS

STORY BY **YUMI HOTTA**

ART BY **TAKESHI OBATA**

Supervised by **YUKARI UMEZAWA (5 Dan)**

Character Introductions

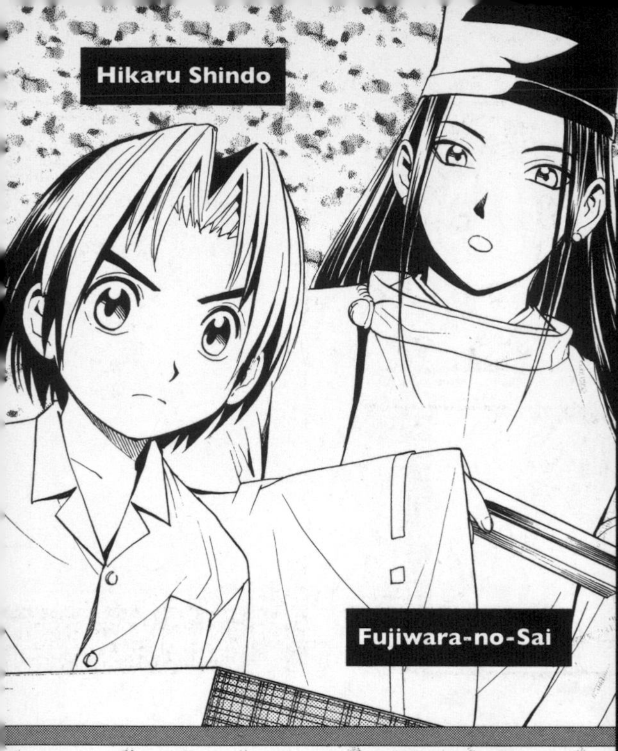
Hikaru Shindo
Fujiwara-no-Sai

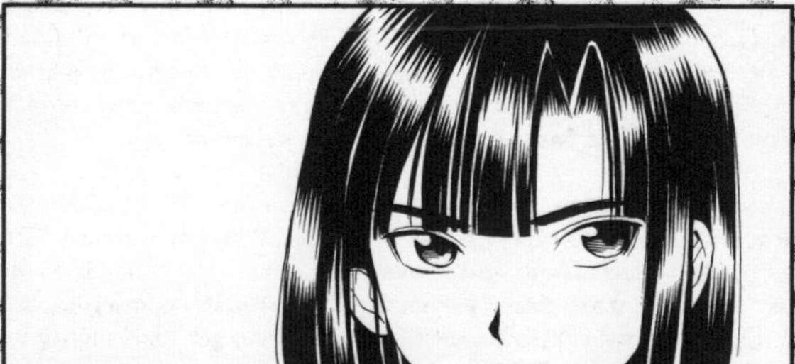
Akira Toya

Akari Fujisaki

Kimihiro Tsutsui

Yuki Mitani

Story Thus Far

Hikaru Shindo is a classic middle school cutup: a poor student and a compulsive prankster. One fateful day, up in his grandfather's attic, he and his friend Akari find an old Go board. Hikaru is the only one who can see the bloodstains on it. He also hears a ghostly voice and sees a misty figure before he faints dead away. When he awakens, Fujiwara-no-Sai, the spirit who haunts the board, has become a part of his consciousness…

Hikaru starts looking for a new member for Haze's Go Club in preparation for another upcoming tournament. Akari discovers that their classmate, Yuki Mitani, can play Go. Unfortunately, Yuki cheats and plays against adults for their money at Shu's Go Salon. Hikaru goes to the salon to make Yuki stop cheating. But Yuki ends up losing big to someone who out-cheats him! Hikaru borrows Sai's strength to get Yuki's money back. By and by, Yuki joins the Haze Go Club. Meanwhile, to face Hikaru in the next tournament, Akira joins Kaio's Go Club. Even if he has to deal with getting picked on by his club mates, Akira perseveres in order to play Hikaru again. When Akira finds out that Hikaru will play in the third position, he forfeits his spot as first position on the Kaio team and his membership in the Club if only he can play Hikaru just once in the third spot. And so the fateful tournament begins!

CONTENTS

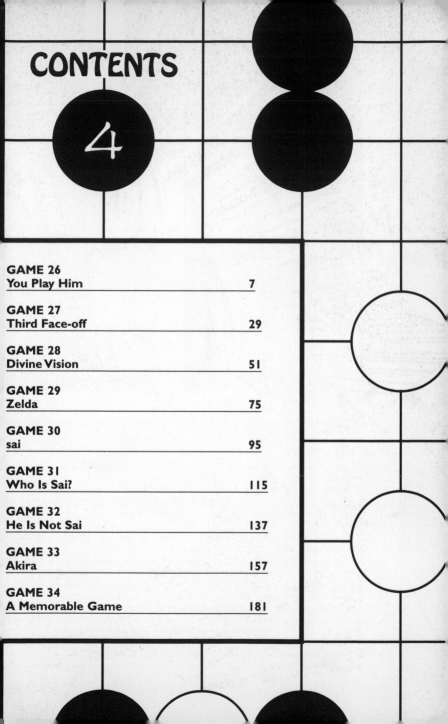

4

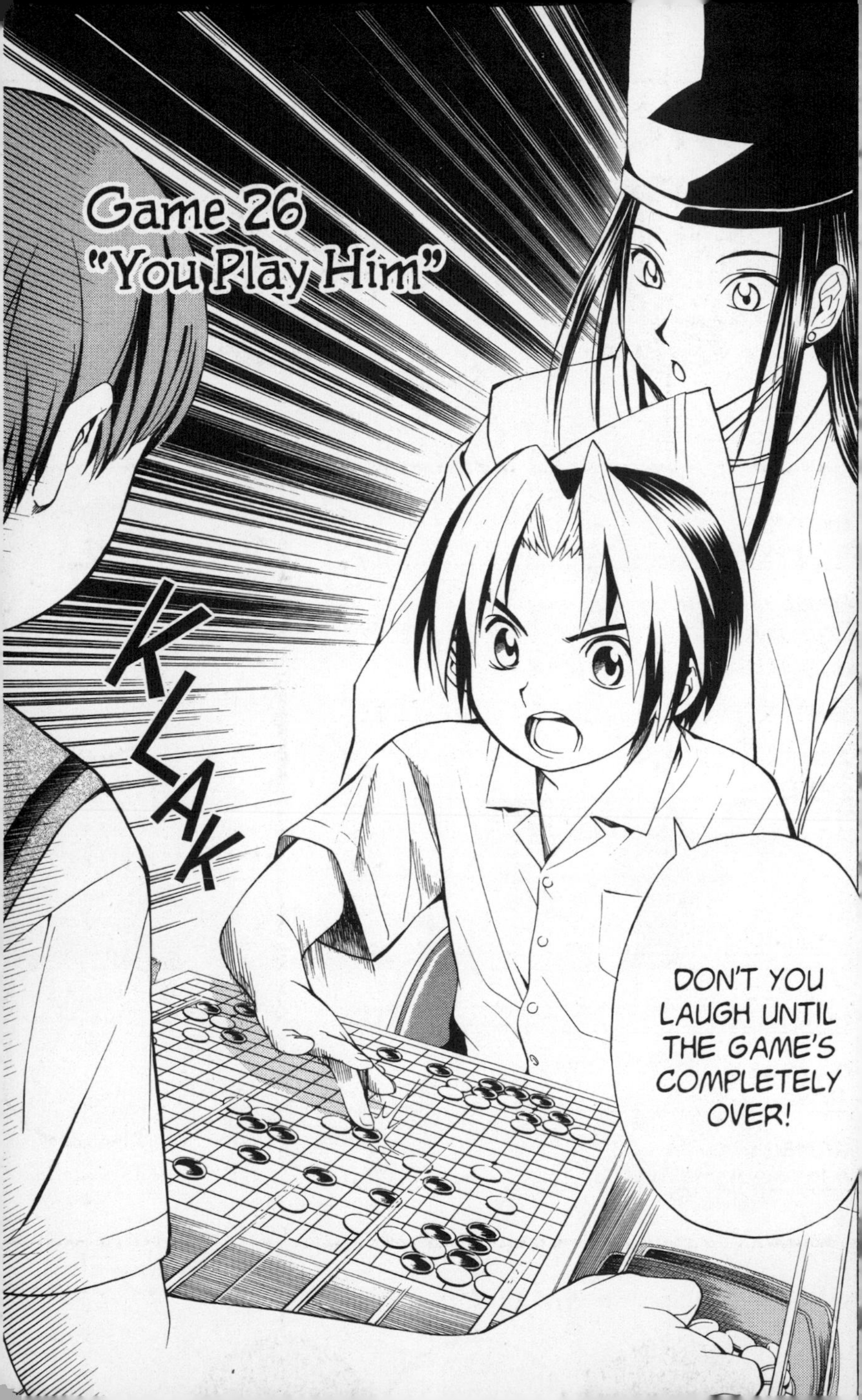
Game 26
"You Play Him"
KLAK
DON'T YOU LAUGH UNTIL THE GAME'S COMPLETELY OVER!

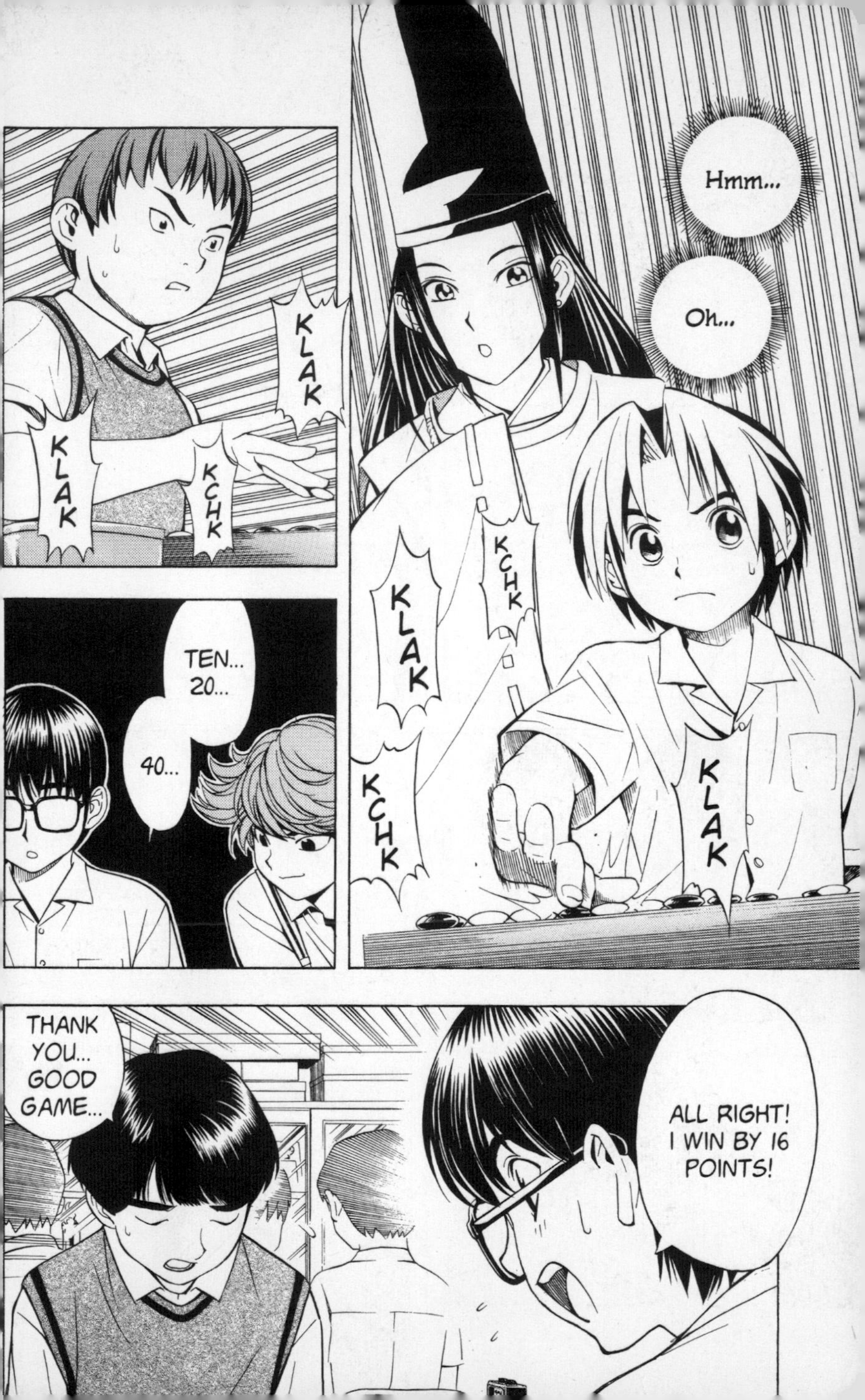
Hmm...
Oh...
KCHK
KLAK
KLAK
KCHK
KLAK
KCHK
KLAK
TEN... 20...
40...
ALL RIGHT! I WIN BY 16 POINTS!
THANK YOU... GOOD GAME...

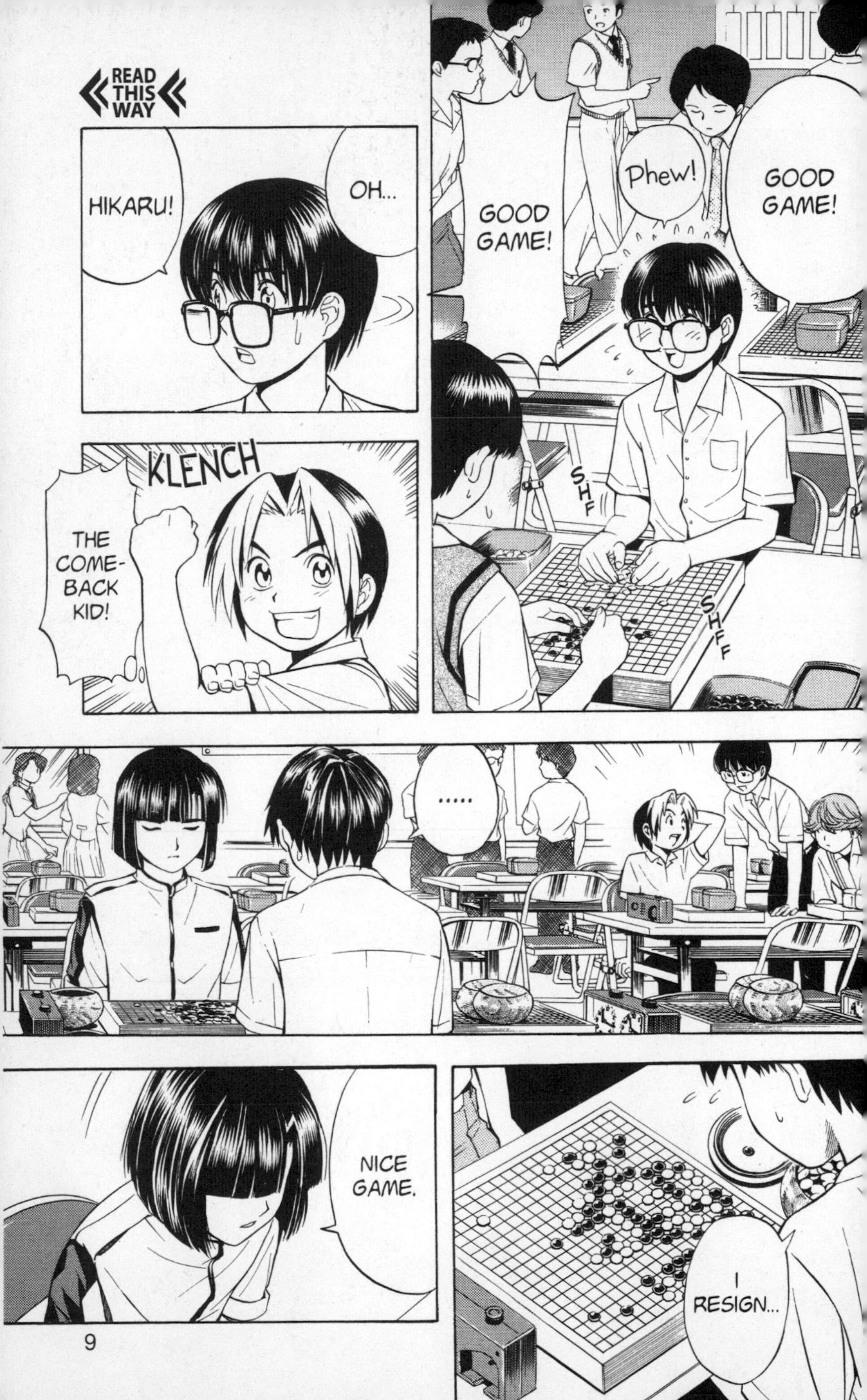

READ THIS WAY
GOOD GAME!
Phew!
GOOD GAME!
SHF
SHFF
OH...
HIKARU!
KLENCH
THE COME-BACK KID!
.....
I RESIGN...
NICE GAME.

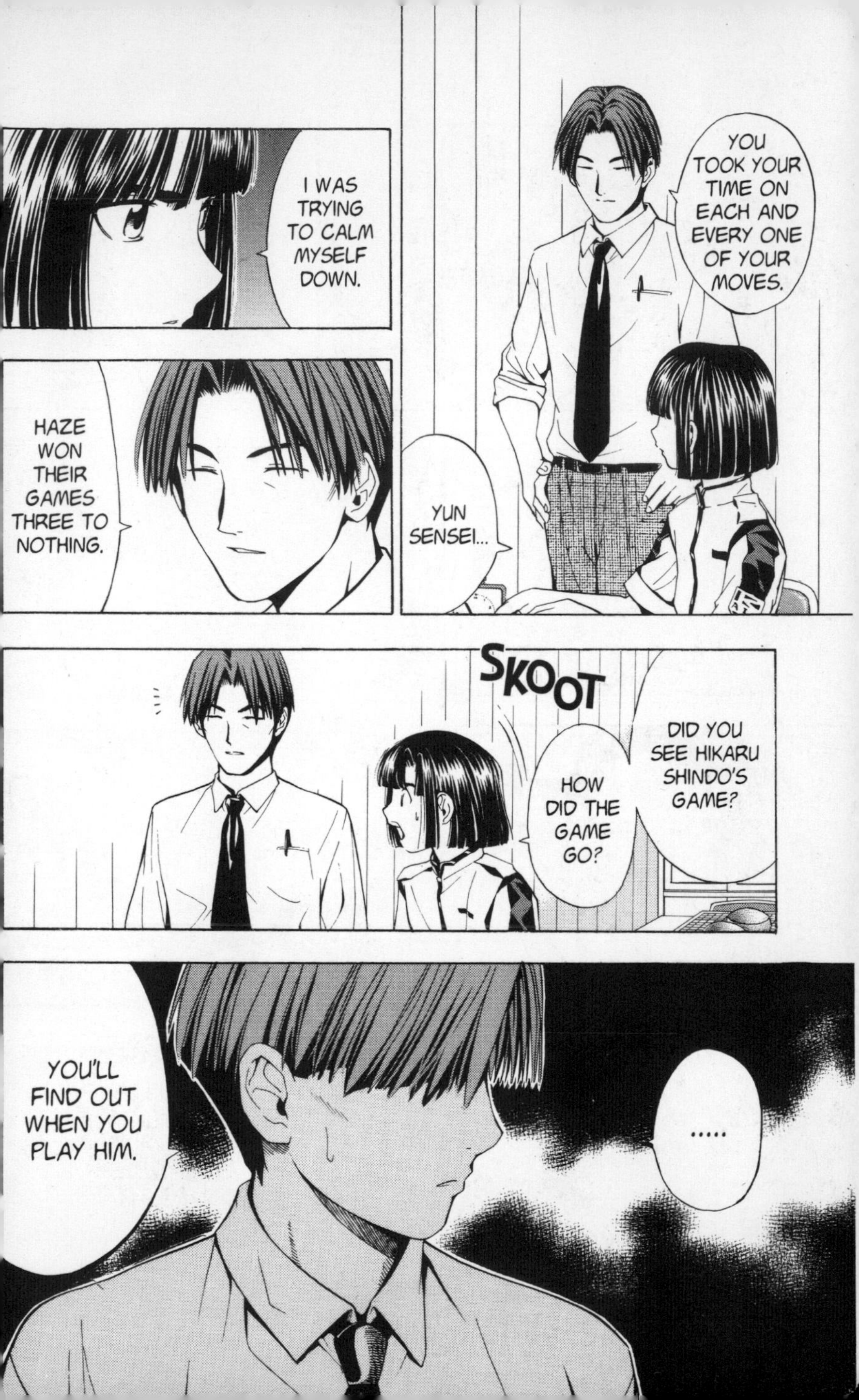
YOU TOOK YOUR TIME ON EACH AND EVERY ONE OF YOUR MOVES.
YUN SENSEI...
I WAS TRYING TO CALM MYSELF DOWN.
HAZE WON THEIR GAMES THREE TO NOTHING.
SKOOT
DID YOU SEE HIKARU SHINDO'S GAME?
HOW DID THE GAME GO?
.....
YOU'LL FIND OUT WHEN YOU PLAY HIM.

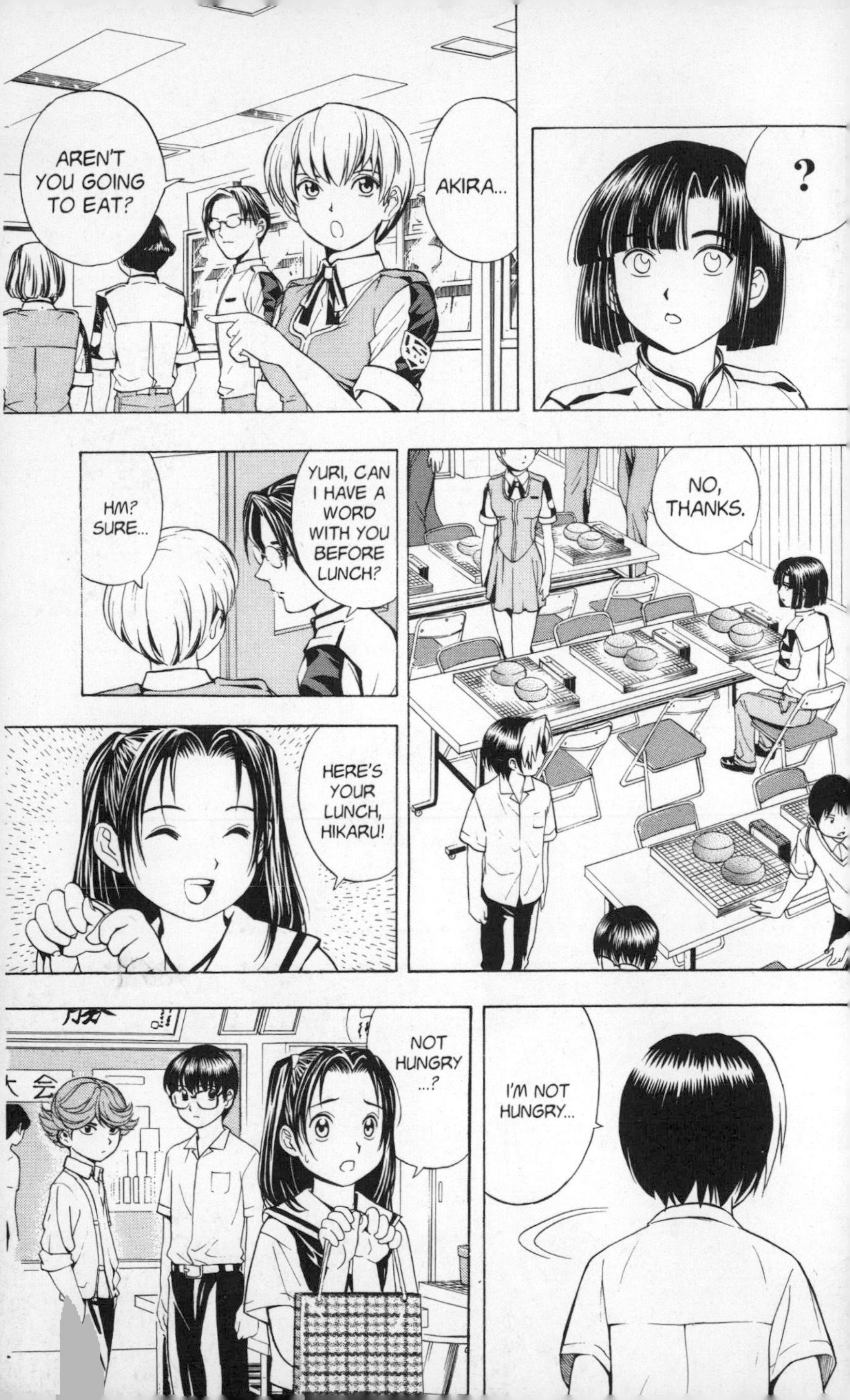
?
AKIRA...
AREN'T YOU GOING TO EAT?
NO, THANKS.
YURI, CAN I HAVE A WORD WITH YOU BEFORE LUNCH?
HM? SURE...
HERE'S YOUR LUNCH, HIKARU!
I'M NOT HUNGRY...
NOT HUNGRY ...?

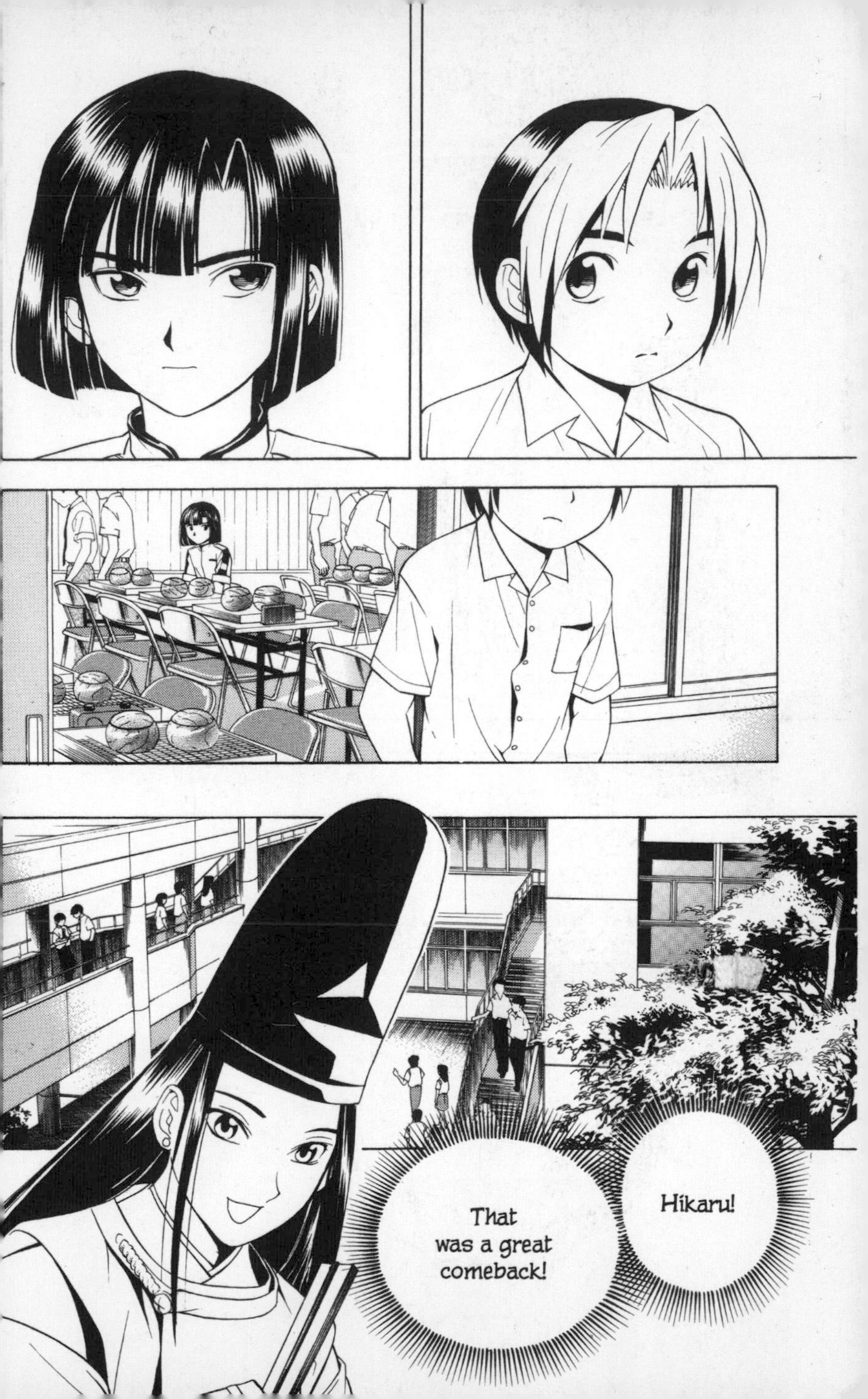
Hikaru!
That was a great comeback!

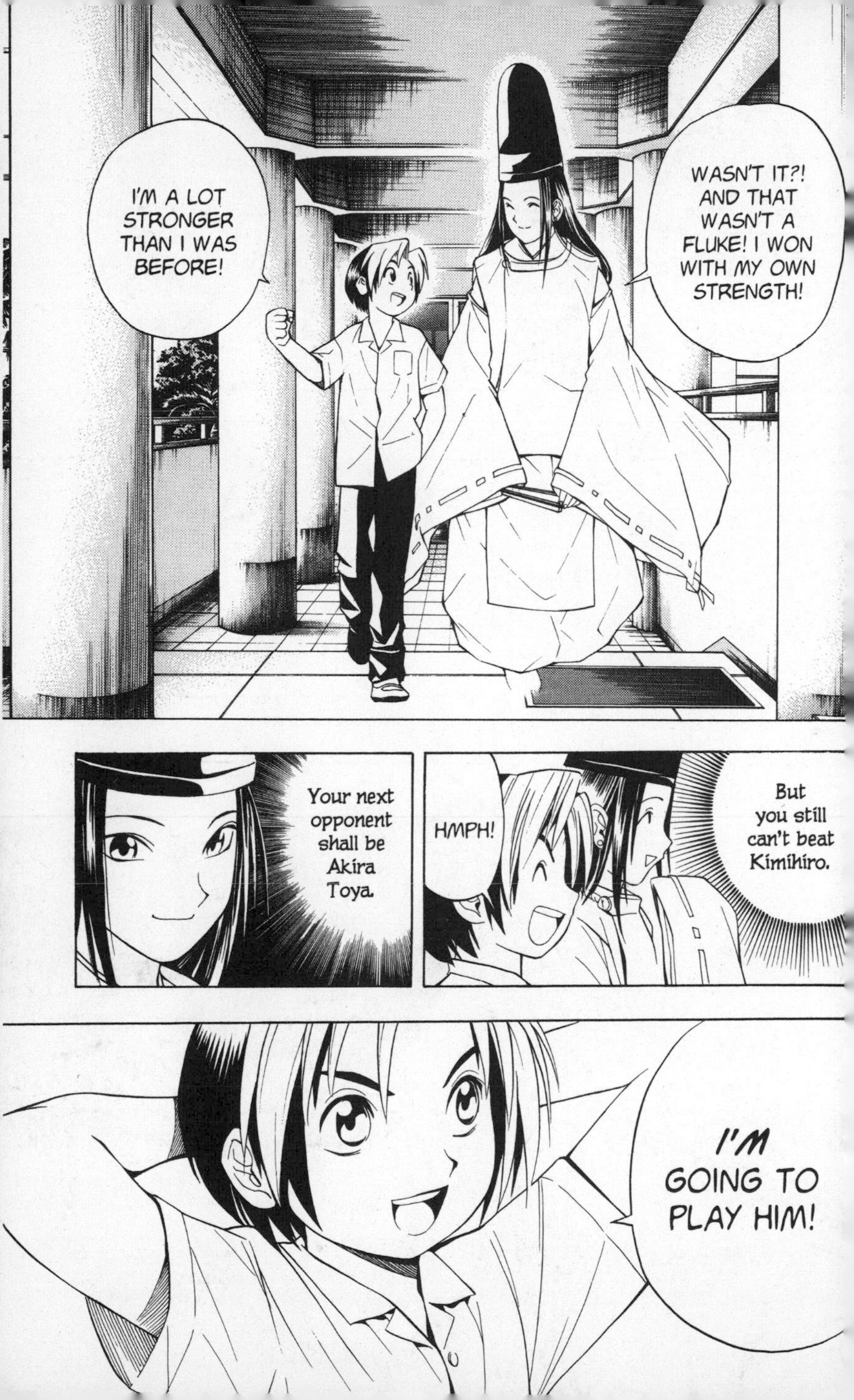
WASN'T IT?! AND THAT WASN'T A FLUKE! I WON WITH MY OWN STRENGTH!
I'M A LOT STRONGER THAN I WAS BEFORE!
But you still can't beat Kimihiro.
HMPH!
Your next opponent shall be Akira Toya.
I'M GOING TO PLAY HIM!

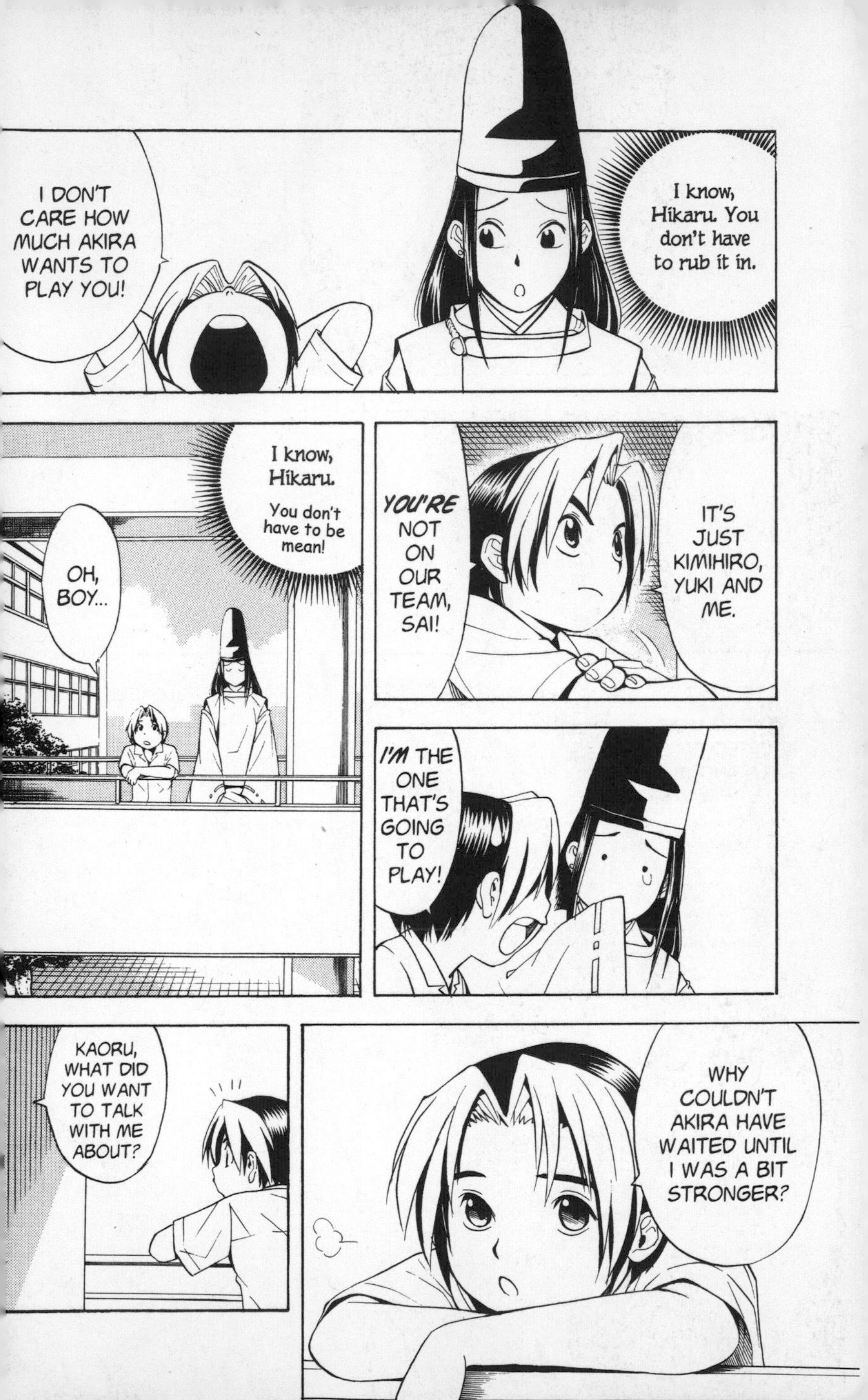
I know, Hikaru. You don't have to rub it in.
I DON'T CARE HOW MUCH AKIRA WANTS TO PLAY YOU!
IT'S JUST KIMIHIRO, YUKI AND ME.
YOU'RE NOT ON OUR TEAM, SAI!
I'M THE ONE THAT'S GOING TO PLAY!
I know, Hikaru. You don't have to be mean!
OH, BOY...
WHY COULDN'T AKIRA HAVE WAITED UNTIL I WAS A BIT STRONGER?
KAORU, WHAT DID YOU WANT TO TALK WITH ME ABOUT?

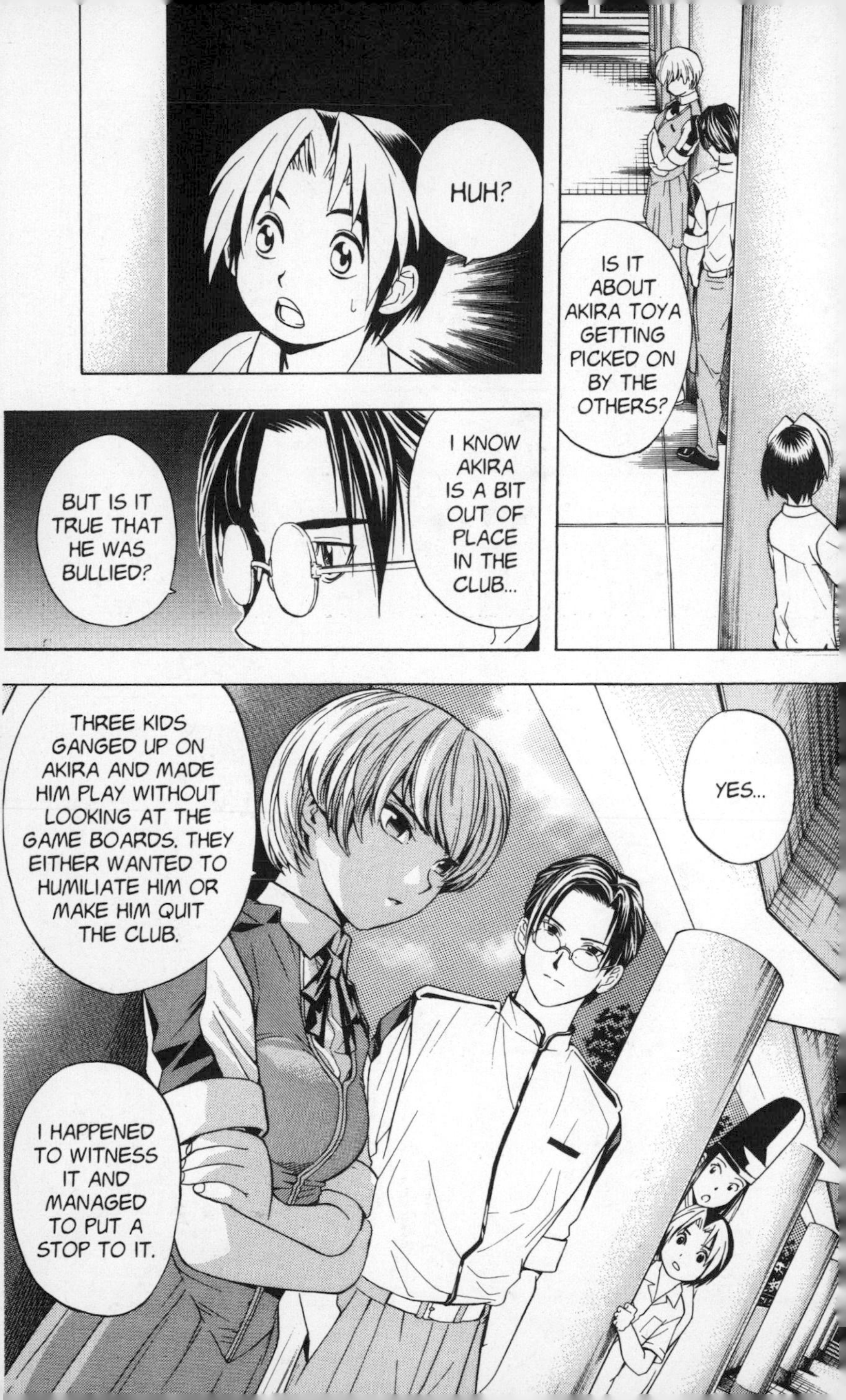
IS IT ABOUT AKIRA TOYA GETTING PICKED ON BY THE OTHERS?
HUH?
I KNOW AKIRA IS A BIT OUT OF PLACE IN THE CLUB...
BUT IS IT TRUE THAT HE WAS BULLIED?
YES...
THREE KIDS GANGED UP ON AKIRA AND MADE HIM PLAY WITHOUT LOOKING AT THE GAME BOARDS. THEY EITHER WANTED TO HUMILIATE HIM OR MAKE HIM QUIT THE CLUB.
I HAPPENED TO WITNESS IT AND MANAGED TO PUT A STOP TO IT.

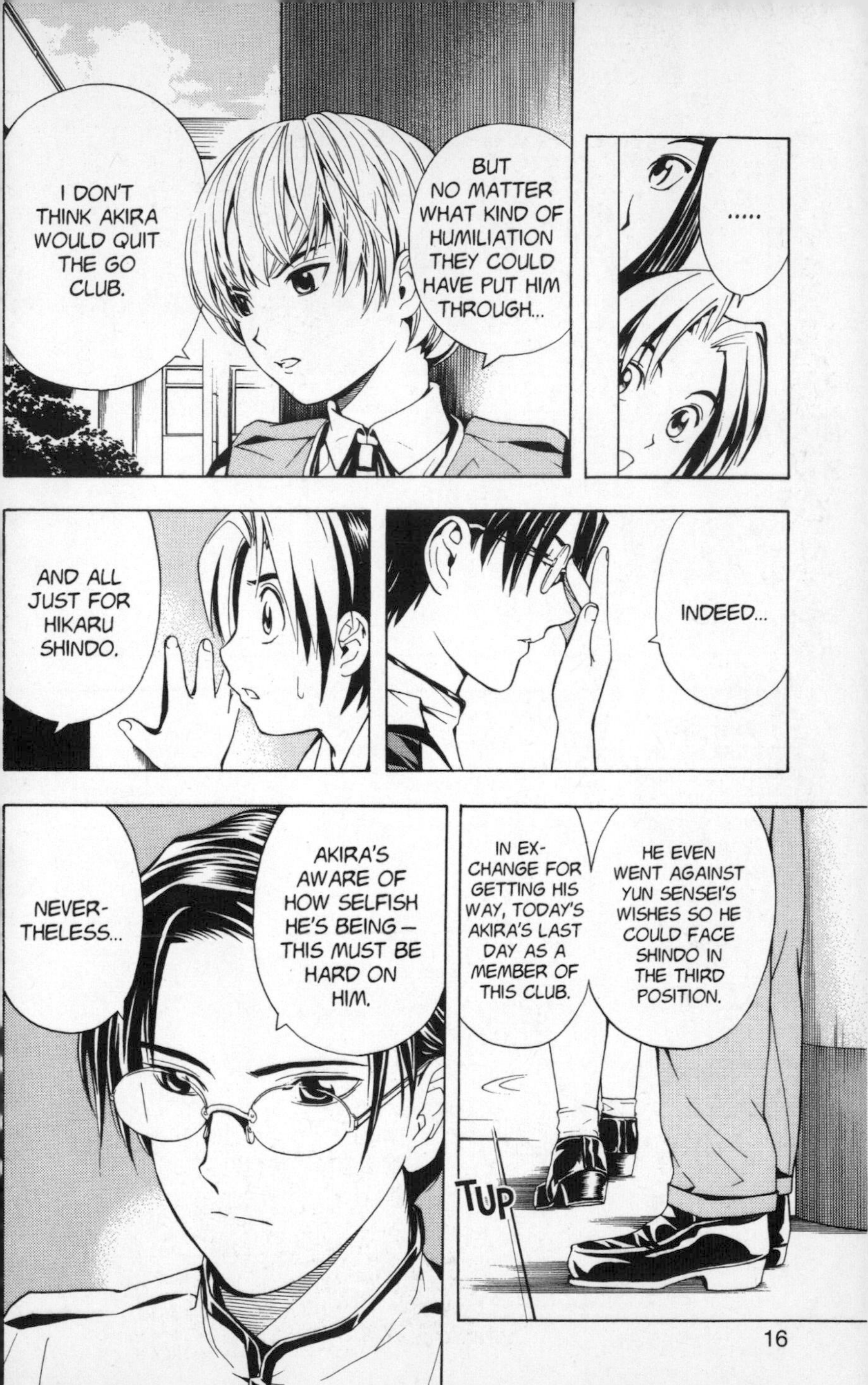
.....
I DON'T THINK AKIRA WOULD QUIT THE GO CLUB.
BUT NO MATTER WHAT KIND OF HUMILIATION THEY COULD HAVE PUT HIM THROUGH...
INDEED...
AND ALL JUST FOR HIKARU SHINDO.
HE EVEN WENT AGAINST YUN SENSEI'S WISHES SO HE COULD FACE SHINDO IN THE THIRD POSITION.
IN EXCHANGE FOR GETTING HIS WAY, TODAY'S AKIRA'S LAST DAY AS A MEMBER OF THIS CLUB.
TUP
AKIRA'S AWARE OF HOW SELFISH HE'S BEING— THIS MUST BE HARD ON HIM.
NEVERTHELESS...

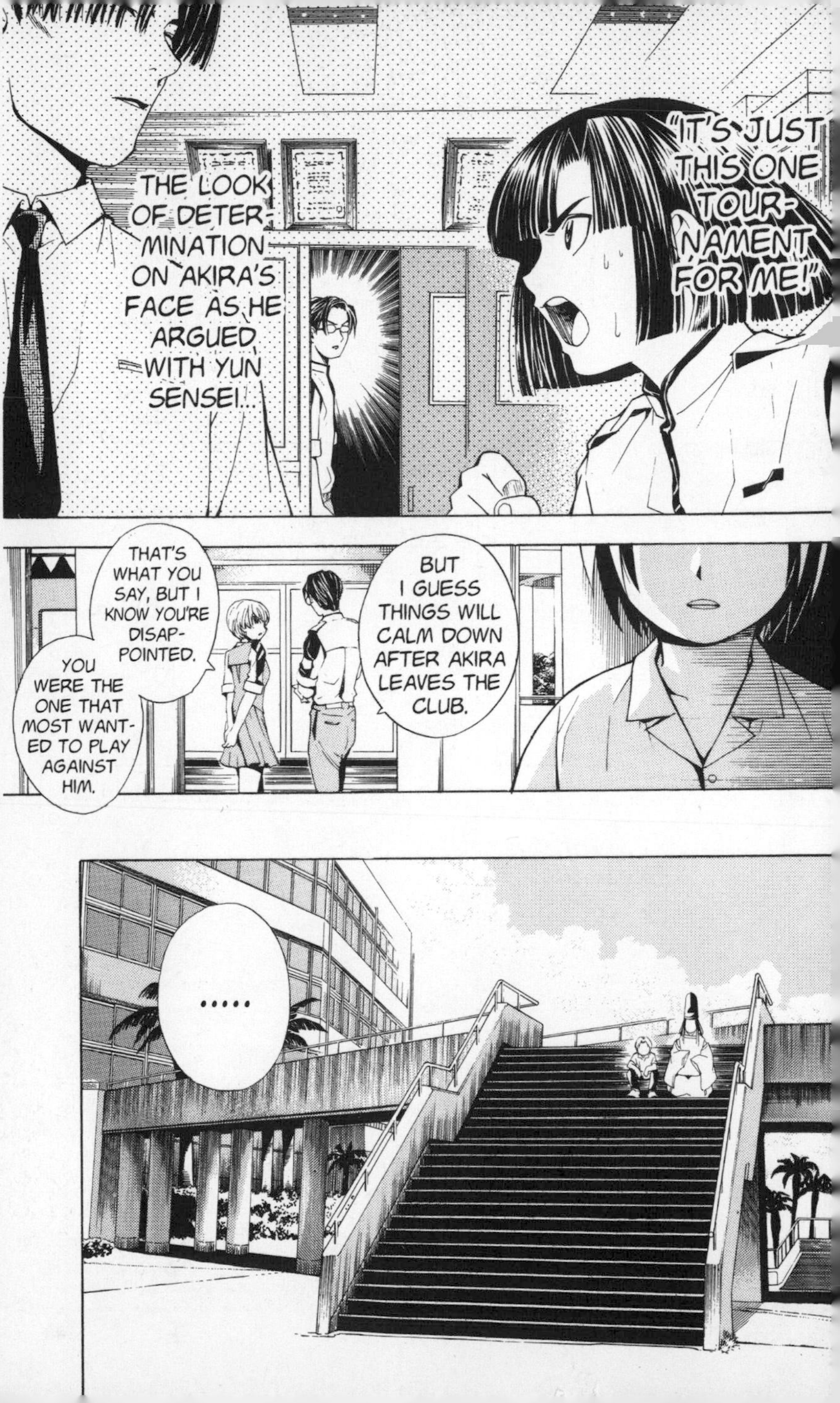
"IT'S JUST THIS ONE TOURNAMENT FOR ME!"
THE LOOK OF DETERMINATION ON AKIRA'S FACE AS HE ARGUED WITH YUN SENSEI...
BUT I GUESS THINGS WILL CALM DOWN AFTER AKIRA LEAVES THE CLUB.
THAT'S WHAT YOU SAY, BUT I KNOW YOU'RE DISAPPOINTED.
YOU WERE THE ONE THAT MOST WANTED TO PLAY AGAINST HIM.
.....

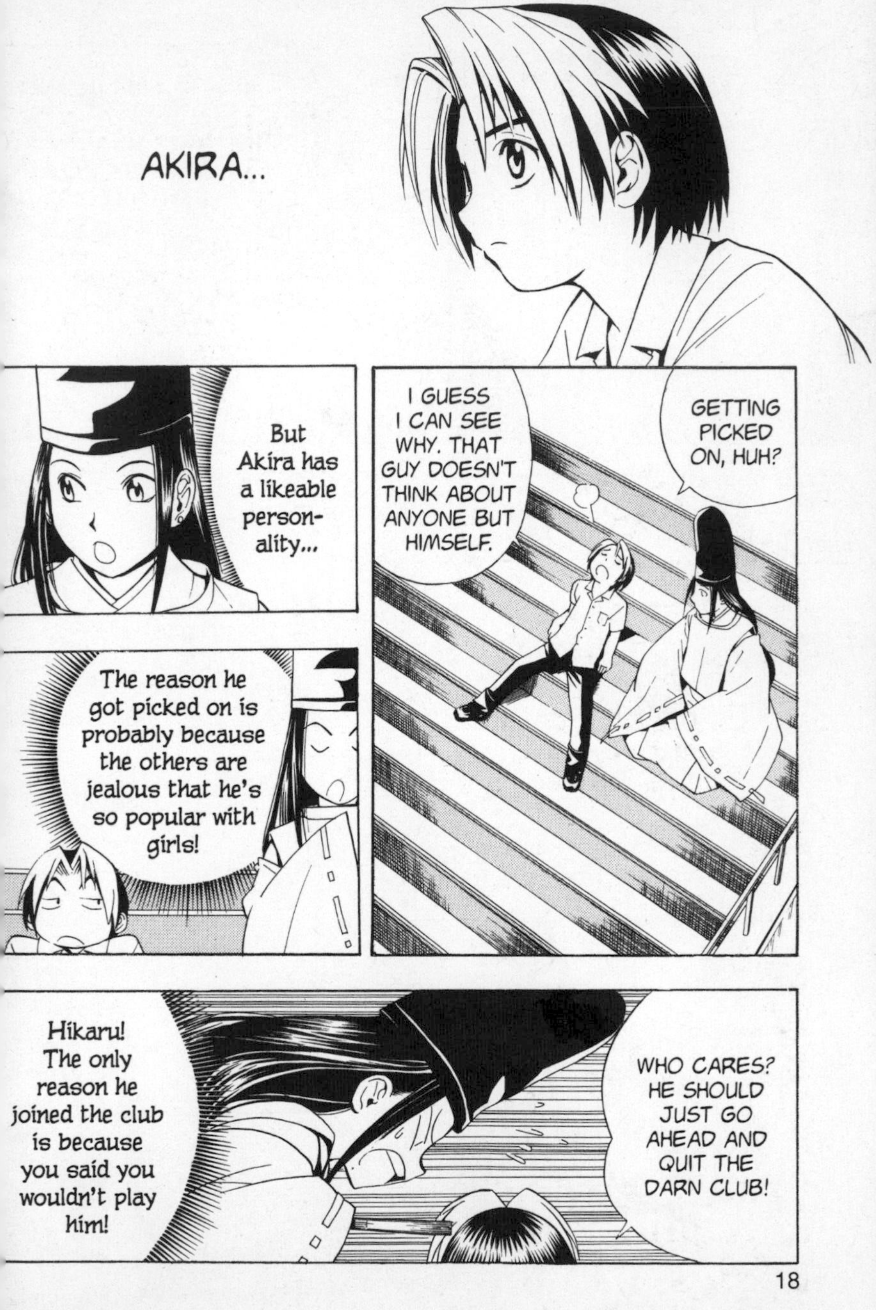
AKIRA...
GETTING PICKED ON, HUH?
I GUESS I CAN SEE WHY. THAT GUY DOESN'T THINK ABOUT ANYONE BUT HIMSELF.
But Akira has a likeable person-ality...
The reason he got picked on is probably because the others are jealous that he's so popular with girls!
WHO CARES? HE SHOULD JUST GO AHEAD AND QUIT THE DARN CLUB!
Hikaru! The only reason he joined the club is because you said you wouldn't play him!

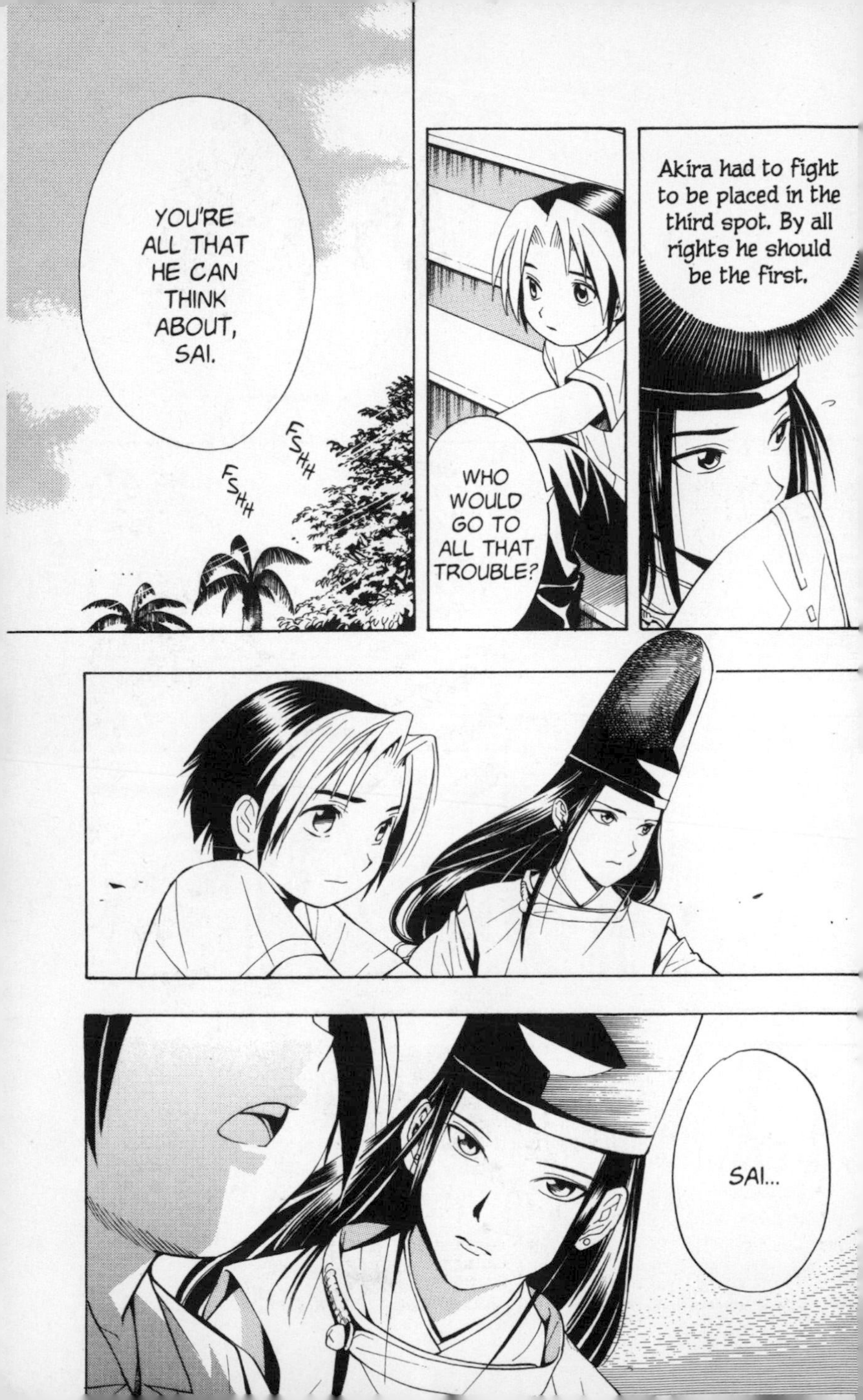
Akira had to fight to be placed in the third spot. By all rights he should be the first.
WHO WOULD GO TO ALL THAT TROUBLE?
YOU'RE ALL THAT HE CAN THINK ABOUT, SAI.
FSHH
FSHH
SAI...

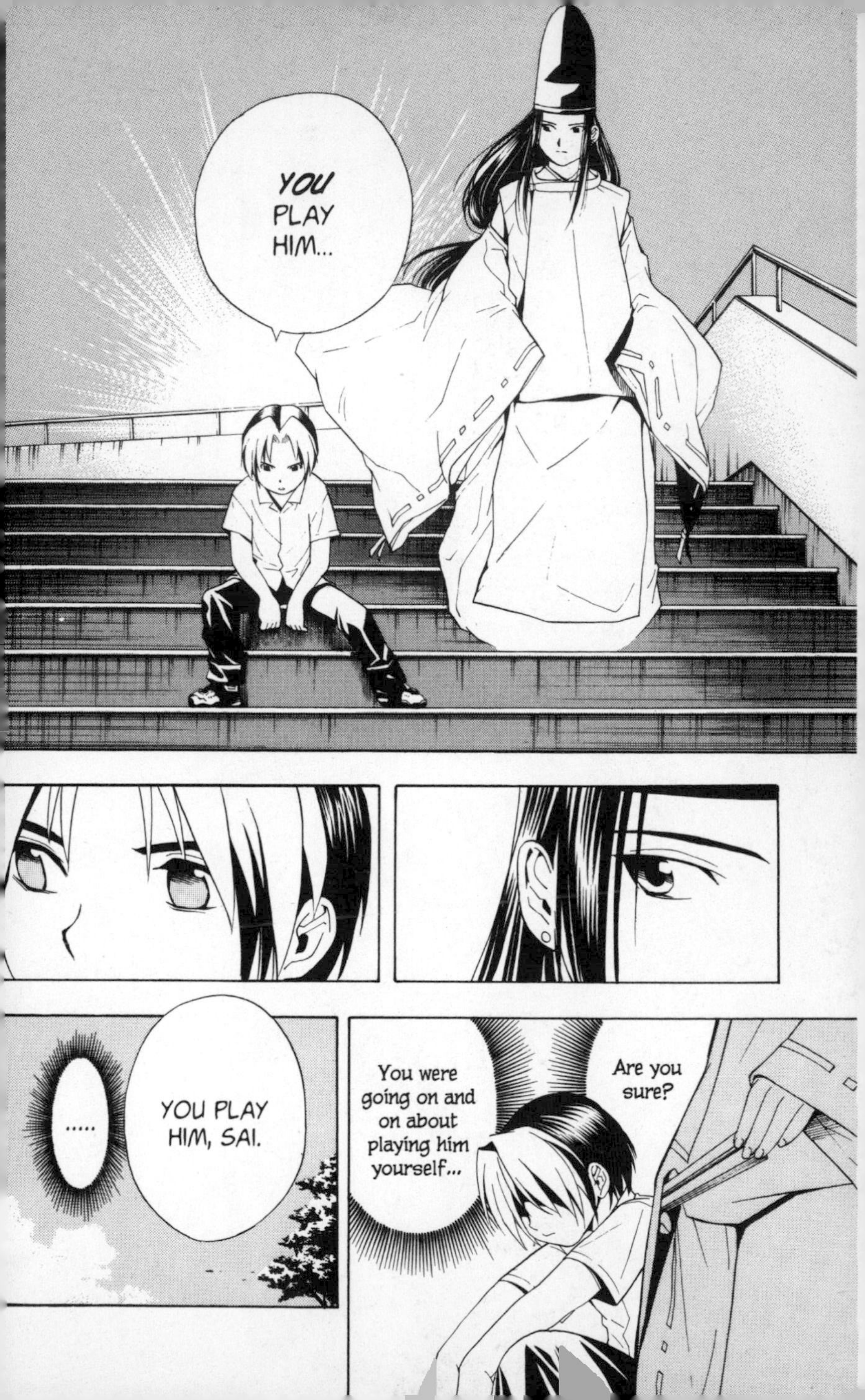
YOU PLAY HIM...
Are you sure?
You were going on and on about playing him yourself...
YOU PLAY HIM, SAI.
......

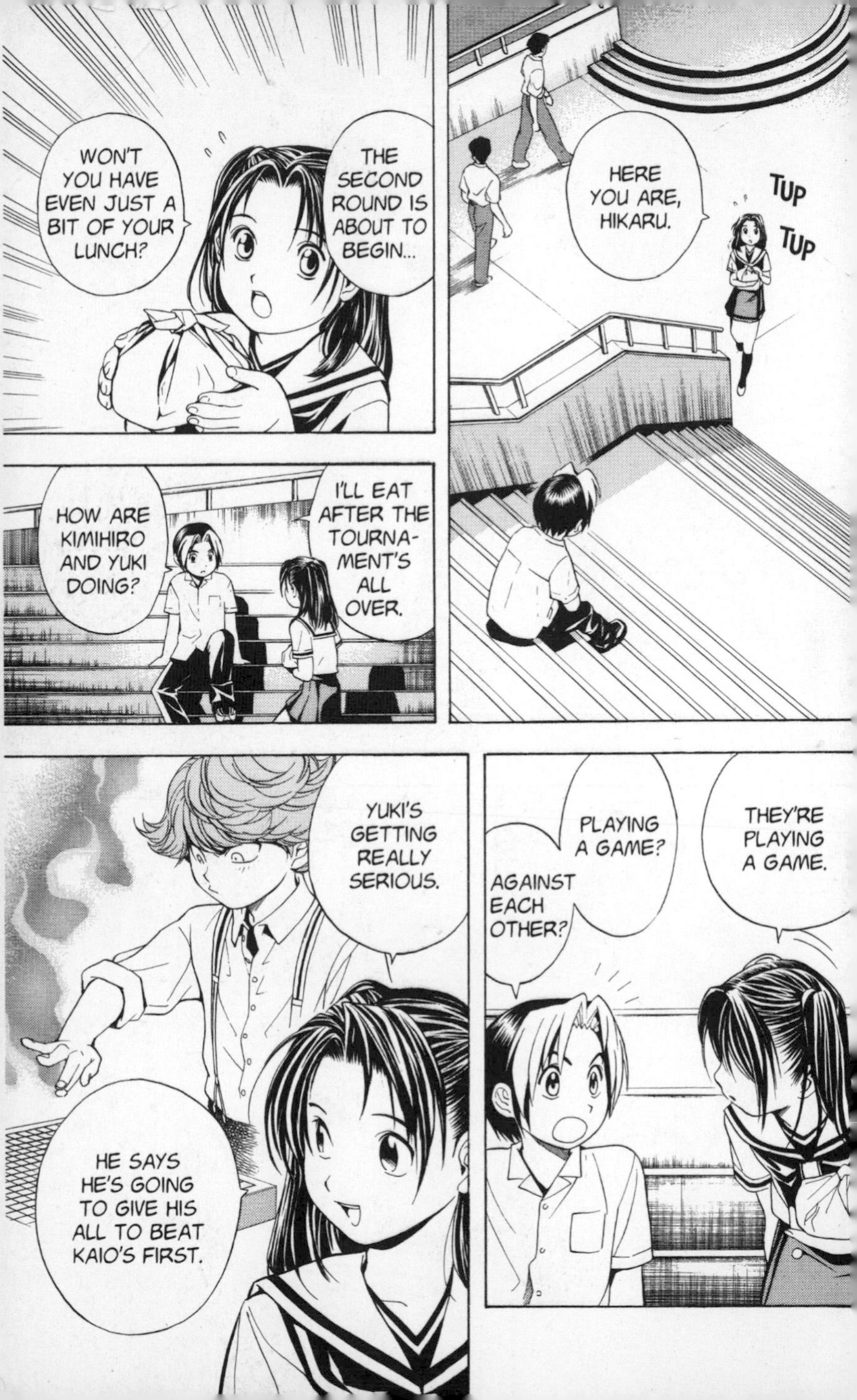
TUP
TUP
HERE YOU ARE, HIKARU.
THE SECOND ROUND IS ABOUT TO BEGIN...
WON'T YOU HAVE EVEN JUST A BIT OF YOUR LUNCH?
I'LL EAT AFTER THE TOURNAMENT'S ALL OVER.
HOW ARE KIMIHIRO AND YUKI DOING?
THEY'RE PLAYING A GAME.
PLAYING A GAME?
AGAINST EACH OTHER?
YUKI'S GETTING REALLY SERIOUS.
HE SAYS HE'S GOING TO GIVE HIS ALL TO BEAT KAIO'S FIRST.

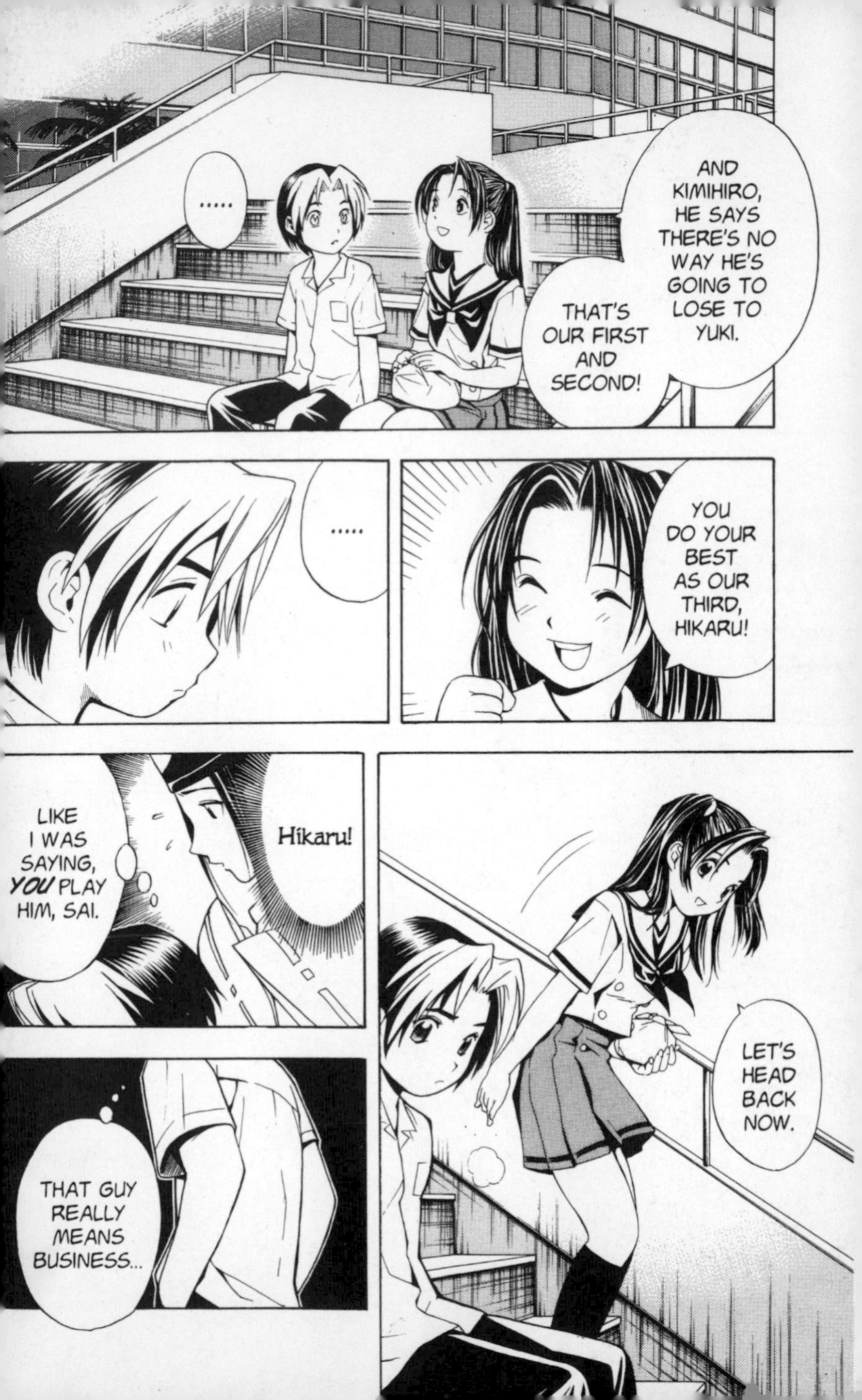
AND KIMIHIRO, HE SAYS THERE'S NO WAY HE'S GOING TO LOSE TO YUKI.
THAT'S OUR FIRST AND SECOND!
.....
YOU DO YOUR BEST AS OUR THIRD, HIKARU!
.....
LET'S HEAD BACK NOW.
Hikaru!
LIKE I WAS SAYING, *YOU* PLAY HIM, SAI.
THAT GUY REALLY MEANS BUSINESS...

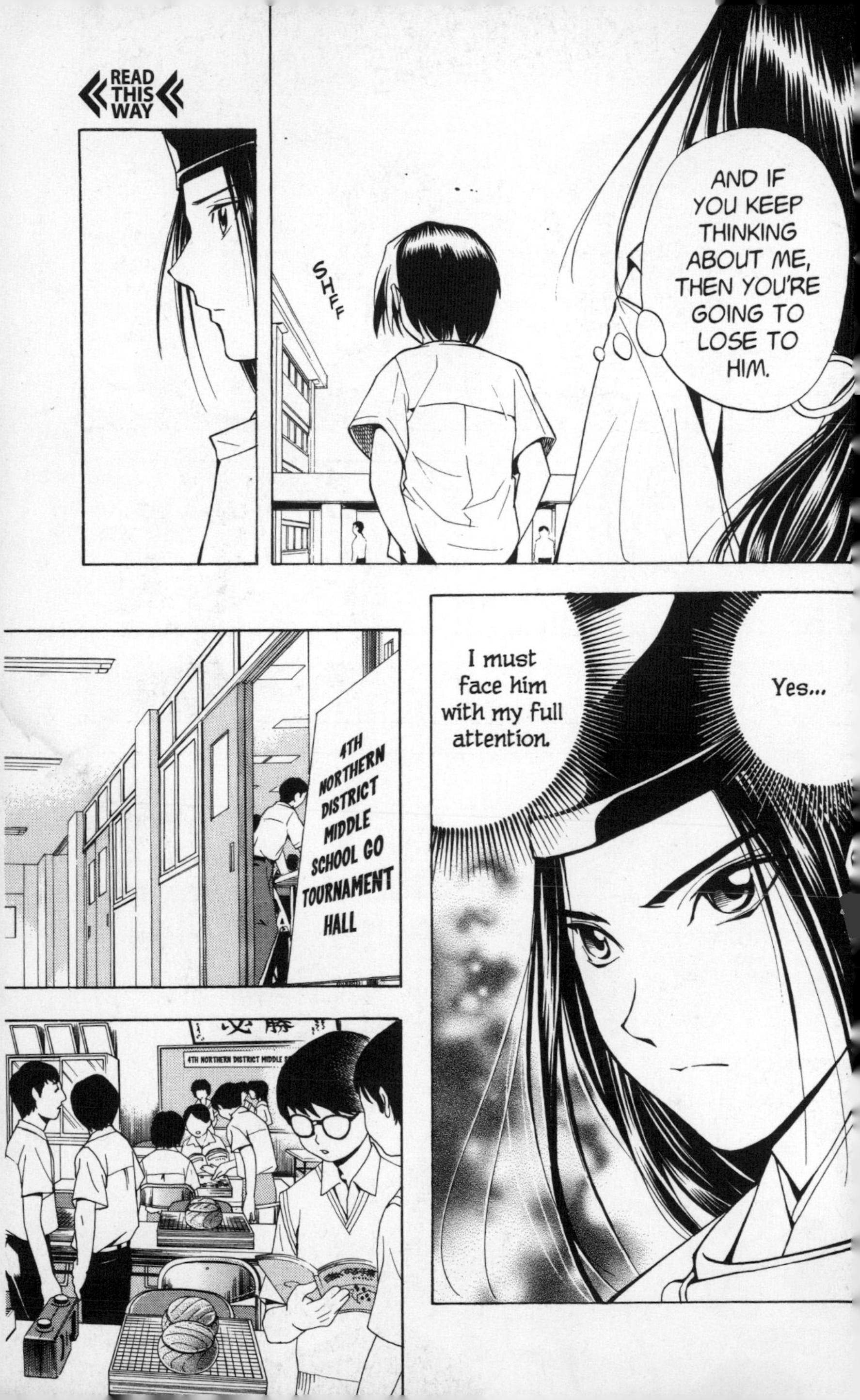

READ THIS WAY
AND IF YOU KEEP THINKING ABOUT ME, THEN YOU'RE GOING TO LOSE TO HIM.
...
SHFF
Yes...
I must face him with my full attention.
4TH NORTHERN DISTRICT MIDDLE SCHOOL GO TOURNAMENT HALL
4TH NORTHERN DISTRICT MIDDLE

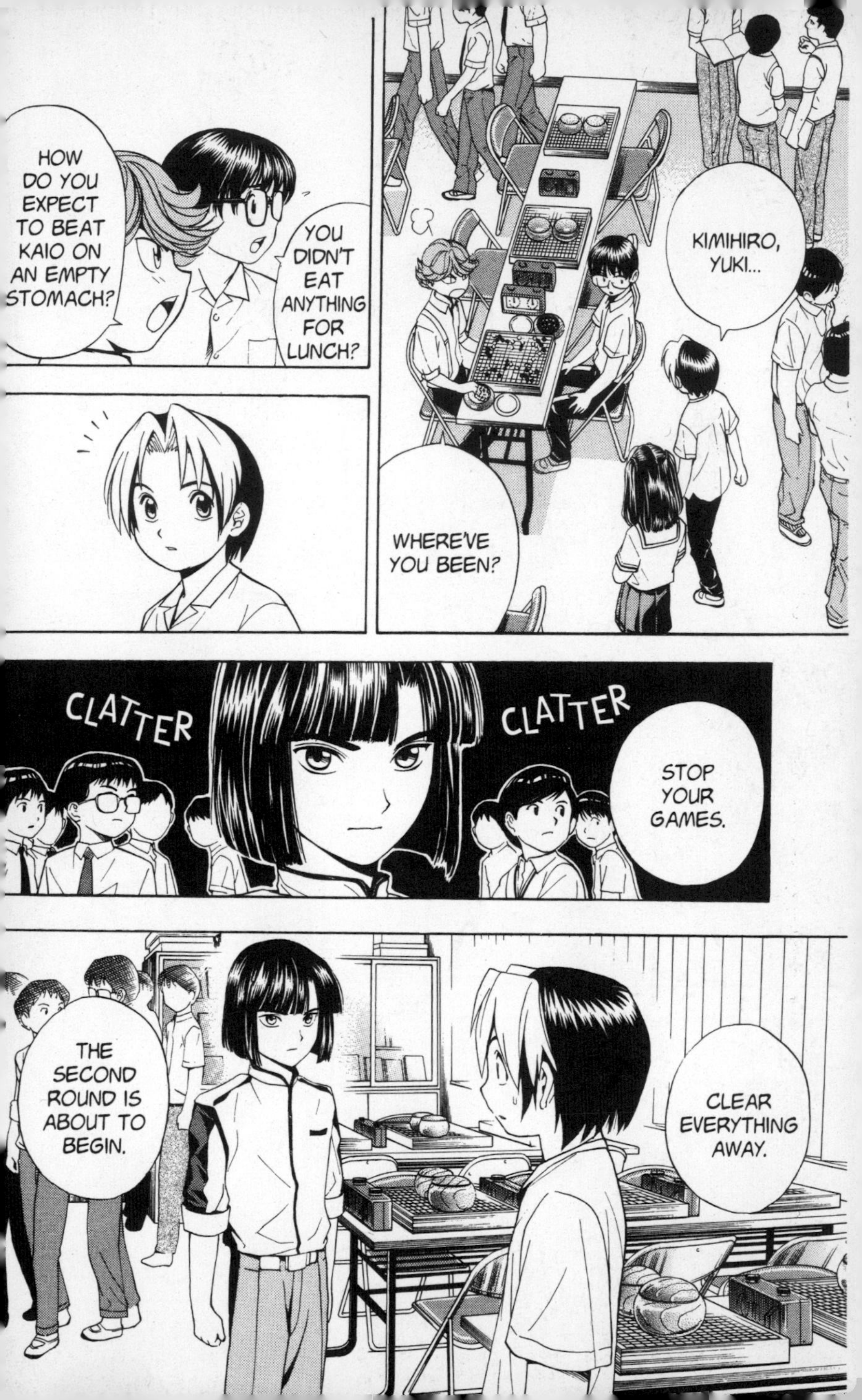
KIMIHIRO, YUKI...
WHERE'VE YOU BEEN?
YOU DIDN'T EAT ANYTHING FOR LUNCH?
HOW DO YOU EXPECT TO BEAT KAIO ON AN EMPTY STOMACH?
CLATTER
STOP YOUR GAMES.
CLATTER
CLEAR EVERYTHING AWAY.
THE SECOND ROUND IS ABOUT TO BEGIN.

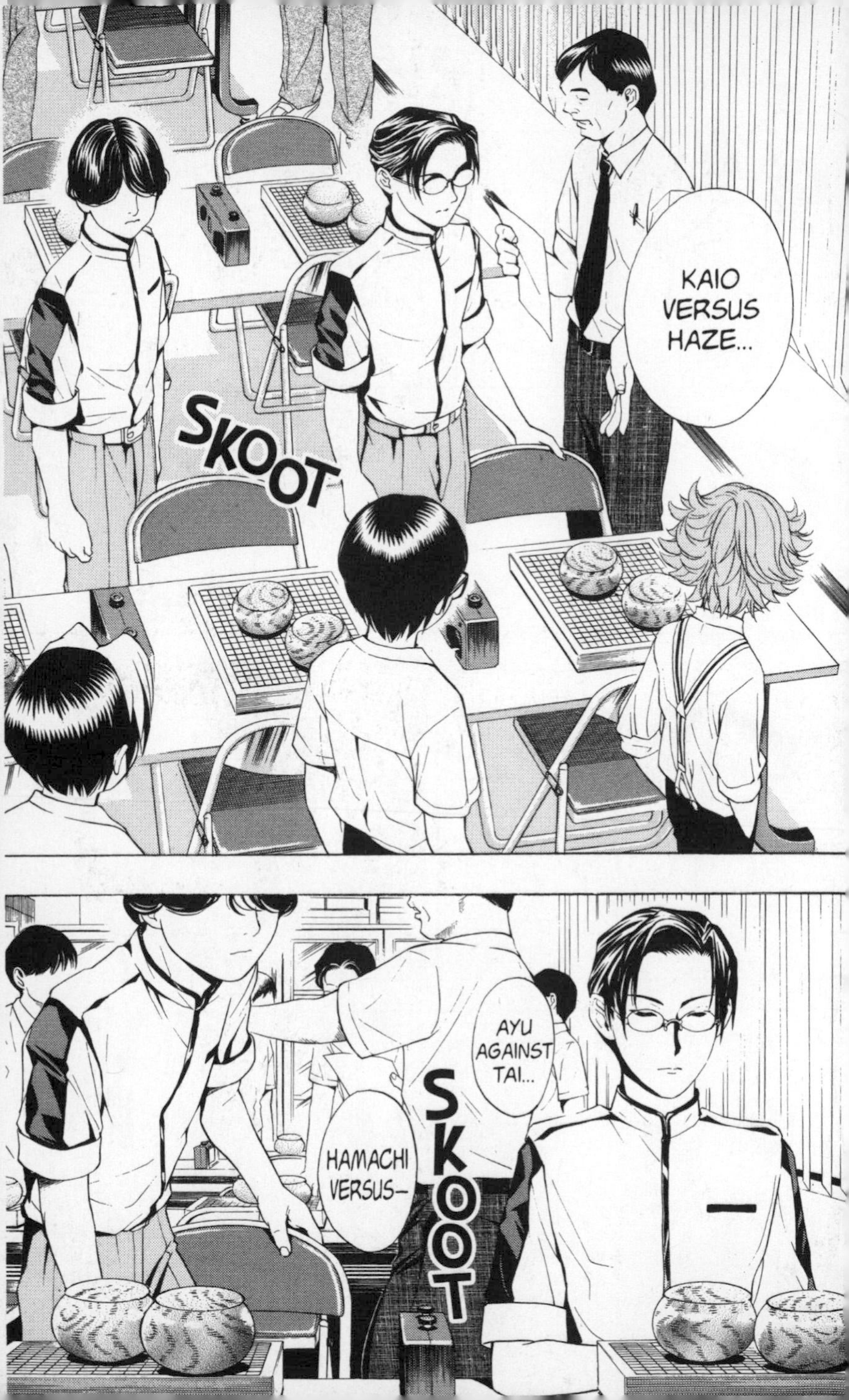
KAIO VERSUS HAZE...
SKOOT
AYU AGAINST TAI...
SKOOT
HAMACHI VERSUS—

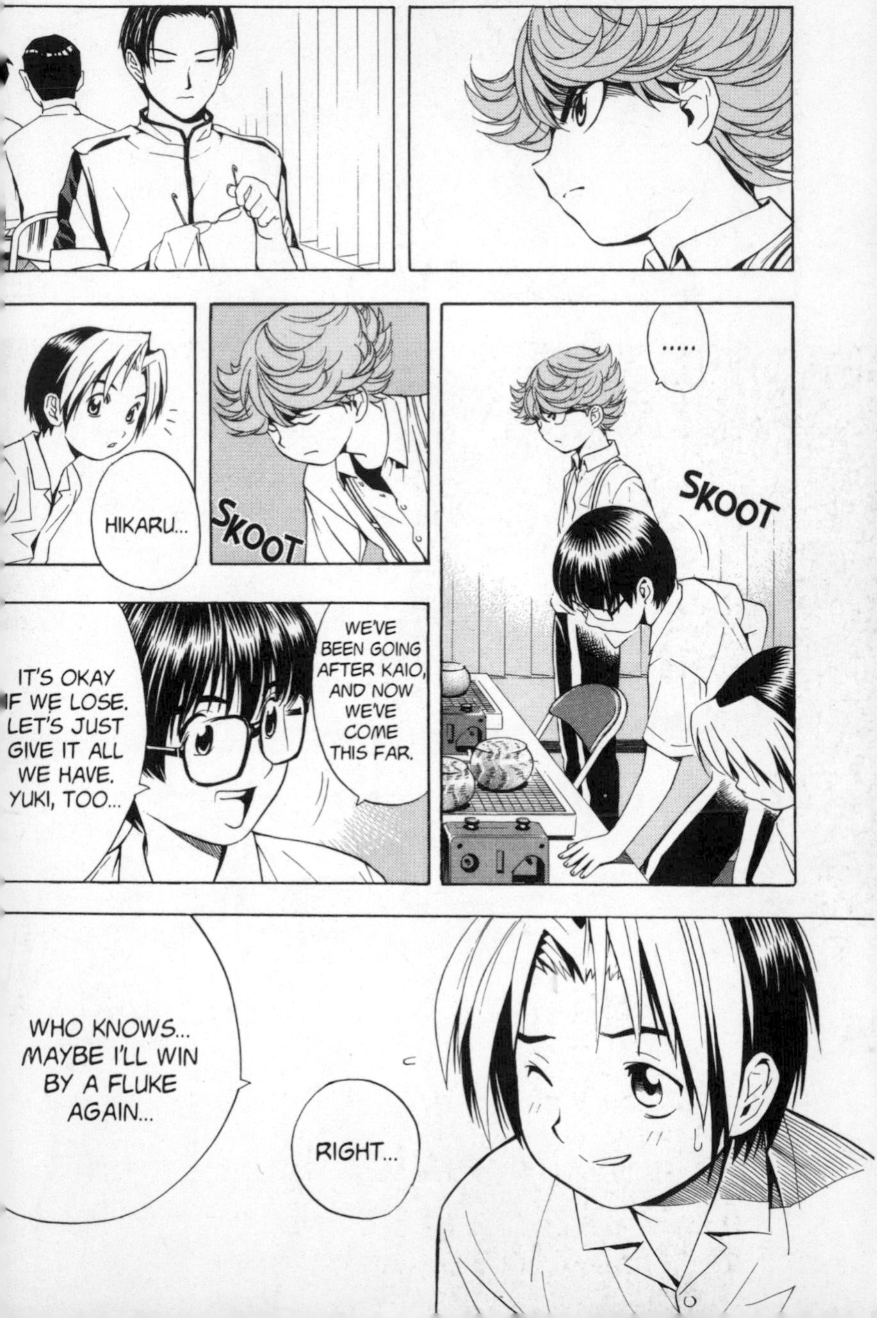
......
SKOOT
SKOOT
HIKARU...
WE'VE BEEN GOING AFTER KAIO, AND NOW WE'VE COME THIS FAR.
IT'S OKAY IF WE LOSE. LET'S JUST GIVE IT ALL WE HAVE. YUKI, TOO...
RIGHT...
WHO KNOWS... MAYBE I'LL WIN BY A FLUKE AGAIN...

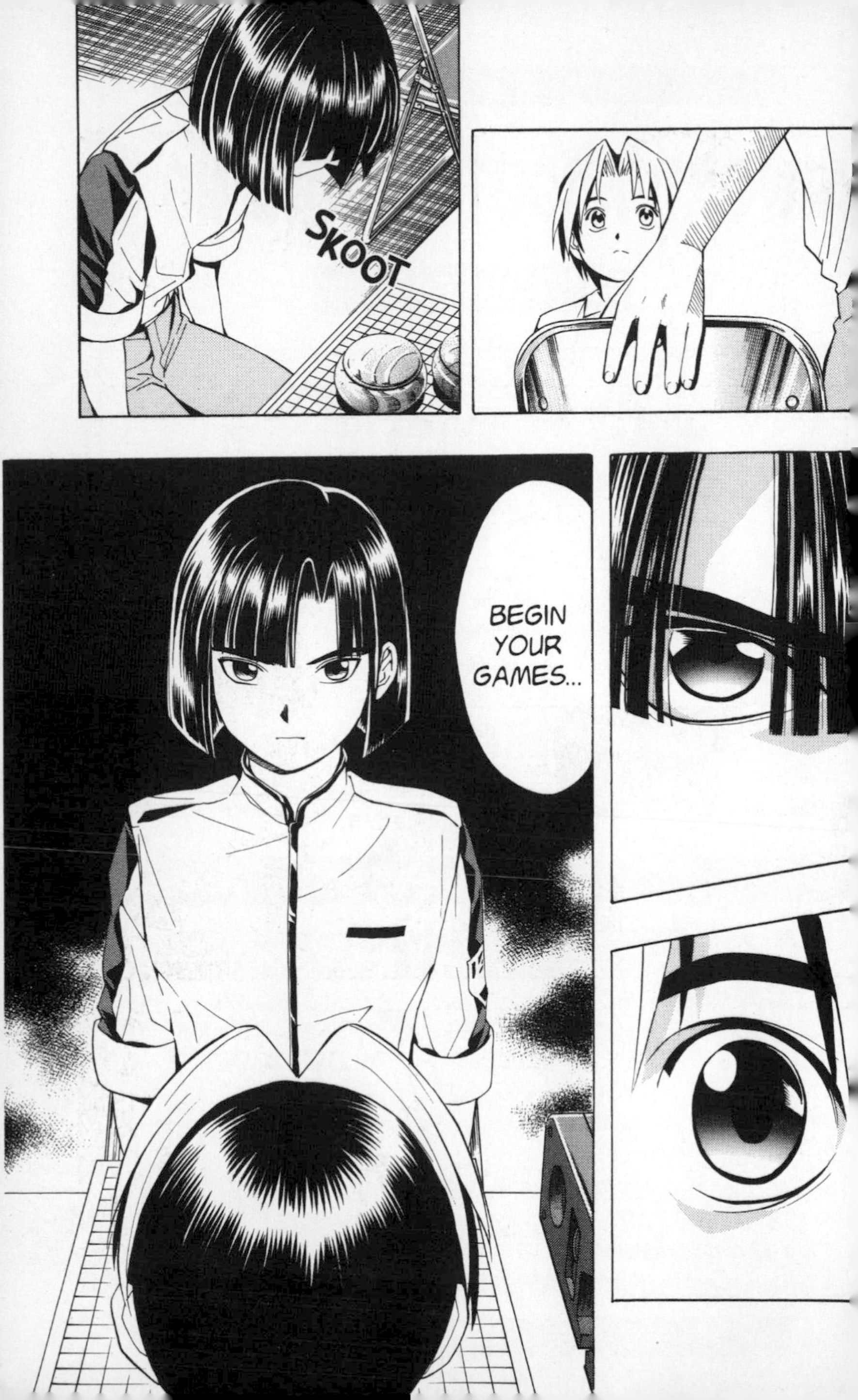
SKOOT
BEGIN YOUR GAMES...

A WORD ABOUT HIKARU NO GO

HAZE

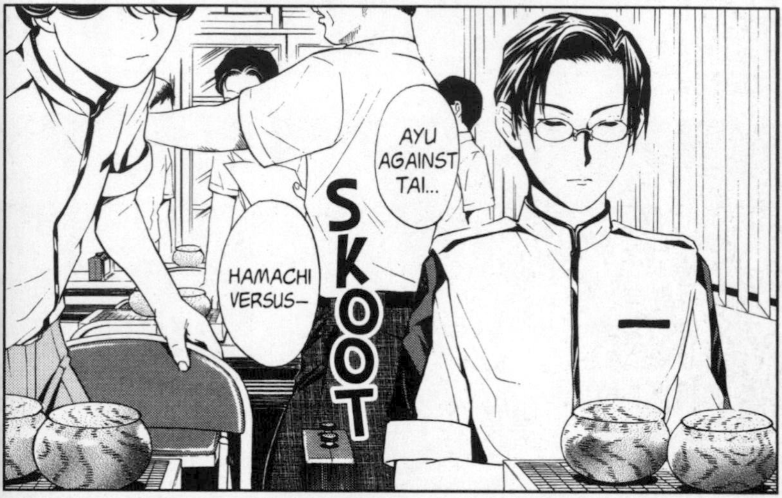
AYU AGAINST TAI...
SKOOT
HAMACHI VERSUS—

HAZE MIDDLE SCHOOL WAS ORIGINALLY GOING TO BE CALLED TARA MIDDLE SCHOOL. BUT THEN I HEARD THAT A TARA MIDDLE SCHOOL ACTUALLY EXISTS SO WE CHANGED IT TO HAZE. I WONDER IF THERE ARE ANY SCHOOLS OUT THERE CALLED AYU, TAI OR HAMACHI? AND MAYBE I SHOULD FIND OUT IF THERE ARE ANY SCHOOLS NAMED IWANA OR KAWAHAGI...

[NOTE: ALL THE MIDDLE SCHOOLS ARE NAMED AFTER DIFFERENT TYPES OF FISH: HAZE=GOBY, TARA=COD, AYU=SWEET SMELT, TAI=SEA BREAM, HAMACHI=YELLOW TAIL, IWANA=CHAR, KAWAHAGI=FILEFISH.]

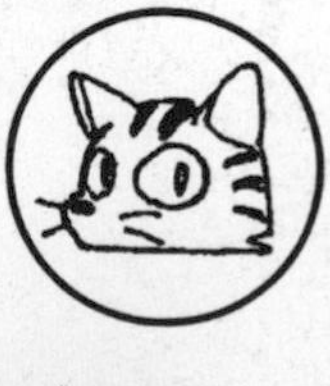

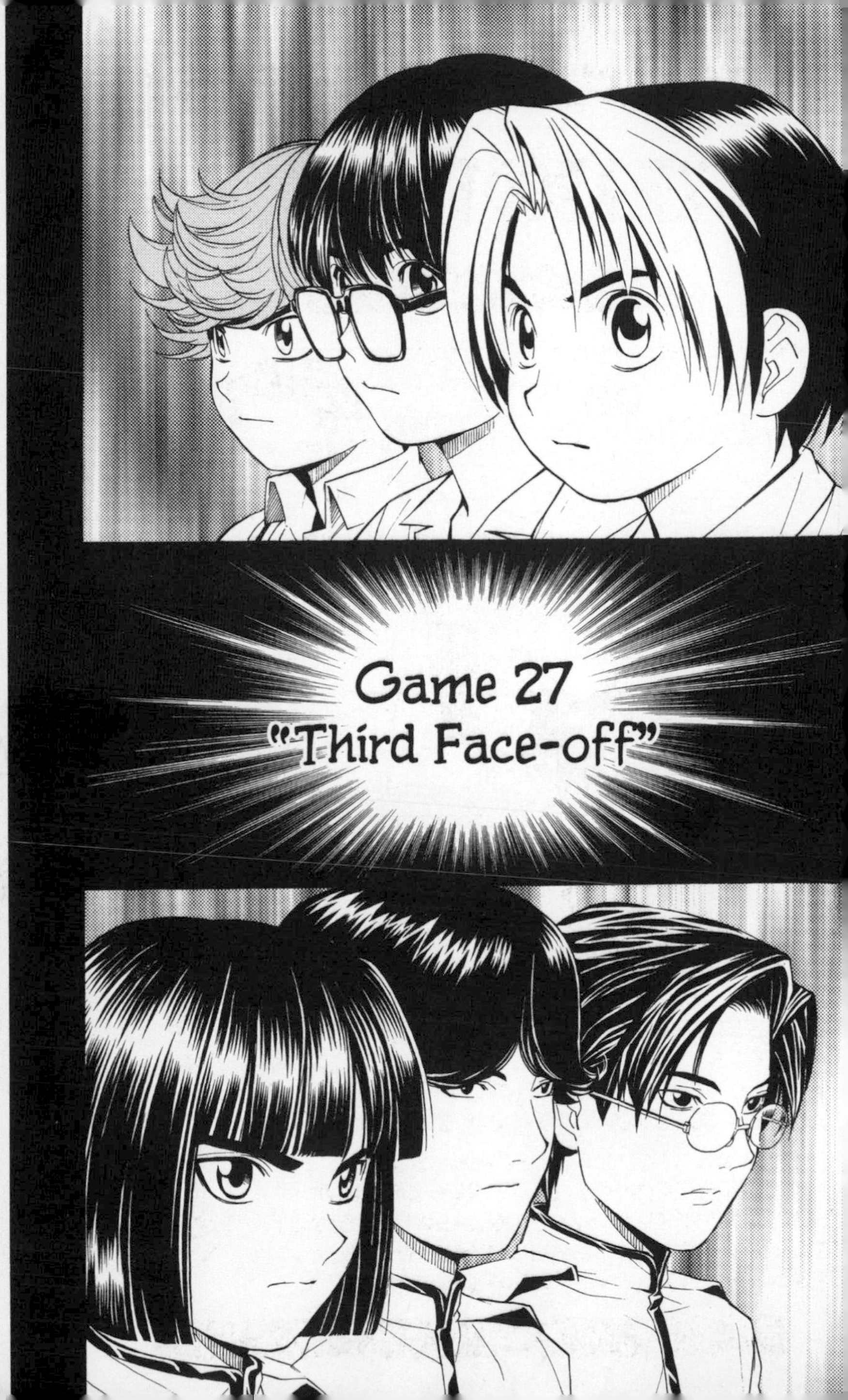
Game 27
"Third Face-off"

LET'S CHOOSE FOR COLOR...

SCHF

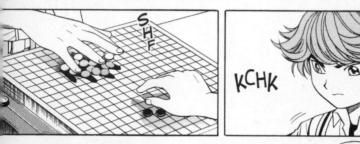

S.H.F

KCHK

YUKI'S BLACK...

TWO, FOUR, SIX... 14.

SO YOU'RE BLACK TOO, HIKARU.

ONEGAI-SHIMASU.

ONEGAI-SHIMASU.

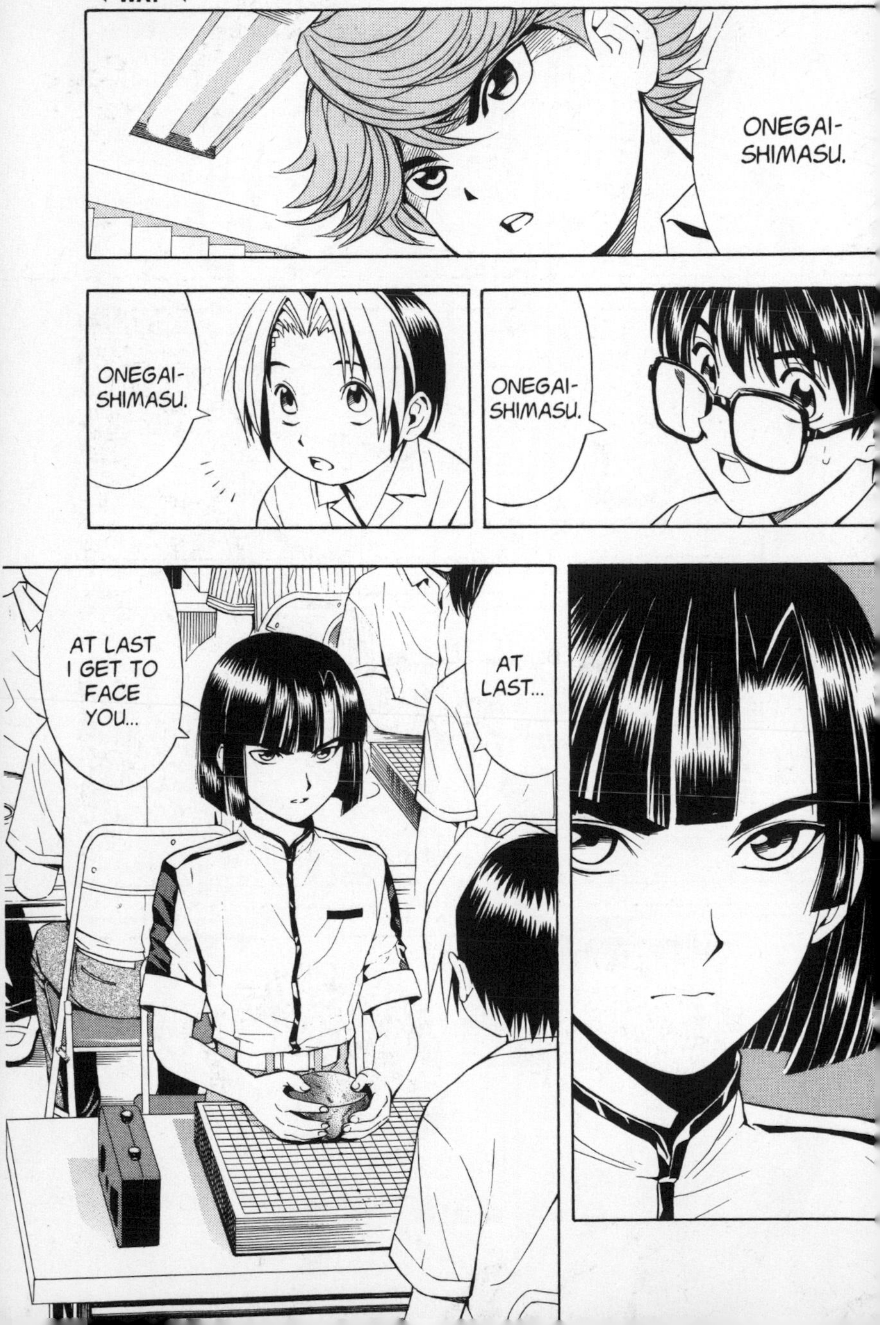
READ THIS WAY
ONEGAI-SHIMASU.
ONEGAI-SHIMASU.
ONEGAI-SHIMASU.
AT LAST...
AT LAST I GET TO FACE YOU...

EVEN THOUGH LAST TIME HE REALLY GOT WHUPPED BY SAI, HE'S NOT AT ALL DISCOURAGED.

I'M SURPRISED HE'S SO OPTIMISTIC.

CLATTER

KTP

!

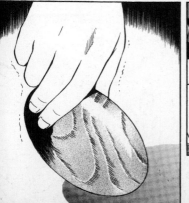

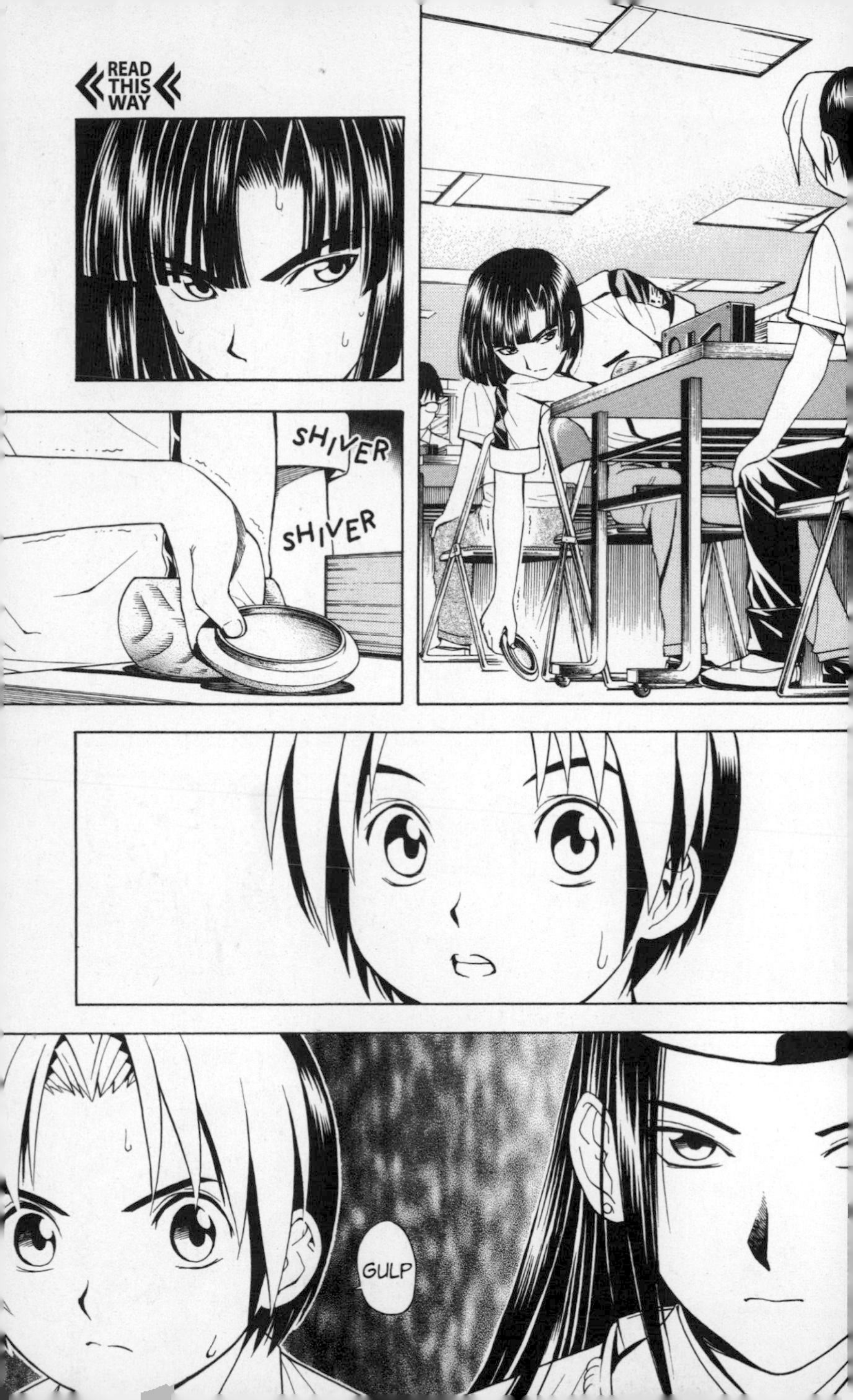
READ THIS WAY
SHIVER
SHIVER
GULP

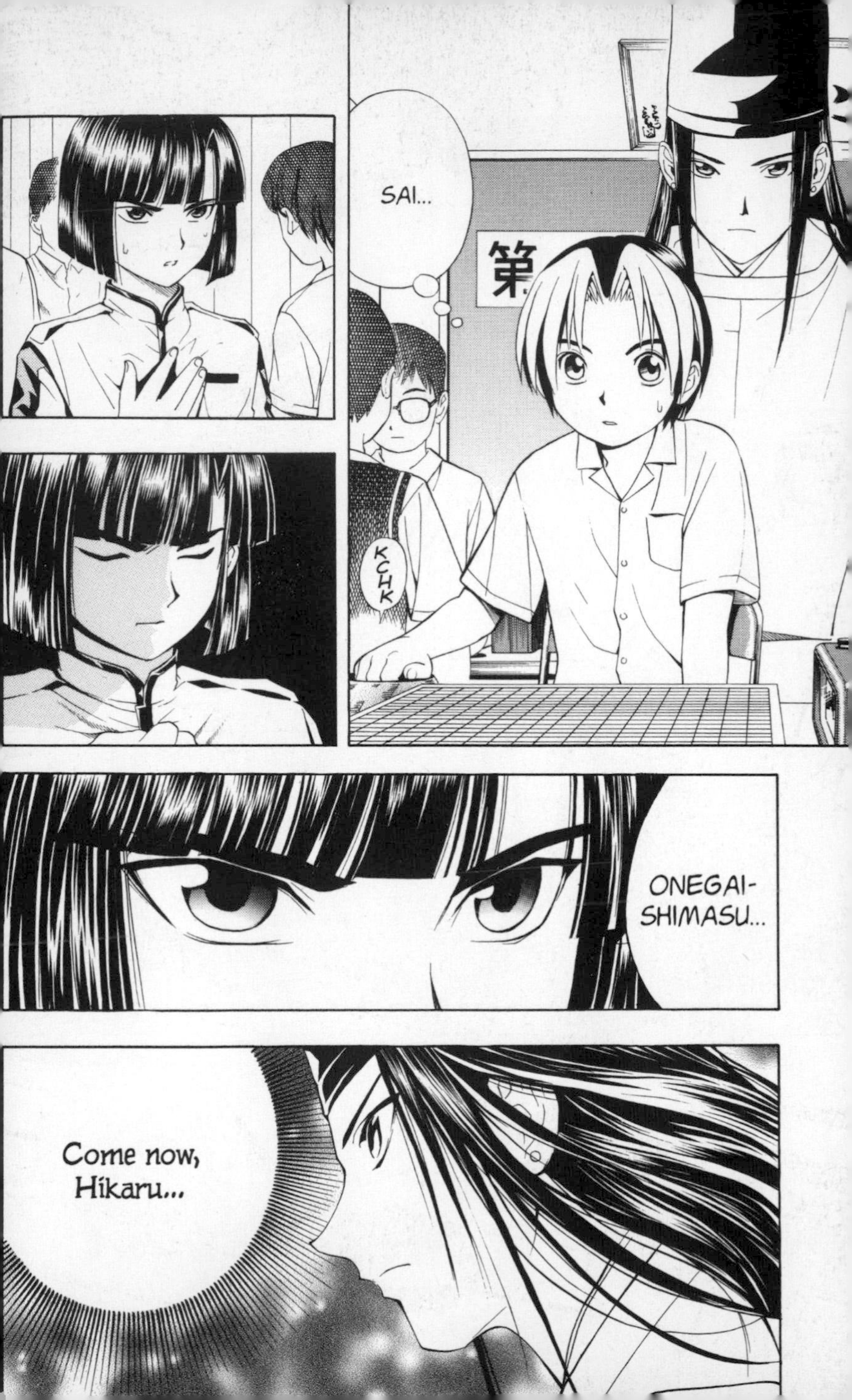
SAI...
第
KCHK
ONEGAI-SHIMASU...
Come now, Hikaru...

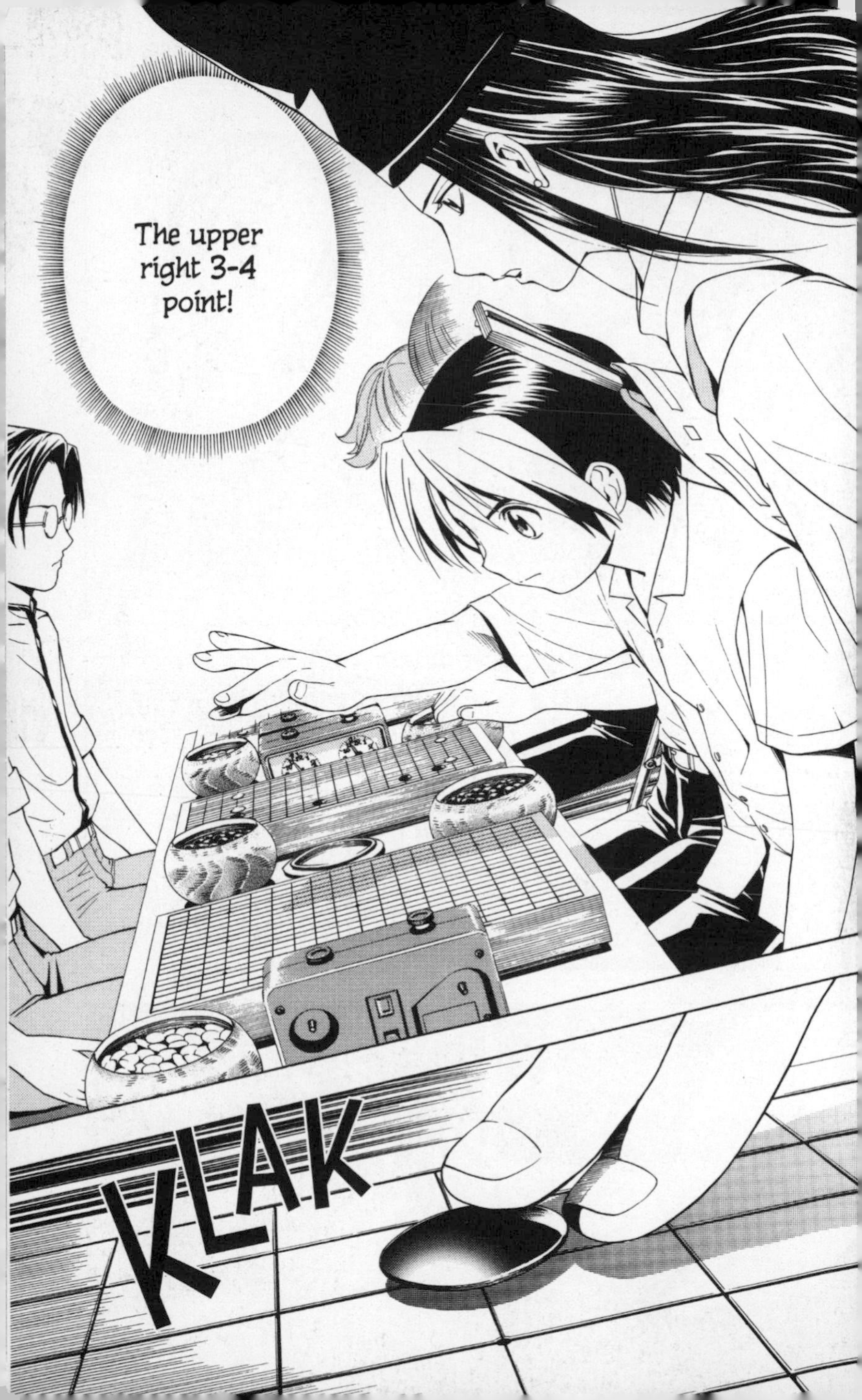
The upper right 3-4 point!
KLAK

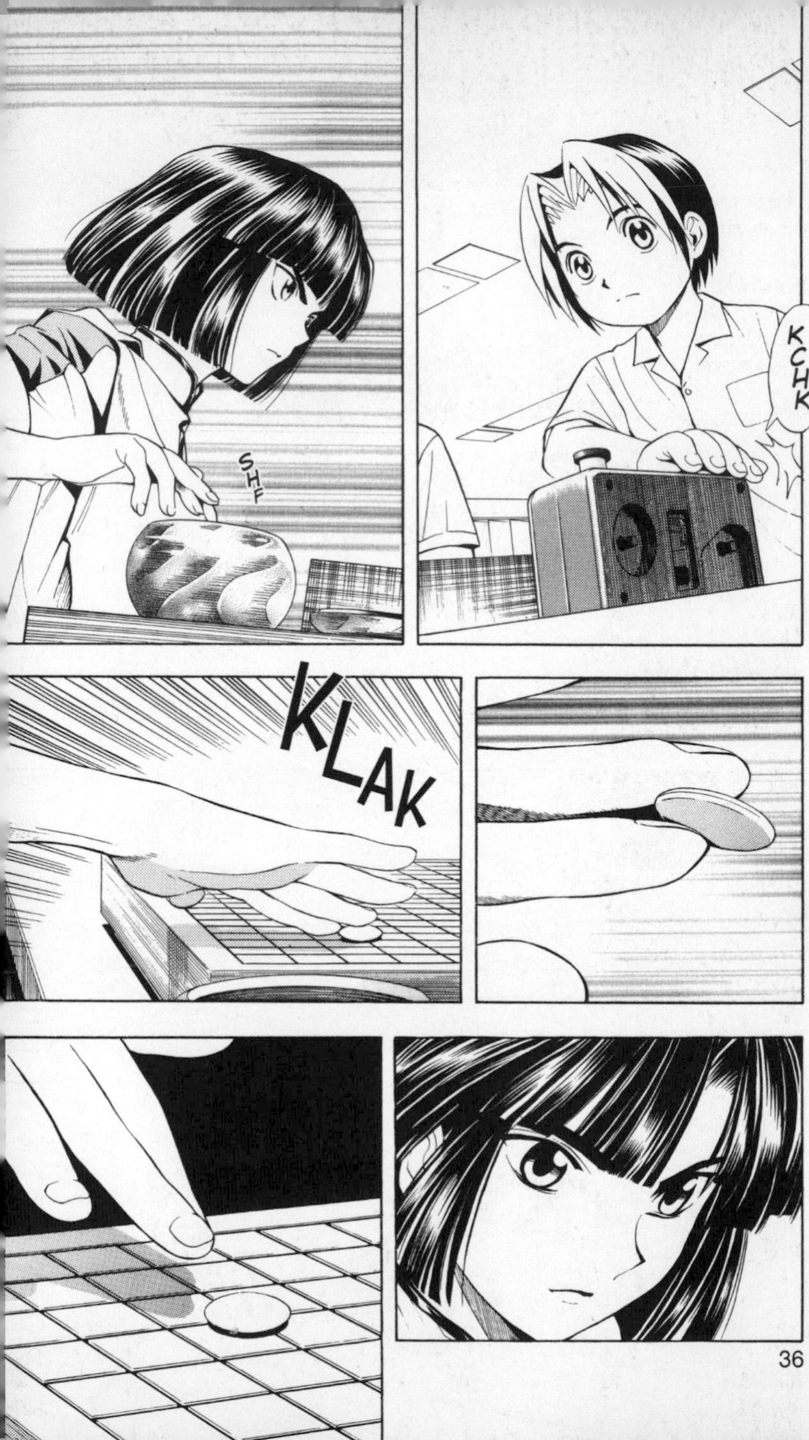
KCHK
SHF
KLAK

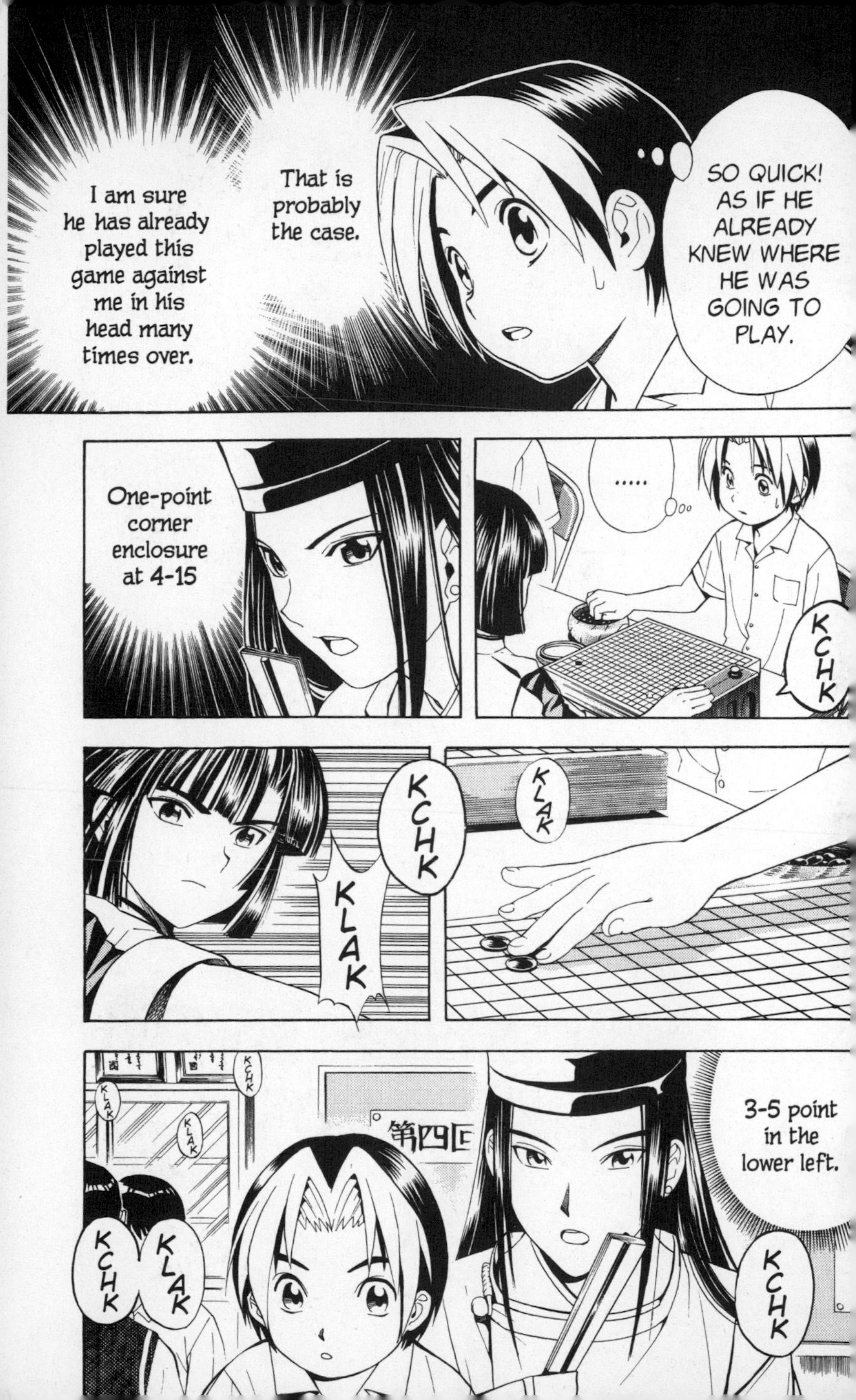
SO QUICK! AS IF HE ALREADY KNEW WHERE HE WAS GOING TO PLAY.
That is probably the case.
I am sure he has already played this game against me in his head many times over.
.....
KCHK
One-point corner enclosure at 4-15
KLAK
KCHK
KLAK
3-5 point in the lower left.
KCHK
KCHK
KLAK
KLAK
KLAK
KCHK

HE'S GOT THAT SAME LOOK IN HIS EYES.

AKIRA...

I GOT DRAWN IN BY THE SERIOUS LOOK IN YOUR EYES WHEN YOU WERE TAKING ON SAI. AND NOW I'VE COME THIS FAR...

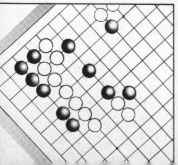

OVER-COMING YOU IS MY DISTANT GOAL...

READ THIS WAY

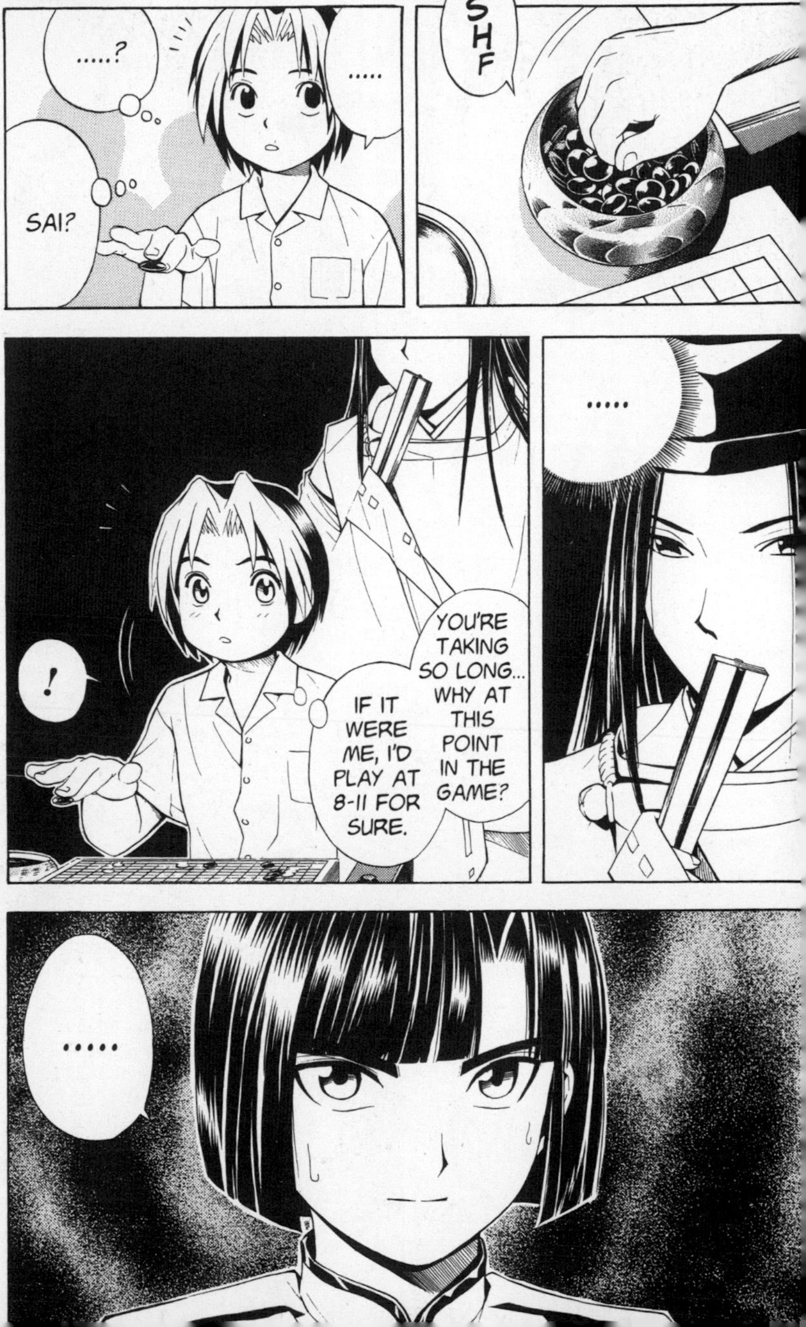
SHF
.....
.....?
SAI?
.....
YOU'RE TAKING SO LONG... WHY AT THIS POINT IN THE GAME?
IF IT WERE ME, I'D PLAY AT 8-11 FOR SURE.
!
.....

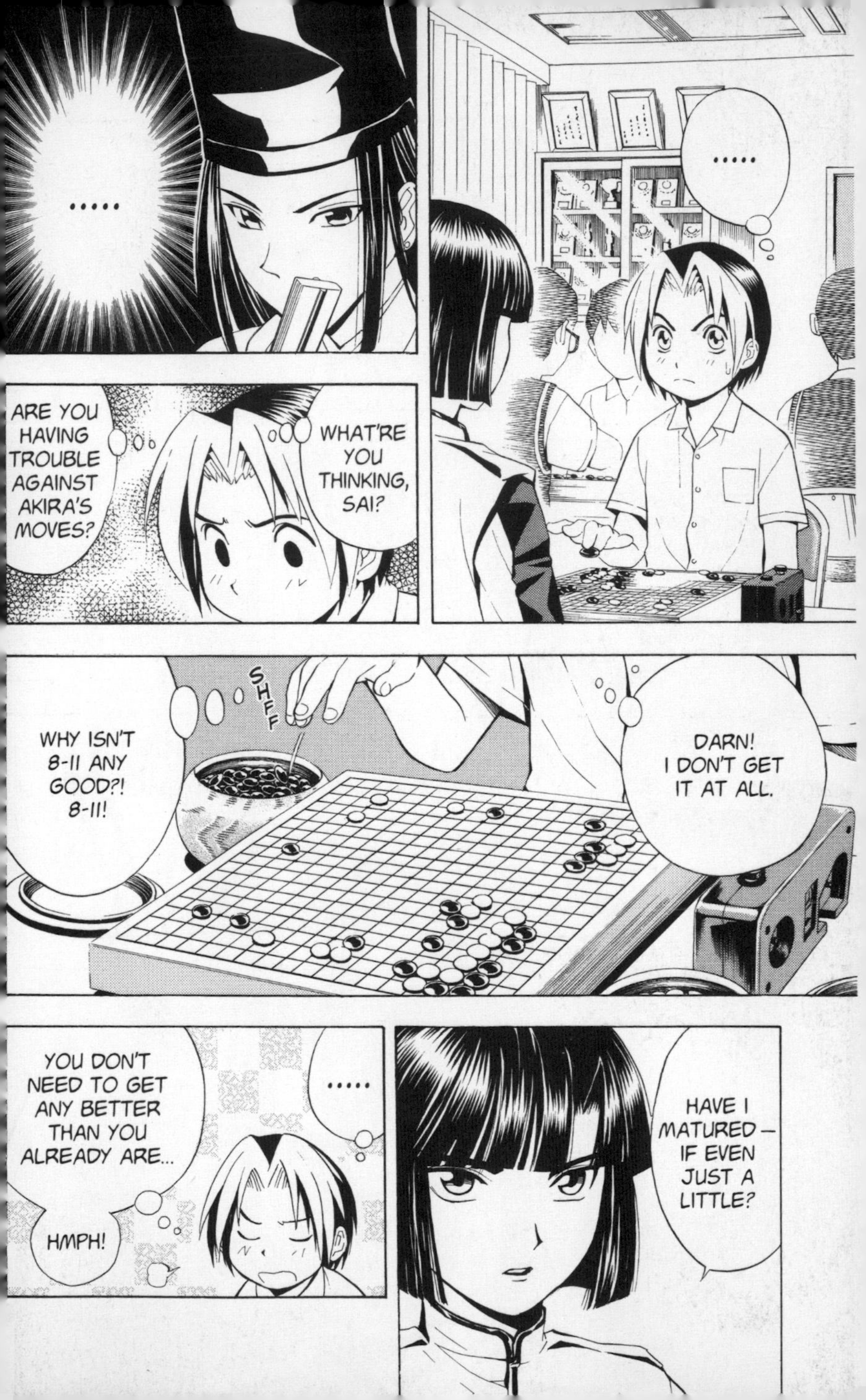
.....
.....
WHAT'RE YOU THINKING, SAI?
ARE YOU HAVING TROUBLE AGAINST AKIRA'S MOVES?
DARN! I DON'T GET IT AT ALL.
SHFF
WHY ISN'T 8-11 ANY GOOD?! 8-11!
HAVE I MATURED— IF EVEN JUST A LITTLE?
.....
YOU DON'T NEED TO GET ANY BETTER THAN YOU ALREADY ARE...
HMPH!

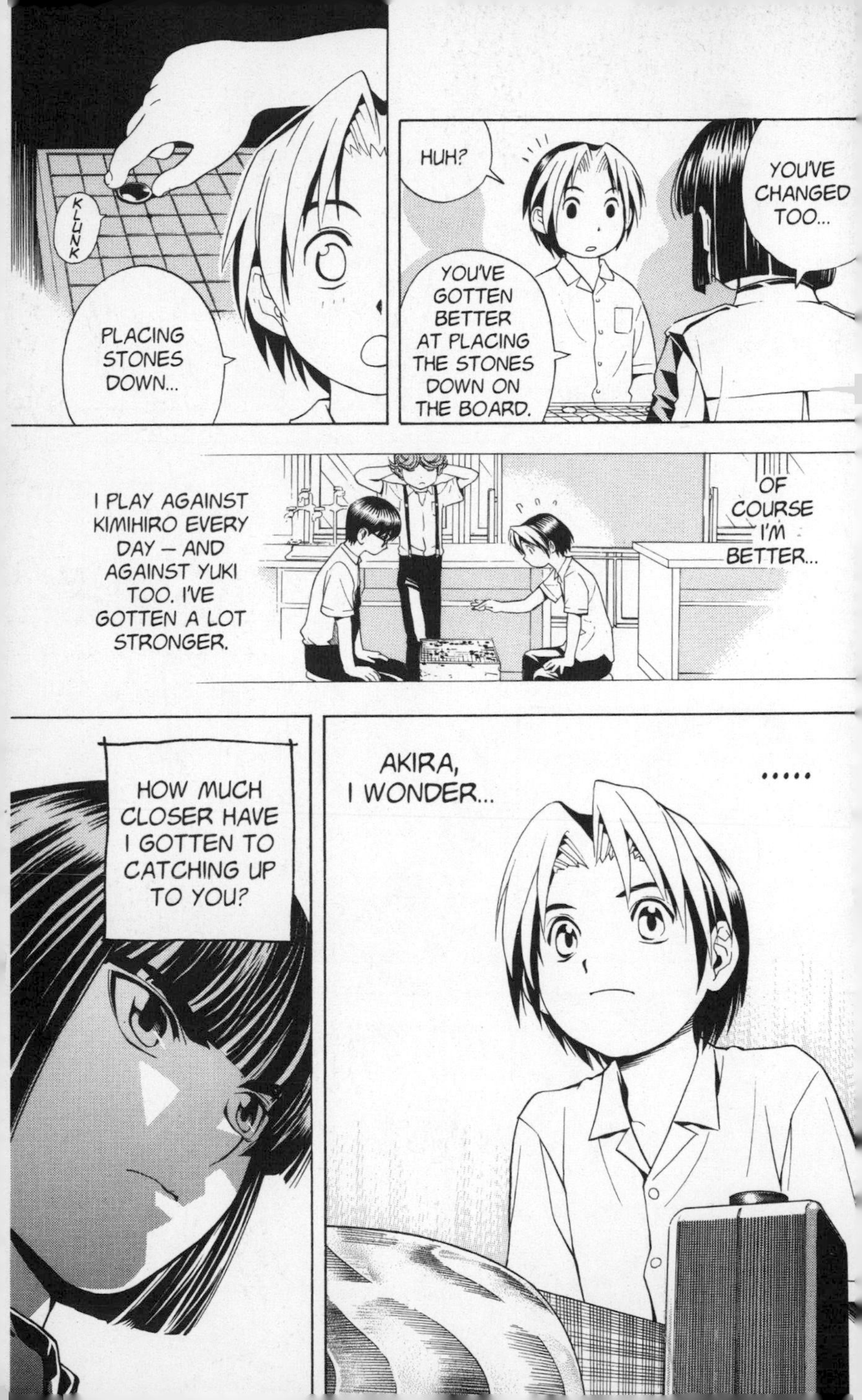
YOU'VE CHANGED TOO...
HUH?
YOU'VE GOTTEN BETTER AT PLACING THE STONES DOWN ON THE BOARD.
KLUNK
PLACING STONES DOWN...
OF COURSE I'M BETTER...
I PLAY AGAINST KIMIHIRO EVERY DAY — AND AGAINST YUKI TOO. I'VE GOTTEN A LOT STRONGER.
.....
AKIRA, I WONDER...
HOW MUCH CLOSER HAVE I GOTTEN TO CATCHING UP TO YOU?

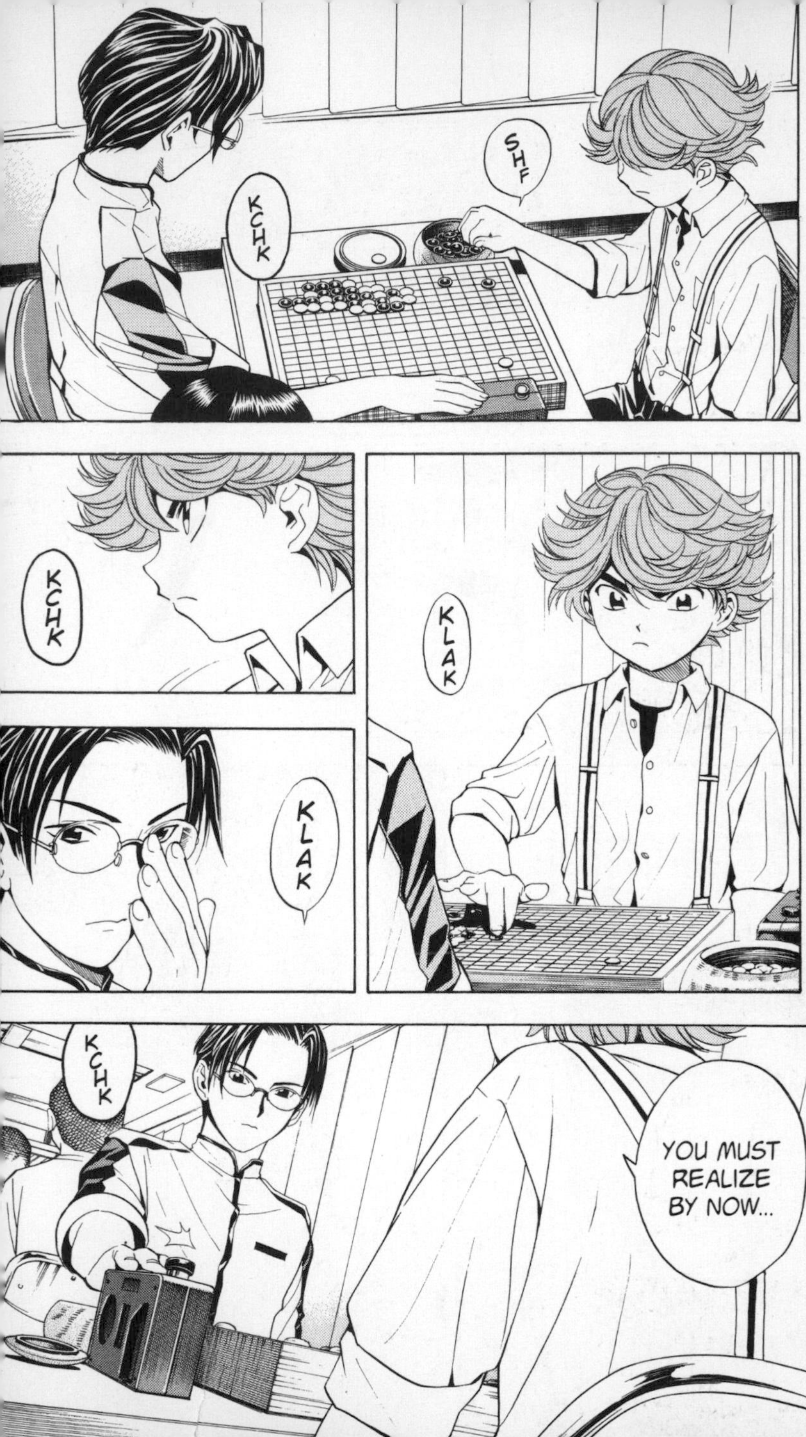
SHF
KCHK
KLAK
KCHK
KLAK
YOU MUST REALIZE BY NOW...
KCHK

READ THIS WAY

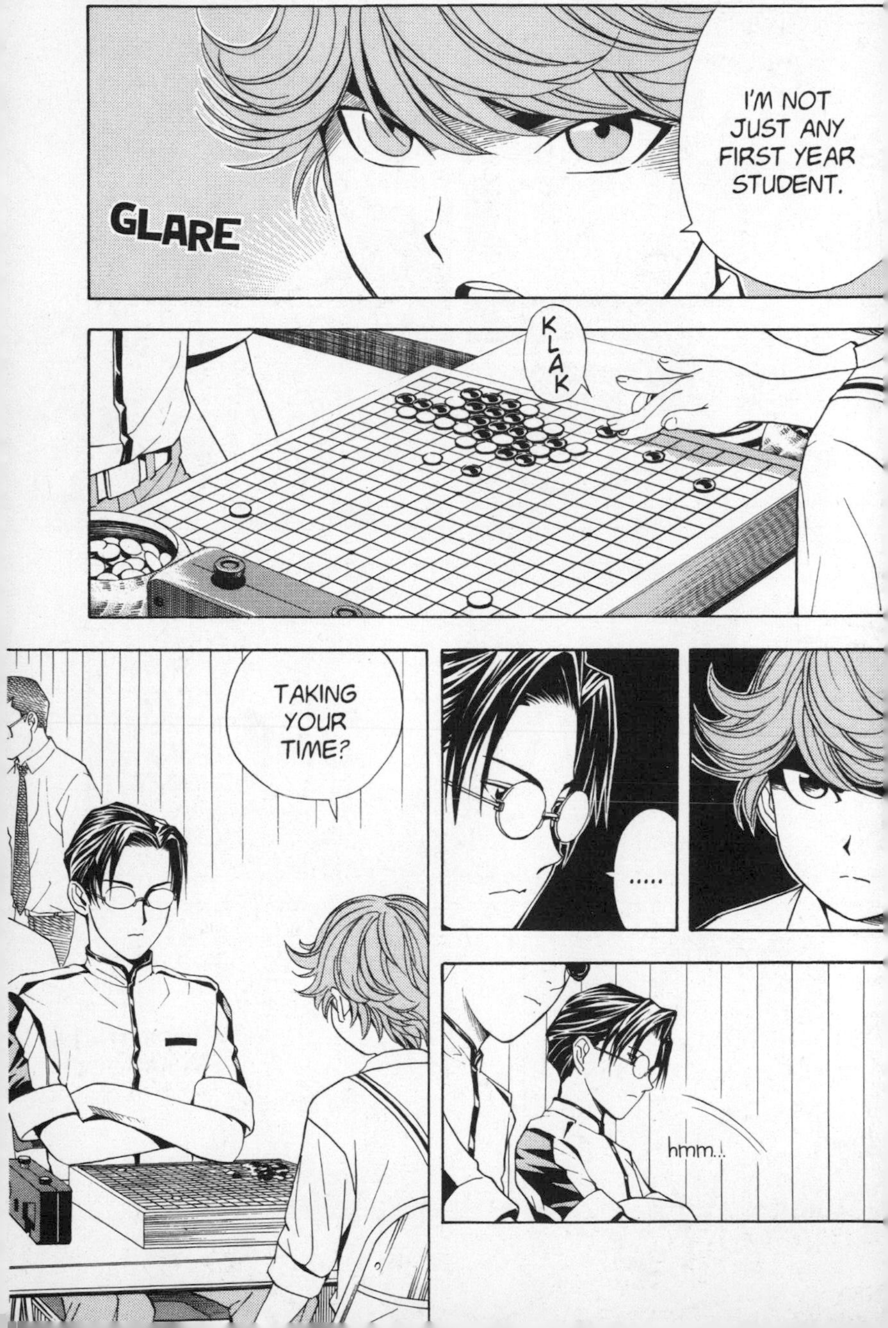
GLARE
I'M NOT JUST ANY FIRST YEAR STUDENT.
KLAK
.....
hmm...
TAKING YOUR TIME?

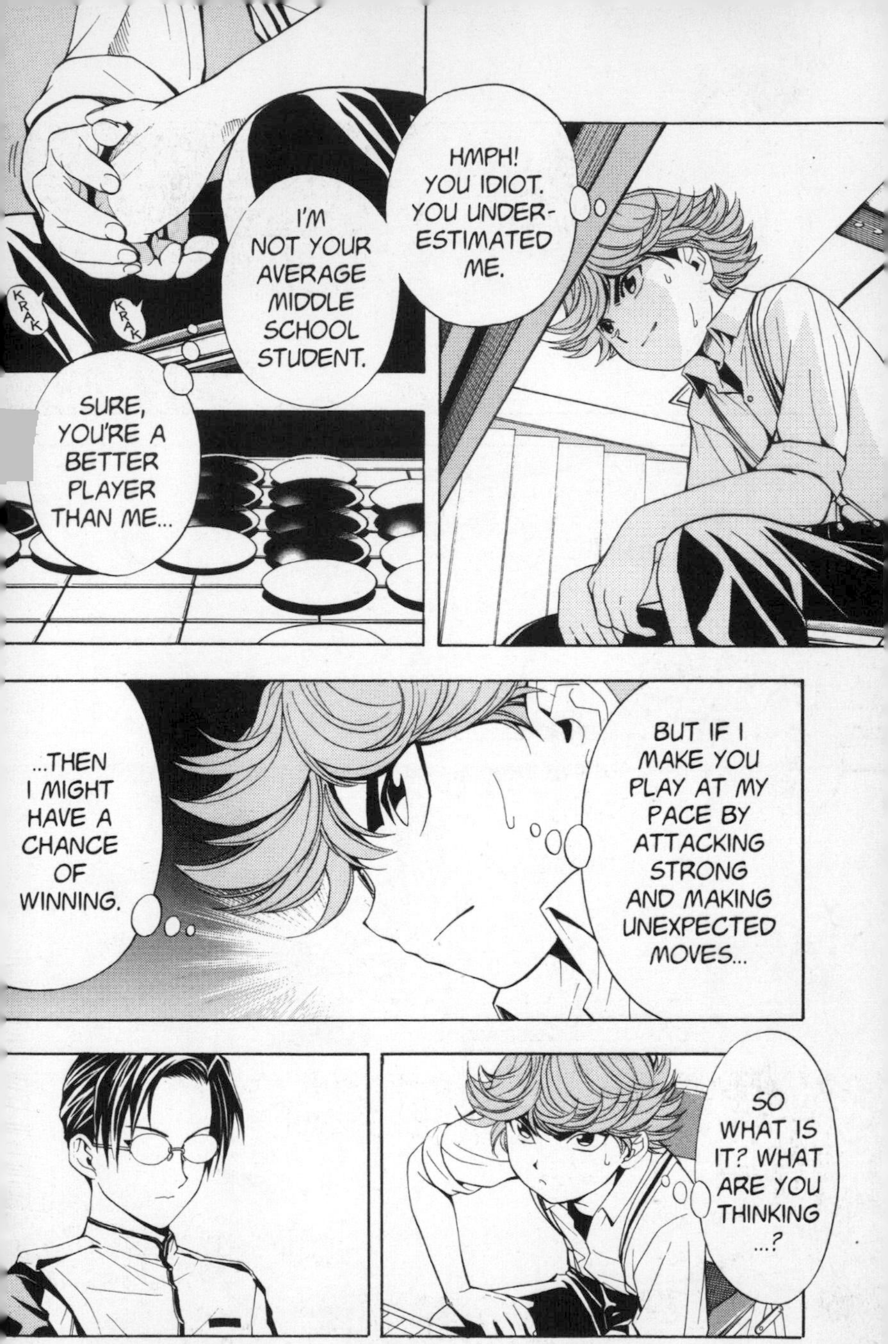
HMPH! YOU IDIOT. YOU UNDER-ESTIMATED ME.
I'M NOT YOUR AVERAGE MIDDLE SCHOOL STUDENT.
KRAK
KRAK
SURE, YOU'RE A BETTER PLAYER THAN ME...
BUT IF I MAKE YOU PLAY AT MY PACE BY ATTACKING STRONG AND MAKING UNEXPECTED MOVES...
...THEN I MIGHT HAVE A CHANCE OF WINNING.
SO WHAT IS IT? WHAT ARE YOU THINKING ...?

READ THIS WAY

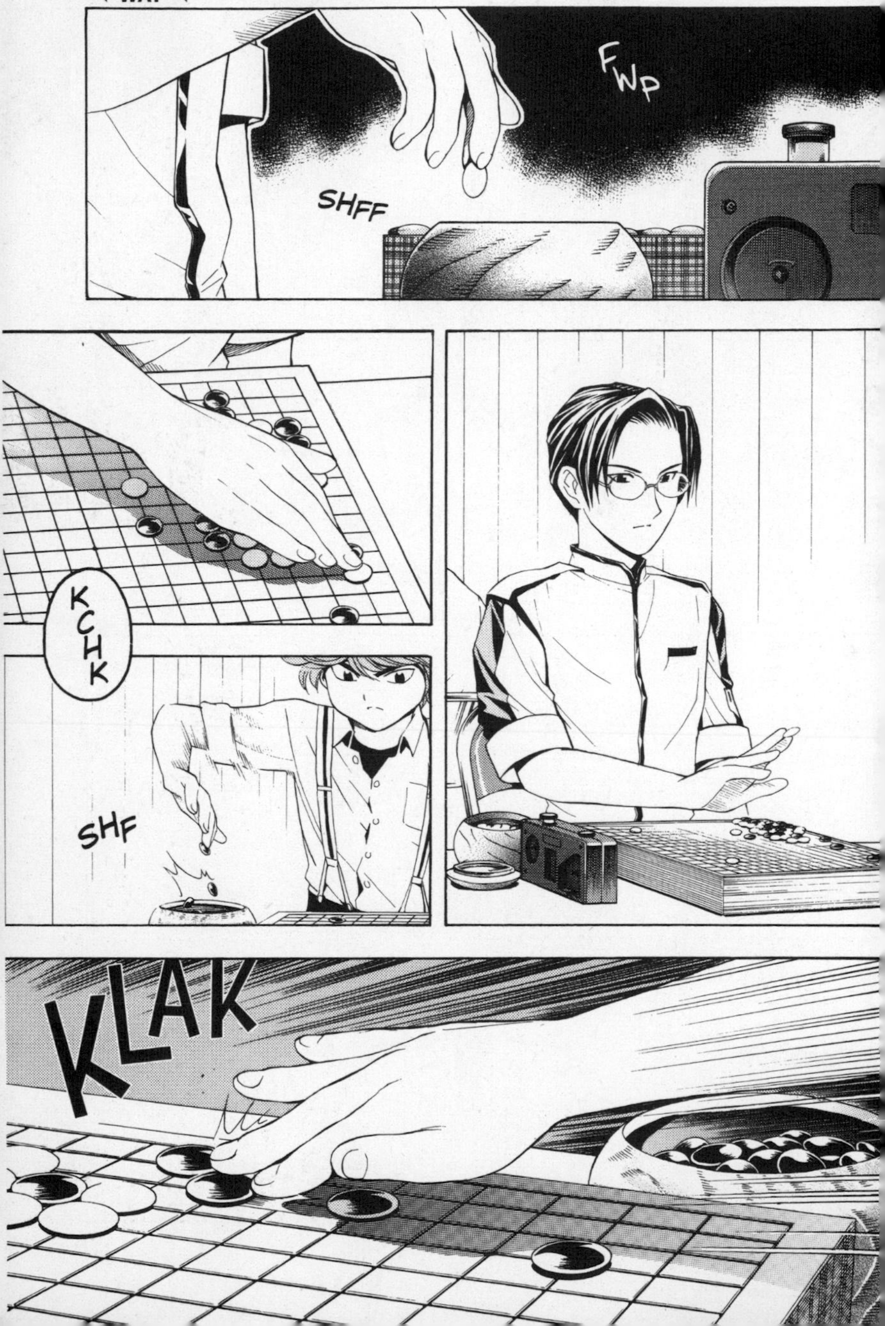
FWP
SHFF
KCHK
SHF
KLAK

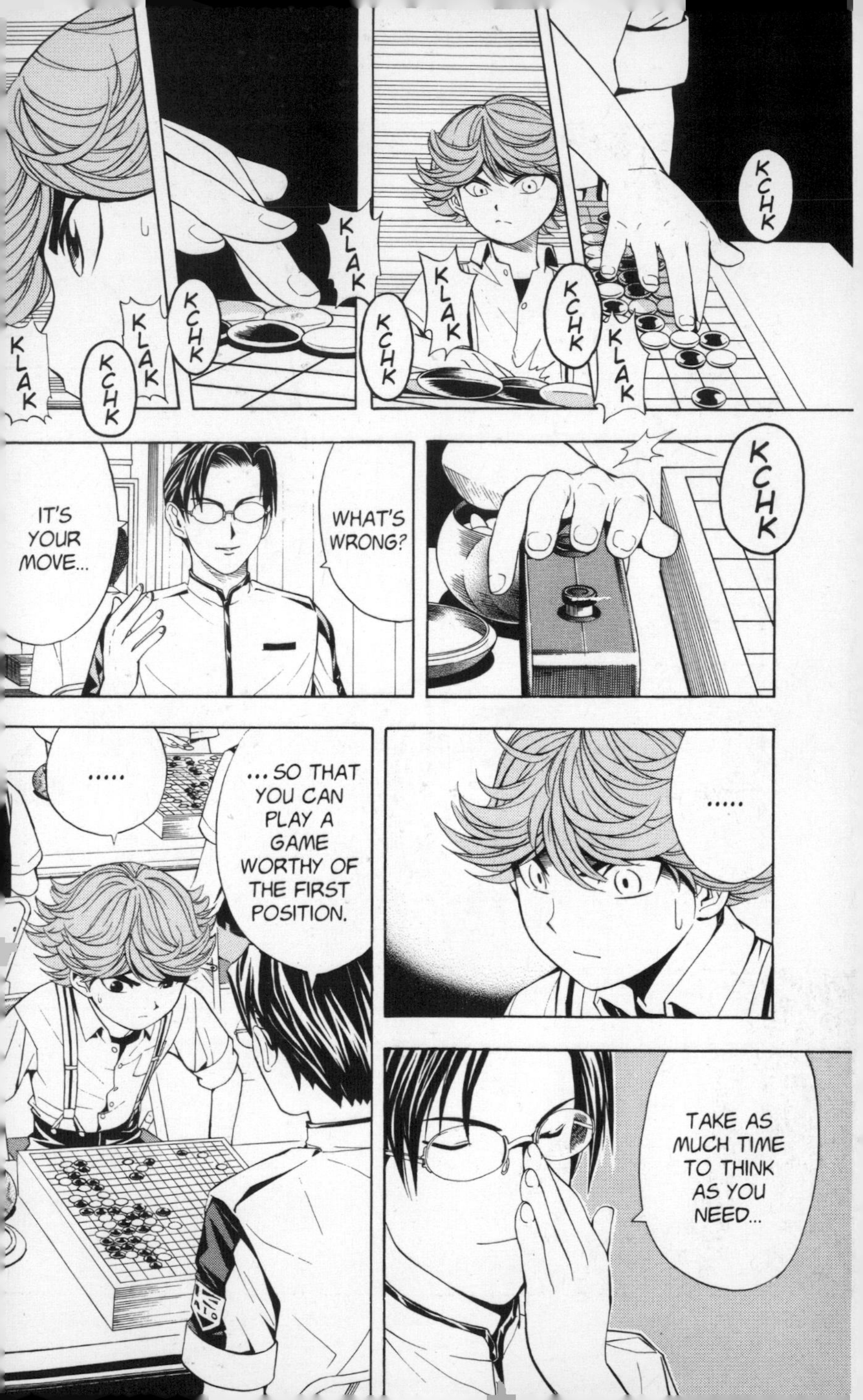
KCHK
KCHK
KLAK
KLAK
KCHK
KLAK
KCHK
KLAK
KCHK
KLAK
KCHK
WHAT'S WRONG?
IT'S YOUR MOVE...
.....
TAKE AS MUCH TIME TO THINK AS YOU NEED...
...SO THAT YOU CAN PLAY A GAME WORTHY OF THE FIRST POSITION.
.....

READ THIS WAY

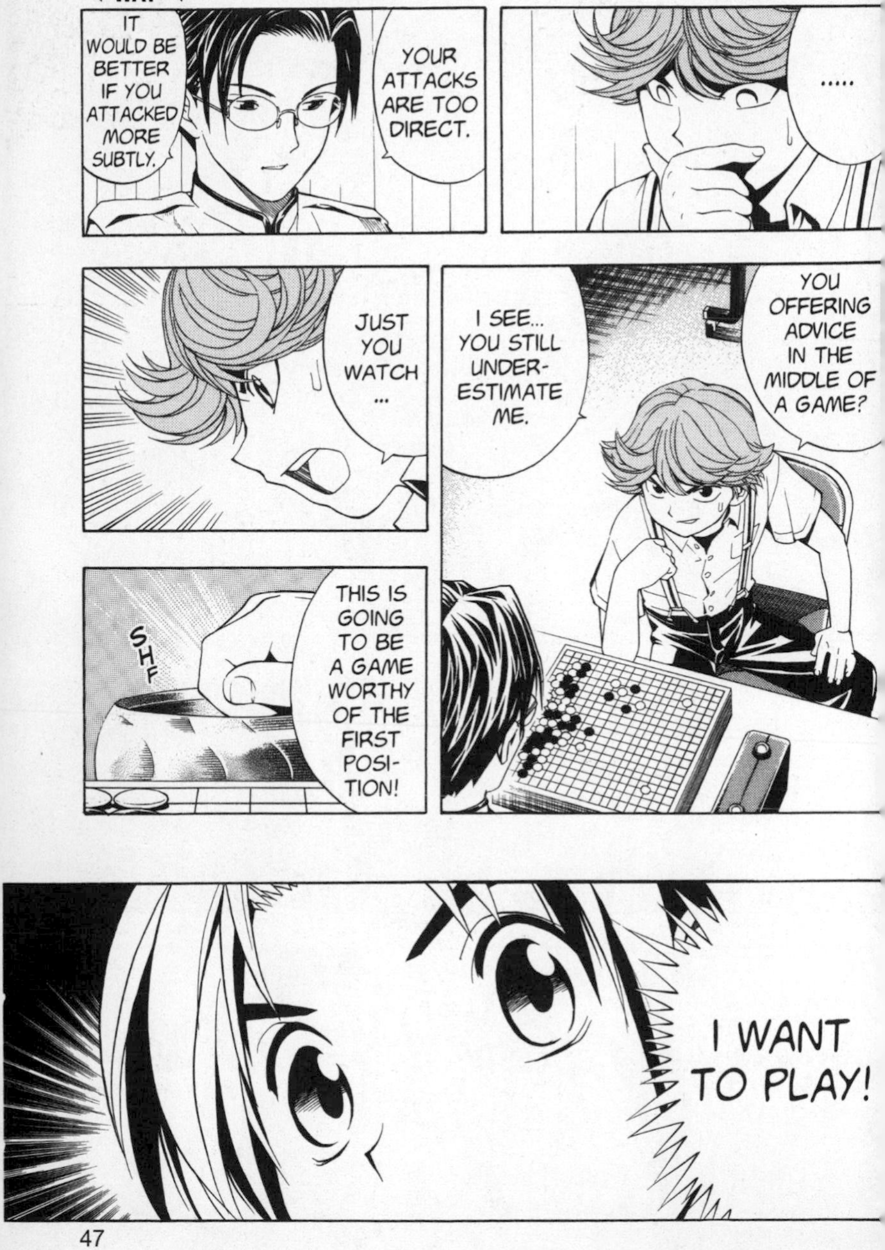
.....
YOUR ATTACKS ARE TOO DIRECT.
IT WOULD BE BETTER IF YOU ATTACKED MORE SUBTLY.
YOU OFFERING ADVICE IN THE MIDDLE OF A GAME?
I SEE... YOU STILL UNDER-ESTIMATE ME.
JUST YOU WATCH ...
THIS IS GOING TO BE A GAME WORTHY OF THE FIRST POSI-TION!
SHF
I WANT TO PLAY!

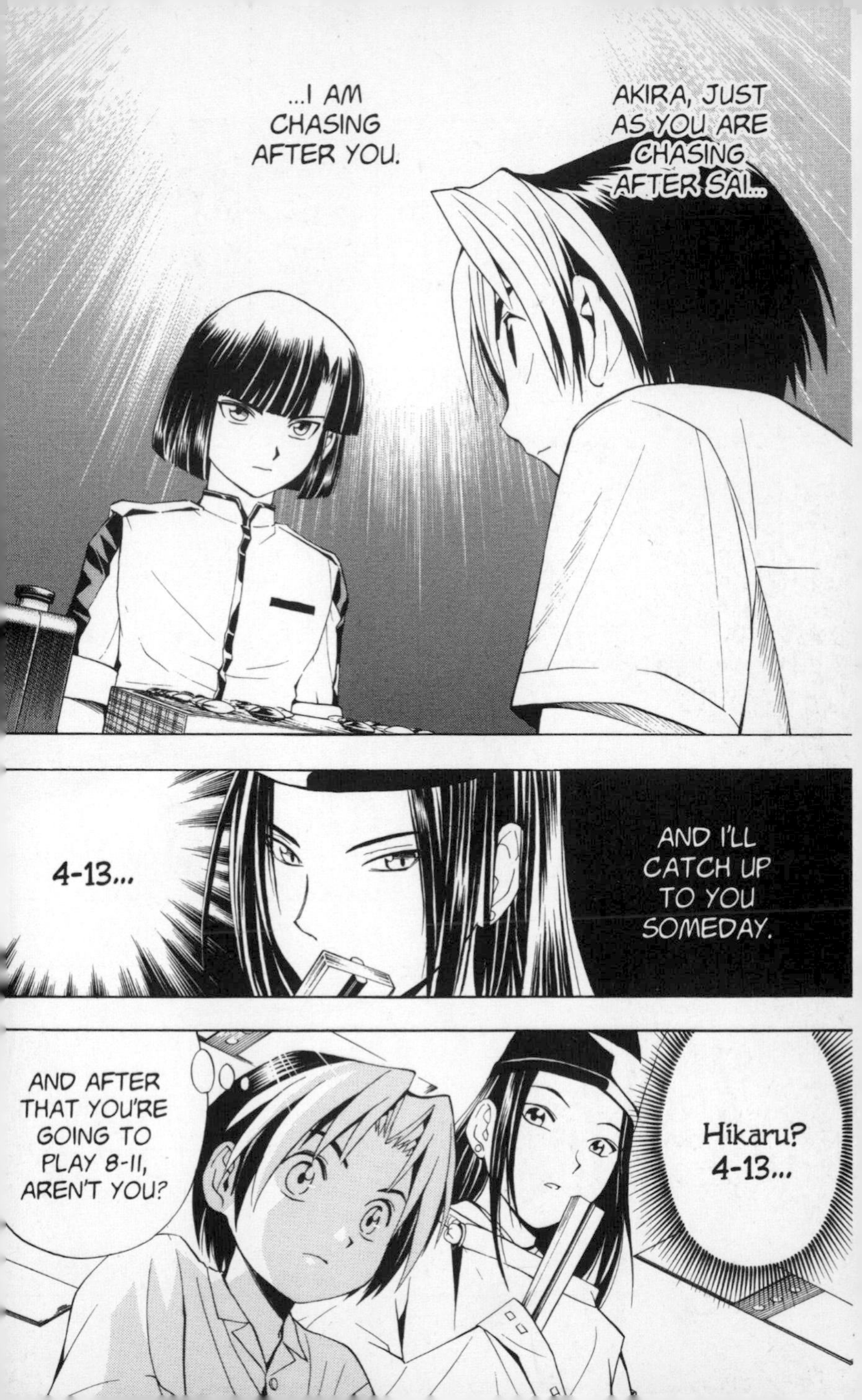
AKIRA, JUST AS YOU ARE CHASING AFTER SAI...
...I AM CHASING AFTER YOU.
AND I'LL CATCH UP TO YOU SOMEDAY.
4-13...
Hikaru? 4-13...
AND AFTER THAT YOU'RE GOING TO PLAY 8-11, AREN'T YOU?

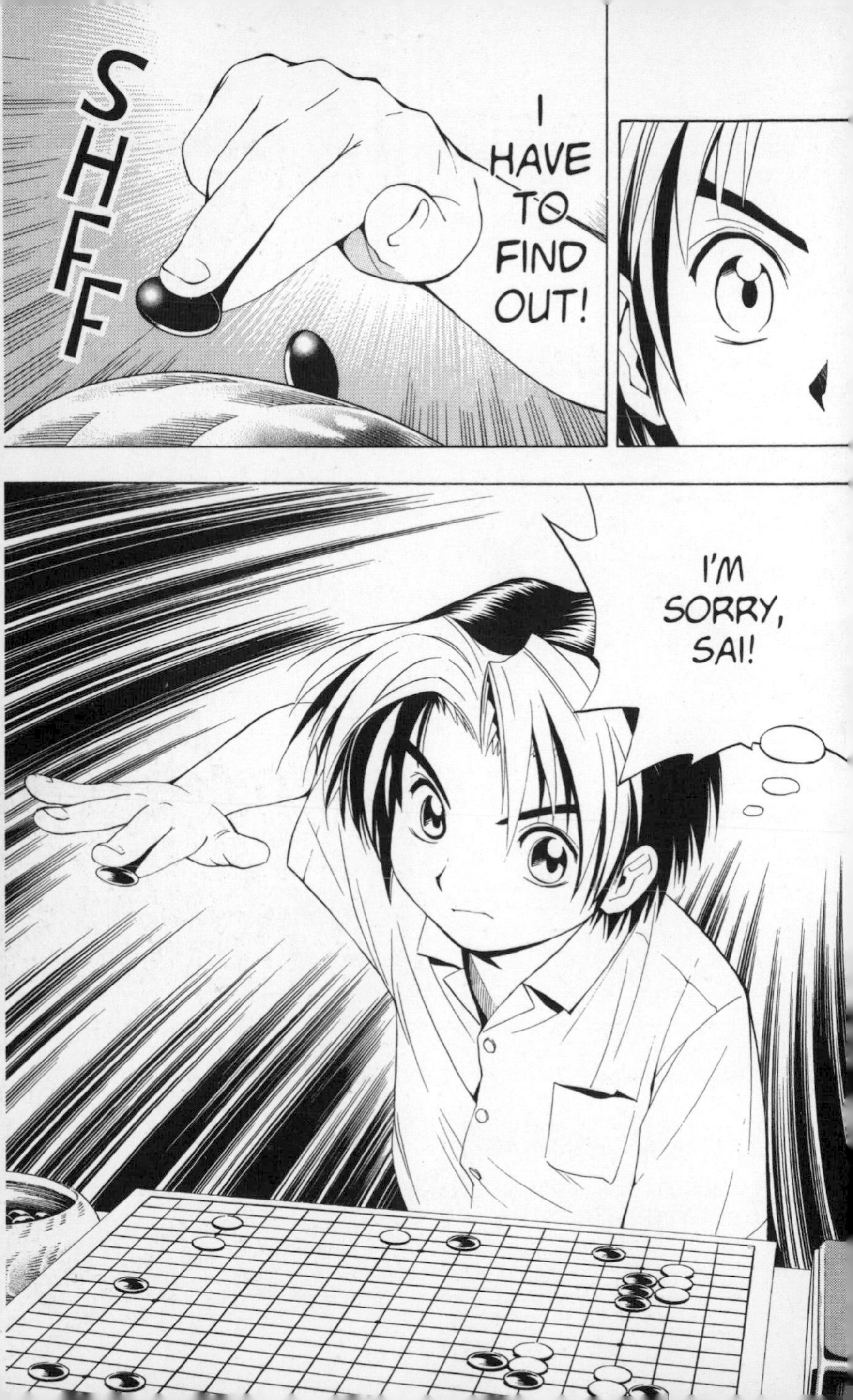
SHFFF
I HAVE TO FIND OUT!
I'M SORRY, SAI!

HIKARU NO GO STORYBOARDS ⑧

YUMI HOTTA

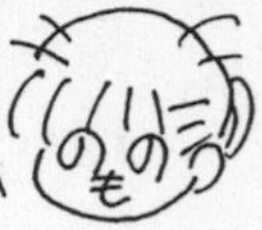

IT'S ALREADY BEEN A YEAR SINCE *HIKARU NO GO* STARTED BEING SERIALIZED.

AND IN THIS TIME I HAVEN'T SEEN THE EDITORIAL DEPARTMENT ONCE.

AND I'VE NEVER SEEN OBATA SENSEI'S FINISHED ARTWORK.

MAYBE IT CAN'T BE HELPED BECAUSE I LIVE FAR AWAY FROM THE CITY. BUT I'D LIKE TO SEE IT ONCE BEFORE THIS SERIES ENDS.

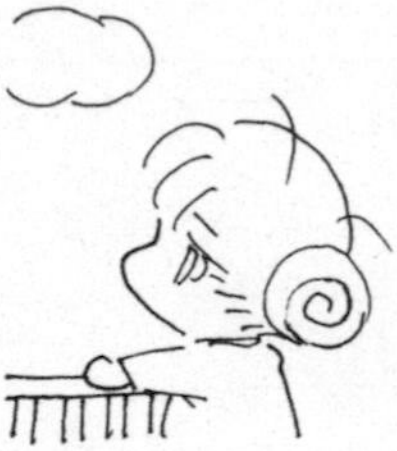

OH... BUT THERE'S LOTS OF FUN THINGS THAT HAPPEN TOO.

ONE TIME THERE WAS PANIC WITH THE COLOR PAGES FROM GAME 18. THERE WAS A CREDITING ERROR!

[STORY BY TAKESHI OBATA
ART BY YUMI HOTTA]

HOW MUCH PANIC WAS THERE? THERE WAS A LOT!

READ THIS "HIKARU NO GO STORYBOARDS" SECTION VERY QUIETLY AND CALMLY.

SO, THAT BEING SAID, EVERYONE...

THIS IS A BONUS PAGE. WE MUSTN'T MAKE IT SO EXCITING THAT IT WILL GET IN THE WAY OF THE MAIN PART OF THIS MANGA.

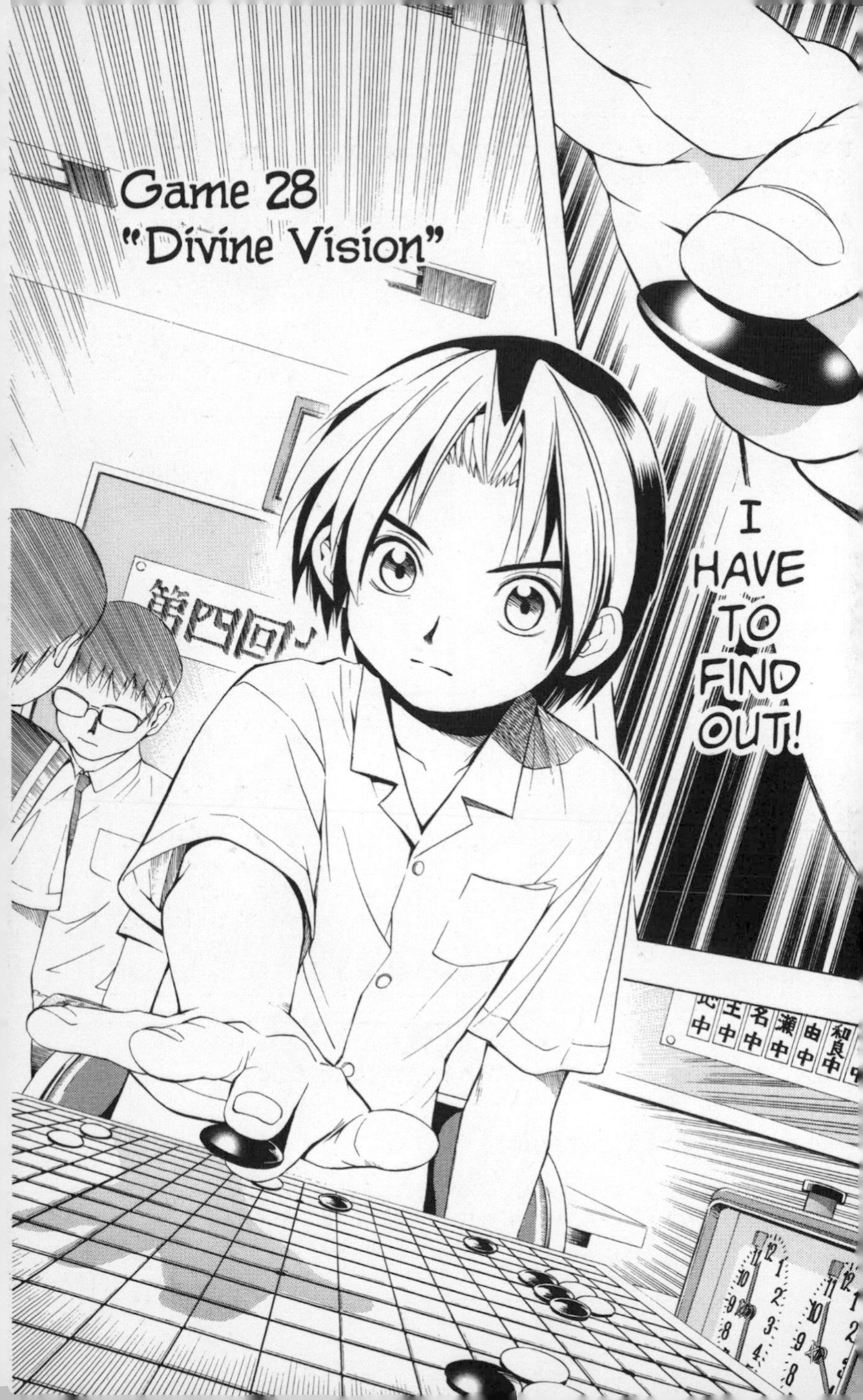
Game 28
"Divine Vision"
I HAVE TO FIND OUT!

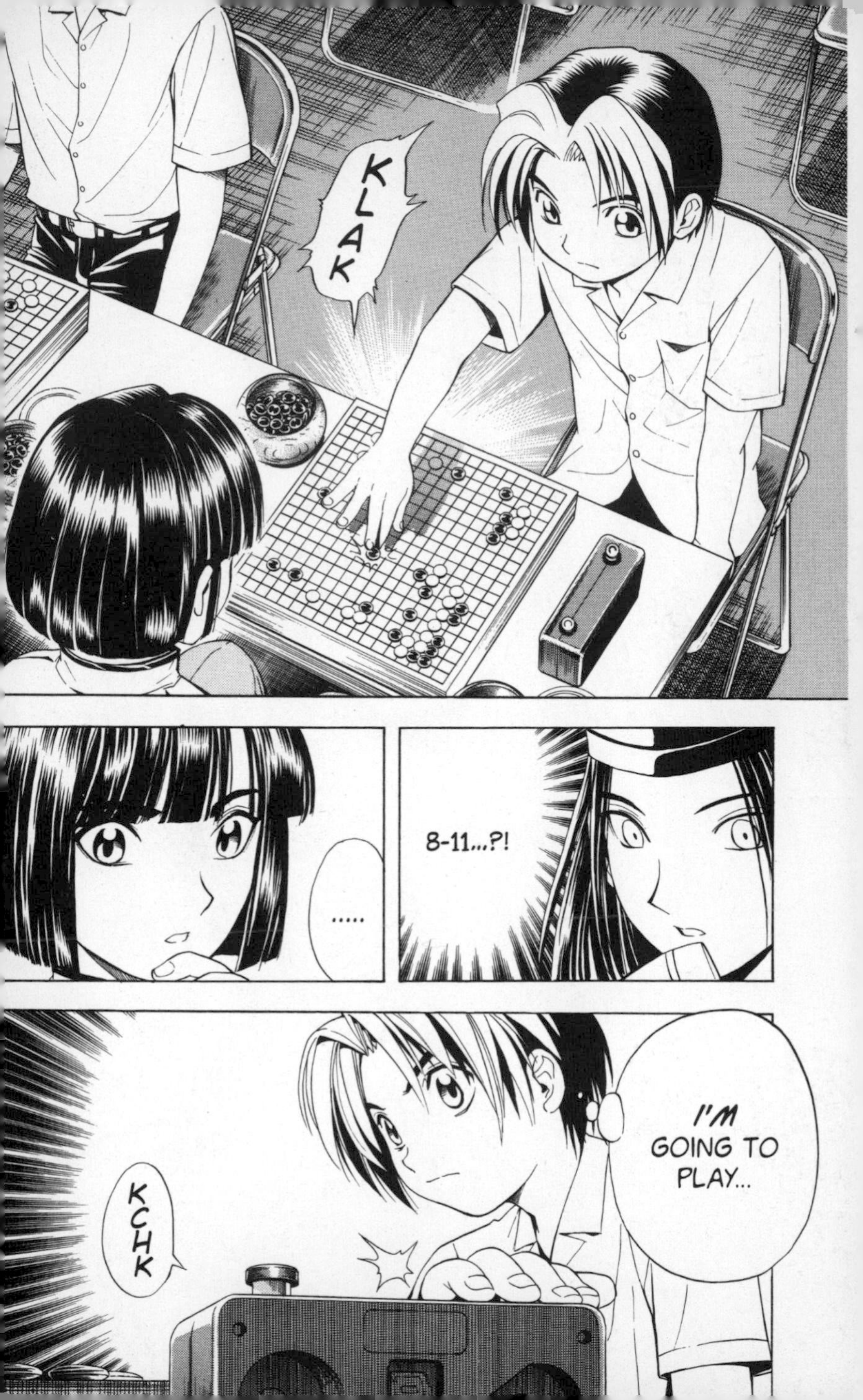
KLAK
8-11...?!
.....
I'M GOING TO PLAY...
KCHK

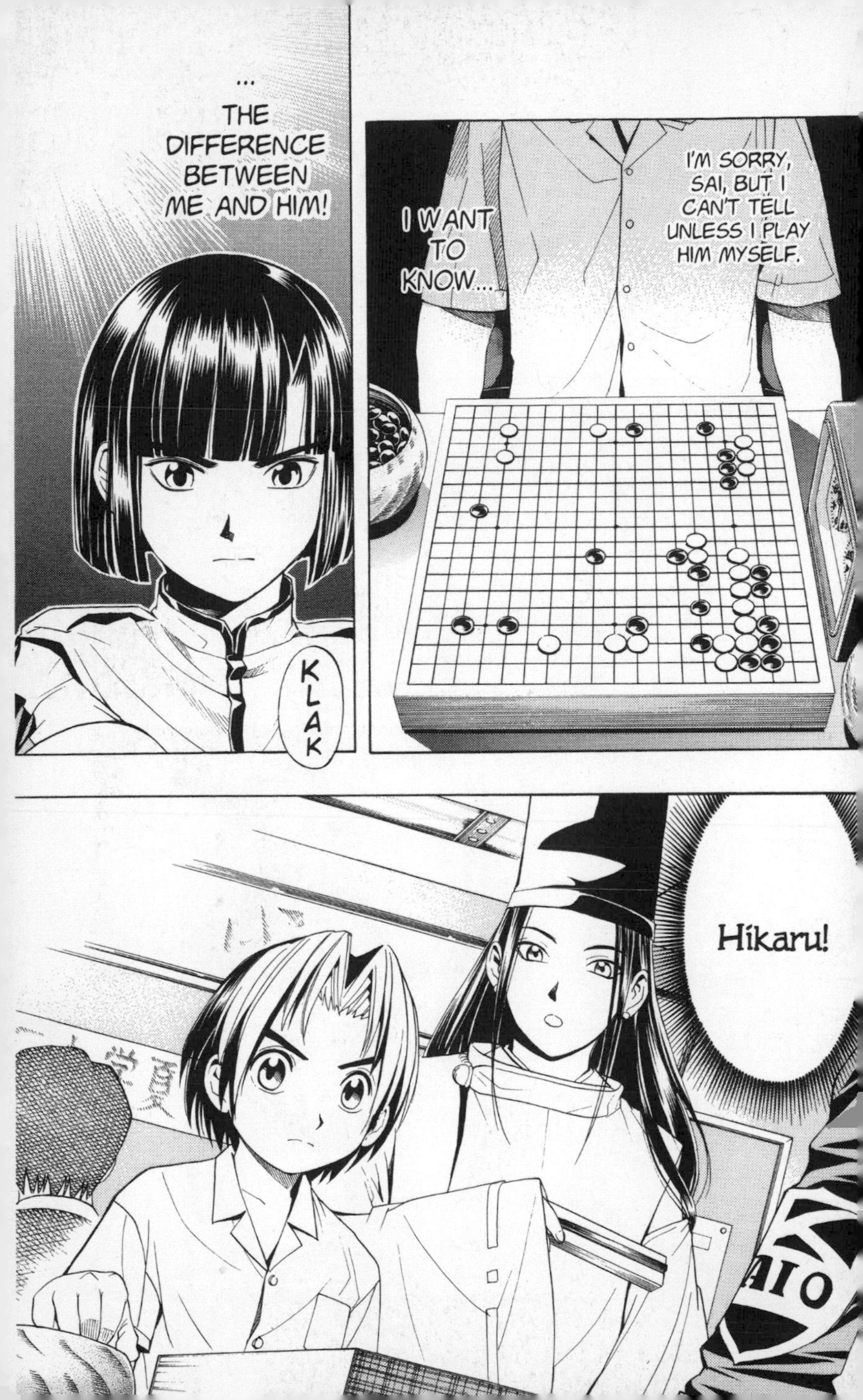
I'M SORRY, SAI, BUT I CAN'T TELL UNLESS I PLAY HIM MYSELF.
I WANT TO KNOW...
... THE DIFFERENCE BETWEEN ME AND HIM!
KLAK
Hikaru!

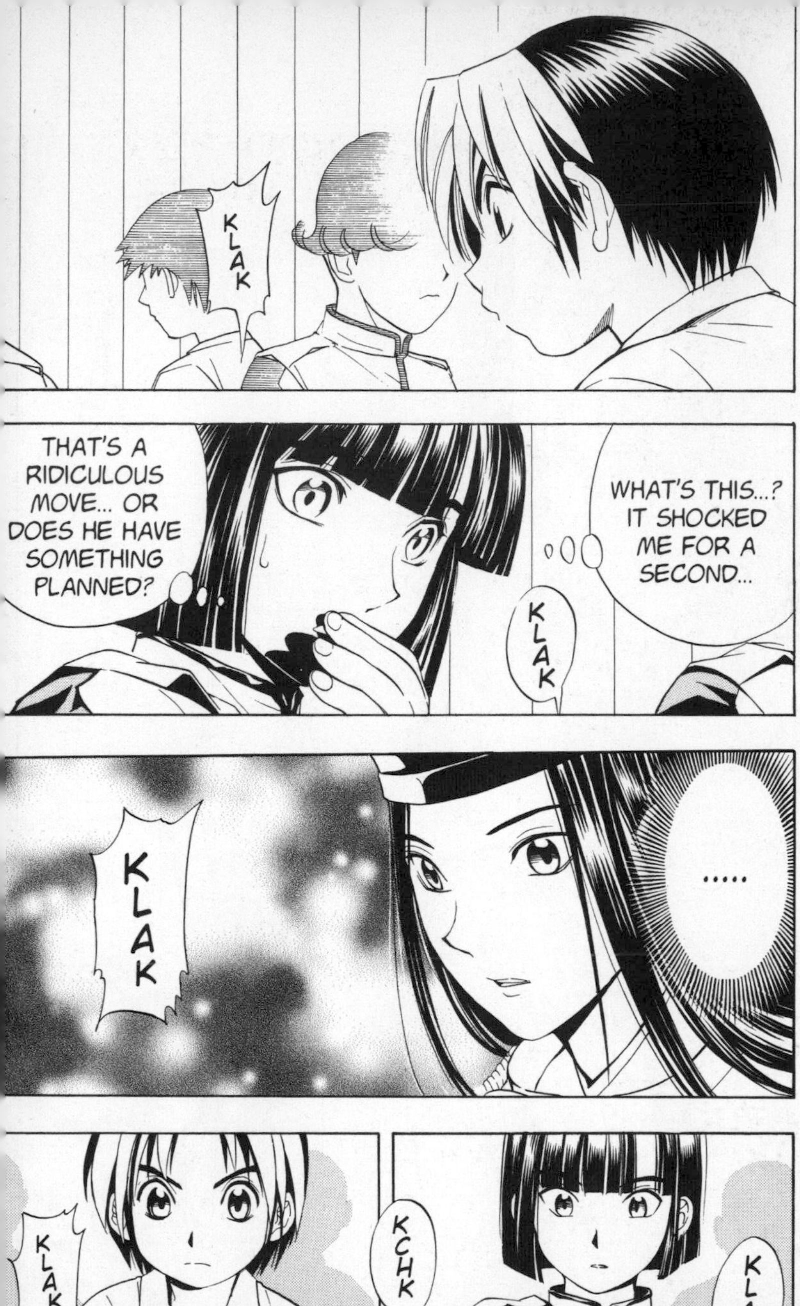
KLAK
WHAT'S THIS...? IT SHOCKED ME FOR A SECOND...
KLAK
THAT'S A RIDICULOUS MOVE... OR DOES HE HAVE SOMETHING PLANNED?
.....
KLAK
KLAK
KCHK
KLAK

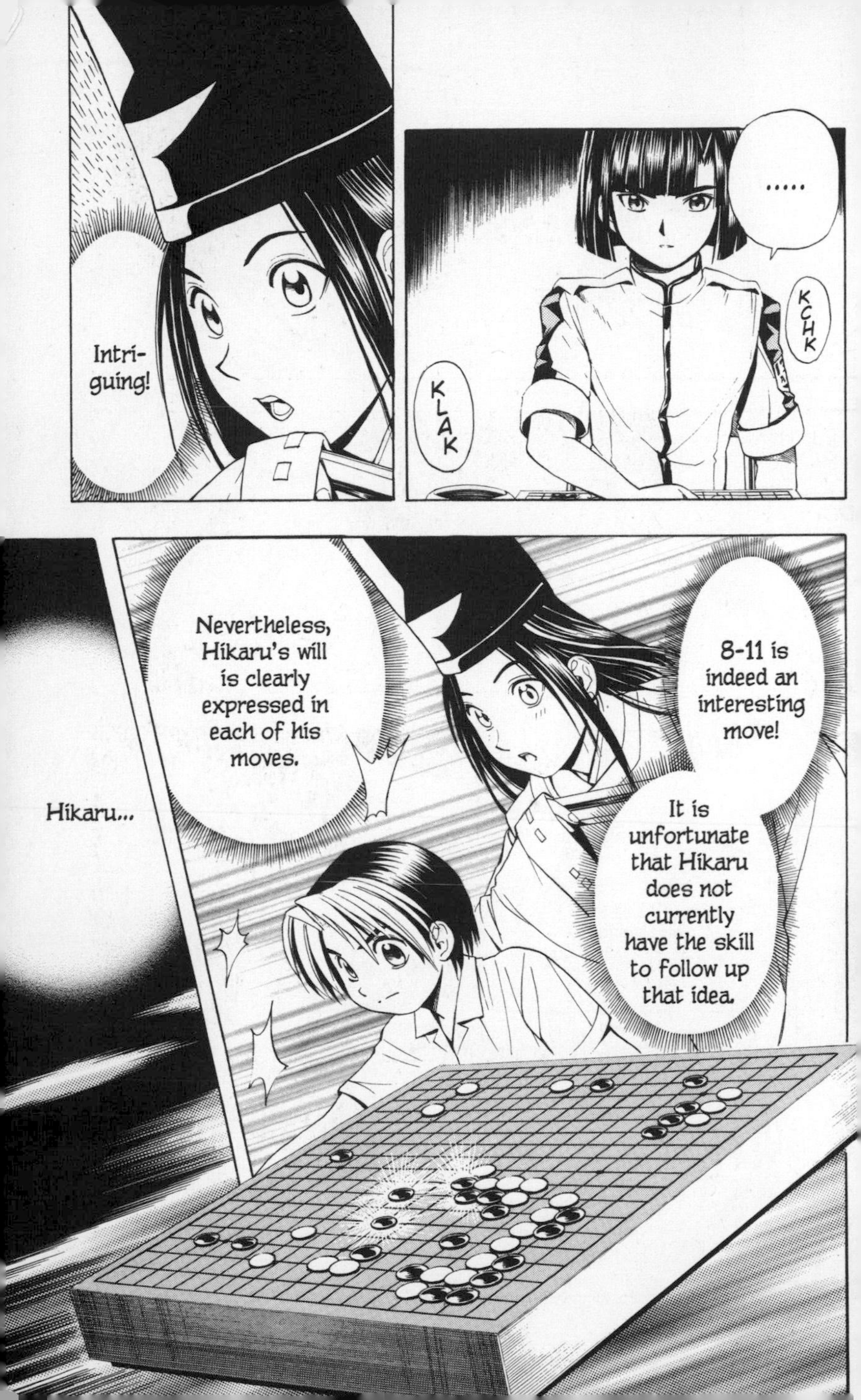
.....
KCHK
KLAK
Intri-guing!
8-11 is indeed an interesting move!
It is unfortunate that Hikaru does not currently have the skill to follow up that idea.
Nevertheless, Hikaru's will is clearly expressed in each of his moves.
Hikaru...

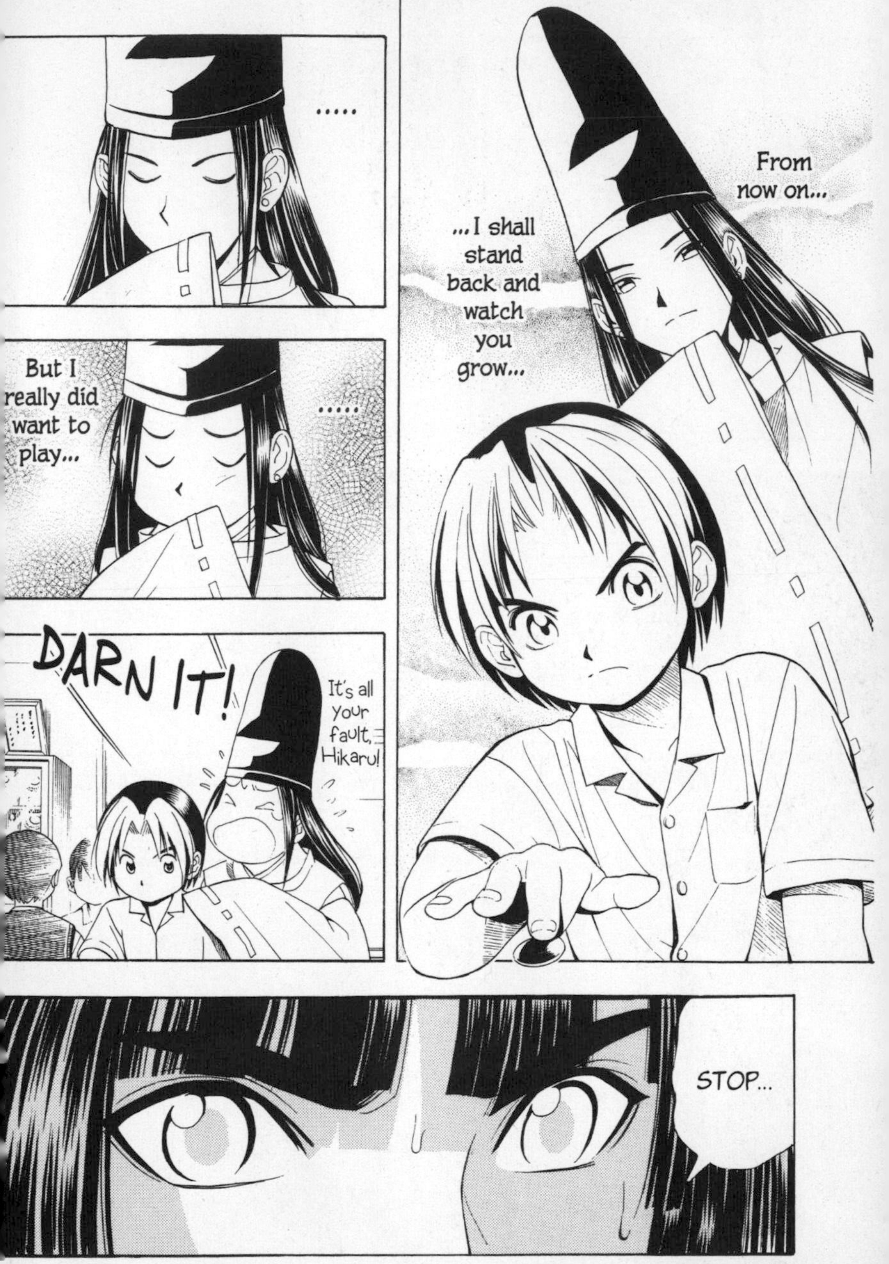
From now on...
...I shall stand back and watch you grow...
.....
.....
But I really did want to play...
DARN IT!
It's all your fault, Hikaru!
STOP...

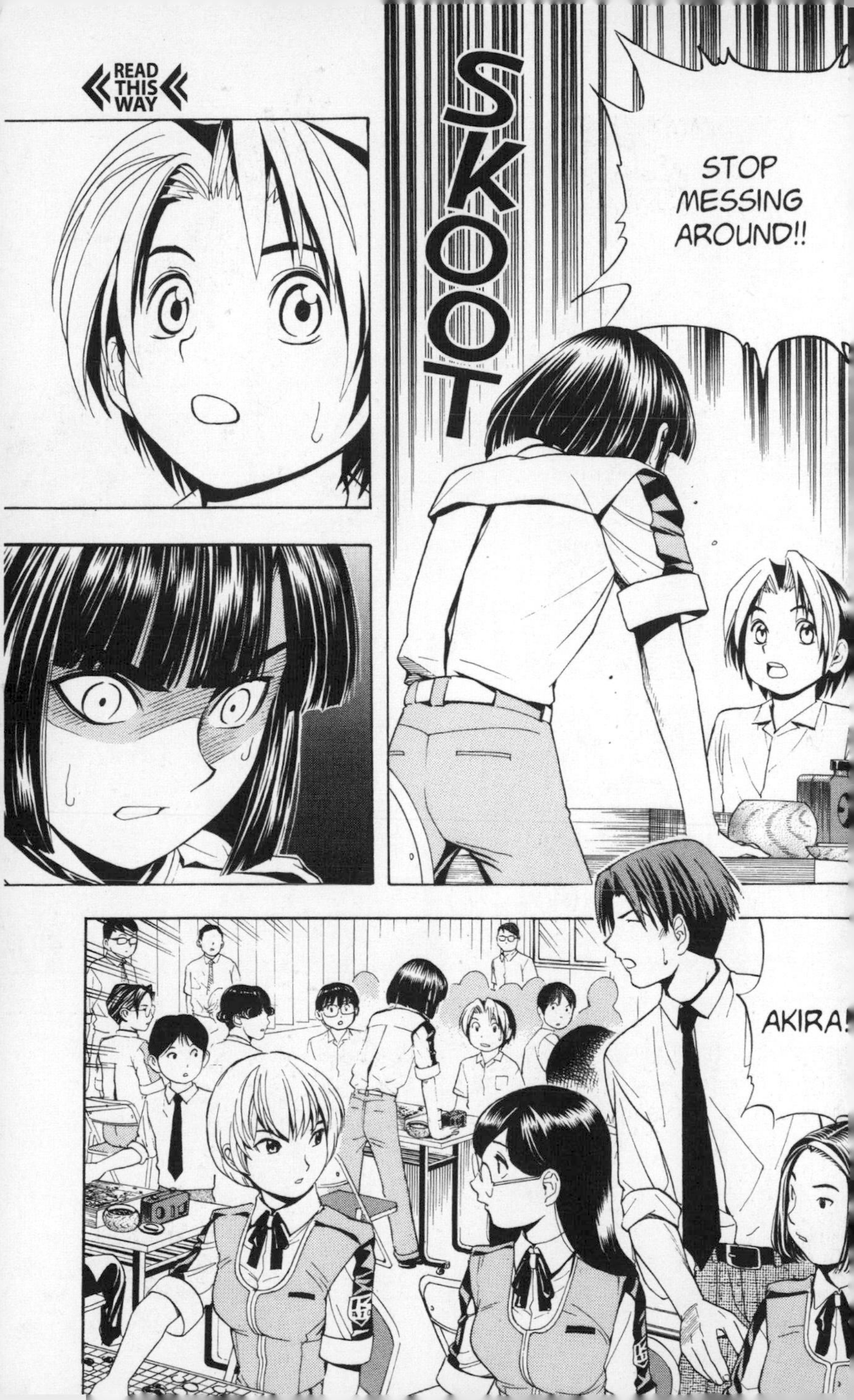
READ THIS WAY
SKOOT
STOP MESSING AROUND!!
AKIRA!

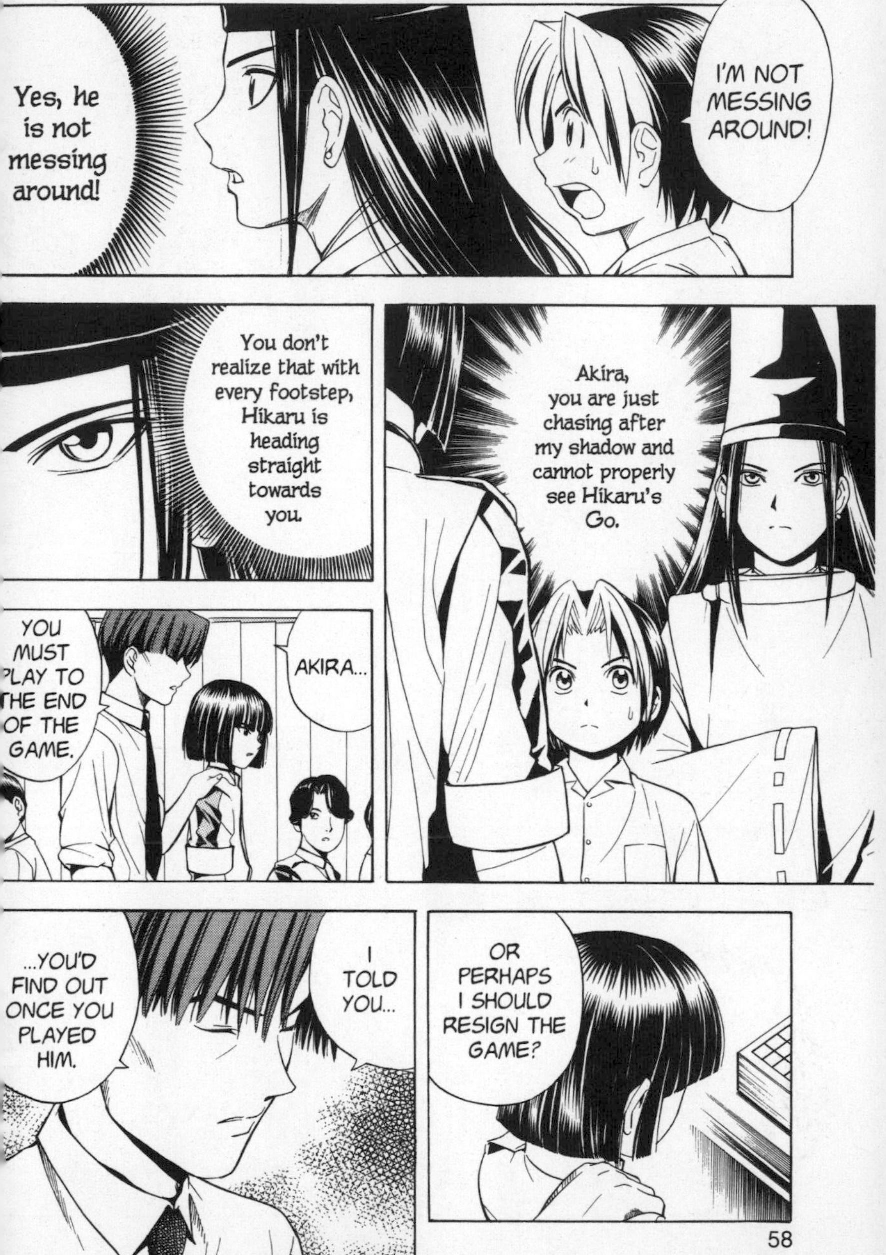
I'M NOT MESSING AROUND!
Yes, he is not messing around!
Akira, you are just chasing after my shadow and cannot properly see Hikaru's Go.
You don't realize that with every footstep, Hikaru is heading straight towards you.
AKIRA...
YOU MUST PLAY TO THE END OF THE GAME.
OR PERHAPS I SHOULD RESIGN THE GAME?
I TOLD YOU...
...YOU'D FIND OUT ONCE YOU PLAYED HIM.

READ THIS WAY

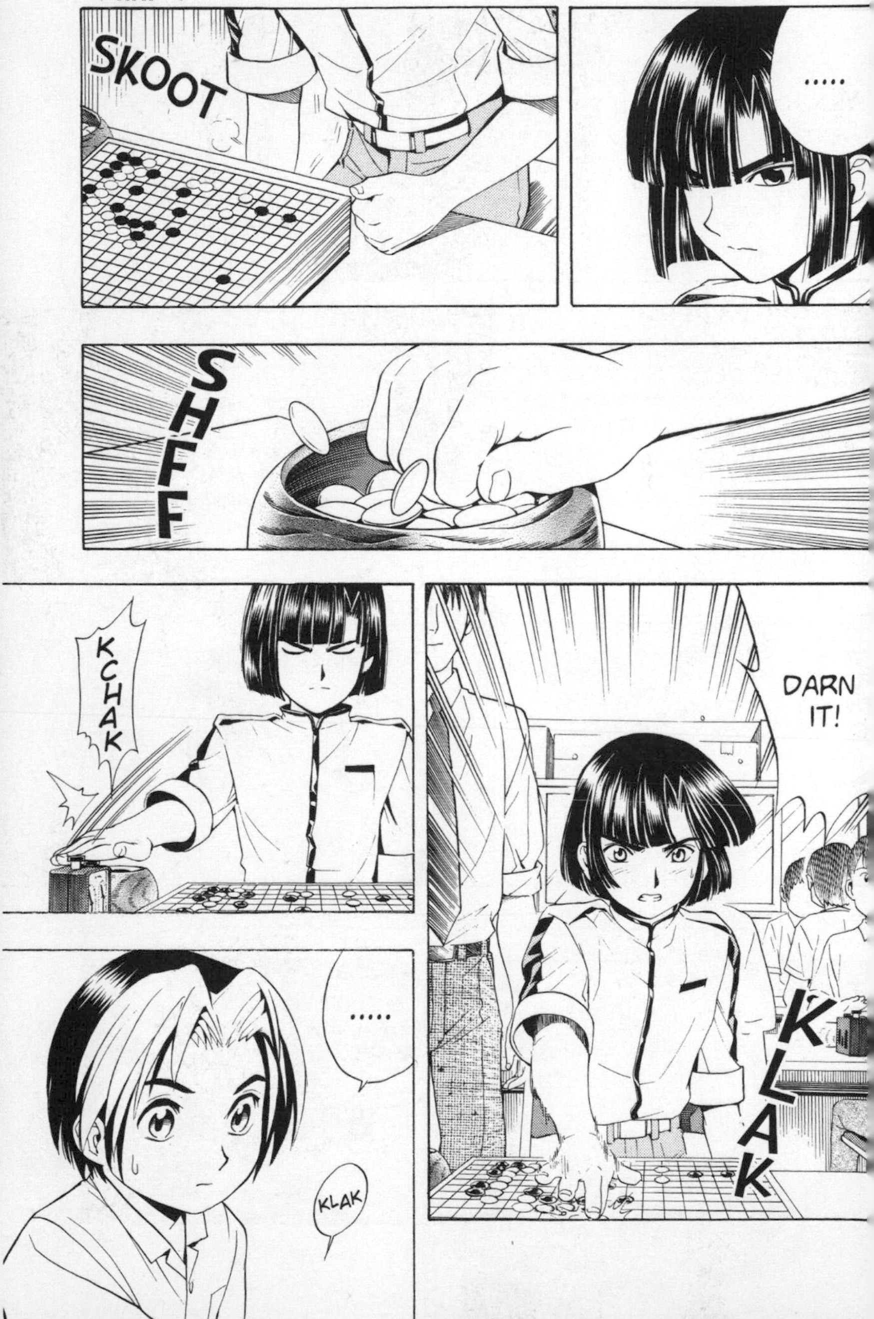
.....
SKOOT
SHFFF
DARN IT!
KLAK
KCHAK
.....
KLAK

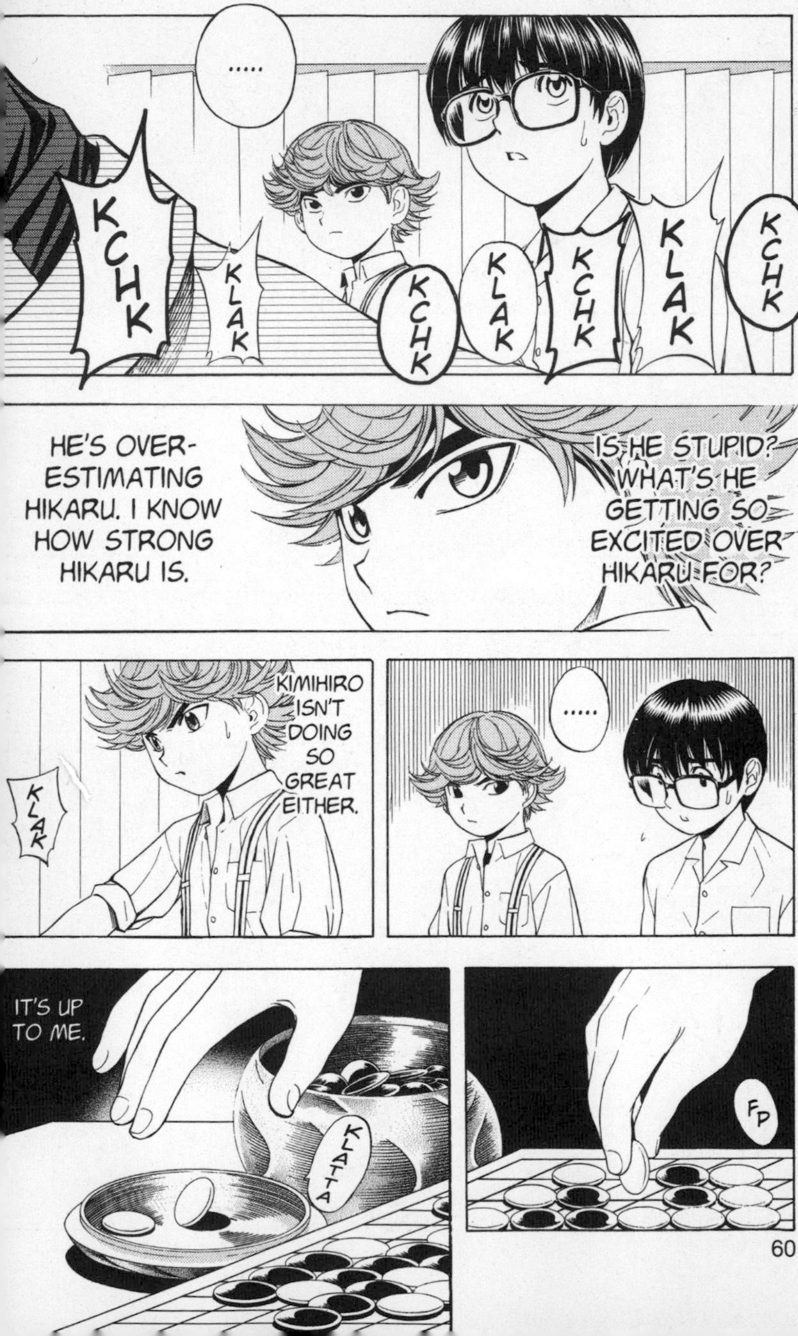
.....
KCHK
KLAK
KCHK
KLAK
KCHK
KLAK
KCHK
IS HE STUPID? WHAT'S HE GETTING SO EXCITED OVER HIKARU FOR?
HE'S OVER-ESTIMATING HIKARU. I KNOW HOW STRONG HIKARU IS.
.....
KIMIHIRO ISN'T DOING SO GREAT EITHER.
KLAK
FP
IT'S UP TO ME.
KLATTA

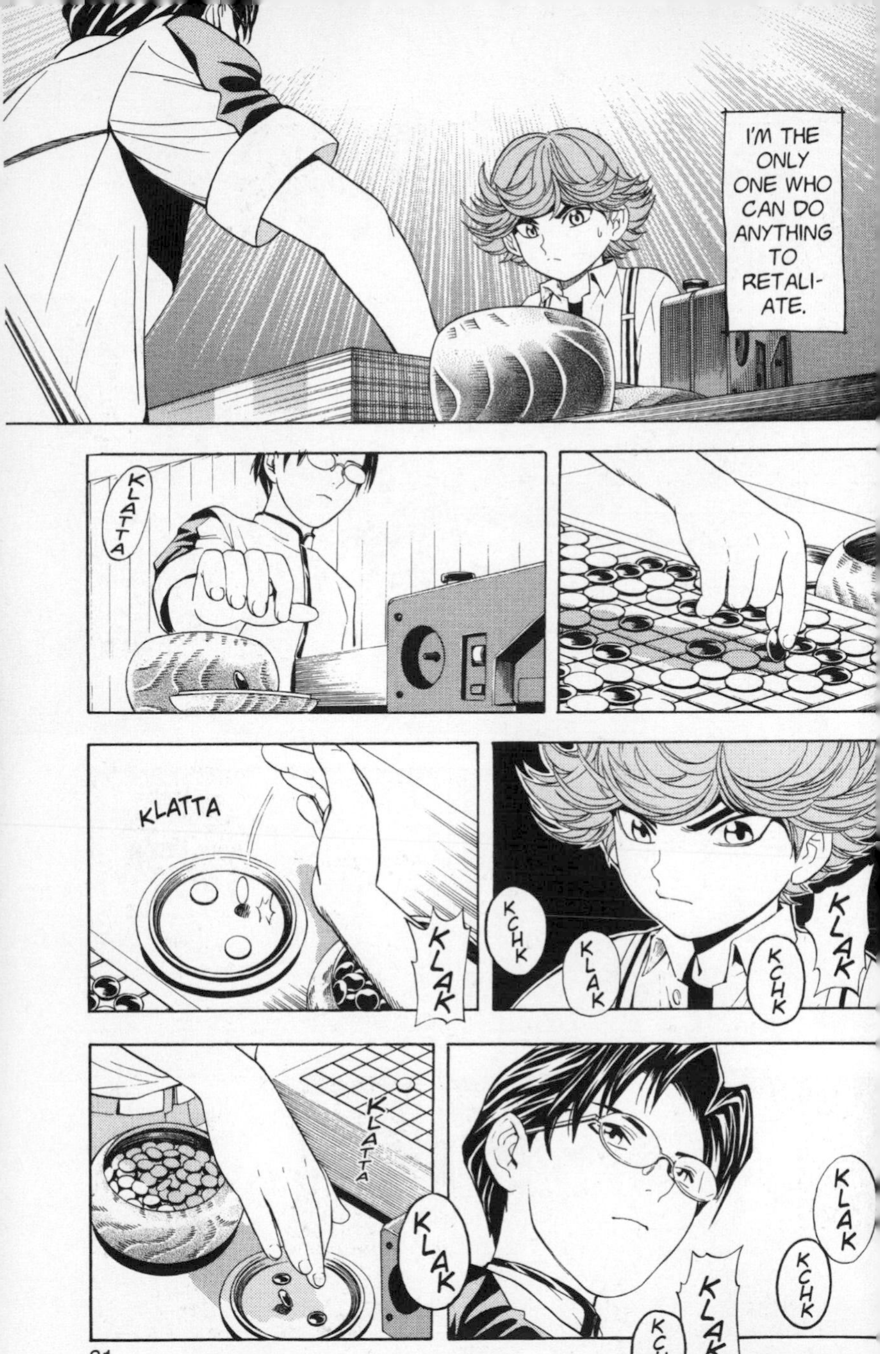
I'M THE ONLY ONE WHO CAN DO ANYTHING TO RETALI-ATE.
KLATTA
KLAK
KCHK
KLAK
KCHK
KLAK
KLATTA
KLAK
KCHK
KLAK
KCHK
KLAK
KLATTA

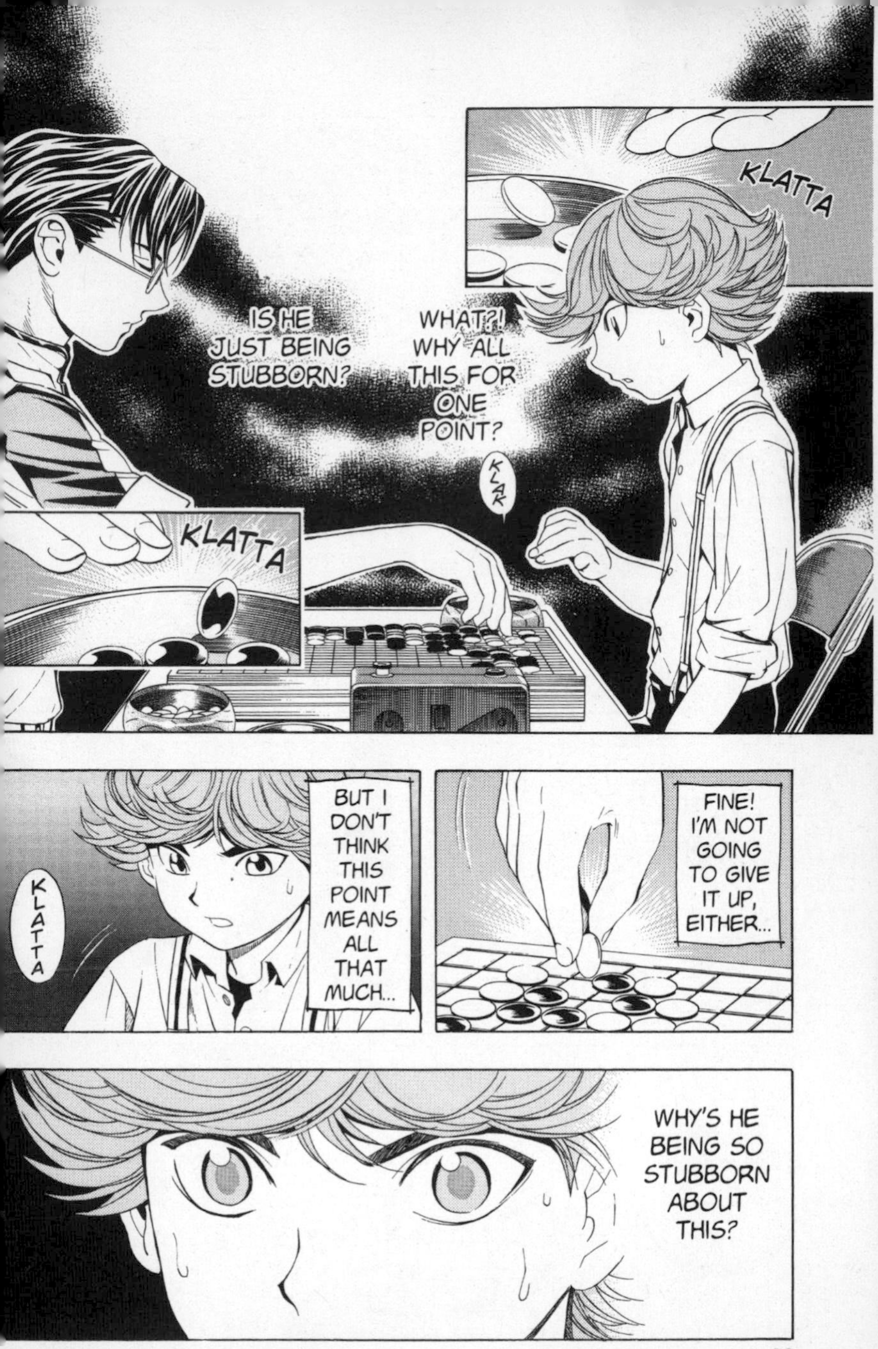
KLATTA
WHAT?! WHY ALL THIS FOR ONE POINT?
IS HE JUST BEING STUBBORN?
KLAK
KLATTA
FINE! I'M NOT GOING TO GIVE IT UP, EITHER...
BUT I DON'T THINK THIS POINT MEANS ALL THAT MUCH...
KLATTA
WHY'S HE BEING SO STUBBORN ABOUT THIS?

READ THIS WAY

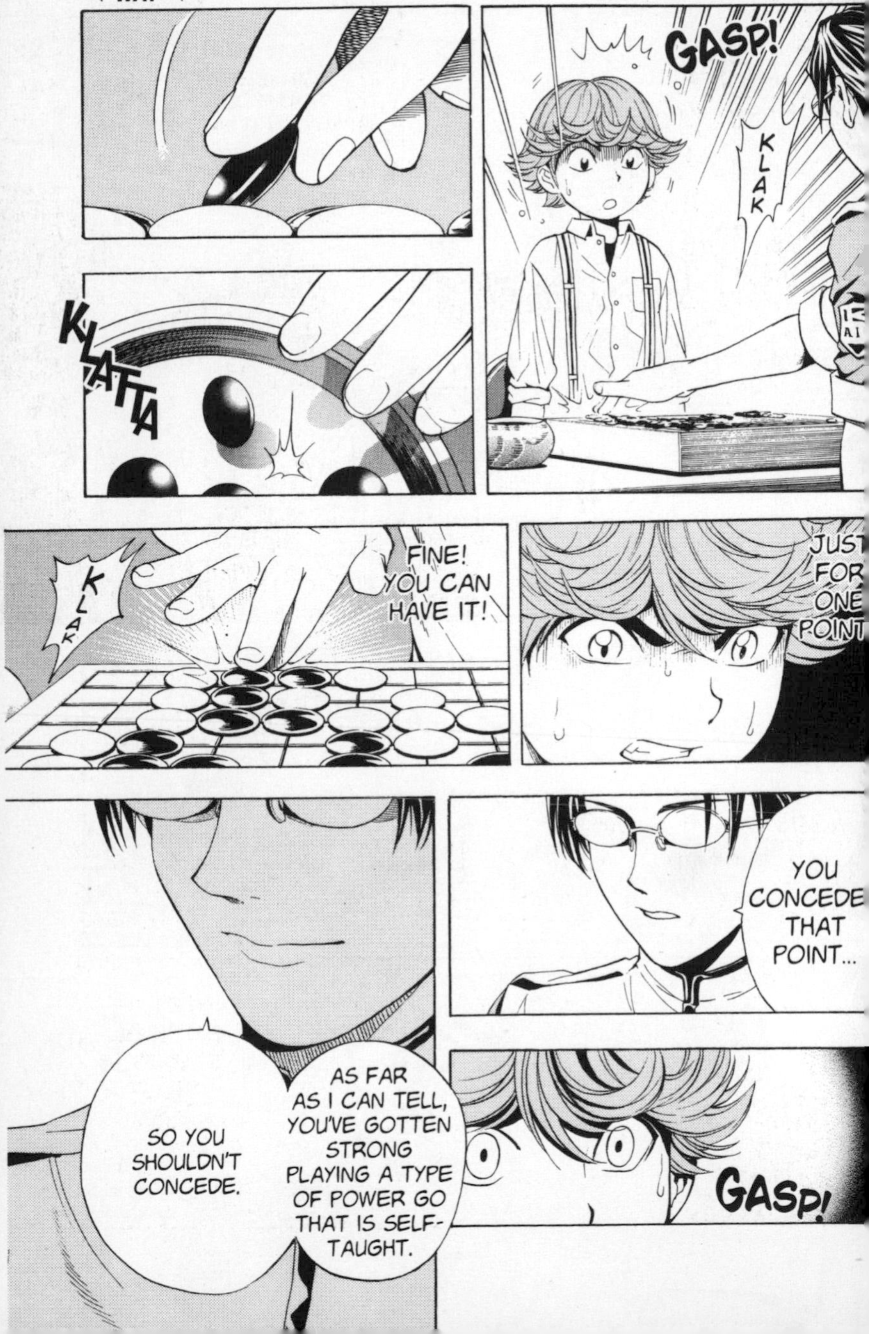
GASP!
KLAK
KLATTA
JUST FOR ONE POINT
FINE! YOU CAN HAVE IT!
KLAK
YOU CONCEDE THAT POINT...
GASP!
AS FAR AS I CAN TELL, YOU'VE GOTTEN STRONG PLAYING A TYPE OF POWER GO THAT IS SELF-TAUGHT.
SO YOU SHOULDN'T CONCEDE.

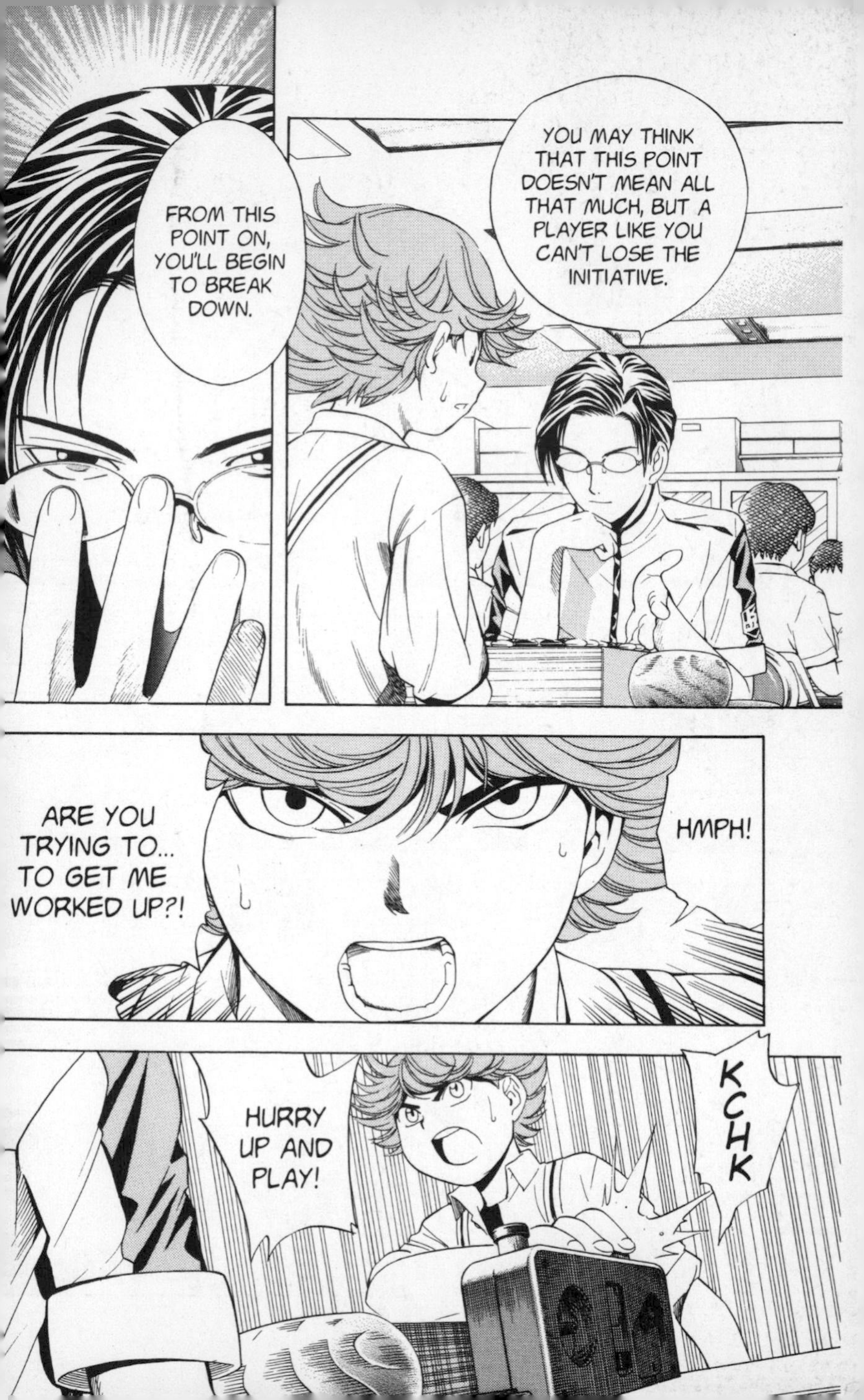
YOU MAY THINK THAT THIS POINT DOESN'T MEAN ALL THAT MUCH, BUT A PLAYER LIKE YOU CAN'T LOSE THE INITIATIVE.
FROM THIS POINT ON, YOU'LL BEGIN TO BREAK DOWN.
HMPH!
ARE YOU TRYING TO... TO GET ME WORKED UP?!
KCHK
HURRY UP AND PLAY!

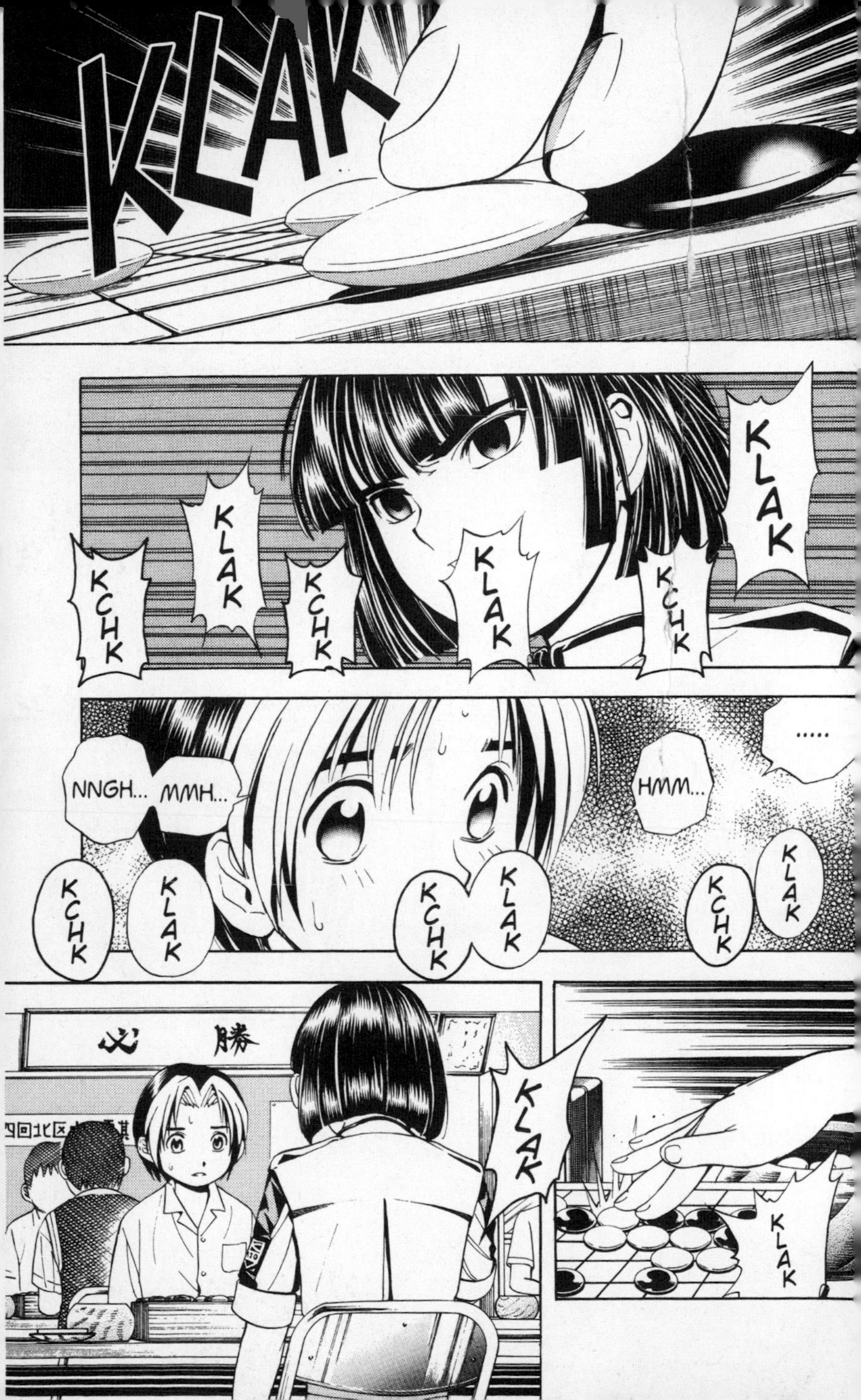
KLAK
KLAK
KCHK
KLAK
KCHK
KLAK
KCHK
.....
HMM...
KLAK
KCHK
KLAK
KCHK
MMH...
NNGH...
KLAK
KCHK
KLAK
KLAK
必勝

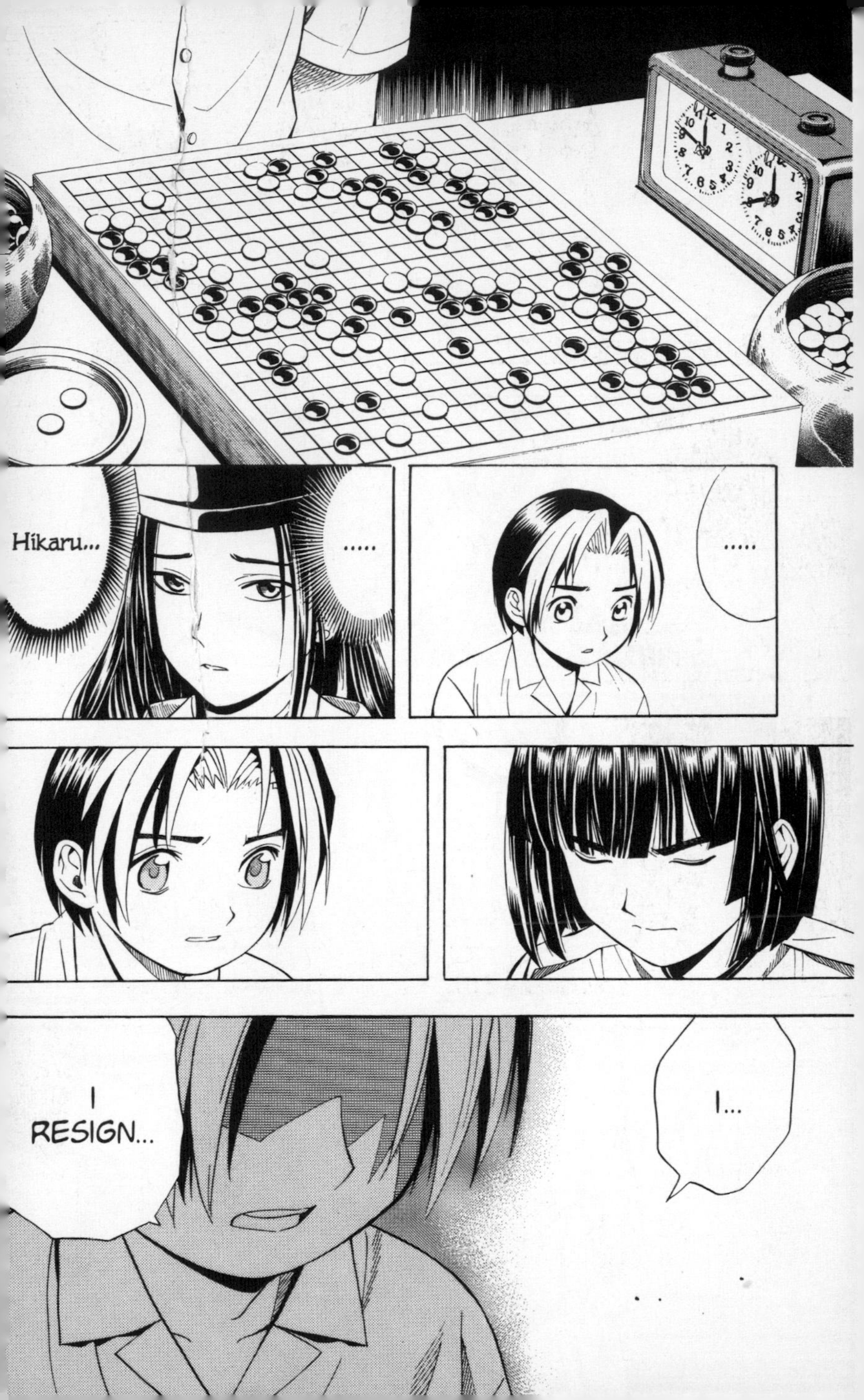
.....
.....
Hikaru...
I...
I RESIGN...

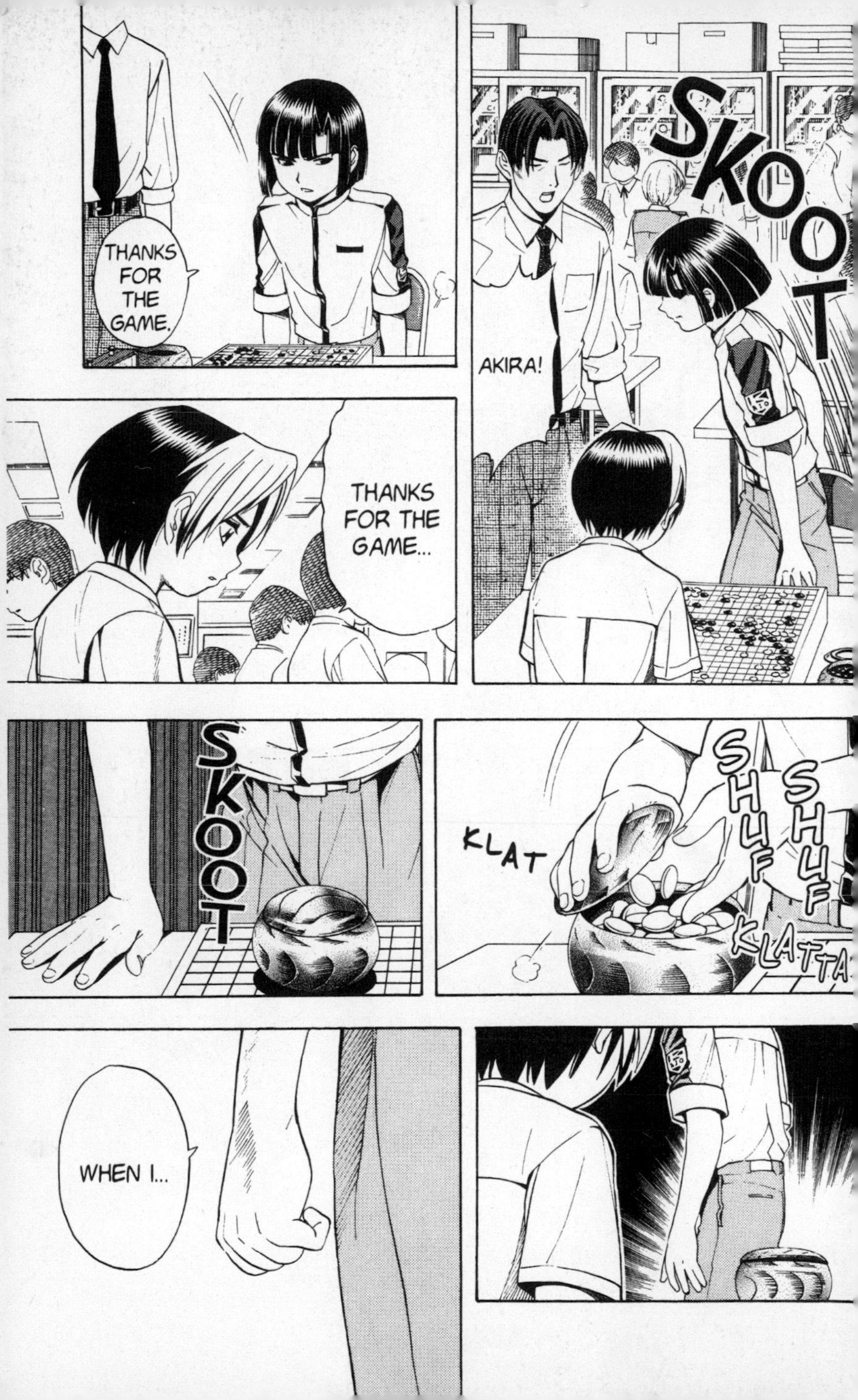
SKOOT
AKIRA!
THANKS FOR THE GAME.
THANKS FOR THE GAME...
SHUF
SHUF
KLAT
KLATTA
SKOOT
WHEN I...

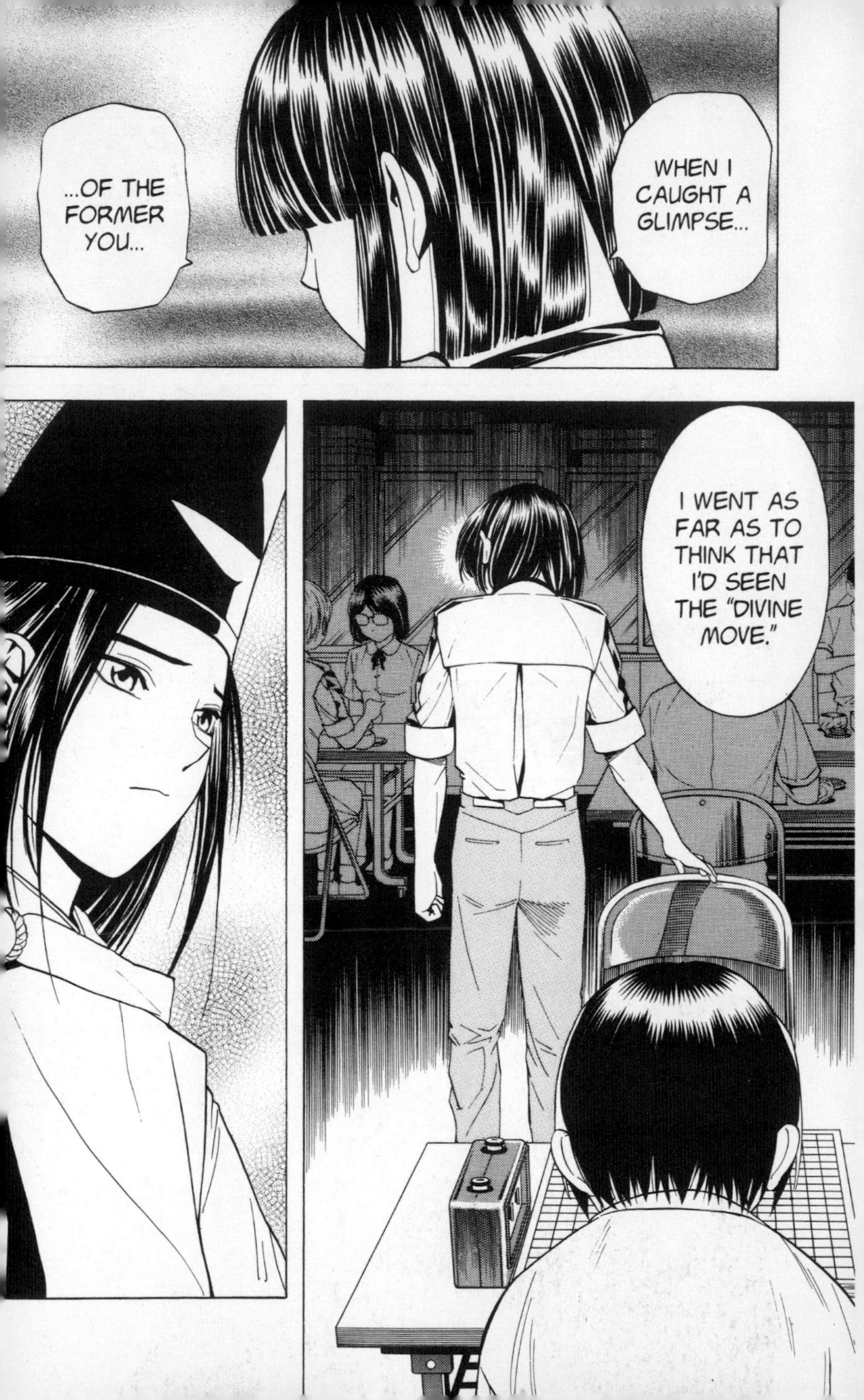
WHEN I CAUGHT A GLIMPSE...
...OF THE FORMER YOU...
I WENT AS FAR AS TO THINK THAT I'D SEEN THE "DIVINE MOVE."

READ THIS WAY

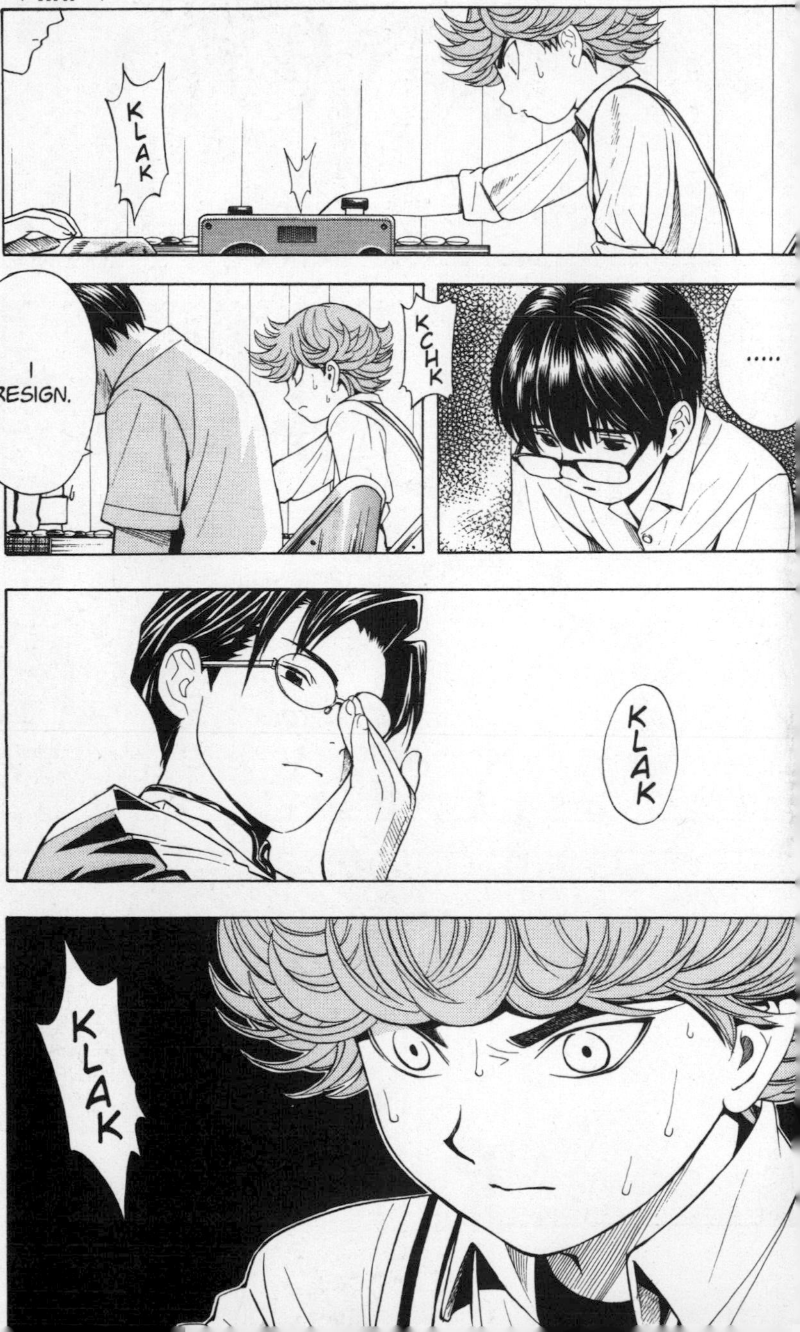

KLAK
.....
KCHK
I RESIGN.
KLAK
KLAK

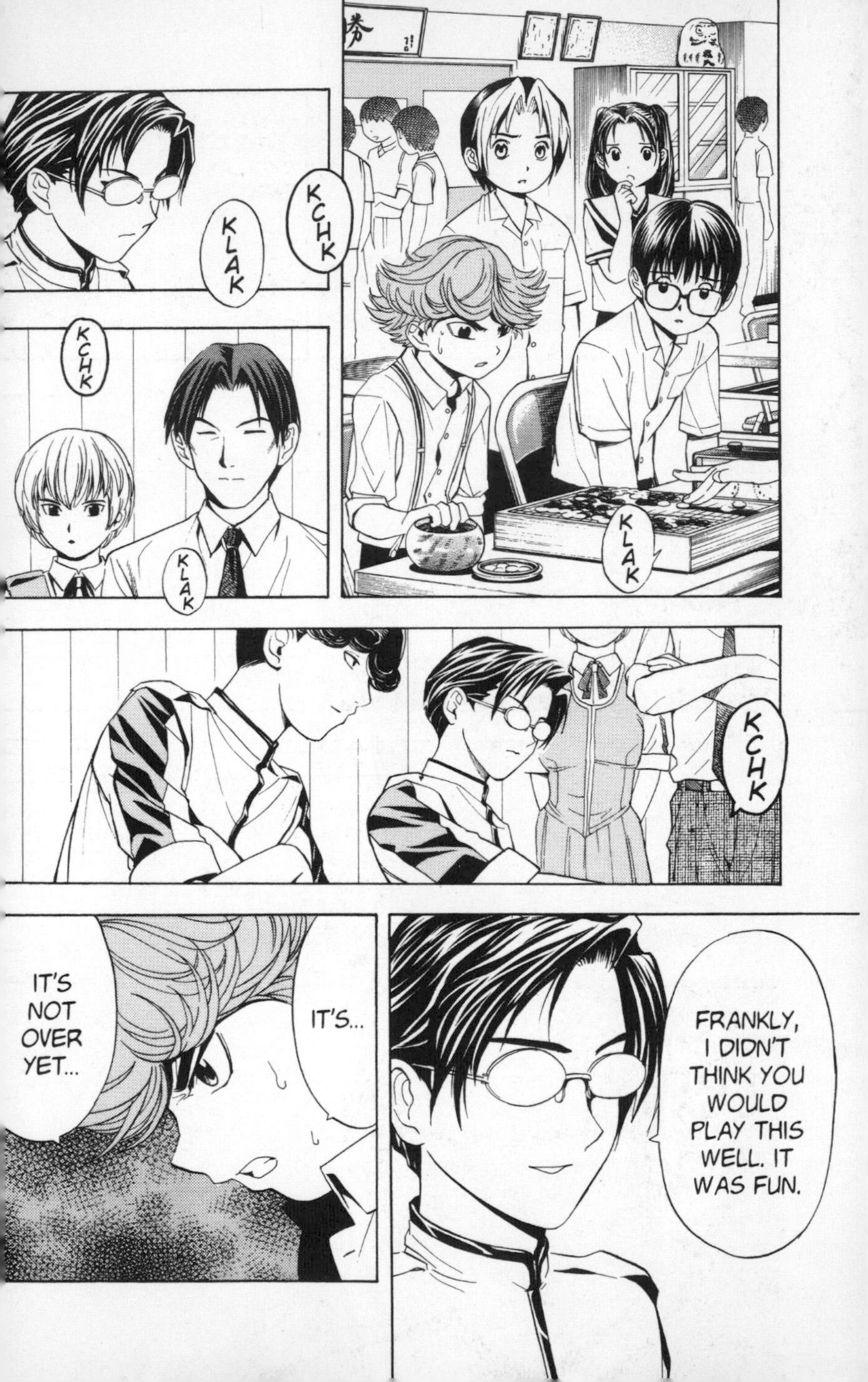
KLAK
KCHK
KLAK
KCHK
KLAK
KCHK
FRANKLY, I DIDN'T THINK YOU WOULD PLAY THIS WELL. IT WAS FUN.
IT'S...
IT'S NOT OVER YET...

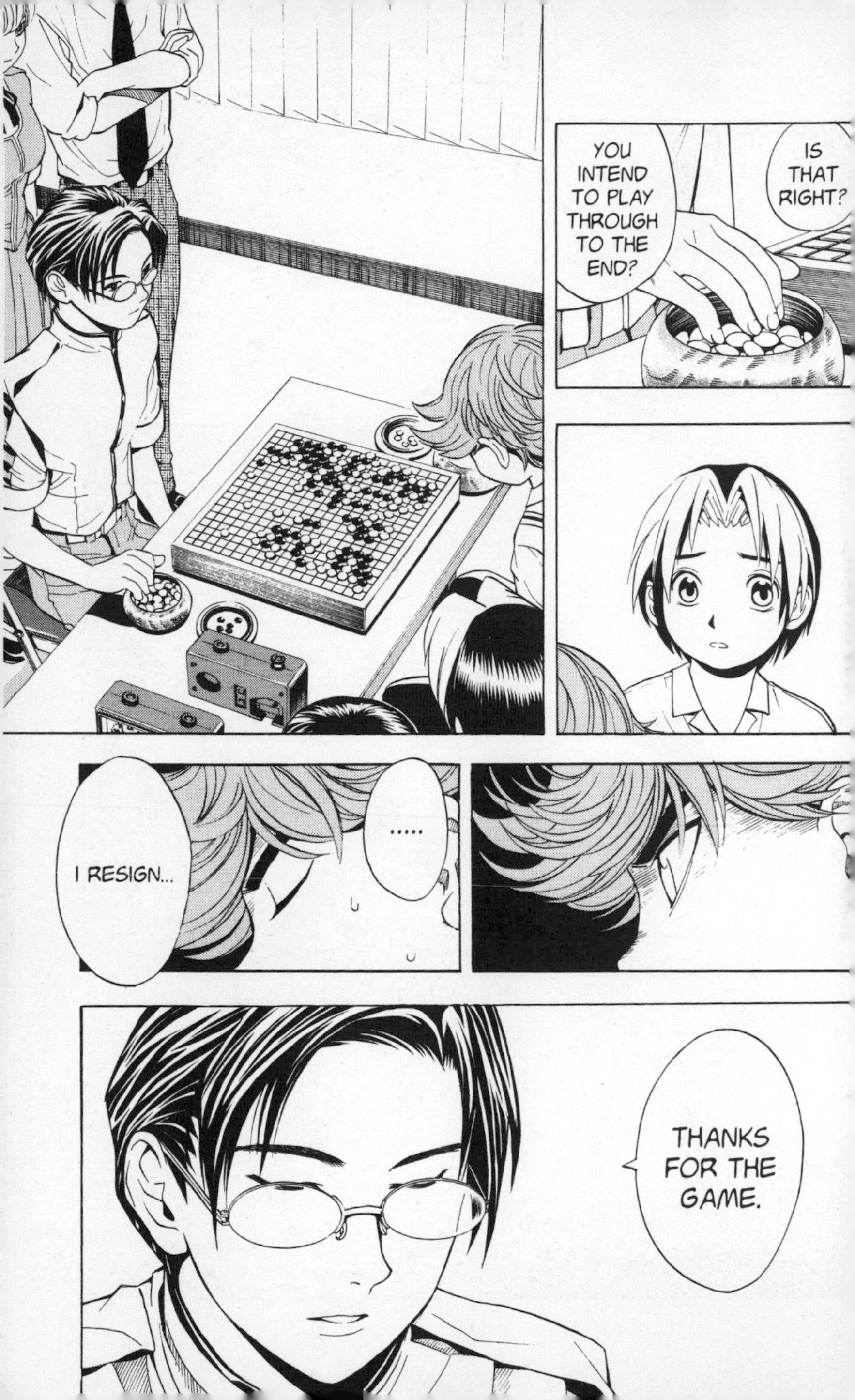
YOU INTEND TO PLAY THROUGH TO THE END?
IS THAT RIGHT?
.....
I RESIGN...
THANKS FOR THE GAME.

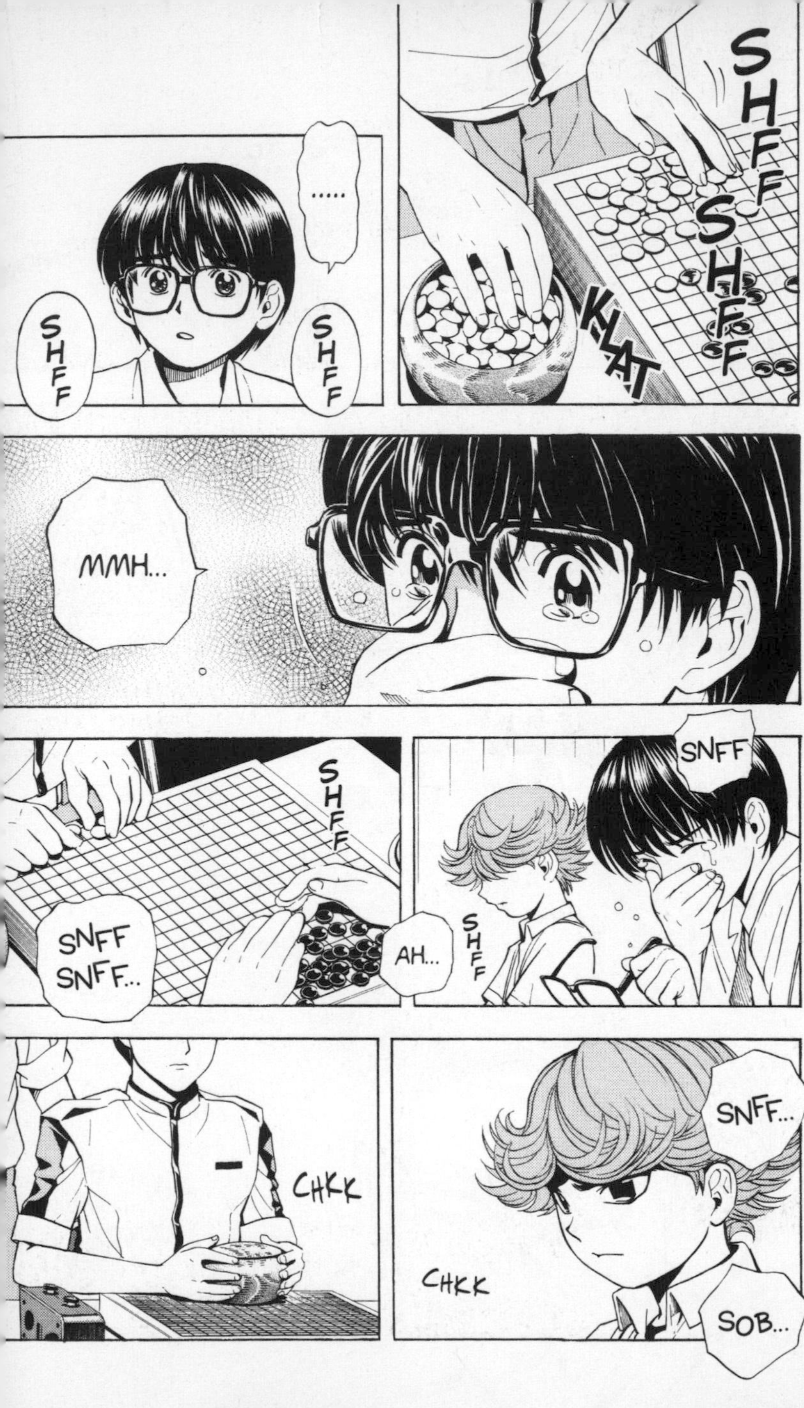
SHFF
SHFF
KLAT
......
SHFF
SHFF
MMH...
SNFF
SHFF
SHFF
AH...
SNFF SNFF...
SNFF...
SOB...
CHKK
CHKK

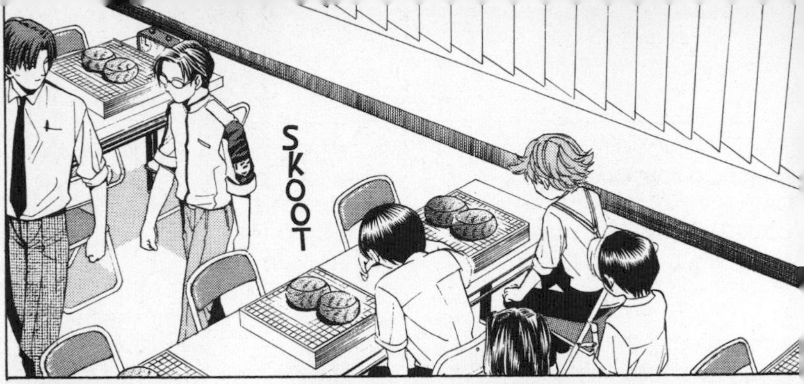
SKOOT

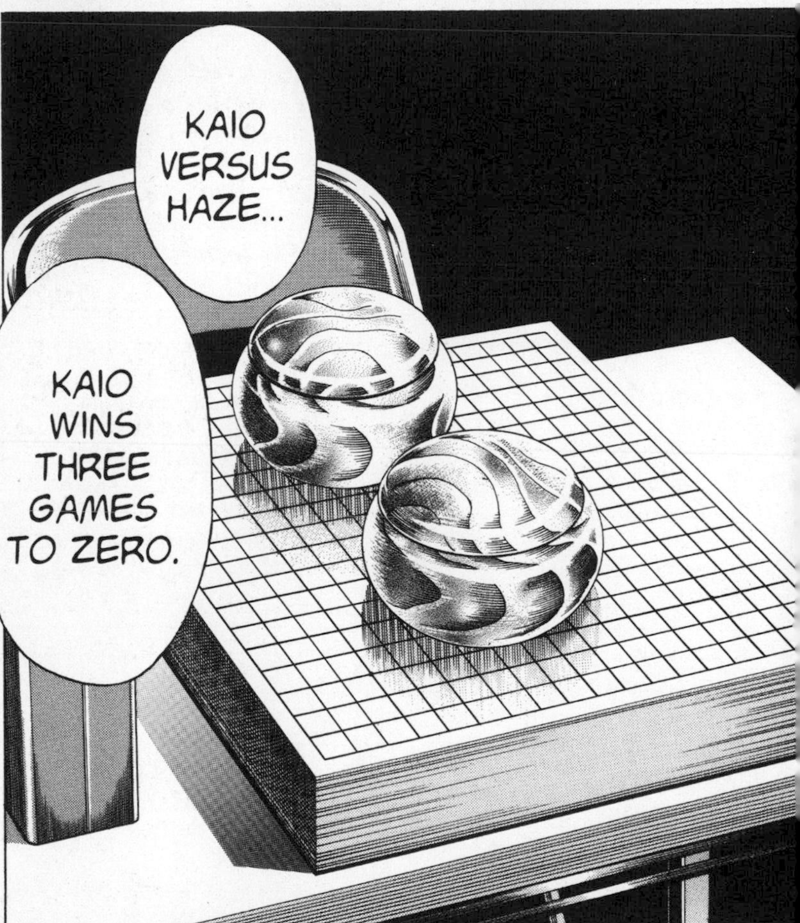
KAIO VERSUS HAZE...
KAIO WINS THREE GAMES TO ZERO.

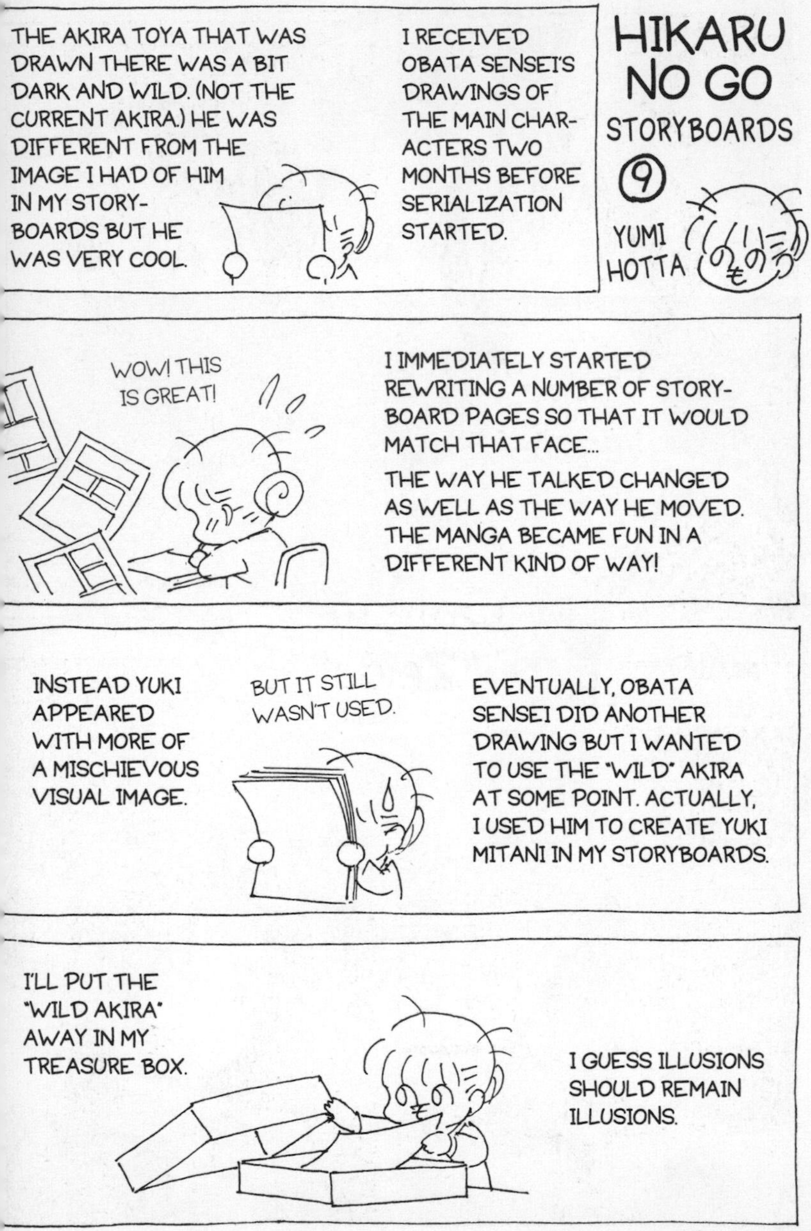
HIKARU NO GO
STORYBOARDS
9
YUMI HOTTA
I RECEIVED OBATA SENSEI'S DRAWINGS OF THE MAIN CHARACTERS TWO MONTHS BEFORE SERIALIZATION STARTED.
THE AKIRA TOYA THAT WAS DRAWN THERE WAS A BIT DARK AND WILD. (NOT THE CURRENT AKIRA.) HE WAS DIFFERENT FROM THE IMAGE I HAD OF HIM IN MY STORYBOARDS BUT HE WAS VERY COOL.
I IMMEDIATELY STARTED REWRITING A NUMBER OF STORYBOARD PAGES SO THAT IT WOULD MATCH THAT FACE...
THE WAY HE TALKED CHANGED AS WELL AS THE WAY HE MOVED. THE MANGA BECAME FUN IN A DIFFERENT KIND OF WAY!
WOW! THIS IS GREAT!
EVENTUALLY, OBATA SENSEI DID ANOTHER DRAWING BUT I WANTED TO USE THE "WILD" AKIRA AT SOME POINT. ACTUALLY, I USED HIM TO CREATE YUKI MITANI IN MY STORYBOARDS.
BUT IT STILL WASN'T USED.
INSTEAD YUKI APPEARED WITH MORE OF A MISCHIEVOUS VISUAL IMAGE.
I GUESS ILLUSIONS SHOULD REMAIN ILLUSIONS.
I'LL PUT THE "WILD AKIRA" AWAY IN MY TREASURE BOX.

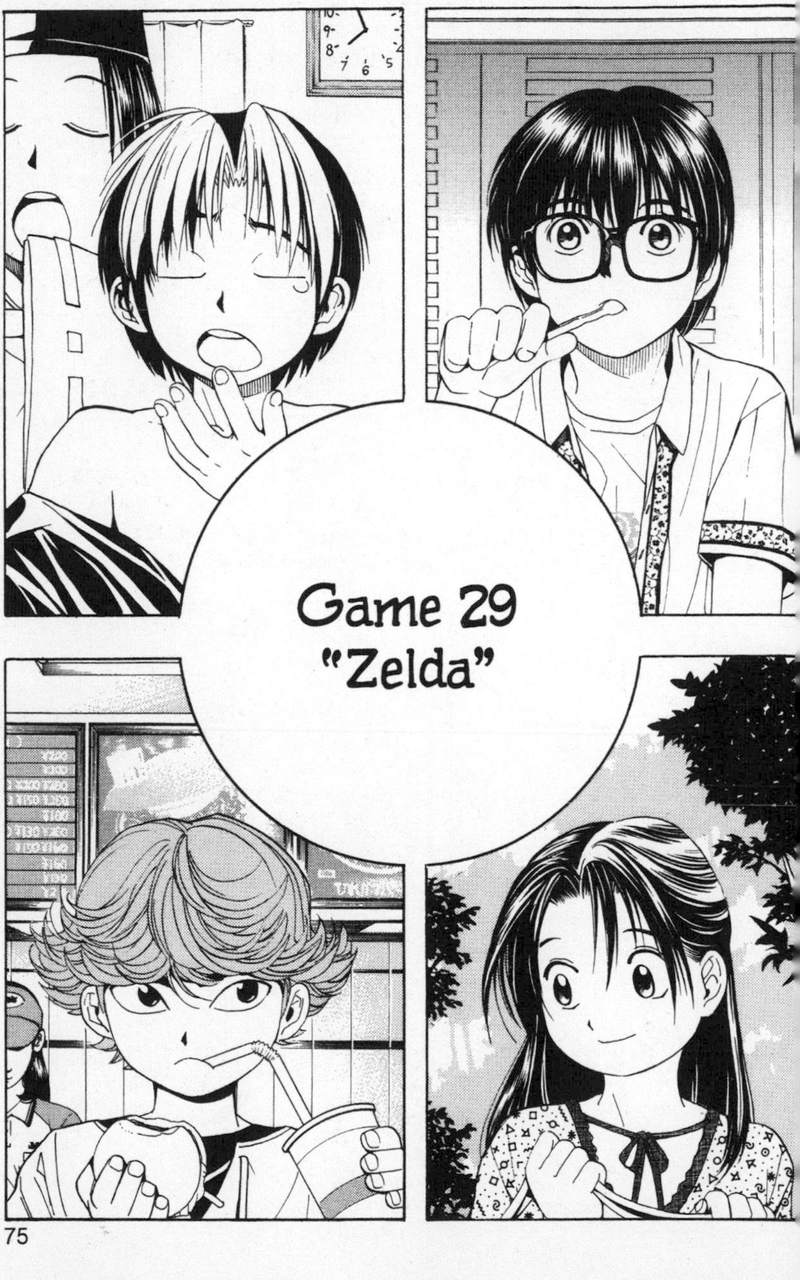

Game 29
"Zelda"

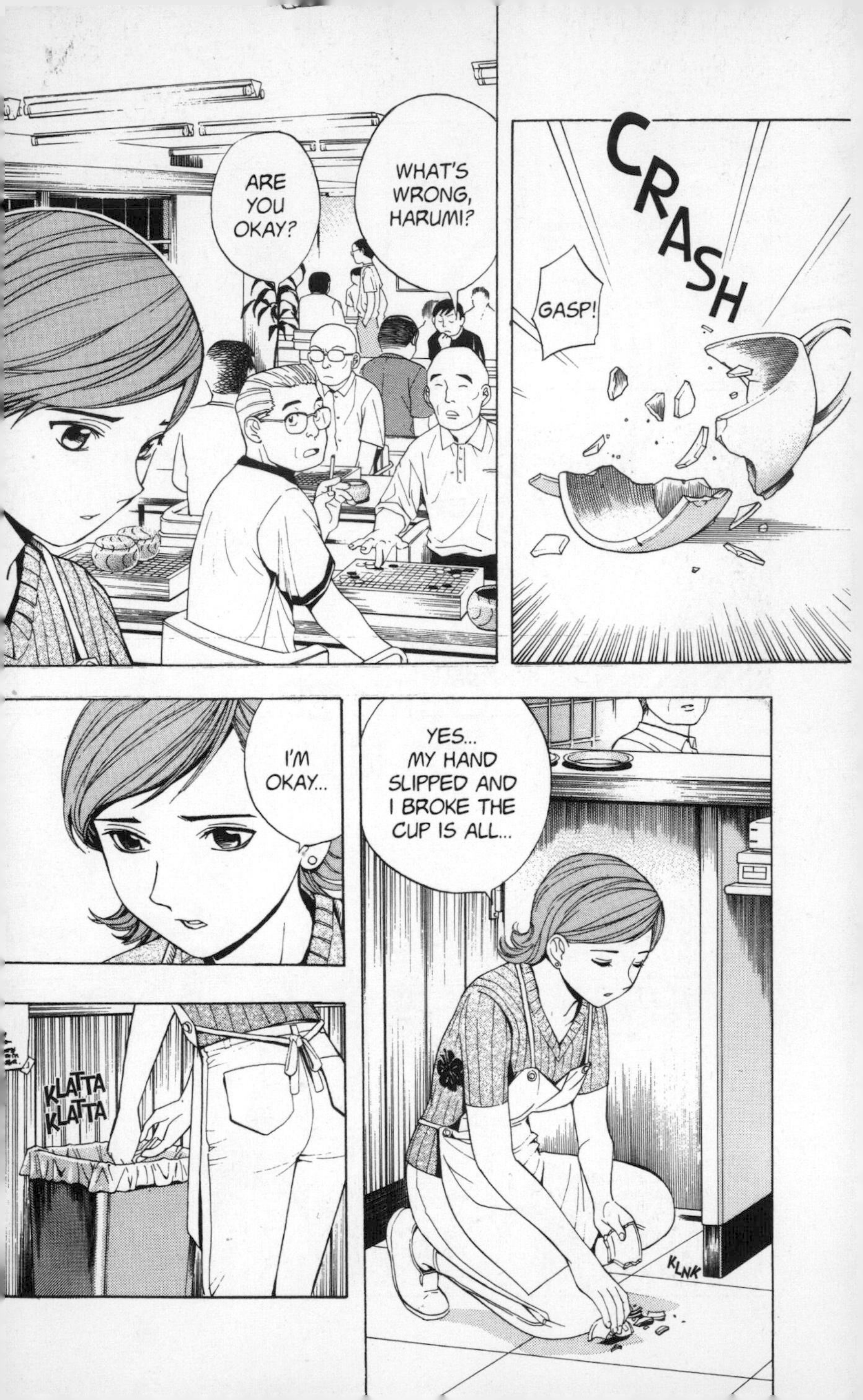
CRASH
GASP!
WHAT'S WRONG, HARUMI?
ARE YOU OKAY?
YES... MY HAND SLIPPED AND I BROKE THE CUP IS ALL...
KLNK
I'M OKAY...
KLATTA KLATTA

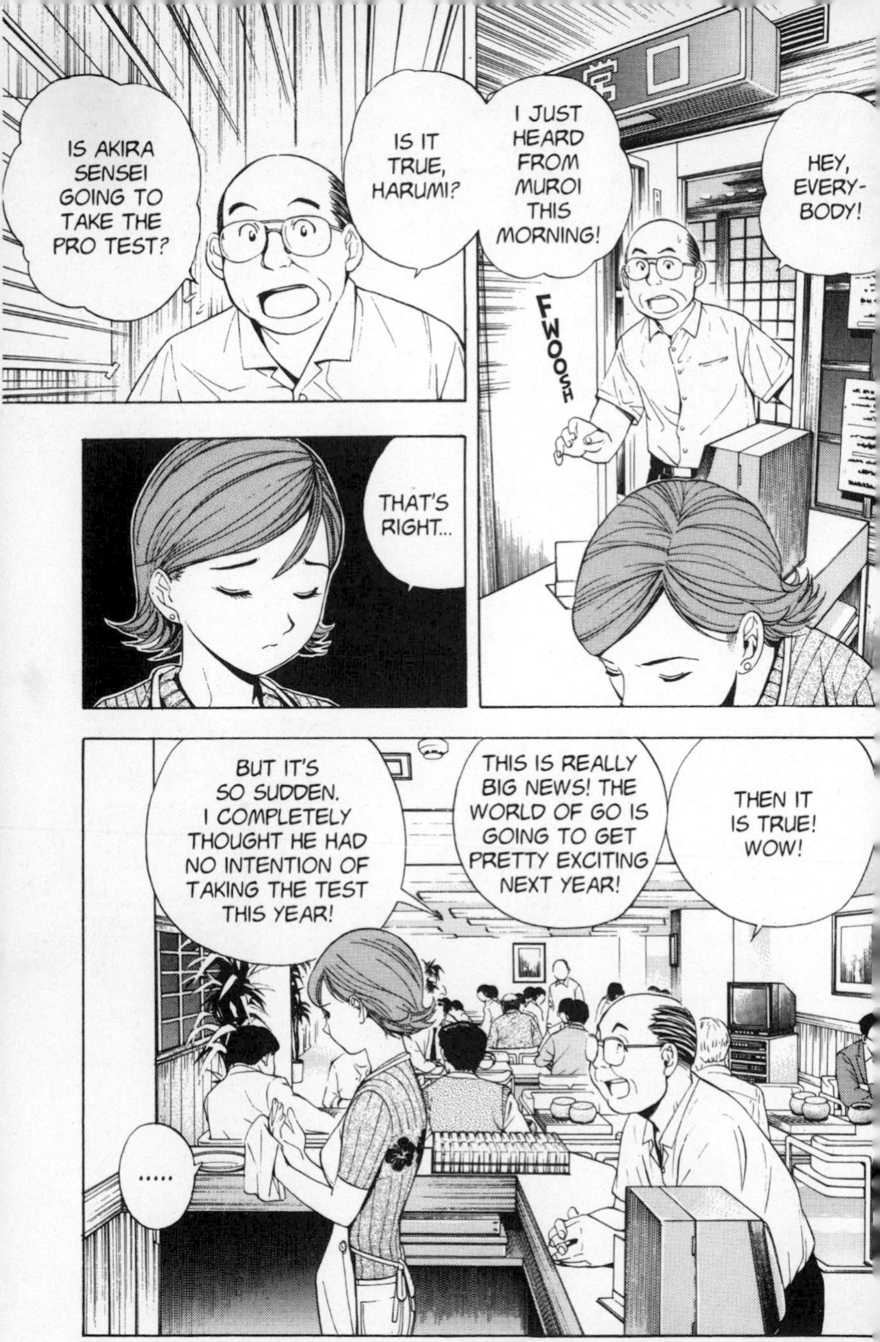
HEY, EVERYBODY!
I JUST HEARD FROM MUROI THIS MORNING!
FWOOSH
IS IT TRUE, HARUMI?
IS AKIRA SENSEI GOING TO TAKE THE PRO TEST?
THAT'S RIGHT...
THEN IT IS TRUE! WOW!
THIS IS REALLY BIG NEWS! THE WORLD OF GO IS GOING TO GET PRETTY EXCITING NEXT YEAR!
BUT IT'S SO SUDDEN. I COMPLETELY THOUGHT HE HAD NO INTENTION OF TAKING THE TEST THIS YEAR!
......

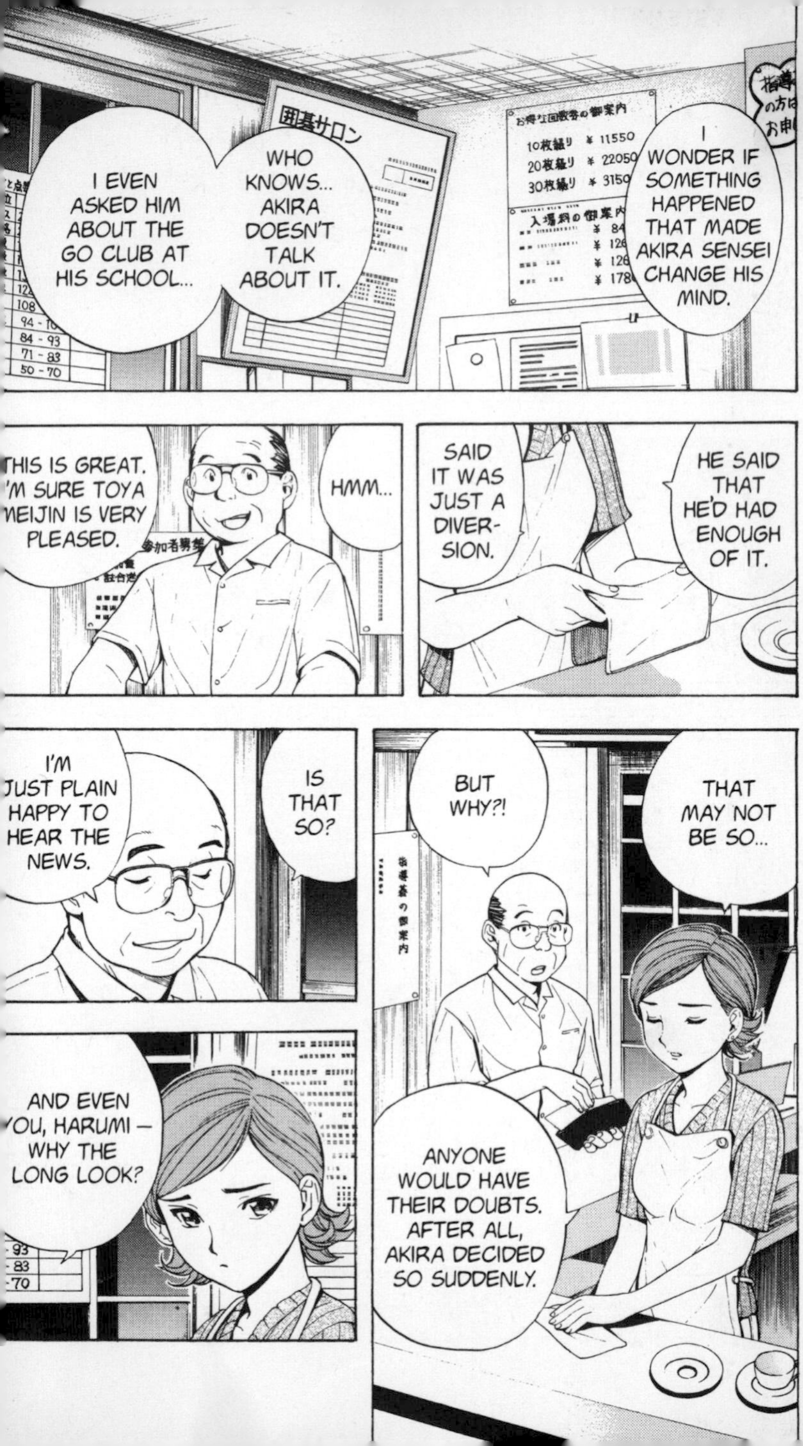
I WONDER IF SOMETHING HAPPENED THAT MADE AKIRA SENSEI CHANGE HIS MIND.
囲碁サロン
WHO KNOWS... AKIRA DOESN'T TALK ABOUT IT.
I EVEN ASKED HIM ABOUT THE GO CLUB AT HIS SCHOOL...
HE SAID THAT HE'D HAD ENOUGH OF IT.
SAID IT WAS JUST A DIVERSION.
HMM...
THIS IS GREAT. I'M SURE TOYA MEIJIN IS VERY PLEASED.
THAT MAY NOT BE SO...
BUT WHY?!
ANYONE WOULD HAVE THEIR DOUBTS. AFTER ALL, AKIRA DECIDED SO SUDDENLY.
IS THAT SO?
I'M JUST PLAIN HAPPY TO HEAR THE NEWS.
AND EVEN YOU, HARUMI — WHY THE LONG LOOK?

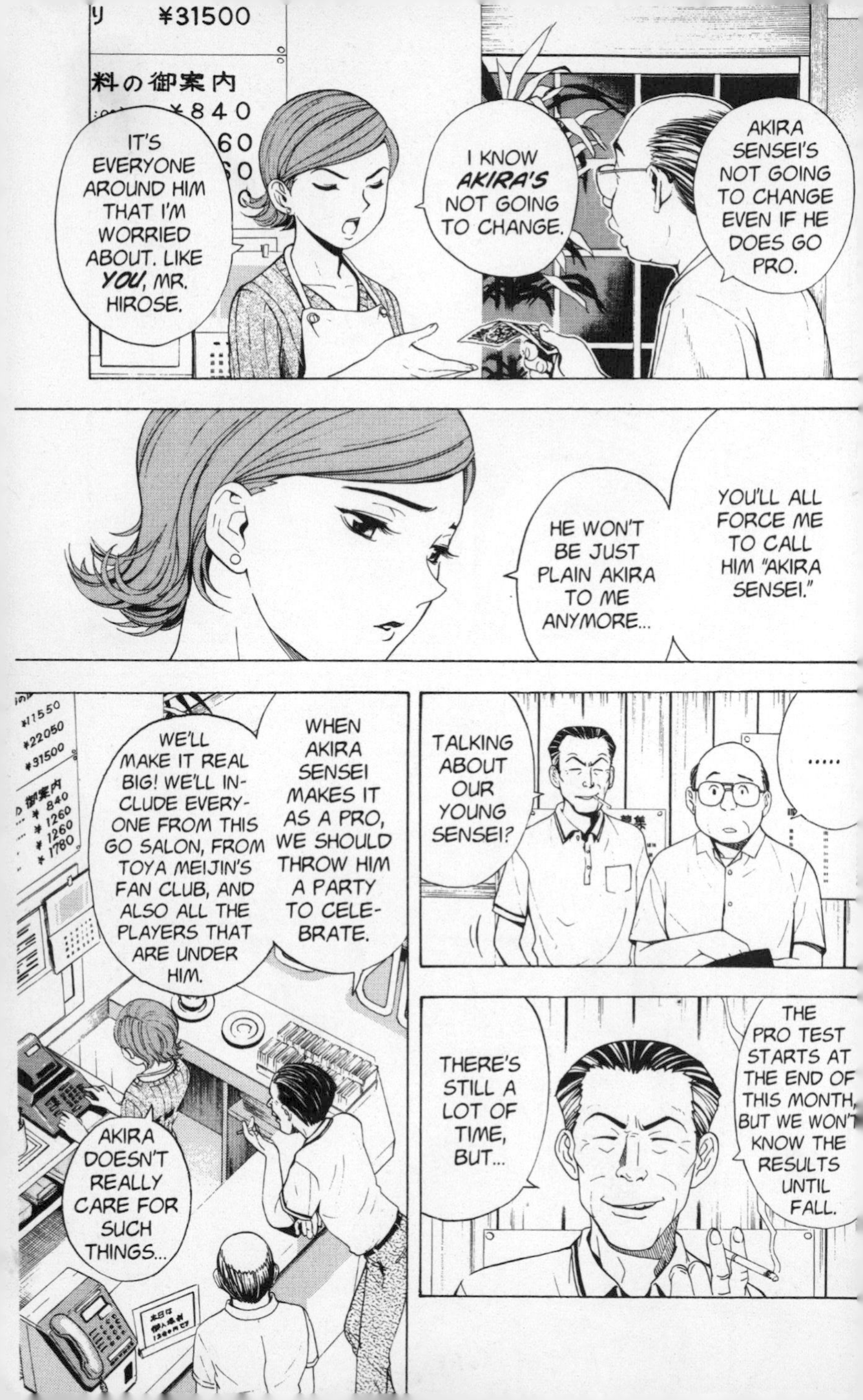

リ ¥31500
料の御案内
AKIRA SENSEI'S NOT GOING TO CHANGE EVEN IF HE DOES GO PRO.
I KNOW *AKIRA'S* NOT GOING TO CHANGE.
IT'S EVERYONE AROUND HIM THAT I'M WORRIED ABOUT. LIKE *YOU*, MR. HIROSE.
YOU'LL ALL FORCE ME TO CALL HIM "AKIRA SENSEI."
HE WON'T BE JUST PLAIN AKIRA TO ME ANYMORE...
.....
TALKING ABOUT OUR YOUNG SENSEI?
THE PRO TEST STARTS AT THE END OF THIS MONTH, BUT WE WON'T KNOW THE RESULTS UNTIL FALL.
THERE'S STILL A LOT OF TIME, BUT...
WHEN AKIRA SENSEI MAKES IT AS A PRO, WE SHOULD THROW HIM A PARTY TO CELEBRATE.
WE'LL MAKE IT REAL BIG! WE'LL INCLUDE EVERYONE FROM THIS GO SALON, FROM TOYA MEIJIN'S FAN CLUB, AND ALSO ALL THE PLAYERS THAT ARE UNDER HIM.
AKIRA DOESN'T REALLY CARE FOR SUCH THINGS...

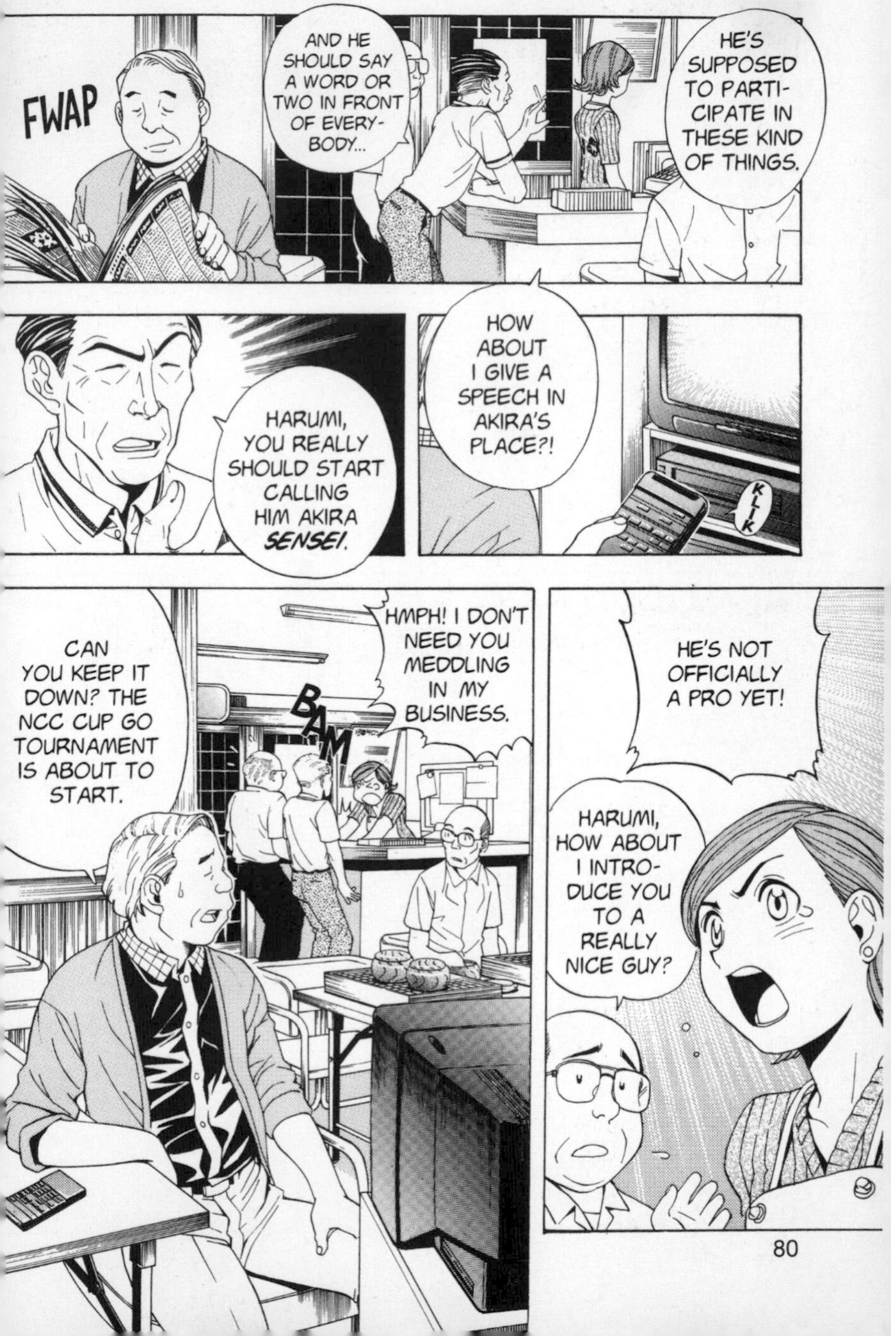
HE'S SUPPOSED TO PARTICIPATE IN THESE KIND OF THINGS.
AND HE SHOULD SAY A WORD OR TWO IN FRONT OF EVERYBODY...
FWAP
HOW ABOUT I GIVE A SPEECH IN AKIRA'S PLACE?!
KLIK
HARUMI, YOU REALLY SHOULD START CALLING HIM AKIRA *SENSEI*.
HE'S NOT OFFICIALLY A PRO YET!
HARUMI, HOW ABOUT I INTRODUCE YOU TO A REALLY NICE GUY?
HMPH! I DON'T NEED YOU MEDDLING IN MY BUSINESS.
BAM
CAN YOU KEEP IT DOWN? THE NCC CUP GO TOURNAMENT IS ABOUT TO START.

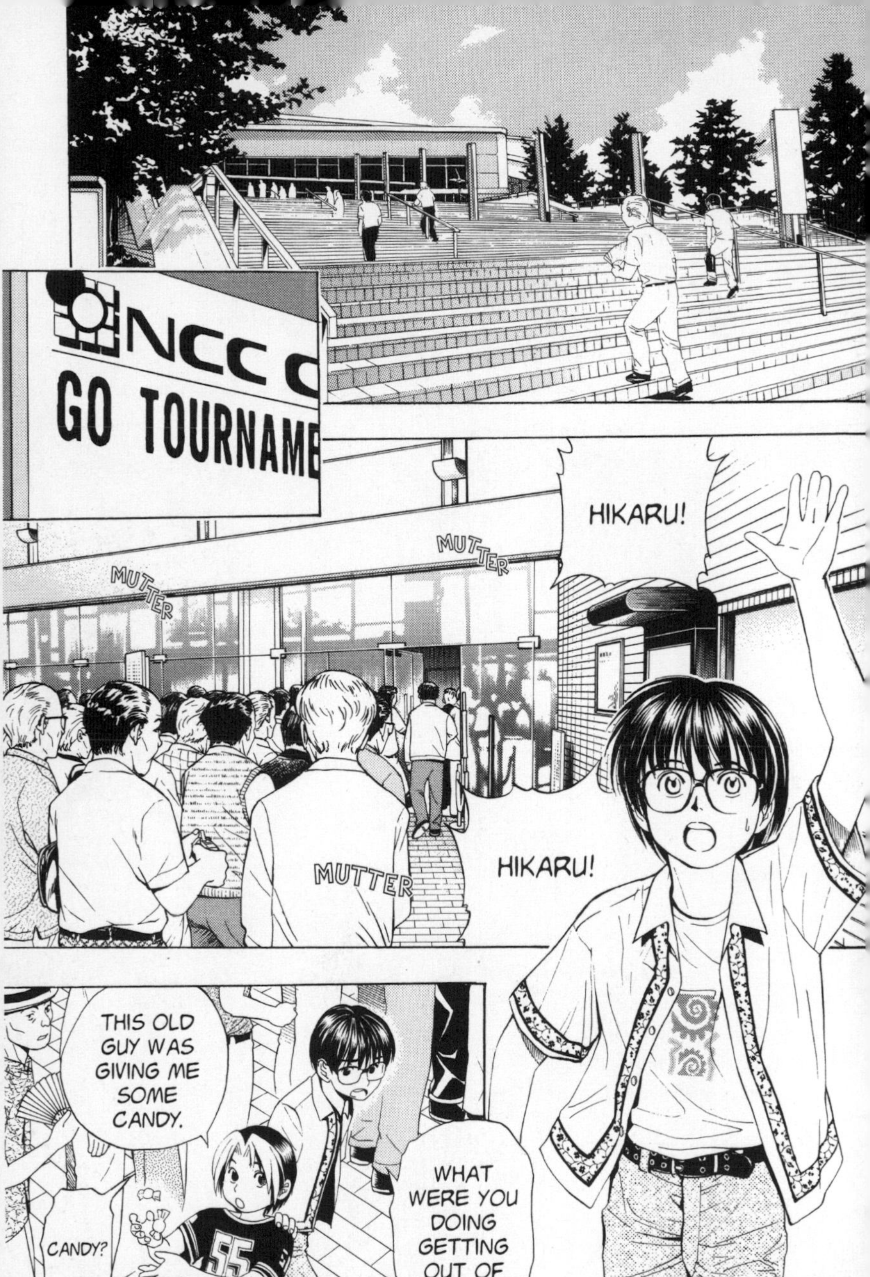
NCC
GO TOURNAME
HIKARU!
HIKARU!
MUTTER
MUTTER
MUTTER
WHAT WERE YOU DOING GETTING OUT OF LINE?
THIS OLD GUY WAS GIVING ME SOME CANDY.
CANDY?

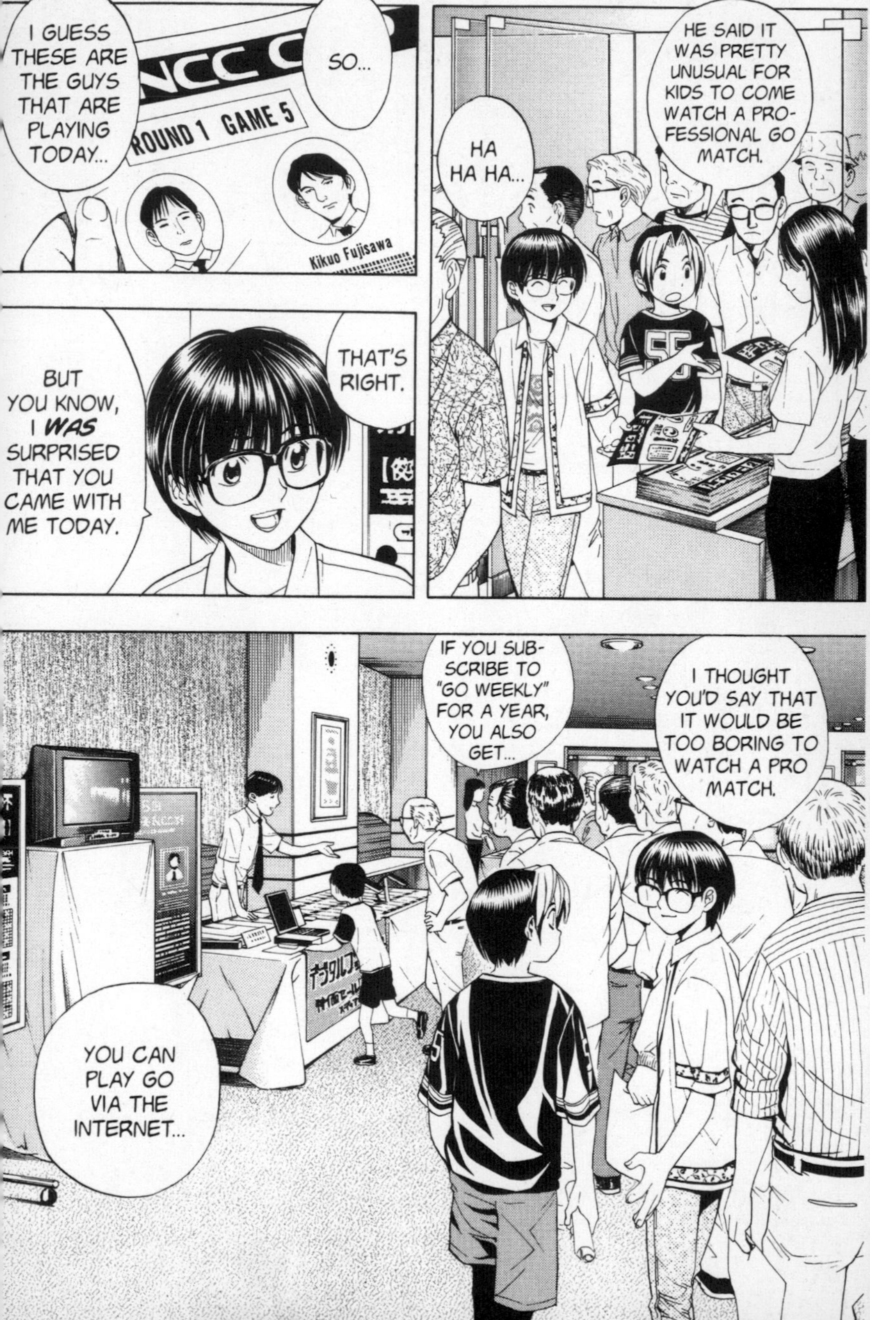
HE SAID IT WAS PRETTY UNUSUAL FOR KIDS TO COME WATCH A PROFESSIONAL GO MATCH.
HA HA HA...
SO...
I GUESS THESE ARE THE GUYS THAT ARE PLAYING TODAY...
ROUND 1 GAME 5
Kikuo Fujisawa
THAT'S RIGHT.
BUT YOU KNOW, I *WAS* SURPRISED THAT YOU CAME WITH ME TODAY.
I THOUGHT YOU'D SAY THAT IT WOULD BE TOO BORING TO WATCH A PRO MATCH.
IF YOU SUBSCRIBE TO "GO WEEKLY" FOR A YEAR, YOU ALSO GET...
YOU CAN PLAY GO VIA THE INTERNET...

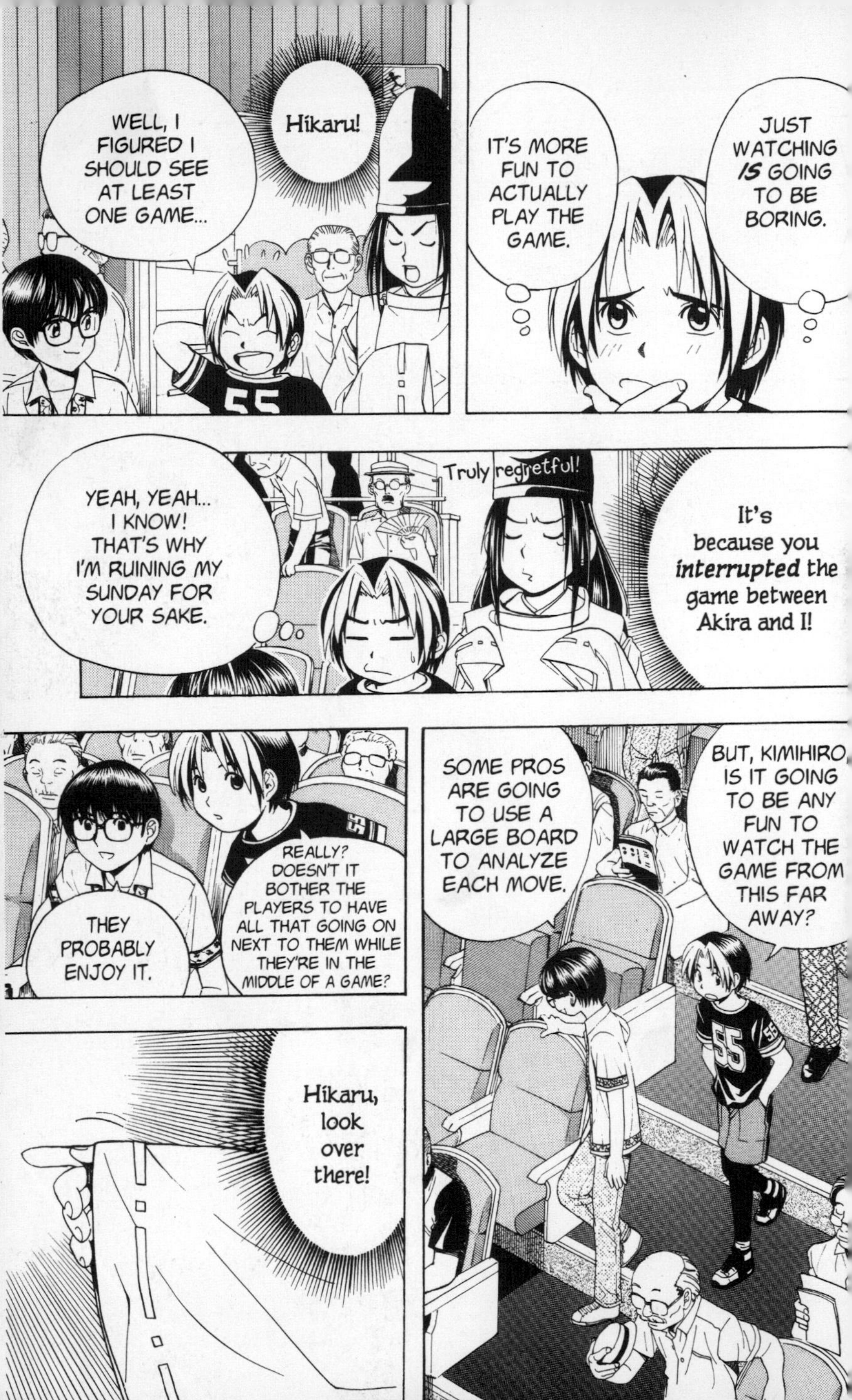

JUST WATCHING *IS* GOING TO BE BORING.
IT'S MORE FUN TO ACTUALLY PLAY THE GAME.
Hikaru!
WELL, I FIGURED I SHOULD SEE AT LEAST ONE GAME...
It's because you *interrupted* the game between Akira and I!
Truly regretful!
YEAH, YEAH... I KNOW! THAT'S WHY I'M RUINING MY SUNDAY FOR YOUR SAKE.
BUT, KIMIHIRO IS IT GOING TO BE ANY FUN TO WATCH THE GAME FROM THIS FAR AWAY?
SOME PROS ARE GOING TO USE A LARGE BOARD TO ANALYZE EACH MOVE.
REALLY? DOESN'T IT BOTHER THE PLAYERS TO HAVE ALL THAT GOING ON NEXT TO THEM WHILE THEY'RE IN THE MIDDLE OF A GAME?
THEY PROBABLY ENJOY IT.
Hikaru, look over there!

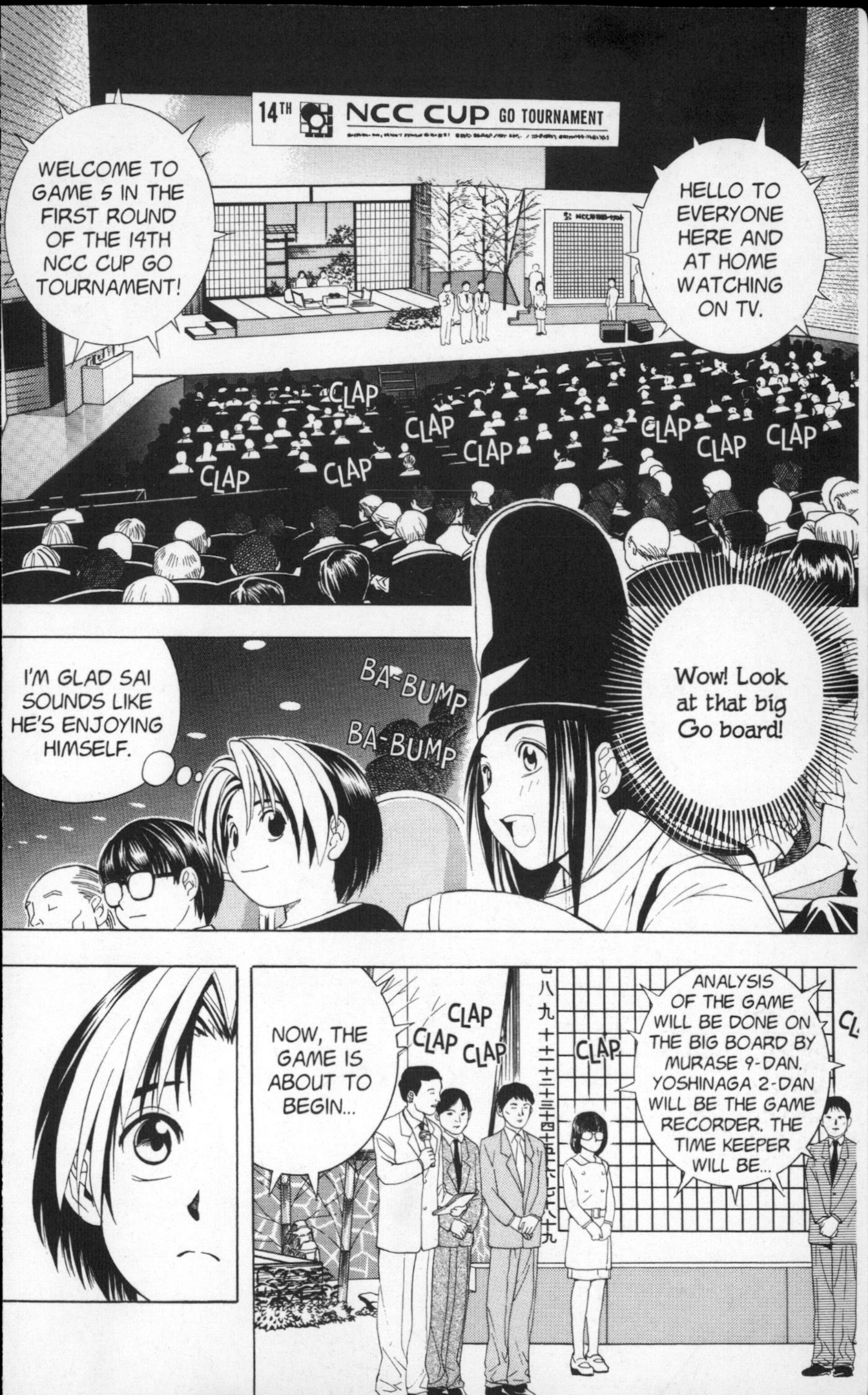

14TH NCC CUP GO TOURNAMENT
HELLO TO EVERYONE HERE AND AT HOME WATCHING ON TV.
WELCOME TO GAME 5 IN THE FIRST ROUND OF THE 14TH NCC CUP GO TOURNAMENT!
CLAP CLAP CLAP CLAP CLAP CLAP CLAP CLAP
Wow! Look at that big Go board!
BA-BUMP
BA-BUMP
I'M GLAD SAI SOUNDS LIKE HE'S ENJOYING HIMSELF.
ANALYSIS OF THE GAME WILL BE DONE ON THE BIG BOARD BY MURASE 9-DAN. YOSHINAGA 2-DAN WILL BE THE GAME RECORDER. THE TIME KEEPER WILL BE...
CLAP
CLAP
CLAP CLAP CLAP
NOW, THE GAME IS ABOUT TO BEGIN...

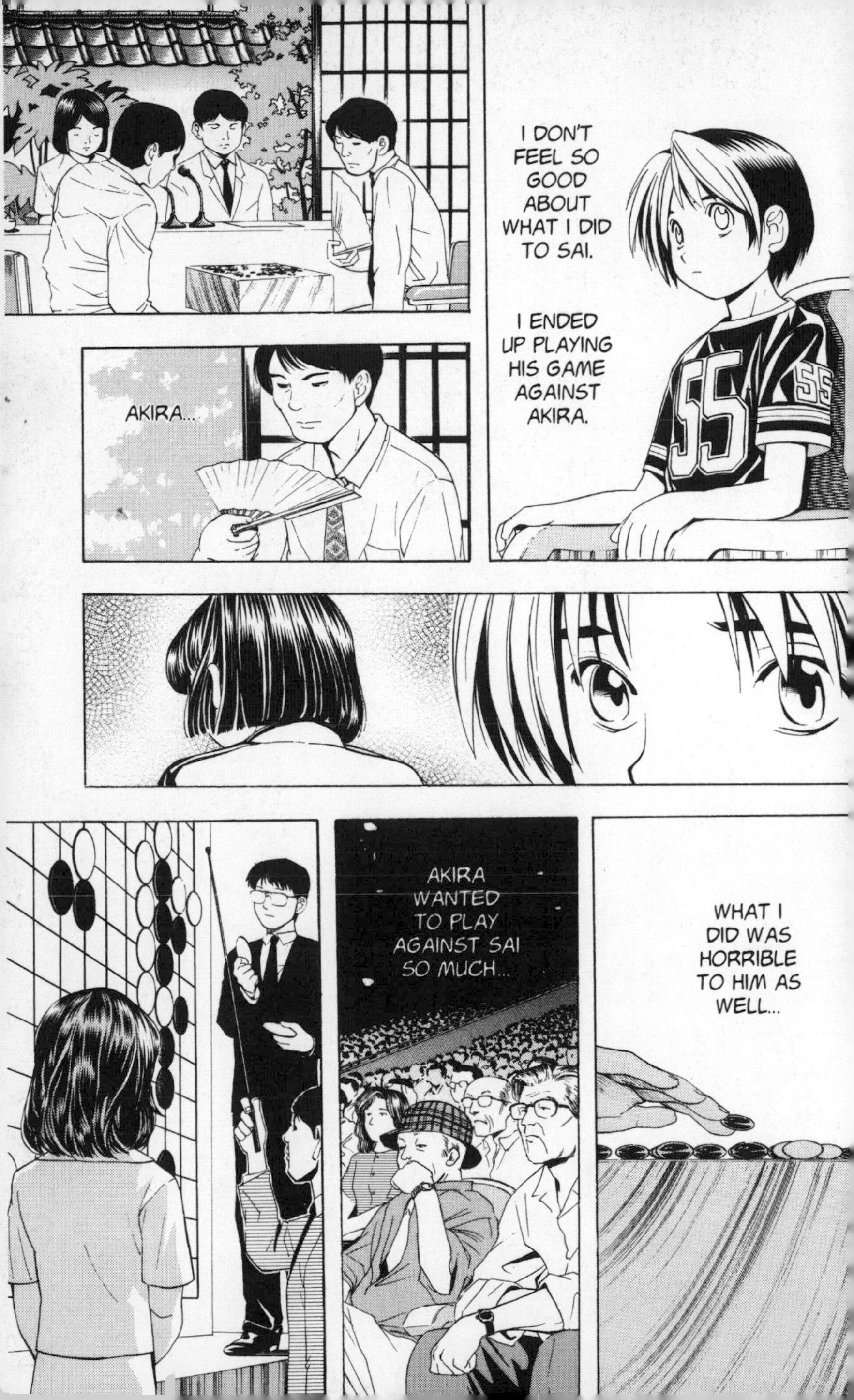
I DON'T FEEL SO GOOD ABOUT WHAT I DID TO SAI.
I ENDED UP PLAYING HIS GAME AGAINST AKIRA.
AKIRA...
WHAT I DID WAS HORRIBLE TO HIM AS WELL...
AKIRA WANTED TO PLAY AGAINST SAI SO MUCH...

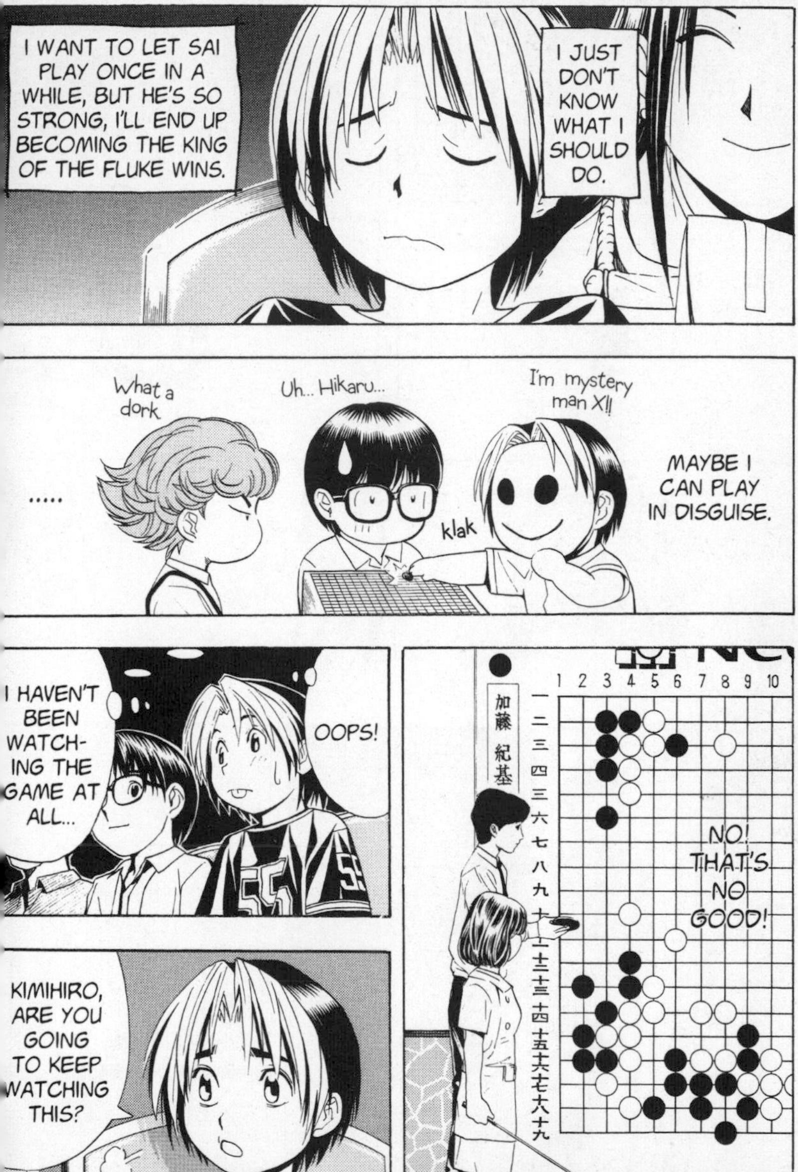
I JUST DON'T KNOW WHAT I SHOULD DO.
I WANT TO LET SAI PLAY ONCE IN A WHILE, BUT HE'S SO STRONG, I'LL END UP BECOMING THE KING OF THE FLUKE WINS.
MAYBE I CAN PLAY IN DISGUISE.
I'm mystery man X!!
klak
Uh... Hikaru...
What a dork
.....
加藤 紀基
NO! THAT'S NO GOOD!
OOPS!
I HAVEN'T BEEN WATCHING THE GAME AT ALL...
KIMIHIRO, ARE YOU GOING TO KEEP WATCHING THIS?

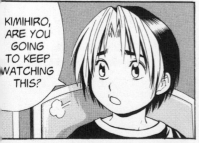

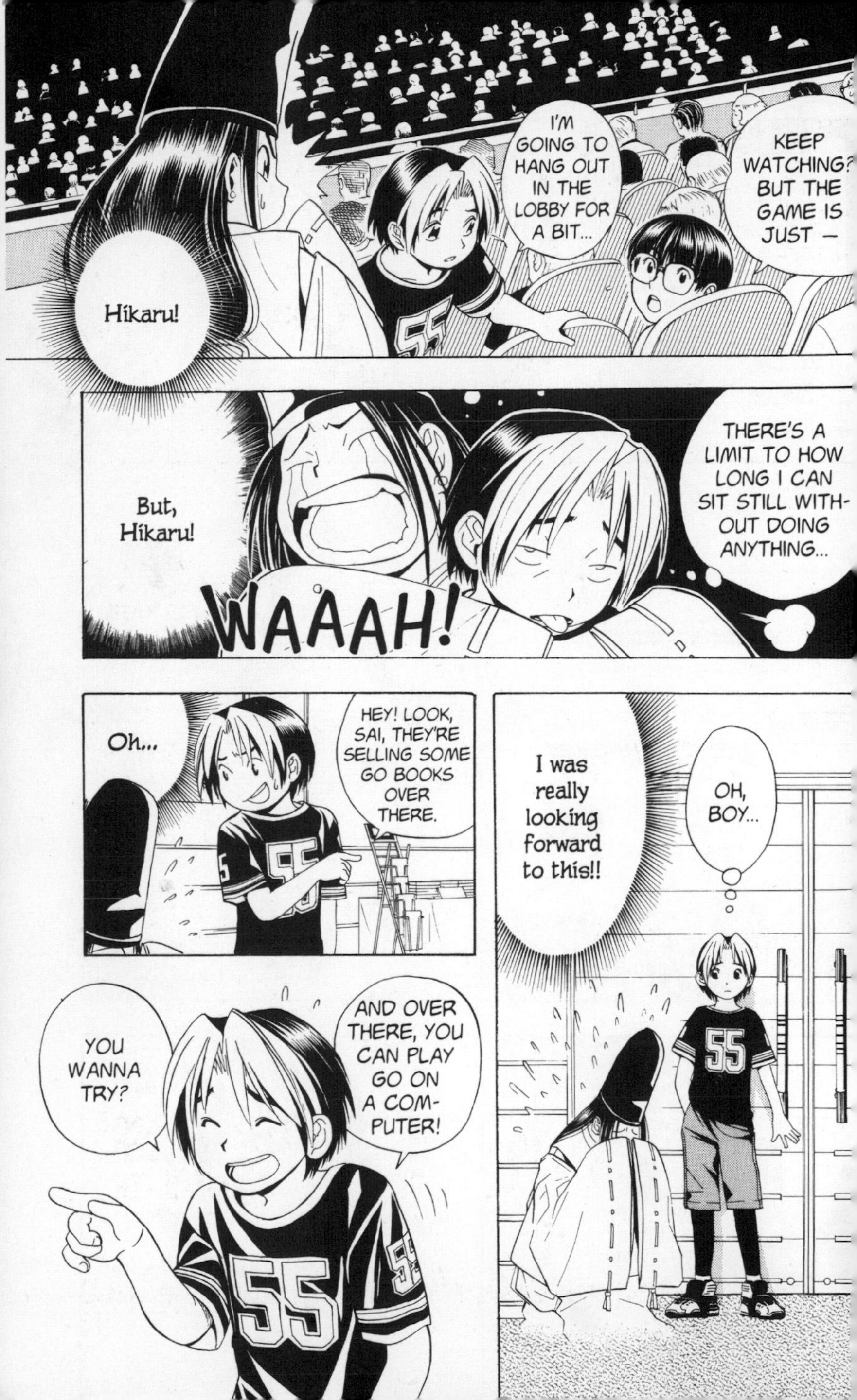
KEEP WATCHING? BUT THE GAME IS JUST –
I'M GOING TO HANG OUT IN THE LOBBY FOR A BIT...
Hikaru!
THERE'S A LIMIT TO HOW LONG I CAN SIT STILL WITHOUT DOING ANYTHING...
But, Hikaru!
WAAAH!
OH, BOY...
I was really looking forward to this!!
HEY! LOOK, SAI, THEY'RE SELLING SOME GO BOOKS OVER THERE.
Oh...
AND OVER THERE, YOU CAN PLAY GO ON A COMPUTER!
YOU WANNA TRY?

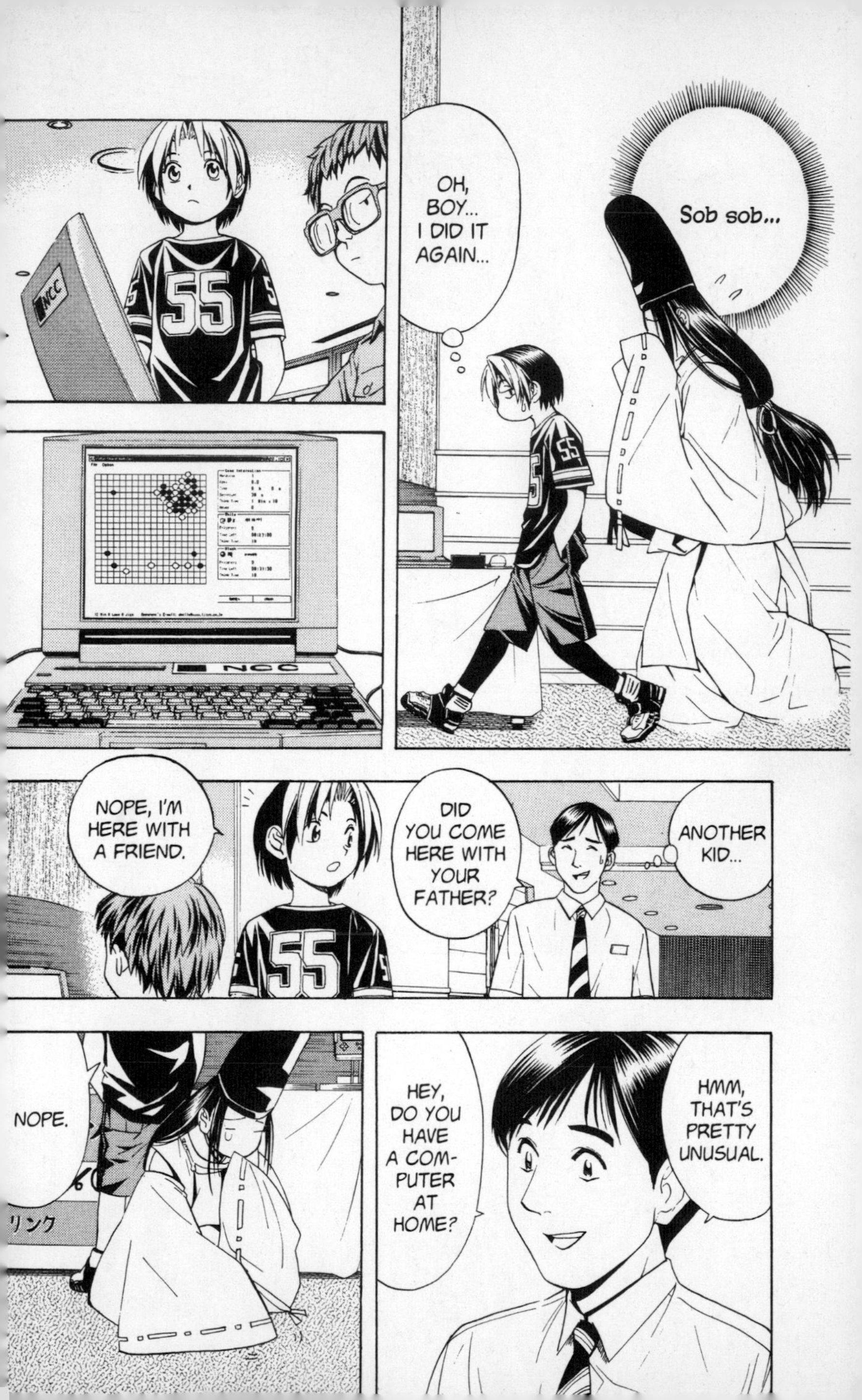
Sob sob...
OH, BOY... I DID IT AGAIN...
NCC
NCC
ANOTHER KID...
DID YOU COME HERE WITH YOUR FATHER?
NOPE, I'M HERE WITH A FRIEND.
HMM, THAT'S PRETTY UNUSUAL.
HEY, DO YOU HAVE A COMPUTER AT HOME?
NOPE.
リンク

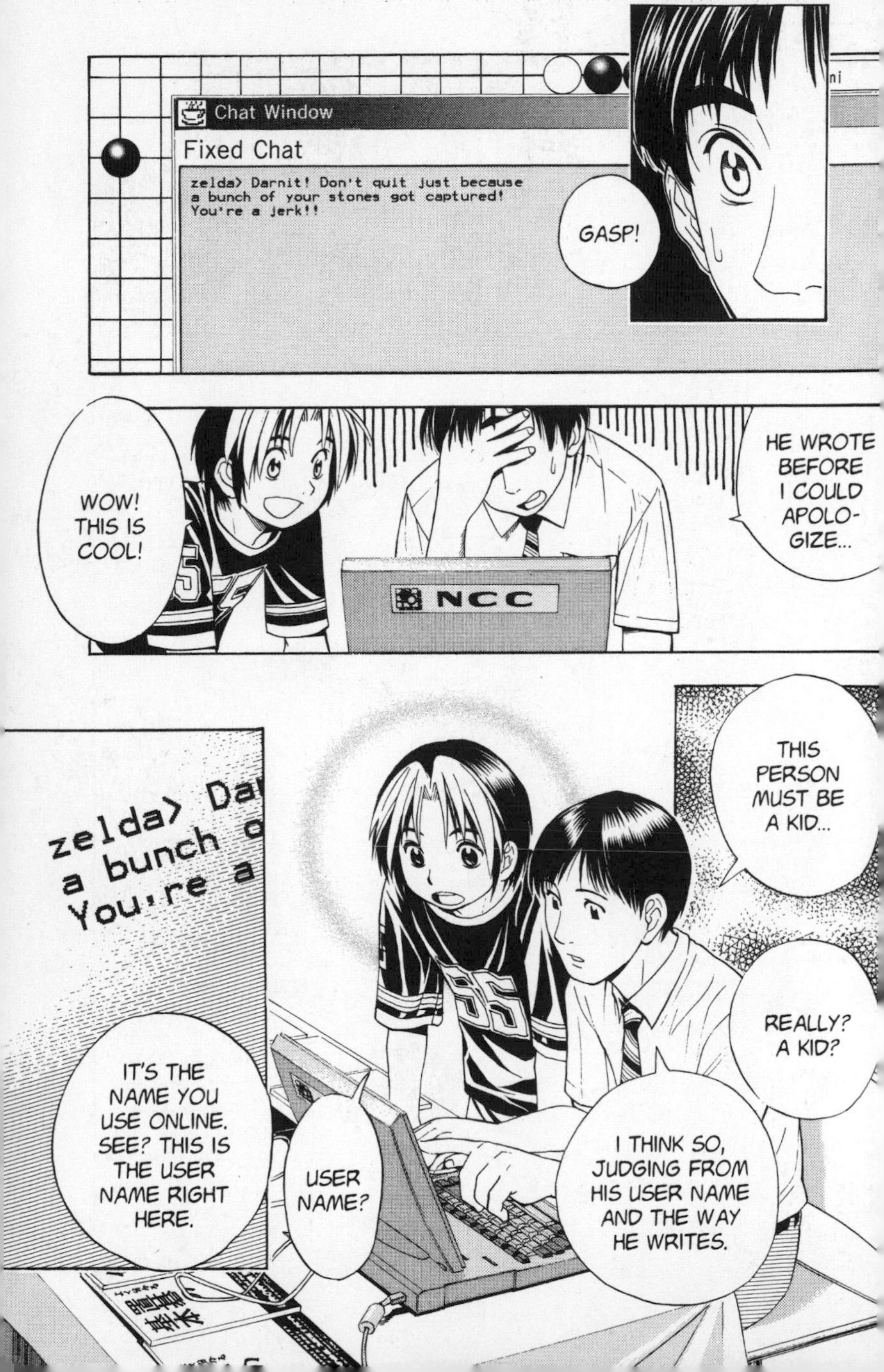
Chat Window
Fixed Chat
zelda> Darnit! Don't quit just because a bunch of your stones got captured! You're a jerk!!
GASP!
HE WROTE BEFORE I COULD APOLOGIZE...
WOW! THIS IS COOL!
NCC
THIS PERSON MUST BE A KID...
REALLY? A KID?
I THINK SO, JUDGING FROM HIS USER NAME AND THE WAY HE WRITES.
USER NAME?
IT'S THE NAME YOU USE ONLINE. SEE? THIS IS THE USER NAME RIGHT HERE.

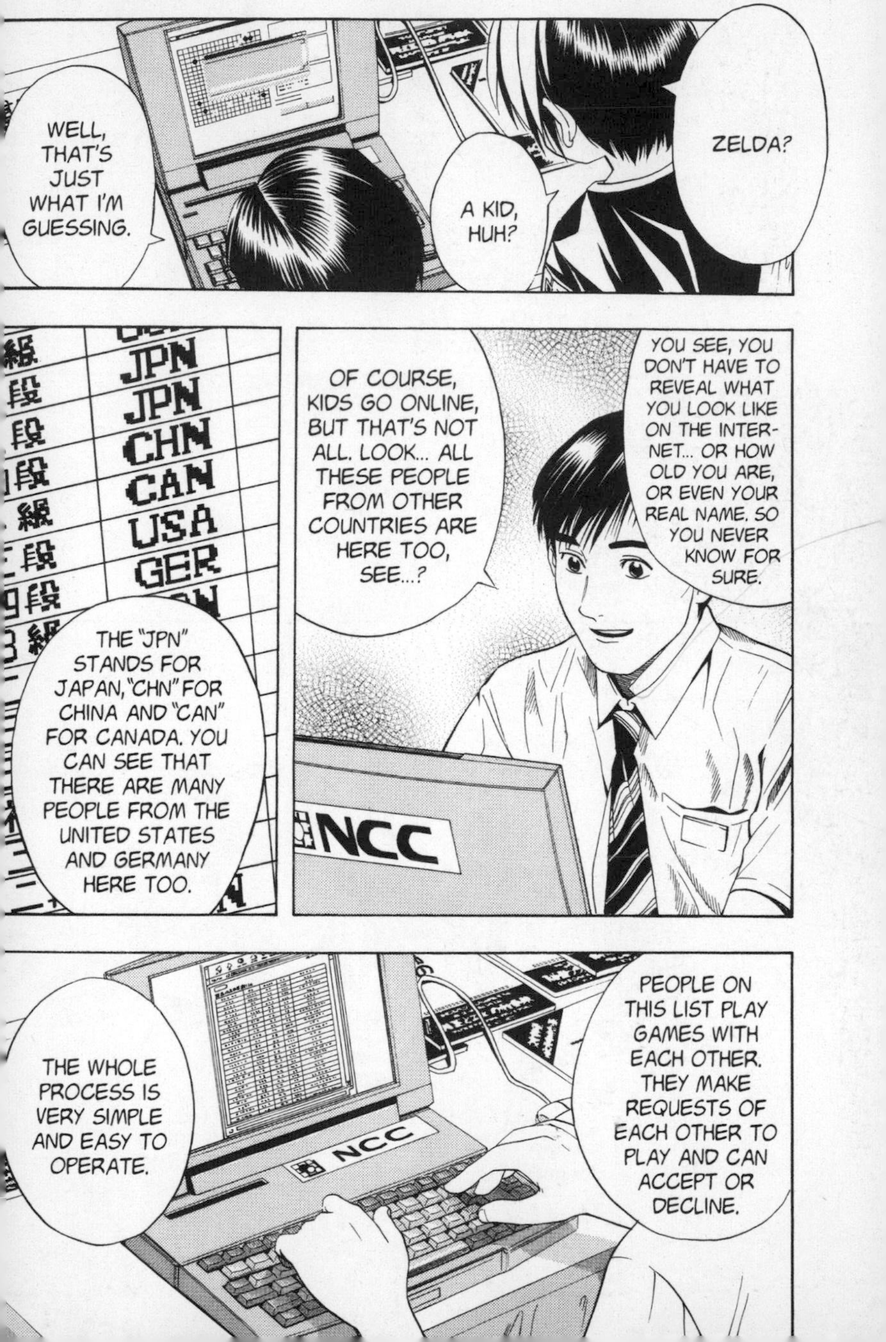

ZELDA?
A KID, HUH?
WELL, THAT'S JUST WHAT I'M GUESSING.
YOU SEE, YOU DON'T HAVE TO REVEAL WHAT YOU LOOK LIKE ON THE INTERNET... OR HOW OLD YOU ARE, OR EVEN YOUR REAL NAME. SO YOU NEVER KNOW FOR SURE.
OF COURSE, KIDS GO ONLINE, BUT THAT'S NOT ALL. LOOK... ALL THESE PEOPLE FROM OTHER COUNTRIES ARE HERE TOO, SEE...?
NCC
JPN
JPN
CHN
CAN
USA
GER
THE "JPN" STANDS FOR JAPAN, "CHN" FOR CHINA AND "CAN" FOR CANADA. YOU CAN SEE THAT THERE ARE MANY PEOPLE FROM THE UNITED STATES AND GERMANY HERE TOO.
PEOPLE ON THIS LIST PLAY GAMES WITH EACH OTHER. THEY MAKE REQUESTS OF EACH OTHER TO PLAY AND CAN ACCEPT OR DECLINE.
THE WHOLE PROCESS IS VERY SIMPLE AND EASY TO OPERATE.
NCC

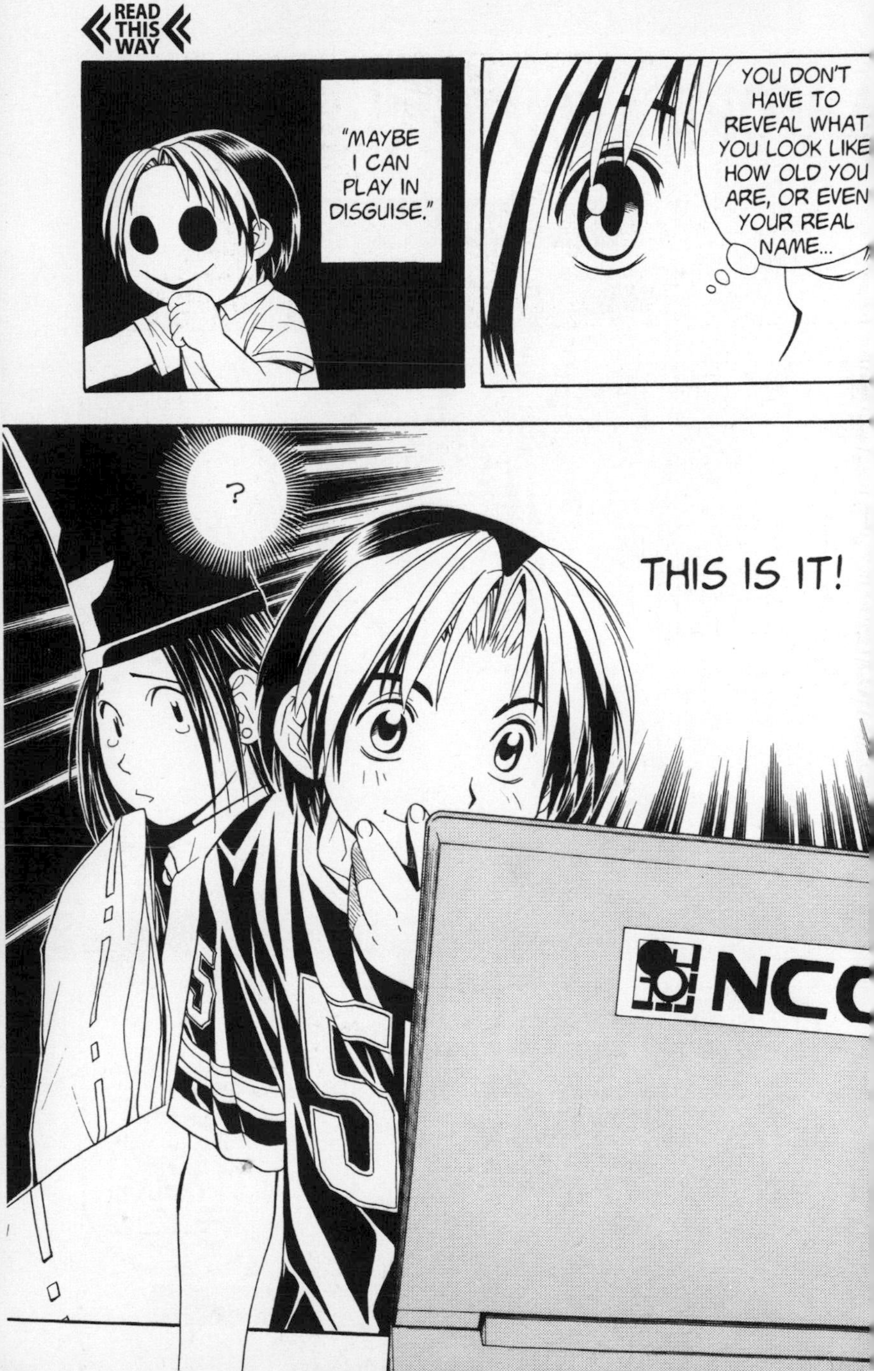
READ THIS WAY
YOU DON'T HAVE TO REVEAL WHAT YOU LOOK LIKE HOW OLD YOU ARE, OR EVEN YOUR REAL NAME...
"MAYBE I CAN PLAY IN DISGUISE."
?
THIS IS IT!
NCC

A WORD ABOUT HIKARU NO GO

SAI

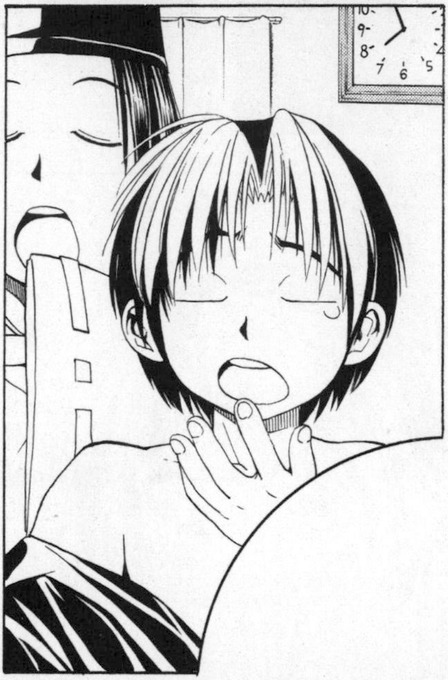

SAI IS YAWNING!

DOES HE GO TO SLEEP AT NIGHT?!

AND DOES HE WAKE UP WHEN HIKARU WAKES UP AND YAWN WHEN HIKARU YAWNS?

IT SEEMS LIKE SO MUCH FUN.

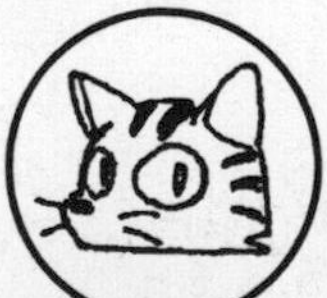

Game 30 "sai"

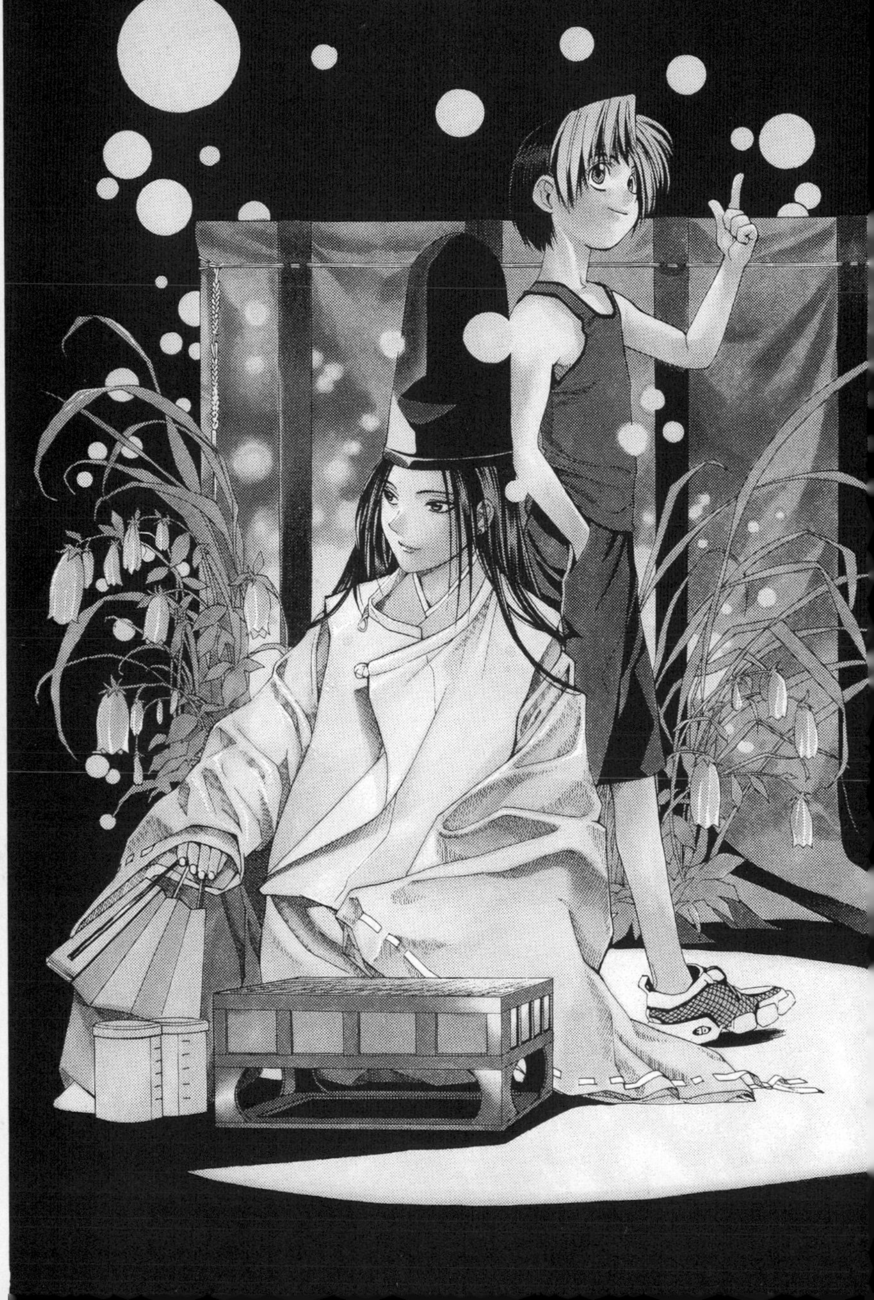

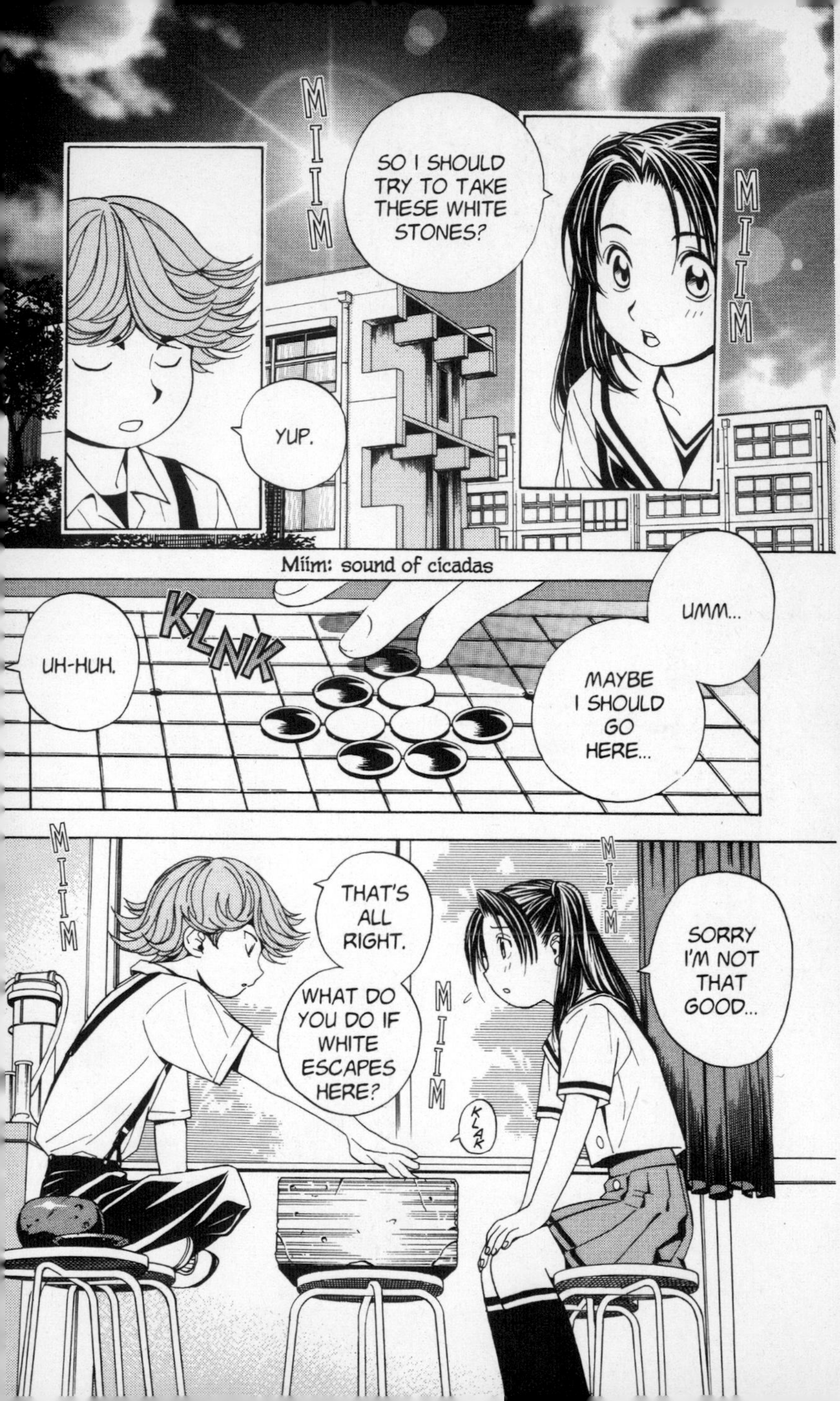
MIIM
MIIM
SO I SHOULD TRY TO TAKE THESE WHITE STONES?
YUP.
UMM...
MAYBE I SHOULD GO HERE...
KLNK
UH-HUH.
SORRY I'M NOT THAT GOOD...
MIIM
KLAK
MIIM
THAT'S ALL RIGHT.
WHAT DO YOU DO IF WHITE ESCAPES HERE?
MIIM
Miim: sound of cicadas

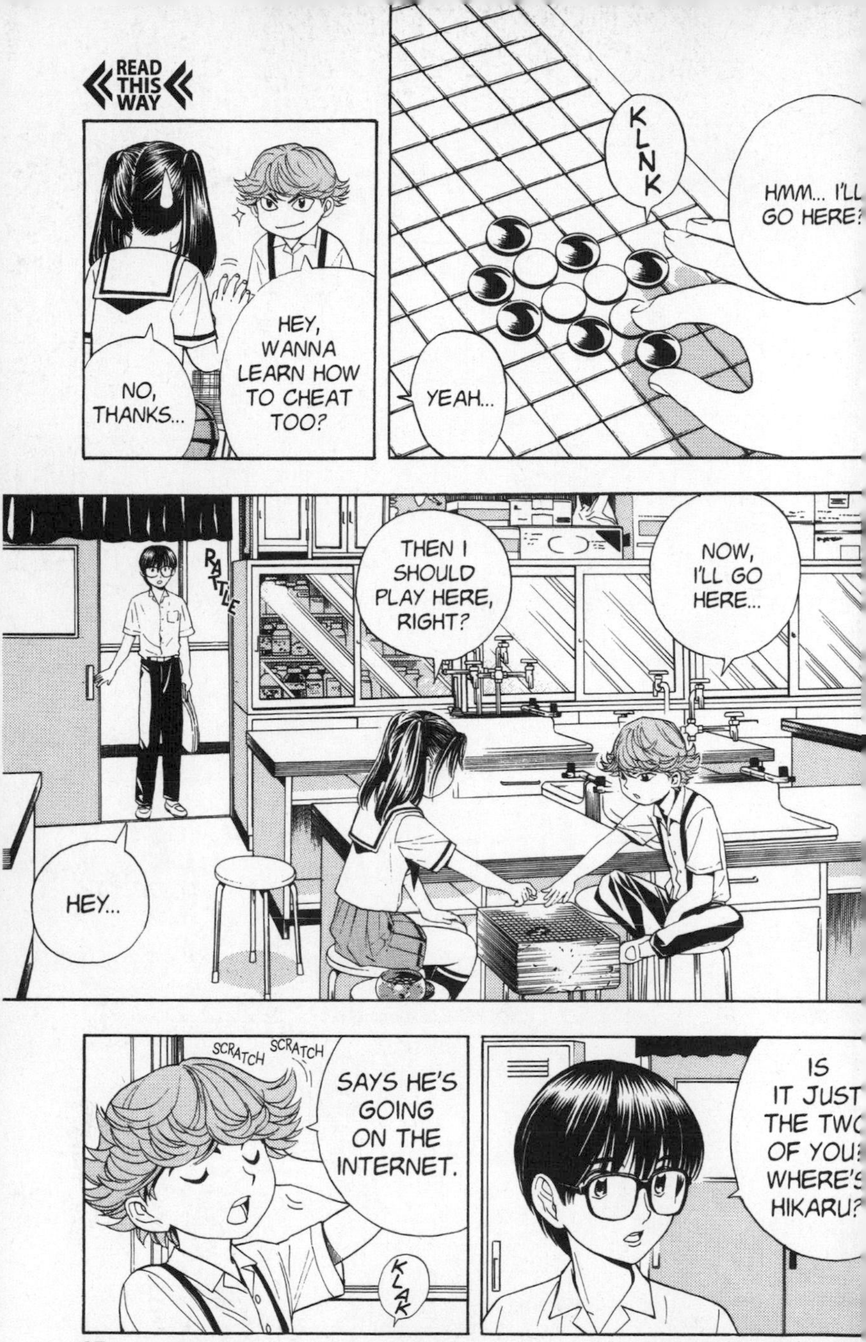
READ THIS WAY
HMM... I'LL GO HERE?
KLNK
YEAH...
HEY, WANNA LEARN HOW TO CHEAT TOO?
NO, THANKS...
NOW, I'LL GO HERE...
THEN I SHOULD PLAY HERE, RIGHT?
RATTLE
HEY...
IS IT JUST THE TWO OF YOU? WHERE'S HIKARU?
SAYS HE'S GOING ON THE INTERNET.
SCRATCH SCRATCH
KLAK

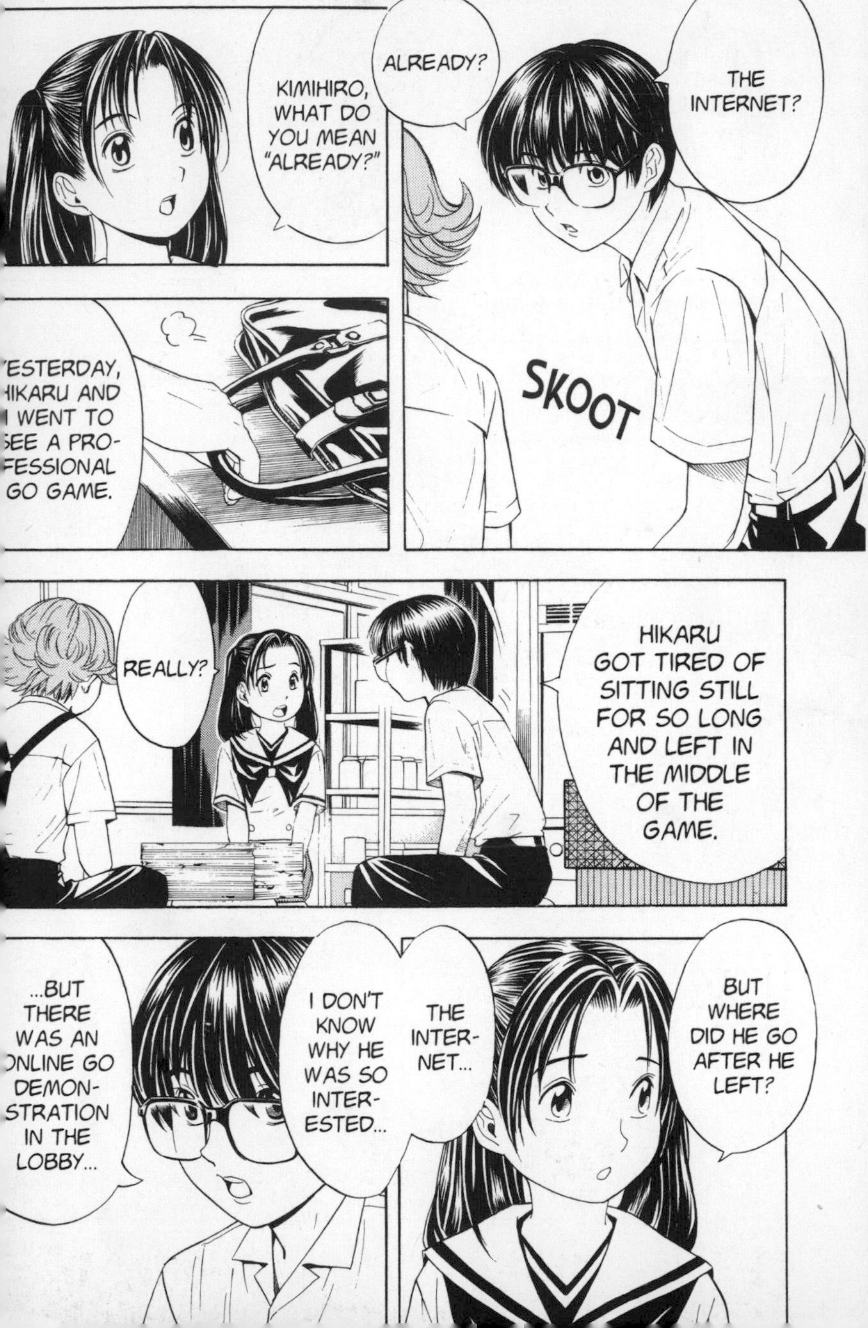
THE INTERNET?
ALREADY?
SKOOT
KIMIHIRO, WHAT DO YOU MEAN "ALREADY?"
YESTERDAY, HIKARU AND I WENT TO SEE A PRO-FESSIONAL GO GAME.
HIKARU GOT TIRED OF SITTING STILL FOR SO LONG AND LEFT IN THE MIDDLE OF THE GAME.
REALLY?
BUT WHERE DID HE GO AFTER HE LEFT?
THE INTER-NET...
I DON'T KNOW WHY HE WAS SO INTER-ESTED...
...BUT THERE WAS AN ONLINE GO DEMON-STRATION IN THE LOBBY...

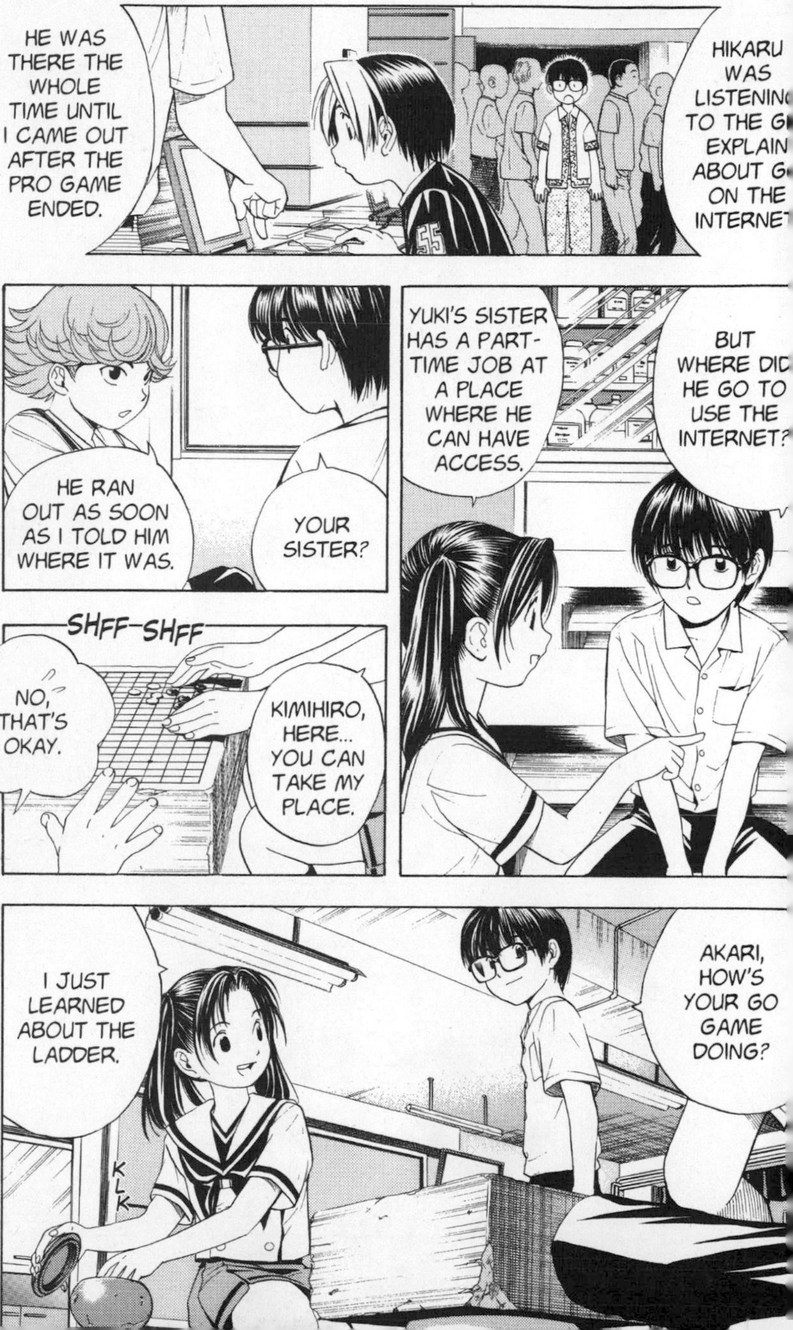
HIKARU WAS LISTENIN TO THE G EXPLAIN ABOUT G ON THE INTERNET
HE WAS THERE THE WHOLE TIME UNTIL I CAME OUT AFTER THE PRO GAME ENDED.
BUT WHERE DID HE GO TO USE THE INTERNET?
YUKI'S SISTER HAS A PART-TIME JOB AT A PLACE WHERE HE CAN HAVE ACCESS.
YOUR SISTER?
HE RAN OUT AS SOON AS I TOLD HIM WHERE IT WAS.
SHFF-SHFF
KIMIHIRO, HERE... YOU CAN TAKE MY PLACE.
NO, THAT'S OKAY.
AKARI, HOW'S YOUR GO GAME DOING?
KLK
I JUST LEARNED ABOUT THE LADDER.

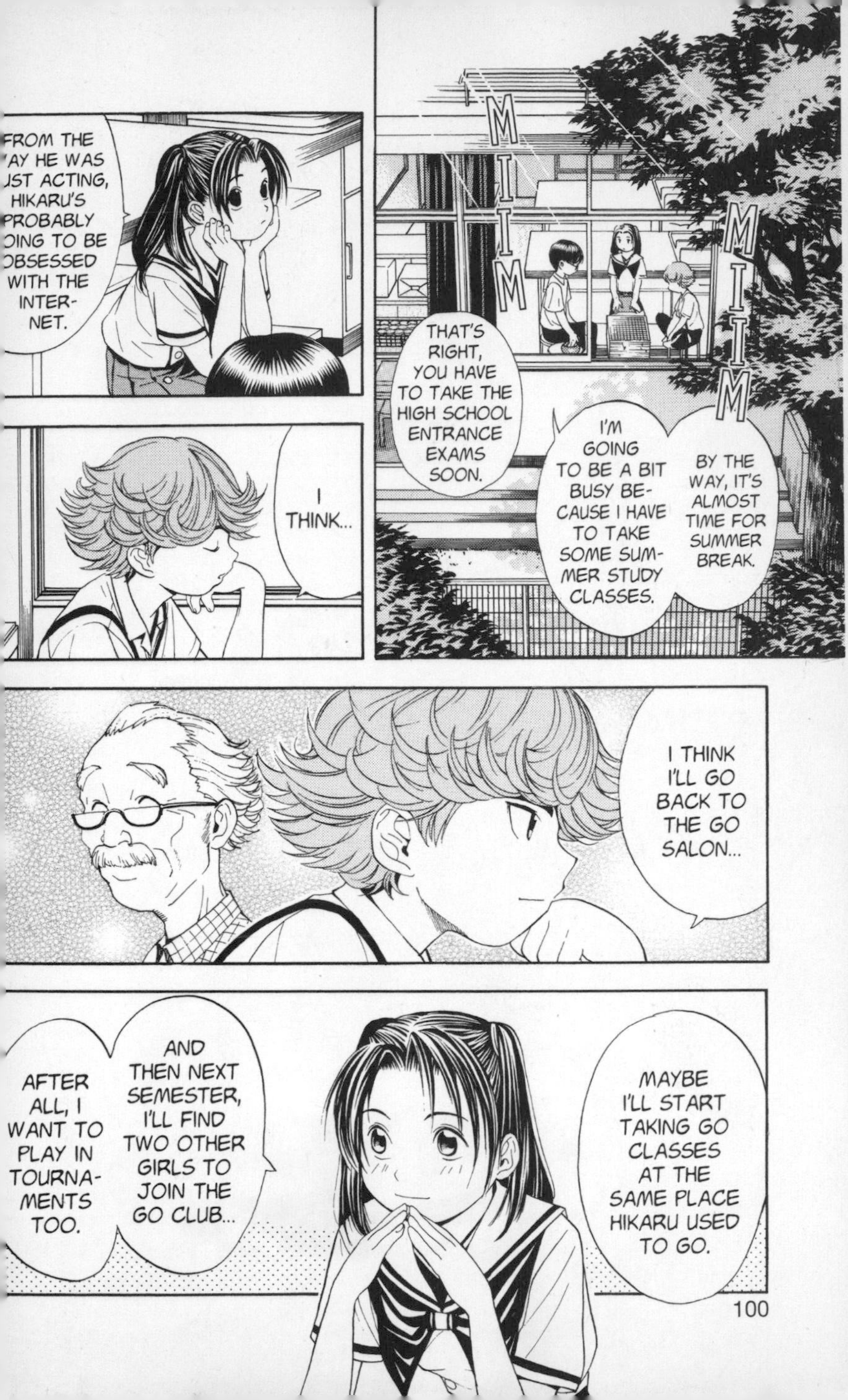
MIIM
MIIM
BY THE WAY, IT'S ALMOST TIME FOR SUMMER BREAK.
I'M GOING TO BE A BIT BUSY BE-CAUSE I HAVE TO TAKE SOME SUM-MER STUDY CLASSES.
THAT'S RIGHT, YOU HAVE TO TAKE THE HIGH SCHOOL ENTRANCE EXAMS SOON.
FROM THE 'AY HE WAS JST ACTING, HIKARU'S PROBABLY OING TO BE BSESSED WITH THE INTER-NET.
I THINK...
I THINK I'LL GO BACK TO THE GO SALON...
MAYBE I'LL START TAKING GO CLASSES AT THE SAME PLACE HIKARU USED TO GO.
AND THEN NEXT SEMESTER, I'LL FIND TWO OTHER GIRLS TO JOIN THE GO CLUB...
AFTER ALL, I WANT TO PLAY IN TOURNA-MENTS TOO.

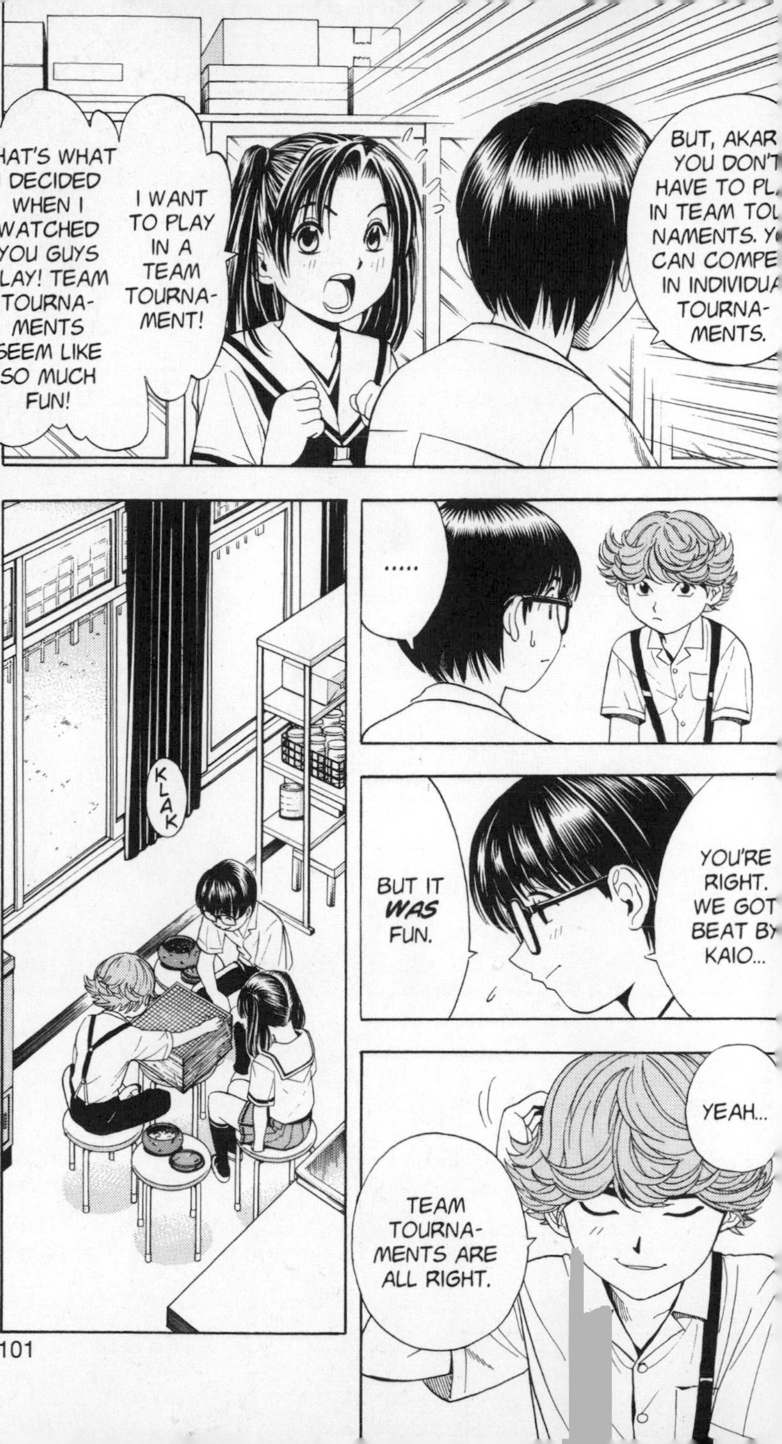
BUT, AKAR YOU DON'T HAVE TO PL IN TEAM TOU NAMENTS. Y CAN COMPE IN INDIVIDU TOURNA- MENTS.
I WANT TO PLAY IN A TEAM TOURNA- MENT!
THAT'S WHAT I DECIDED WHEN I WATCHED YOU GUYS PLAY! TEAM TOURNA- MENTS SEEM LIKE SO MUCH FUN!
.....
YOU'RE RIGHT. WE GOT BEAT B KAIO...
BUT IT *WAS* FUN.
YEAH...
TEAM TOURNA- MENTS ARE ALL RIGHT.
KLAK

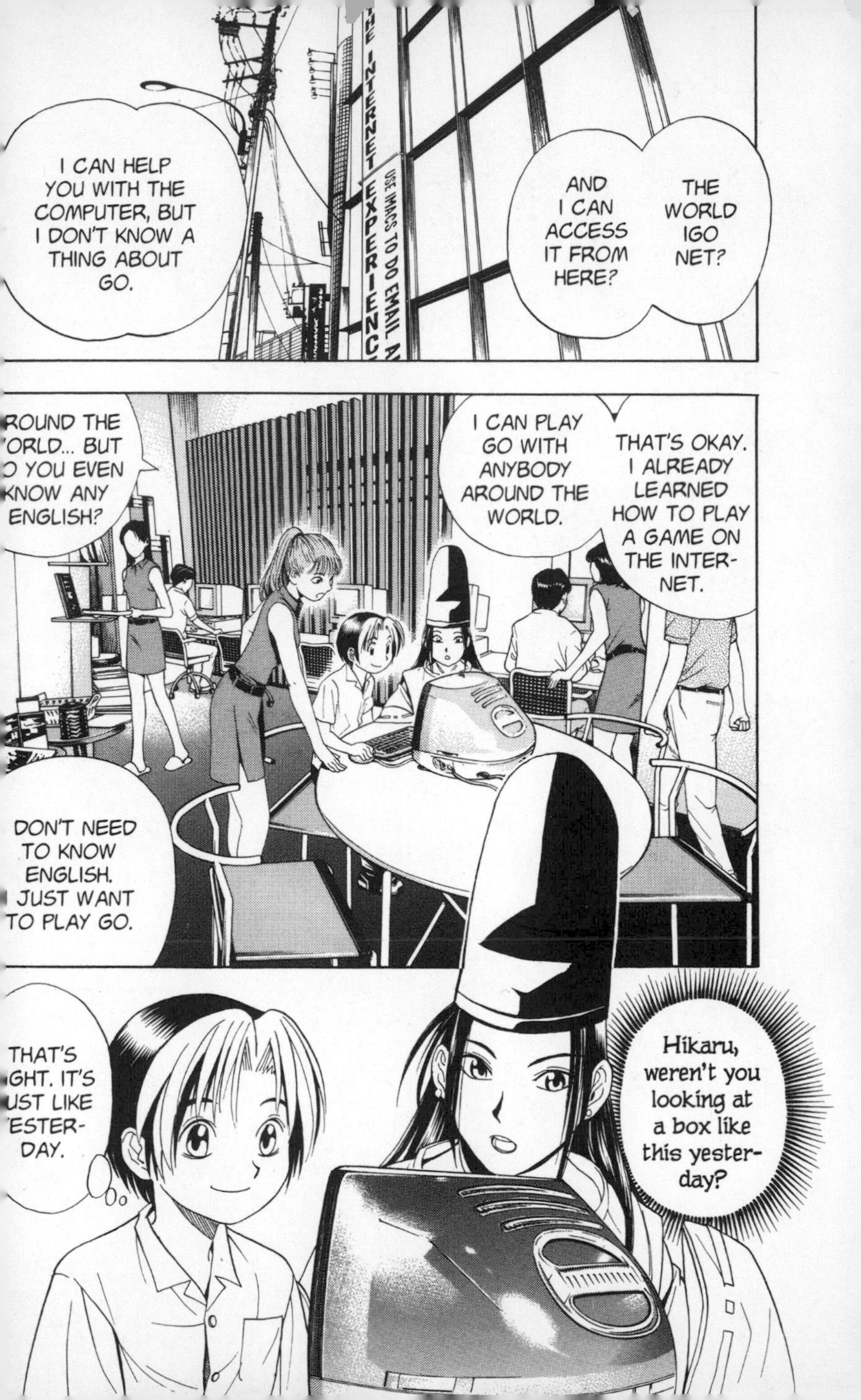
THE WORLD IGO NET?
AND I CAN ACCESS IT FROM HERE?
I CAN HELP YOU WITH THE COMPUTER, BUT I DON'T KNOW A THING ABOUT GO.
THAT'S OKAY. I ALREADY LEARNED HOW TO PLAY A GAME ON THE INTER-NET.
I CAN PLAY GO WITH ANYBODY AROUND THE WORLD.
ROUND THE 'ORLD... BUT O YOU EVEN KNOW ANY ENGLISH?
DON'T NEED TO KNOW ENGLISH. JUST WANT TO PLAY GO.
Hikaru, weren't you looking at a box like this yester-day?
THAT'S GHT. IT'S UST LIKE 'ESTER-DAY.

READ THIS WAY

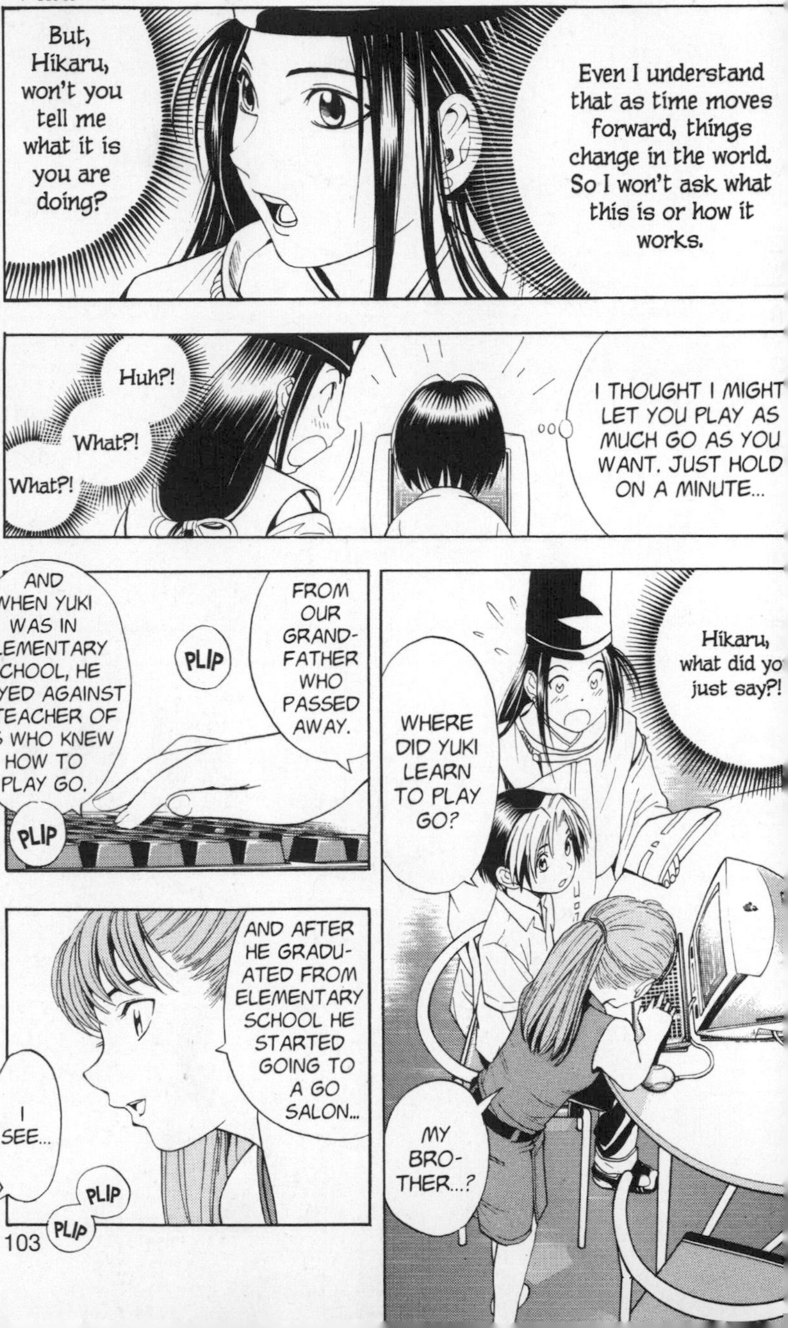
Even I understand that as time moves forward, things change in the world. So I won't ask what this is or how it works.
But, Hikaru, won't you tell me what it is you are doing?
I THOUGHT I MIGHT LET YOU PLAY AS MUCH GO AS YOU WANT. JUST HOLD ON A MINUTE...
Huh?!
What?!
What?!
Hikaru, what did yo just say?!
WHERE DID YUKI LEARN TO PLAY GO?
MY BRO-THER...?
FROM OUR GRAND-FATHER WHO PASSED AWAY.
PLIP
AND WHEN YUKI WAS IN ELEMENTARY SCHOOL, HE PLAYED AGAINST A TEACHER OF HIS WHO KNEW HOW TO PLAY GO.
PLIP
AND AFTER HE GRADU-ATED FROM ELEMENTARY SCHOOL HE STARTED GOING TO A GO SALON...
I SEE...
PLIP
PLIP

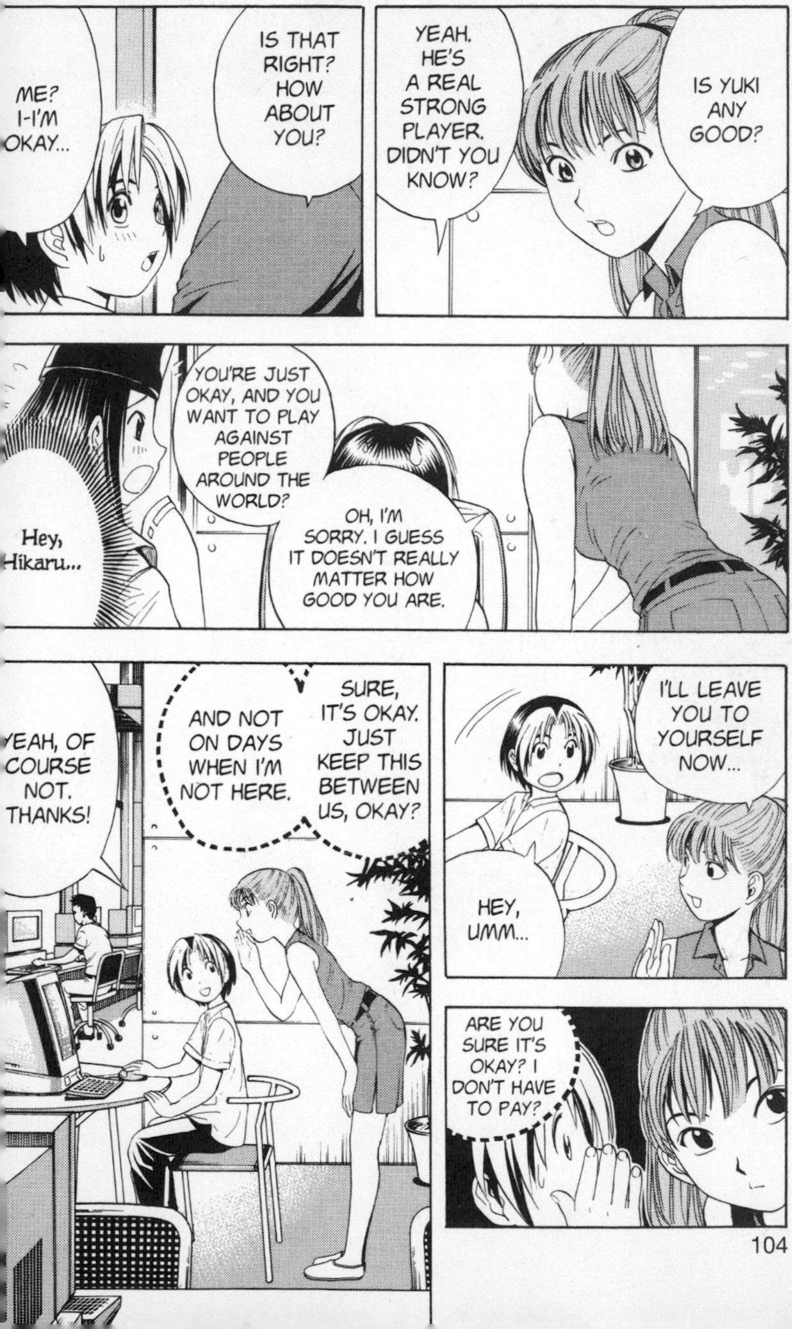
IS YUKI ANY GOOD?
YEAH. HE'S A REAL STRONG PLAYER. DIDN'T YOU KNOW?
IS THAT RIGHT? HOW ABOUT YOU?
ME? I-I'M OKAY...
YOU'RE JUST OKAY, AND YOU WANT TO PLAY AGAINST PEOPLE AROUND THE WORLD?
OH, I'M SORRY. I GUESS IT DOESN'T REALLY MATTER HOW GOOD YOU ARE.
Hey, Hikaru...
I'LL LEAVE YOU TO YOURSELF NOW...
HEY, UMM...
ARE YOU SURE IT'S OKAY? I DON'T HAVE TO PAY?
SURE, IT'S OKAY. JUST KEEP THIS BETWEEN US, OKAY?
AND NOT ON DAYS WHEN I'M NOT HERE.
EAH, OF COURSE NOT. THANKS!

READ THIS WAY

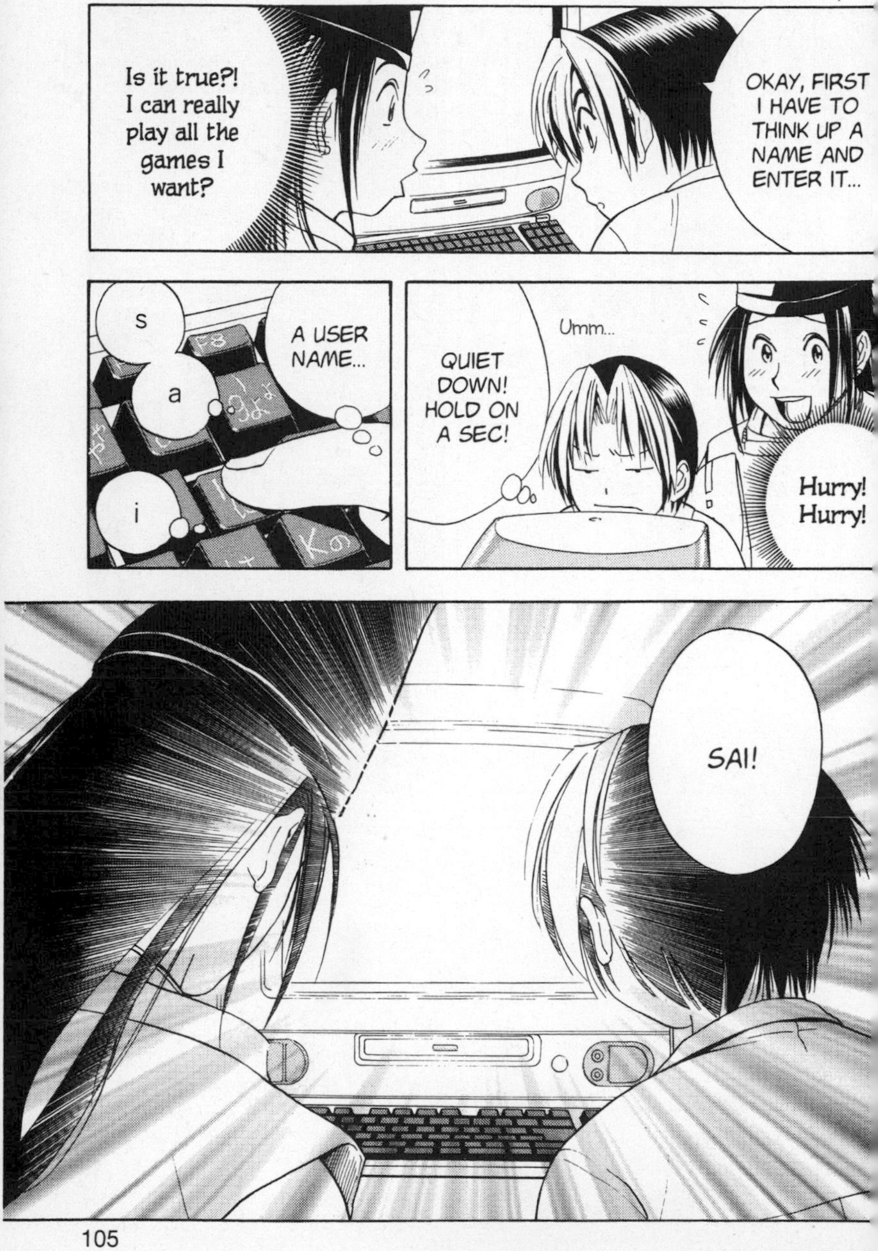
OKAY, FIRST I HAVE TO THINK UP A NAME AND ENTER IT...
Is it true?! I can really play all the games I want?
Hurry! Hurry!
QUIET DOWN! HOLD ON A SEC!
Umm...
A USER NAME...
s
a
i
SAI!

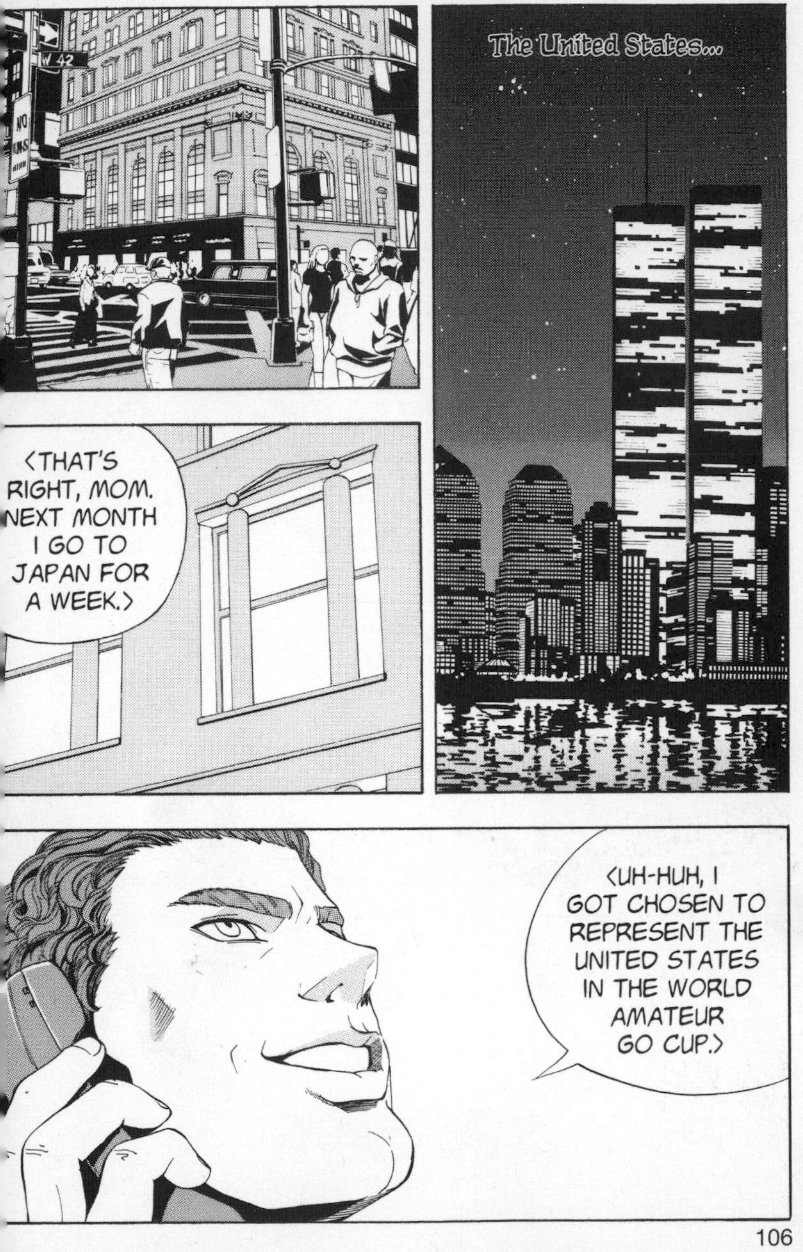
The United States...
W 42
<THAT'S RIGHT, MOM. NEXT MONTH I GO TO JAPAN FOR A WEEK.>
<UH-HUH, I GOT CHOSEN TO REPRESENT THE UNITED STATES IN THE WORLD AMATEUR GO CUP.>

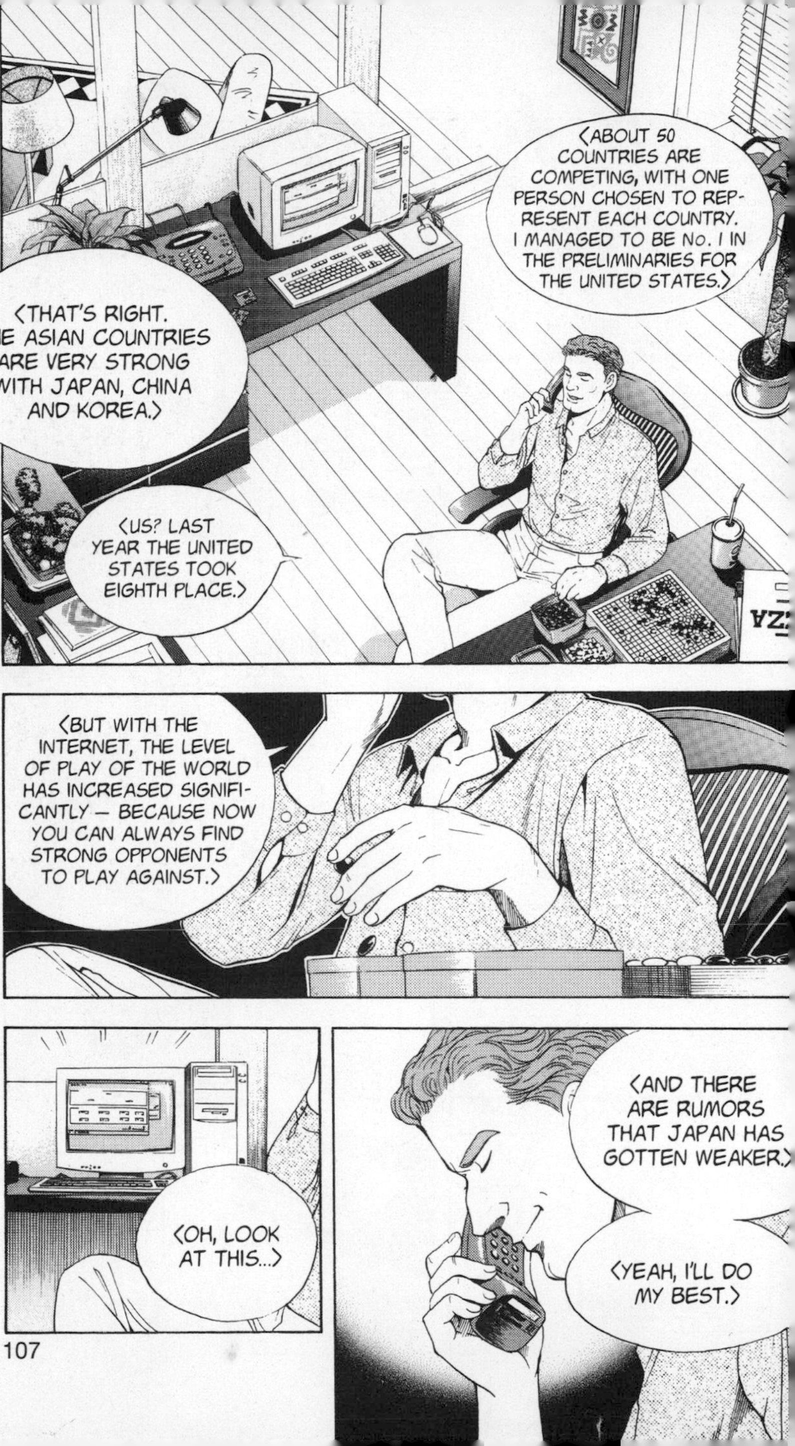
〈ABOUT 50 COUNTRIES ARE COMPETING, WITH ONE PERSON CHOSEN TO REPRESENT EACH COUNTRY. I MANAGED TO BE No. 1 IN THE PRELIMINARIES FOR THE UNITED STATES.〉
〈THAT'S RIGHT. THE ASIAN COUNTRIES ARE VERY STRONG WITH JAPAN, CHINA AND KOREA.〉
〈US? LAST YEAR THE UNITED STATES TOOK EIGHTH PLACE.〉
〈BUT WITH THE INTERNET, THE LEVEL OF PLAY OF THE WORLD HAS INCREASED SIGNIFICANTLY — BECAUSE NOW YOU CAN ALWAYS FIND STRONG OPPONENTS TO PLAY AGAINST.〉
〈AND THERE ARE RUMORS THAT JAPAN HAS GOTTEN WEAKER.〉
〈YEAH, I'LL DO MY BEST.〉
〈OH, LOOK AT THIS...〉

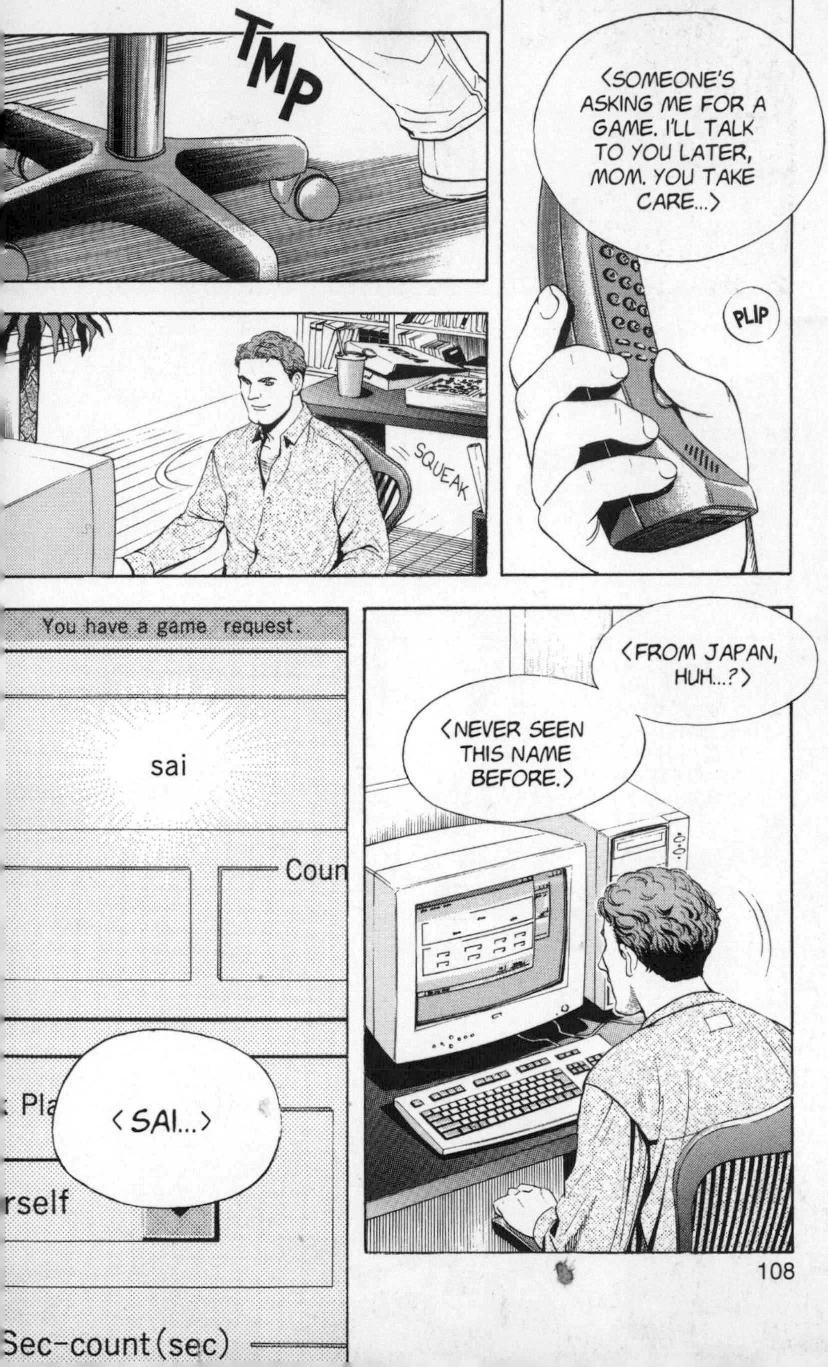
<SOMEONE'S ASKING ME FOR A GAME. I'LL TALK TO YOU LATER, MOM. YOU TAKE CARE...>
PLIP
TMP
SQUEAK
<FROM JAPAN, HUH...?>
<NEVER SEEN THIS NAME BEFORE.>
You have a game request.
sai
Coun
Pla
rself
Sec-count(sec)
<SAI...>

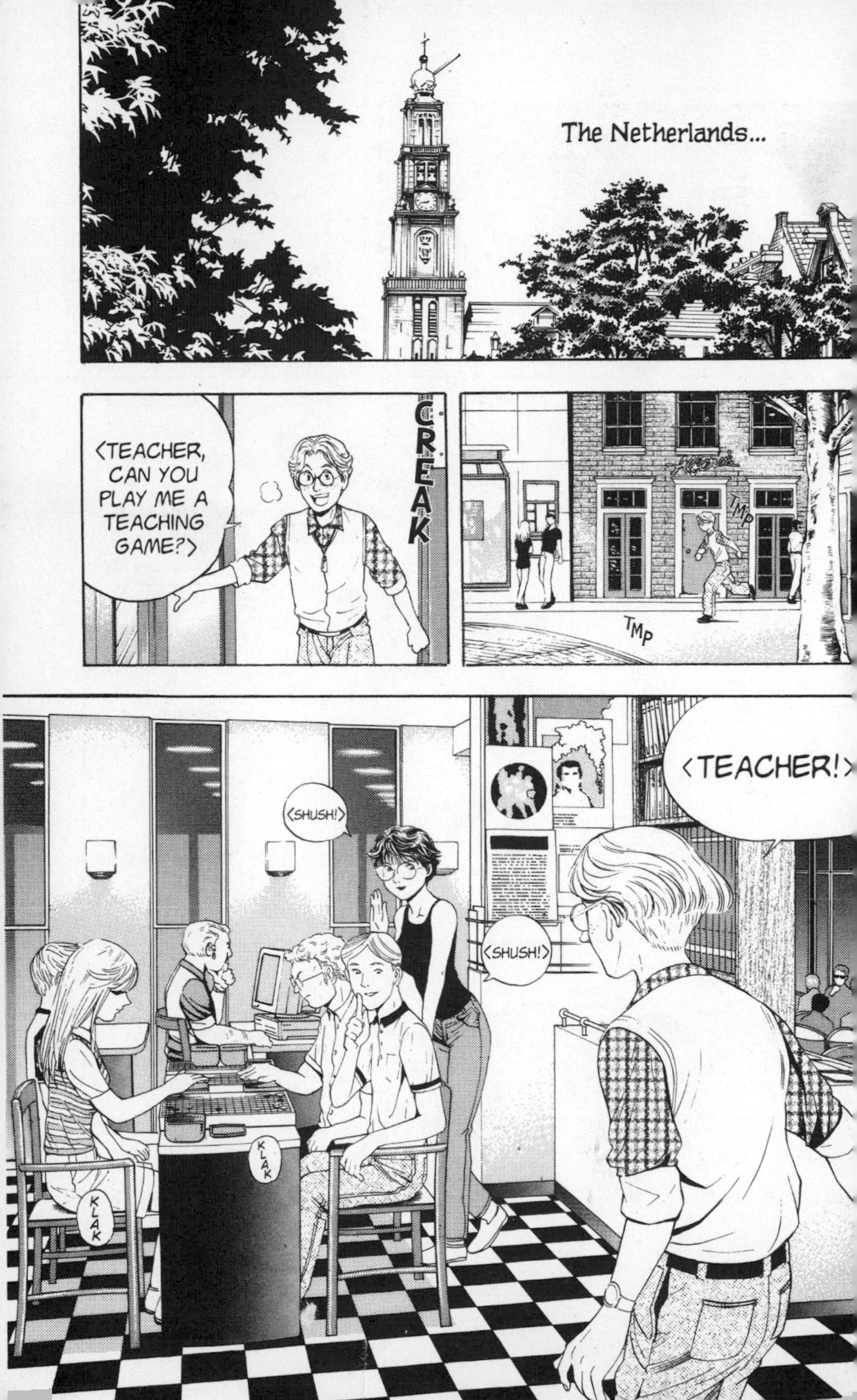
The Netherlands...
TMP
TMP
CREAK
〈TEACHER, CAN YOU PLAY ME A TEACHING GAME?〉
〈TEACHER!〉
〈SHUSH!〉
〈SHUSH!〉
KLAK
KLAK

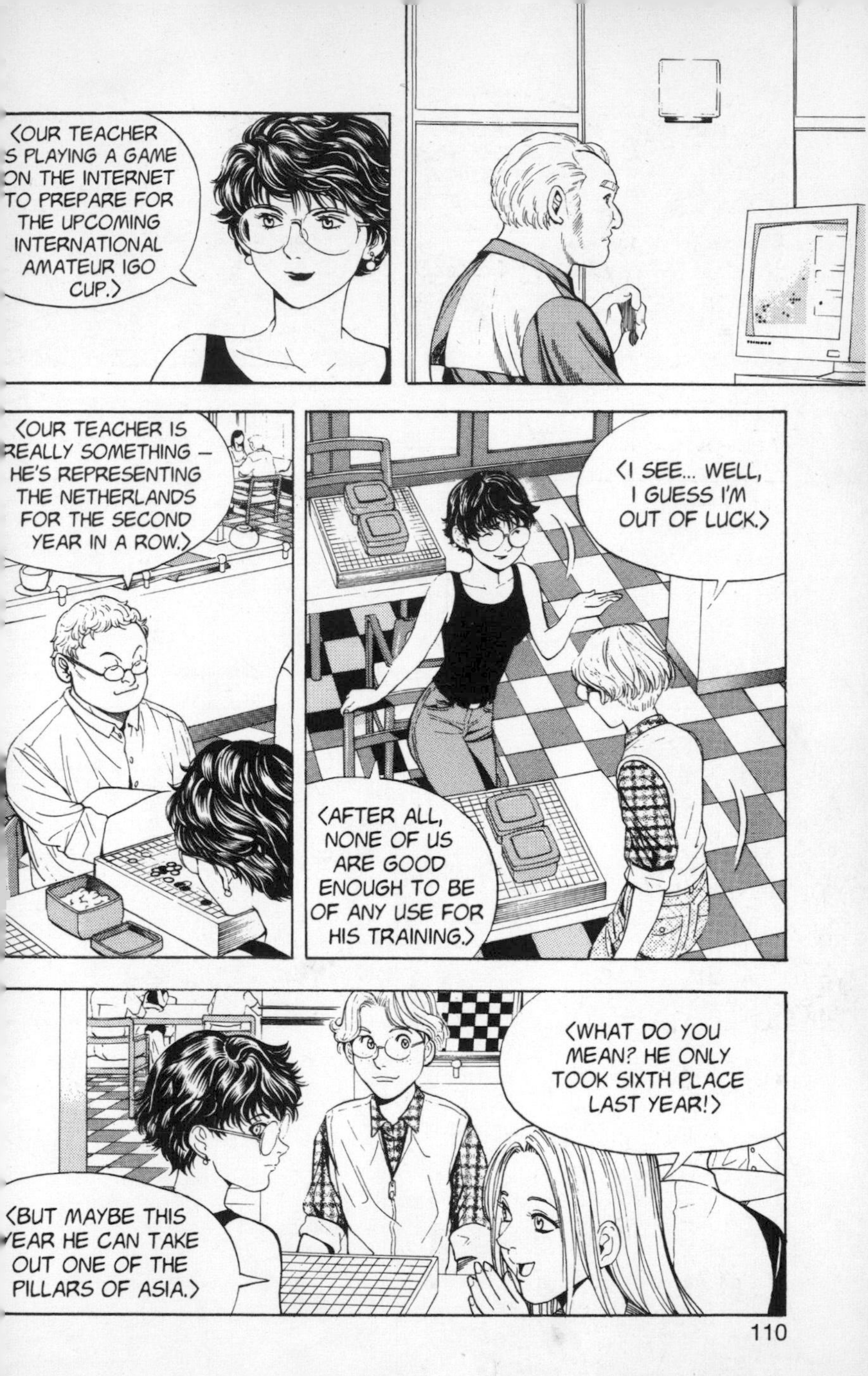
〈OUR TEACHER IS PLAYING A GAME ON THE INTERNET TO PREPARE FOR THE UPCOMING INTERNATIONAL AMATEUR IGO CUP.〉
〈I SEE... WELL, I GUESS I'M OUT OF LUCK.〉
〈AFTER ALL, NONE OF US ARE GOOD ENOUGH TO BE OF ANY USE FOR HIS TRAINING.〉
〈OUR TEACHER IS REALLY SOMETHING — HE'S REPRESENTING THE NETHERLANDS FOR THE SECOND YEAR IN A ROW.〉
〈WHAT DO YOU MEAN? HE ONLY TOOK SIXTH PLACE LAST YEAR!〉
〈BUT MAYBE THIS YEAR HE CAN TAKE OUT ONE OF THE PILLARS OF ASIA.〉

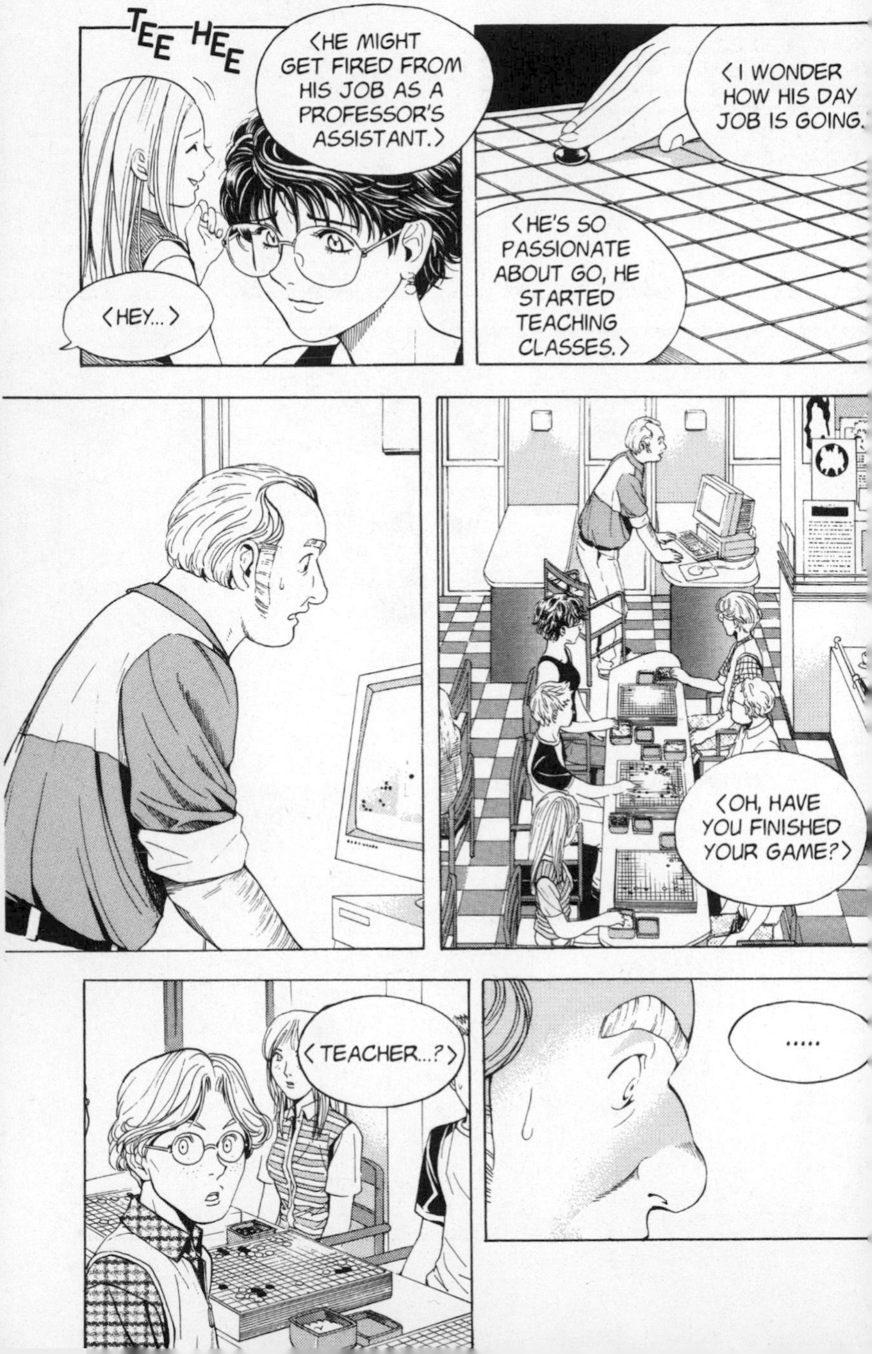
<I WONDER HOW HIS DAY JOB IS GOING.>
<HE'S SO PASSIONATE ABOUT GO, HE STARTED TEACHING CLASSES.>
<HE MIGHT GET FIRED FROM HIS JOB AS A PROFESSOR'S ASSISTANT.>
TEE HEE
<HEY...>
<OH, HAVE YOU FINISHED YOUR GAME?>
.....
<TEACHER...?>

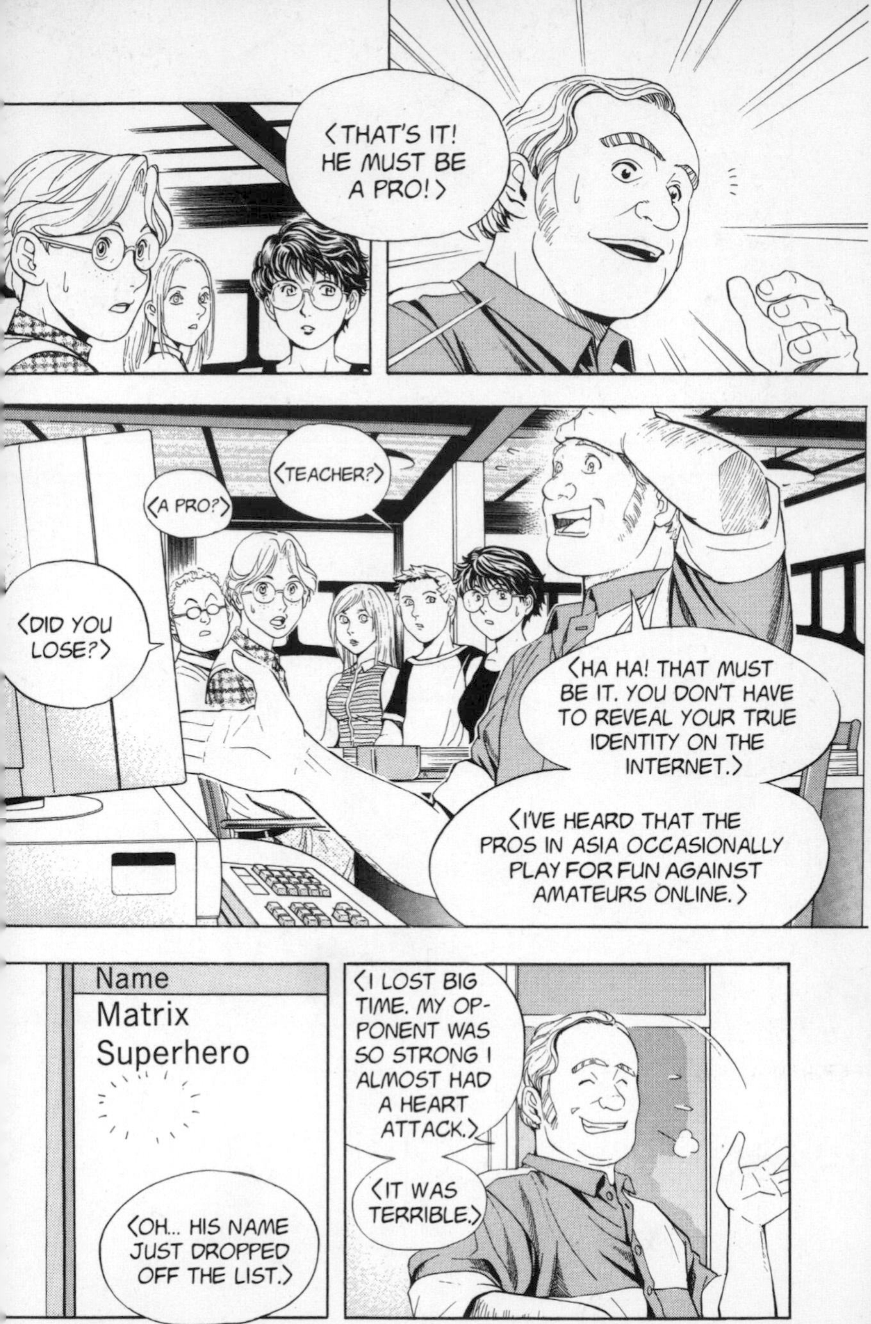

〈THAT'S IT! HE MUST BE A PRO!〉
〈TEACHER?〉
〈A PRO?〉
〈HA HA! THAT MUST BE IT. YOU DON'T HAVE TO REVEAL YOUR TRUE IDENTITY ON THE INTERNET.〉
〈I'VE HEARD THAT THE PROS IN ASIA OCCASIONALLY PLAY FOR FUN AGAINST AMATEURS ONLINE.〉
〈DID YOU LOSE?〉
〈I LOST BIG TIME. MY OPPONENT WAS SO STRONG I ALMOST HAD A HEART ATTACK.〉
〈IT WAS TERRIBLE.〉
Name
Matrix
Superhero
〈OH... HIS NAME JUST DROPPED OFF THE LIST.〉

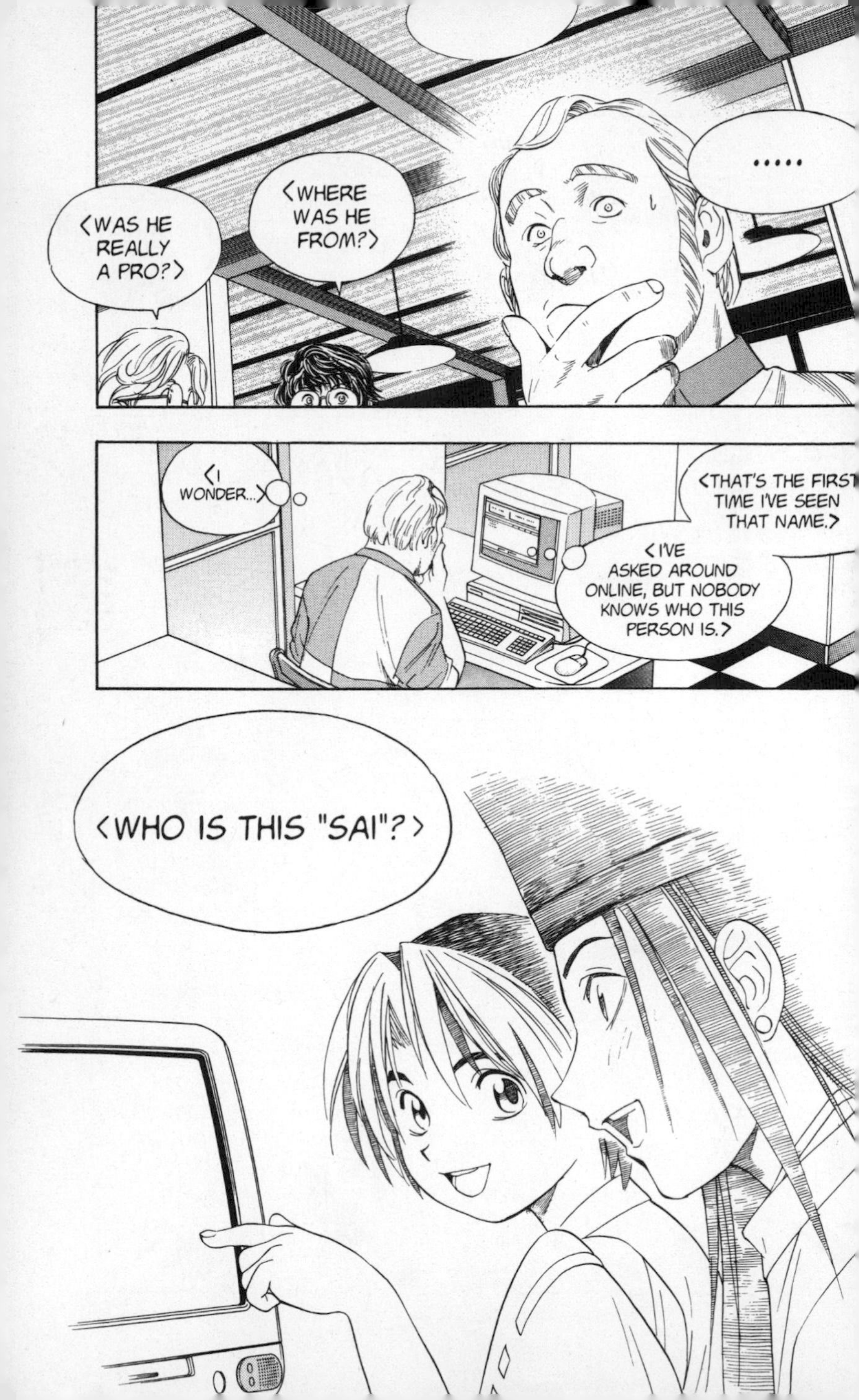
.....
<WHERE WAS HE FROM?>
<WAS HE REALLY A PRO?>
<THAT'S THE FIRST TIME I'VE SEEN THAT NAME.>
<I'VE ASKED AROUND ONLINE, BUT NOBODY KNOWS WHO THIS PERSON IS.>
<I WONDER...>
<WHO IS THIS "SAI"?>

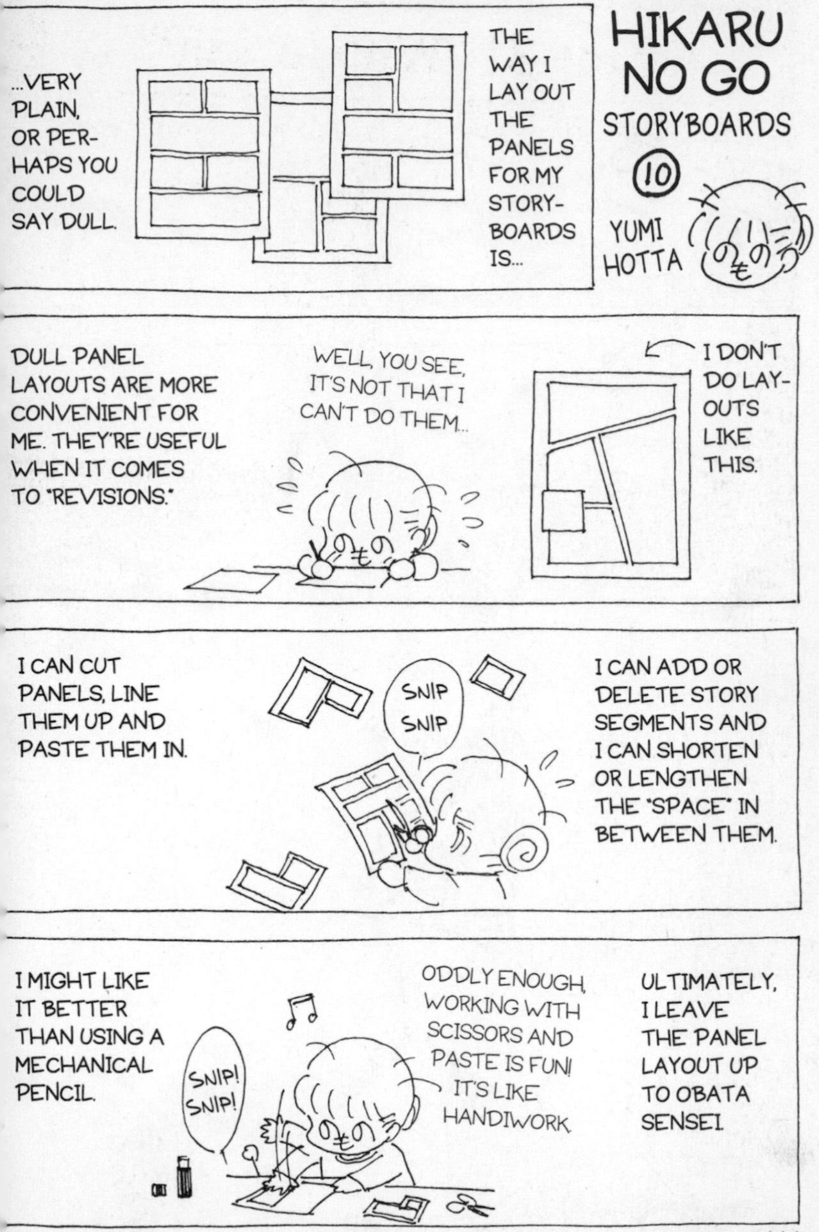
HIKARU NO GO
STORYBOARDS
10
YUMI HOTTA
THE WAY I LAY OUT THE PANELS FOR MY STORY-BOARDS IS...
...VERY PLAIN, OR PER-HAPS YOU COULD SAY DULL.
I DON'T DO LAY-OUTS LIKE THIS.
WELL, YOU SEE, IT'S NOT THAT I CAN'T DO THEM...
DULL PANEL LAYOUTS ARE MORE CONVENIENT FOR ME. THEY'RE USEFUL WHEN IT COMES TO "REVISIONS."
I CAN ADD OR DELETE STORY SEGMENTS AND I CAN SHORTEN OR LENGTHEN THE "SPACE" IN BETWEEN THEM.
SNIP SNIP
I CAN CUT PANELS, LINE THEM UP AND PASTE THEM IN.
ULTIMATELY, I LEAVE THE PANEL LAYOUT UP TO OBATA SENSEI.
ODDLY ENOUGH, WORKING WITH SCISSORS AND PASTE IS FUN! IT'S LIKE HANDIWORK.
SNIP! SNIP!
I MIGHT LIKE IT BETTER THAN USING A MECHANICAL PENCIL.

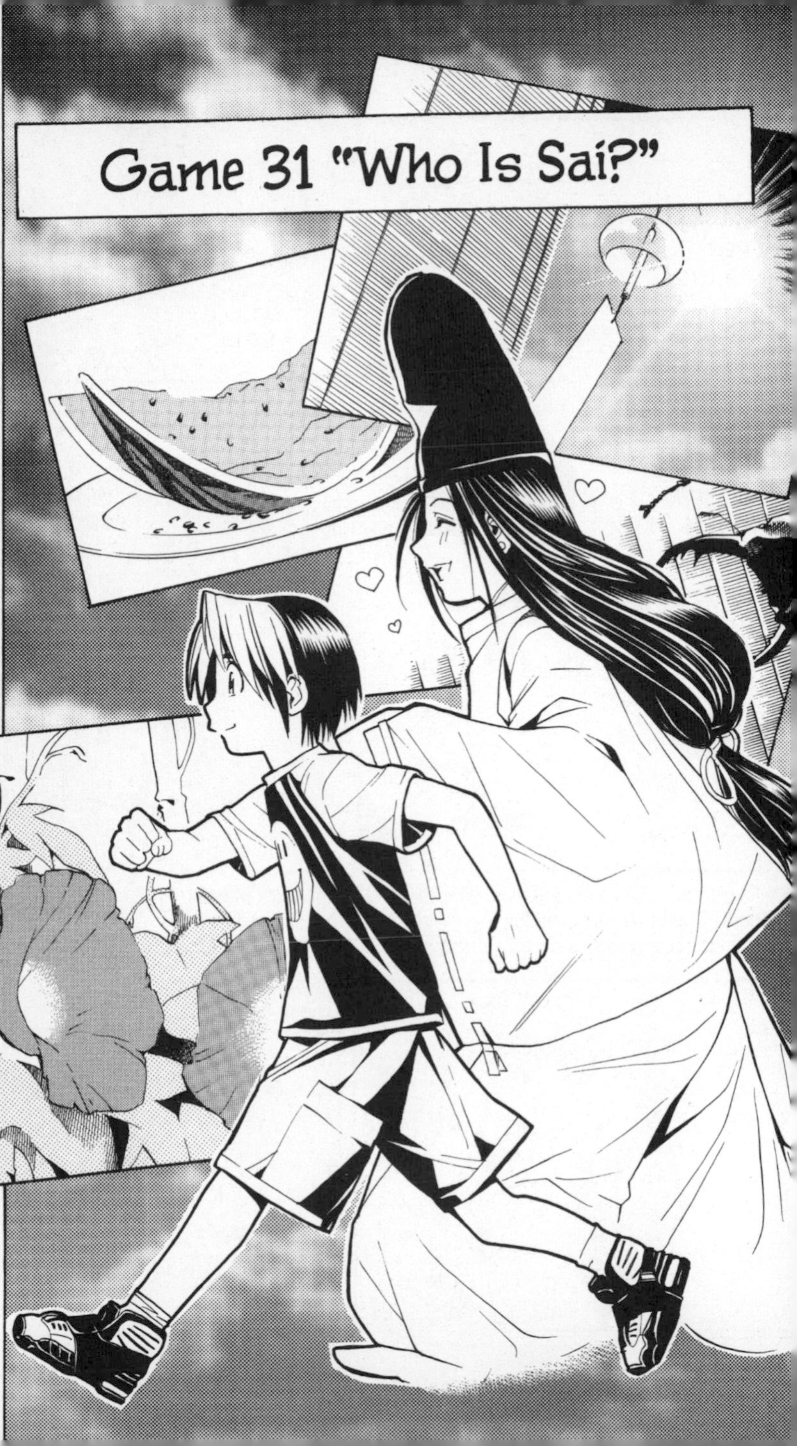
Game 31 "Who Is Sai?"

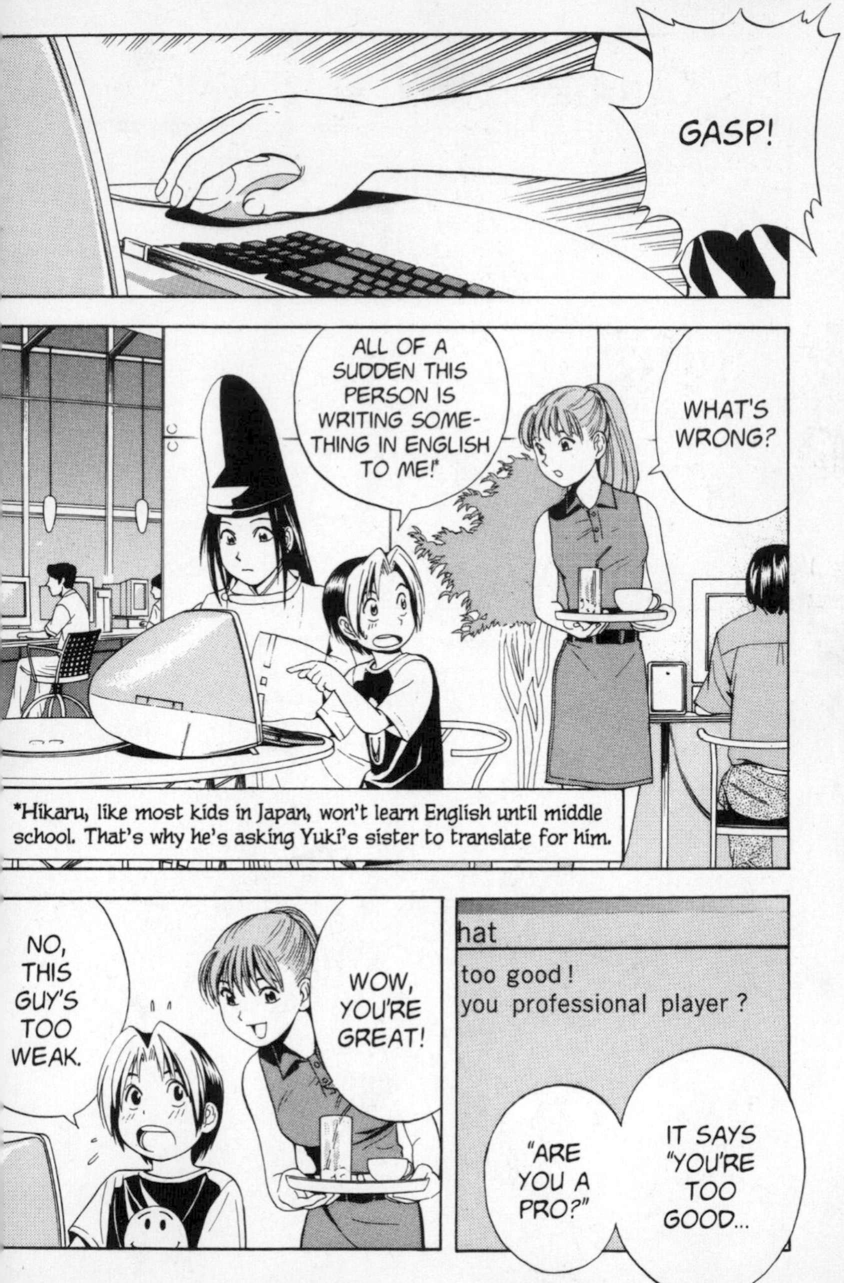
GASP!
WHAT'S WRONG?
ALL OF A SUDDEN THIS PERSON IS WRITING SOME-THING IN ENGLISH TO ME!*
*Hikaru, like most kids in Japan, won't learn English until middle school. That's why he's asking Yuki's sister to translate for him.
hat
too good !
you professional player ?
IT SAYS "YOU'RE TOO GOOD...
"ARE YOU A PRO?"
WOW, YOU'RE GREAT!
NO, THIS GUY'S TOO WEAK.

READ THIS WAY

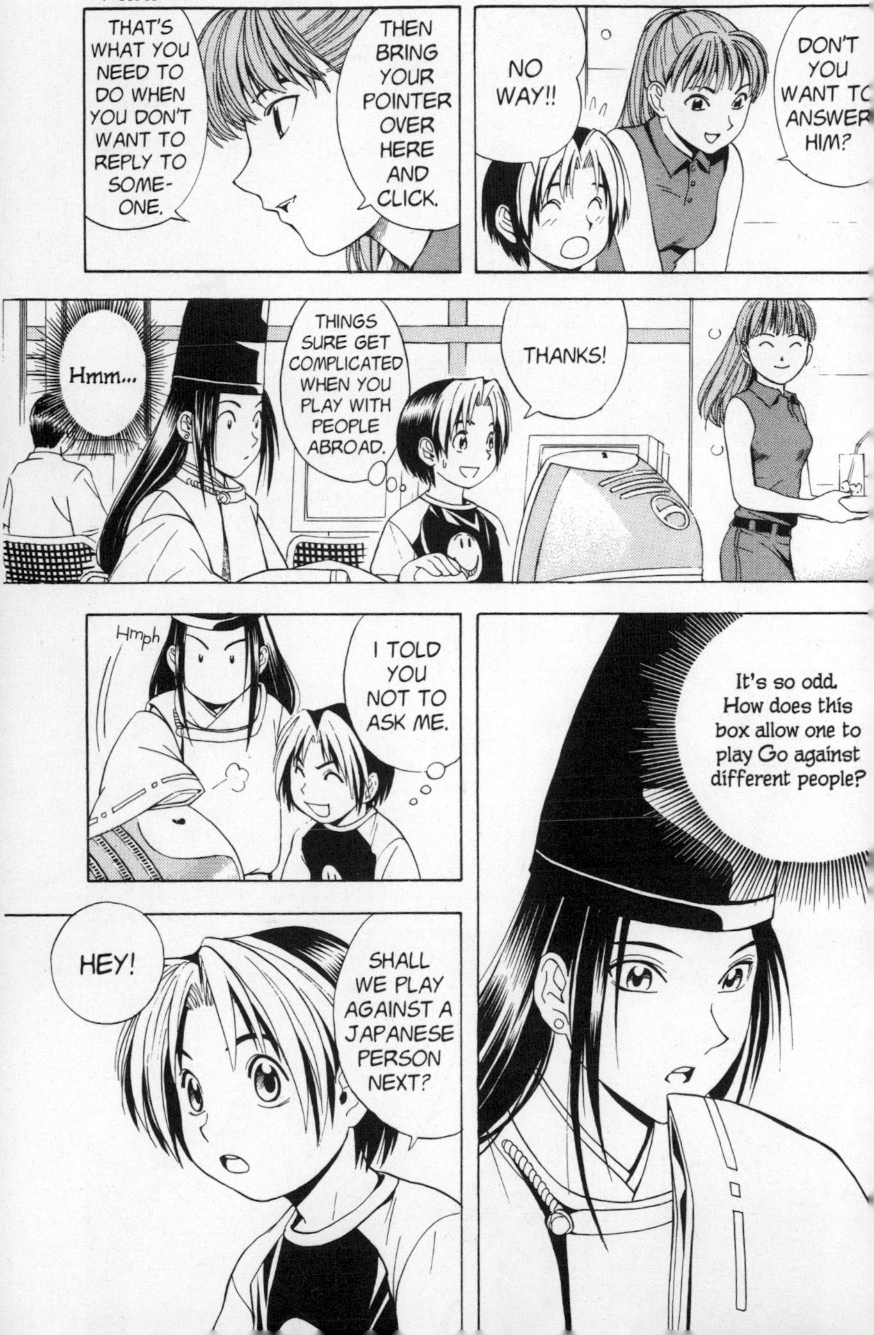
DON'T YOU WANT TO ANSWER HIM?
NO WAY!!
THEN BRING YOUR POINTER OVER HERE AND CLICK.
THAT'S WHAT YOU NEED TO DO WHEN YOU DON'T WANT TO REPLY TO SOME-ONE.
THANKS!
THINGS SURE GET COMPLICATED WHEN YOU PLAY WITH PEOPLE ABROAD.
Hmm...
It's so odd. How does this box allow one to play Go against different people?
I TOLD YOU NOT TO ASK ME.
Hmph
SHALL WE PLAY AGAINST A JAPANESE PERSON NEXT?
HEY!

Name
N.ko
mamo
zelda
ssu
kenji
sweet boy

FROM THE OTHER DAY!

IT'S ZELDA!

Yes, indeed!

LOOKS LIKE YOU'RE ENJOYING YOURSELF, SAI.

Yay! Another game! ♡

LET'S PLAY AGAINST HIM!

YOU CAN PLAY FOR A WHILE. AFTER ALL, IT'S SUMMER.

A kid?

THIS GUY'S JAPANESE. HE MIGHT EVEN BE A KID!

WOW! WOW!

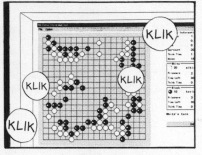

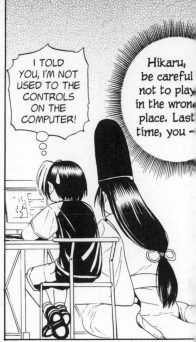

READ THIS WAY

Hikaru, be careful not to pla in the wron place. Last time, you -
I TOLD YOU, I'M NOT USED TO THE CONTROLS ON THE COMPUTER!
KLIK
KLIK
KLIK
KLIK
KLIK
KLIK
KLIK
KLIK
KLIK
KLIK
KLIK
KLIK
KLIK
KLIK

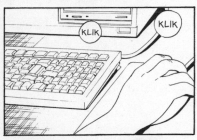

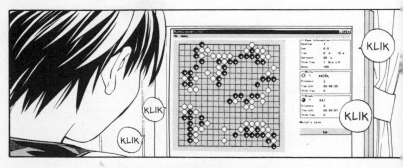

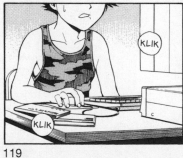

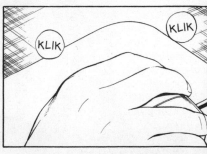

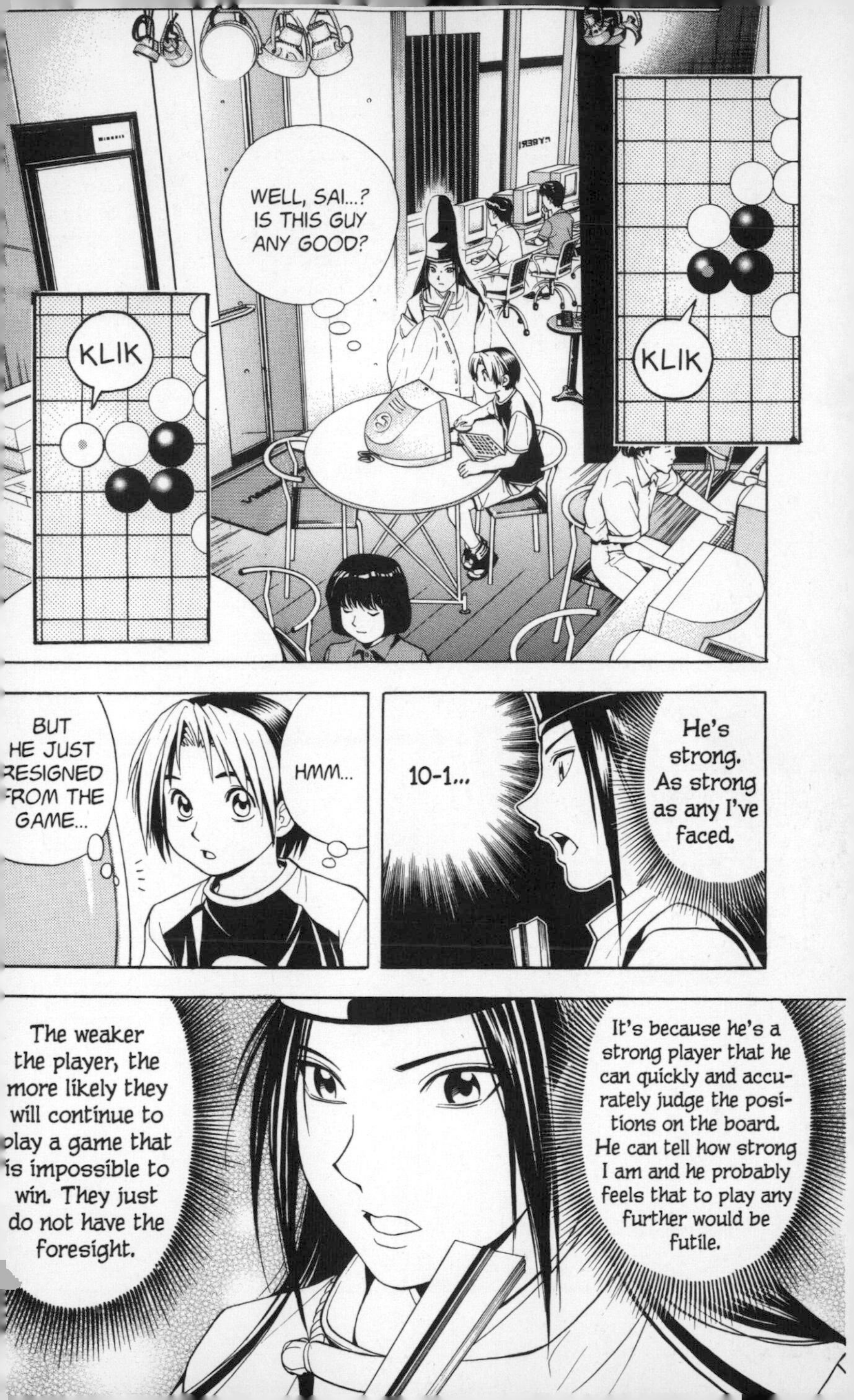
KLIK
WELL, SAI...? IS THIS GUY ANY GOOD?
KLIK
He's strong. As strong as any I've faced.
10-1...
HMM...
BUT HE JUST RESIGNED FROM THE GAME...
It's because he's a strong player that he can quickly and accurately judge the positions on the board. He can tell how strong I am and he probably feels that to play any further would be futile.
The weaker the player, the more likely they will continue to play a game that is impossible to win. They just do not have the foresight.

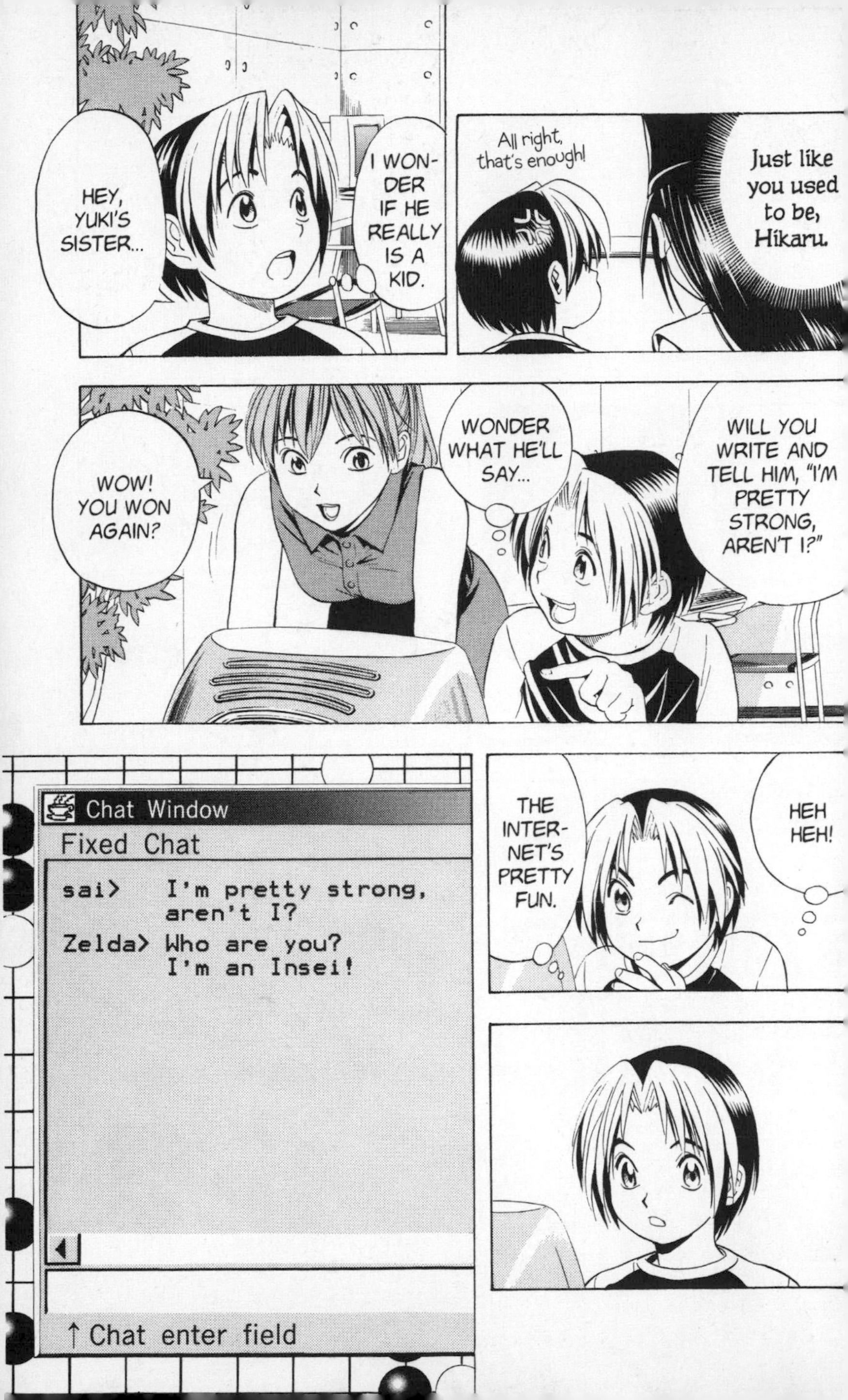
Just like you used to be, Hikaru.
All right, that's enough!
I WONDER IF HE REALLY IS A KID.
HEY, YUKI'S SISTER...
WILL YOU WRITE AND TELL HIM, "I'M PRETTY STRONG, AREN'T I?"
WONDER WHAT HE'LL SAY...
WOW! YOU WON AGAIN?
HEH HEH!
THE INTERNET'S PRETTY FUN.
Chat Window
Fixed Chat
sai> I'm pretty strong, aren't I?
Zelda> Who are you? I'm an Insei!
↑ Chat enter field

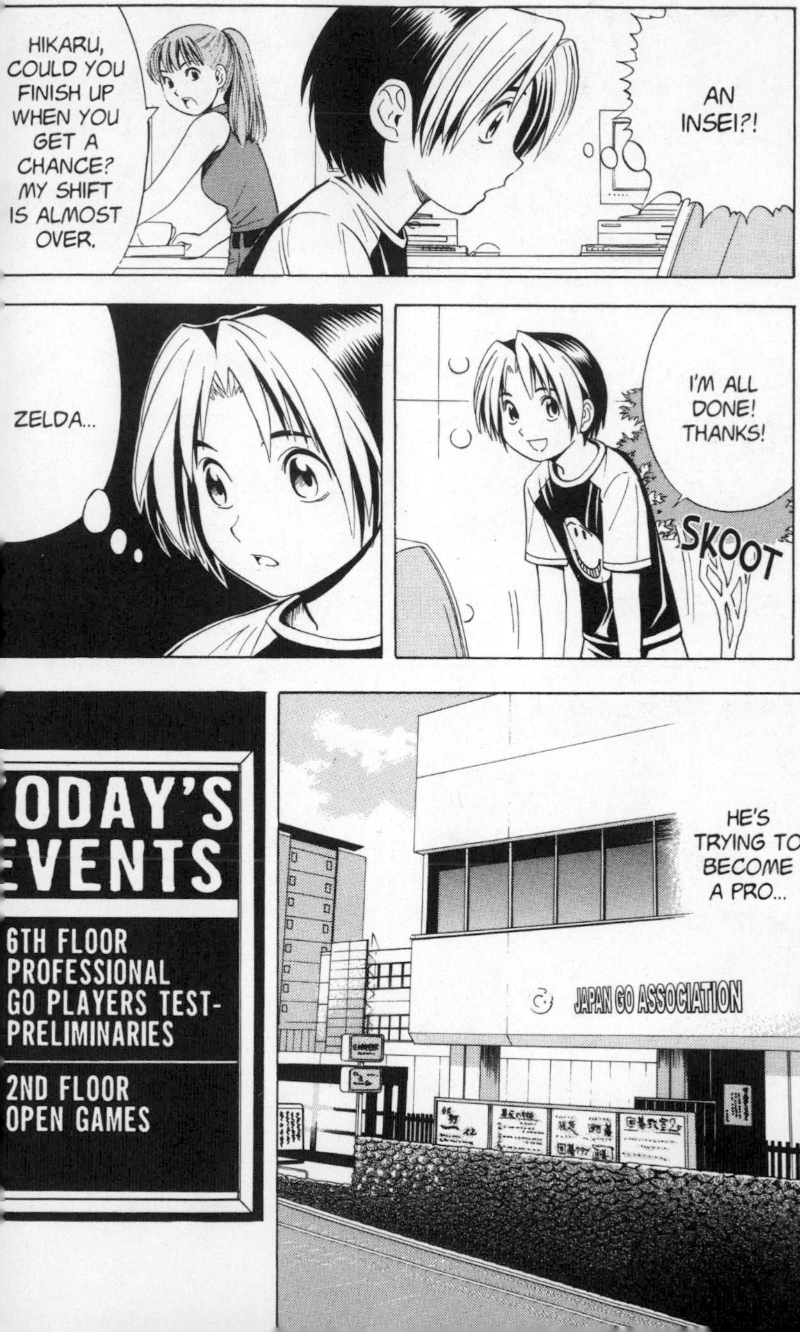
AN INSEI?!
HIKARU, COULD YOU FINISH UP WHEN YOU GET A CHANCE? MY SHIFT IS ALMOST OVER.
I'M ALL DONE! THANKS!
SKOOT
ZELDA...
HE'S TRYING TO BECOME A PRO...
JAPAN GO ASSOCIATION
ODAY'S
EVENTS
6TH FLOOR PROFESSIONAL GO PLAYERS TEST-PRELIMINARIES
2ND FLOOR OPEN GAMES

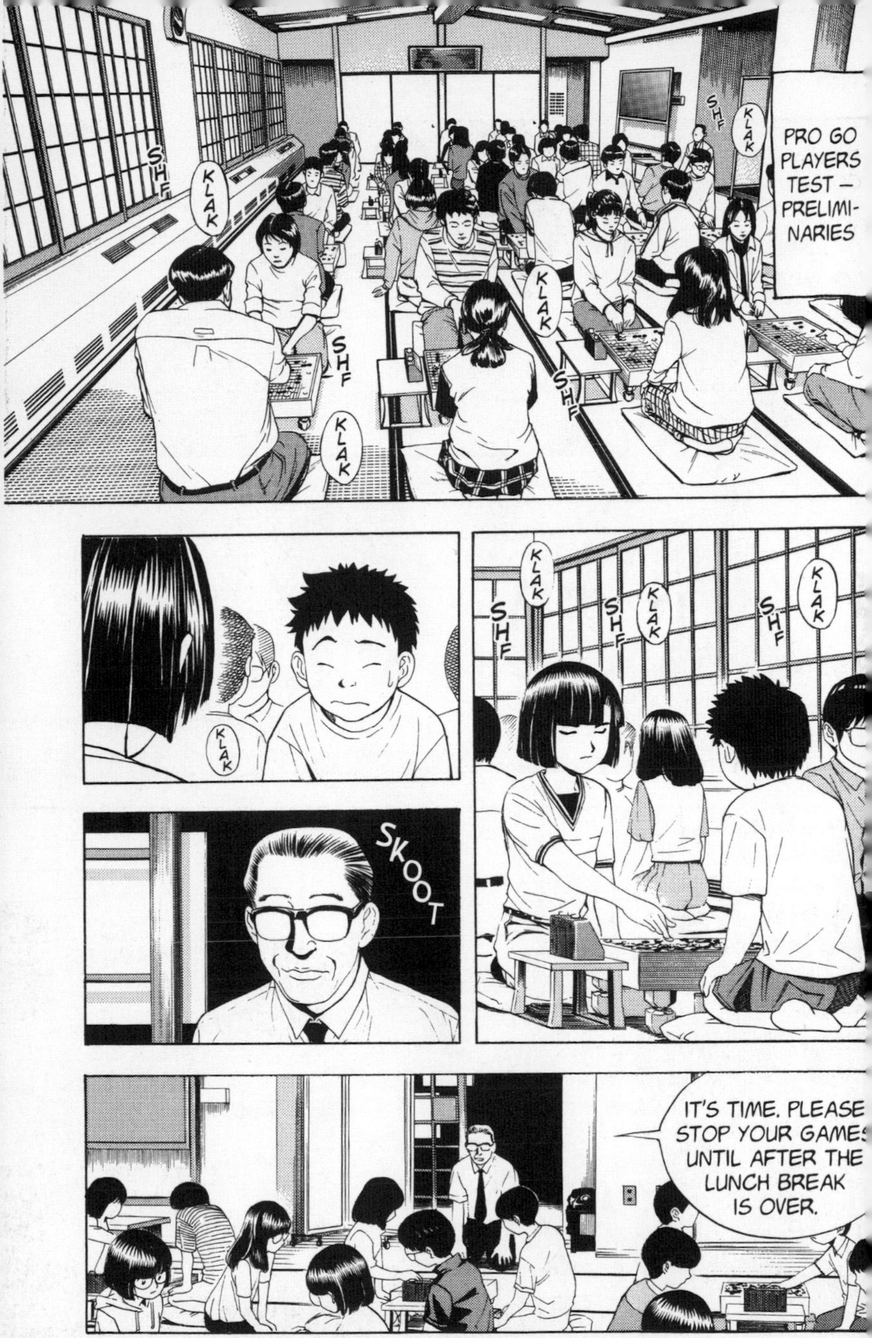
PRO GO PLAYERS TEST — PRELIMINARIES
KLAK
SHF
KLAK
SHF
KLAK
SHF
KLAK
SHF
KLAK
KLAK
SHF
KLAK
SHF
KLAK
SHF
KLAK
SKOOT
IT'S TIME. PLEASE STOP YOUR GAMES UNTIL AFTER THE LUNCH BREAK IS OVER.

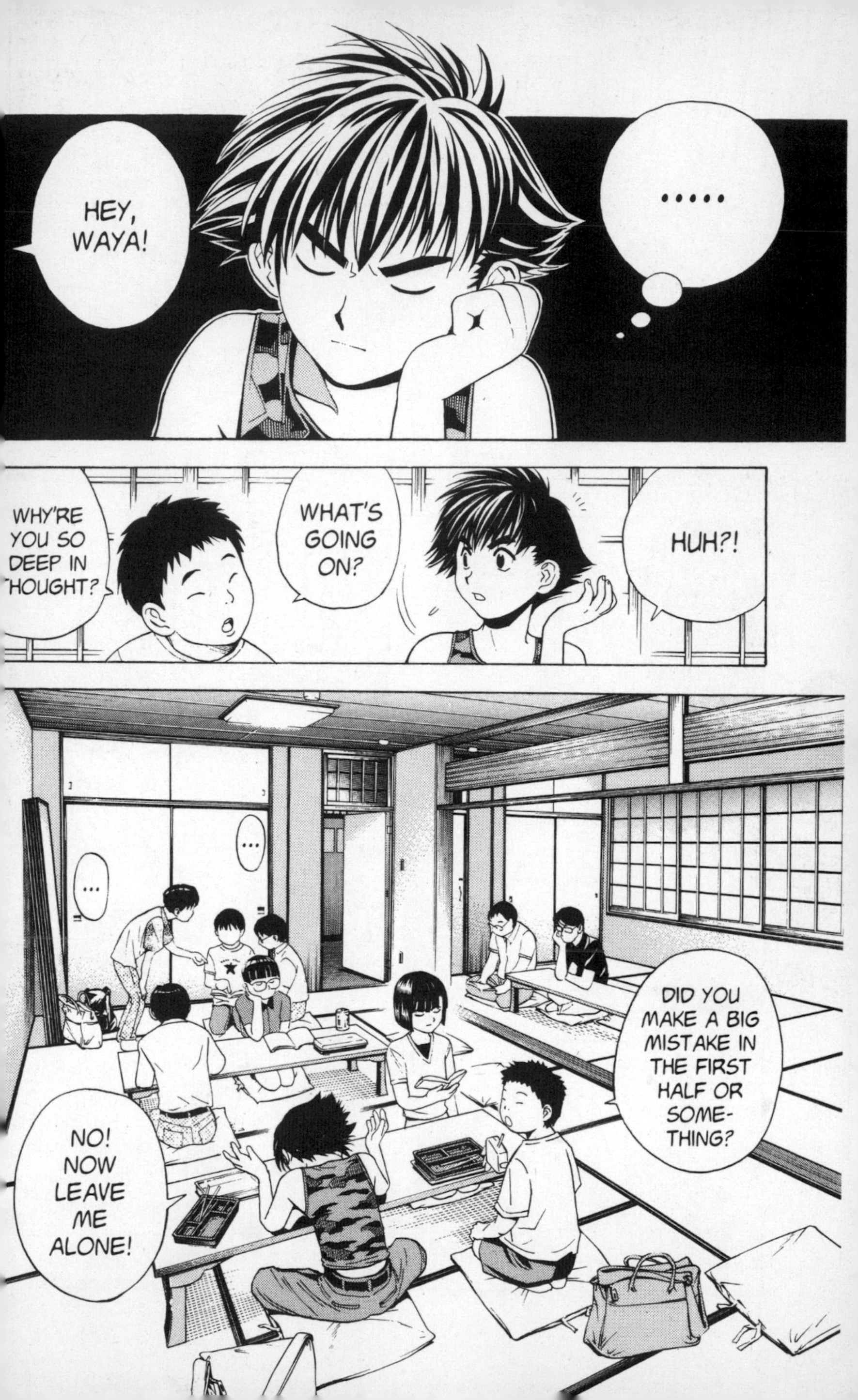
.....
HEY, WAYA!
HUH?!
WHAT'S GOING ON?
WHY'RE YOU SO DEEP IN THOUGHT?
...
...
DID YOU MAKE A BIG MISTAKE IN THE FIRST HALF OR SOME-THING?
NO! NOW LEAVE ME ALONE!

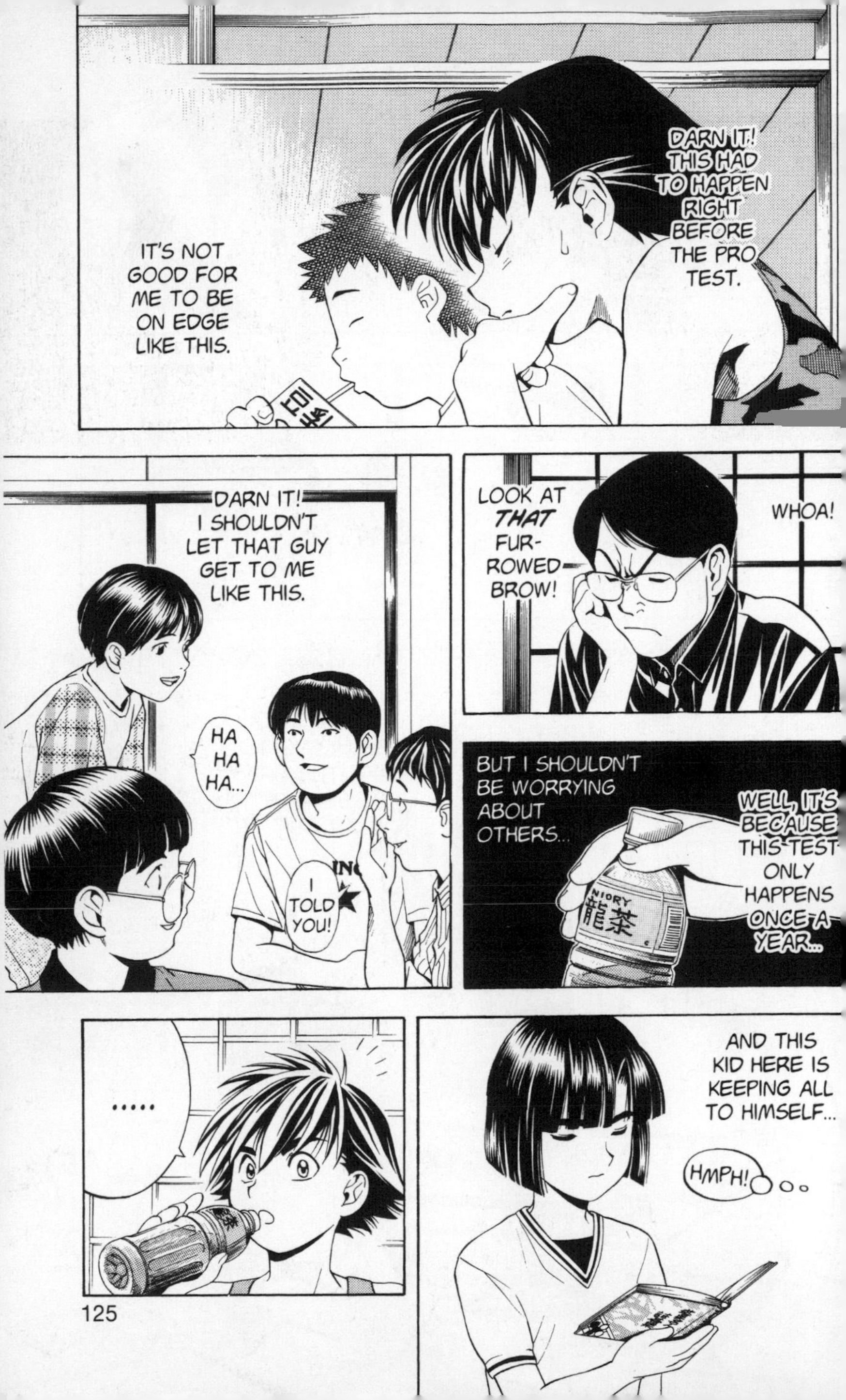

DARN IT! THIS HAD TO HAPPEN RIGHT BEFORE THE PRO TEST.
IT'S NOT GOOD FOR ME TO BE ON EDGE LIKE THIS.
WHOA!
LOOK AT *THAT* FUR-ROWED BROW!
WELL, IT'S BECAUSE THIS TEST ONLY HAPPENS ONCE A YEAR...
BUT I SHOULDN'T BE WORRYING ABOUT OTHERS...
DARN IT! I SHOULDN'T LET THAT GUY GET TO ME LIKE THIS.
HA HA HA...
I TOLD YOU!
AND THIS KID HERE IS KEEPING ALL TO HIMSELF...
HMPH!
.....

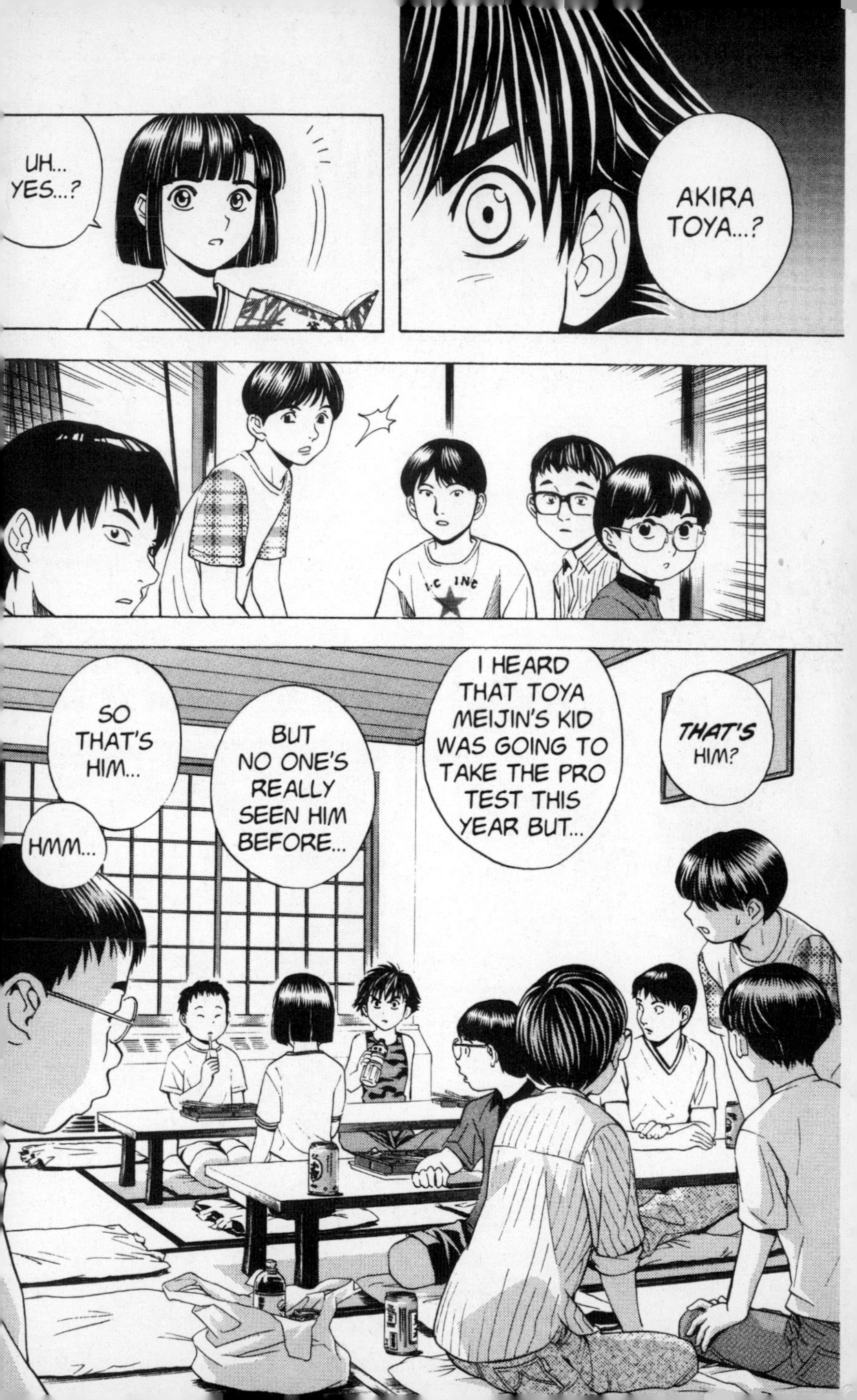
AKIRA TOYA...?
UH... YES...?
THAT'S HIM?
I HEARD THAT TOYA MEIJIN'S KID WAS GOING TO TAKE THE PRO TEST THIS YEAR BUT...
BUT NO ONE'S REALLY SEEN HIM BEFORE...
SO THAT'S HIM...
HMM...

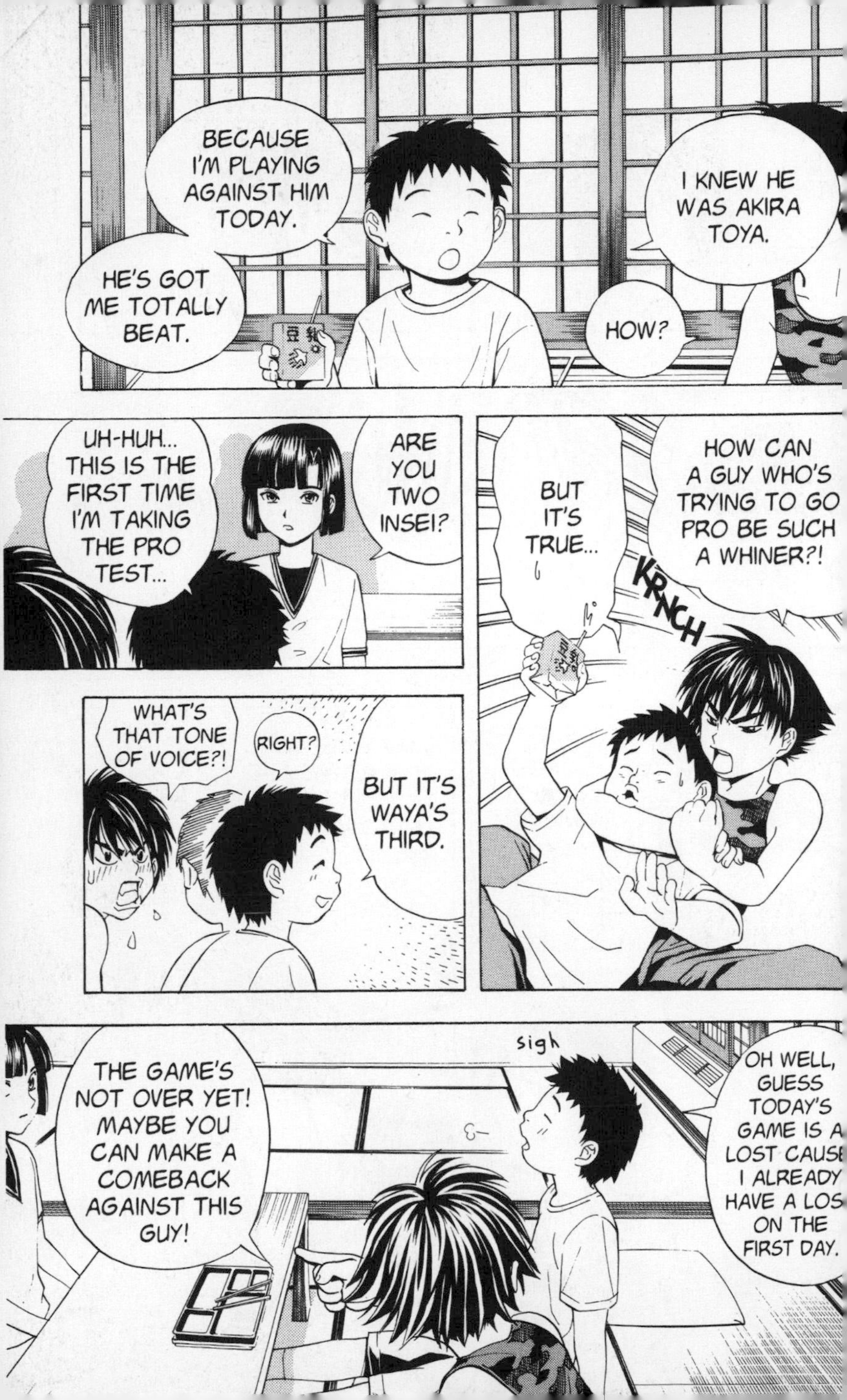
I KNEW HE WAS AKIRA TOYA.
HOW?
BECAUSE I'M PLAYING AGAINST HIM TODAY.
HE'S GOT ME TOTALLY BEAT.
HOW CAN A GUY WHO'S TRYING TO GO PRO BE SUCH A WHINER?!
KRNCH
BUT IT'S TRUE...
ARE YOU TWO INSEI?
UH-HUH... THIS IS THE FIRST TIME I'M TAKING THE PRO TEST...
BUT IT'S WAYA'S THIRD.
RIGHT?
WHAT'S THAT TONE OF VOICE?!
OH WELL, GUESS TODAY'S GAME IS A LOST CAUS I ALREADY HAVE A LOS ON THE FIRST DAY.
sigh
THE GAME'S NOT OVER YET! MAYBE YOU CAN MAKE A COMEBACK AGAINST THIS GUY!

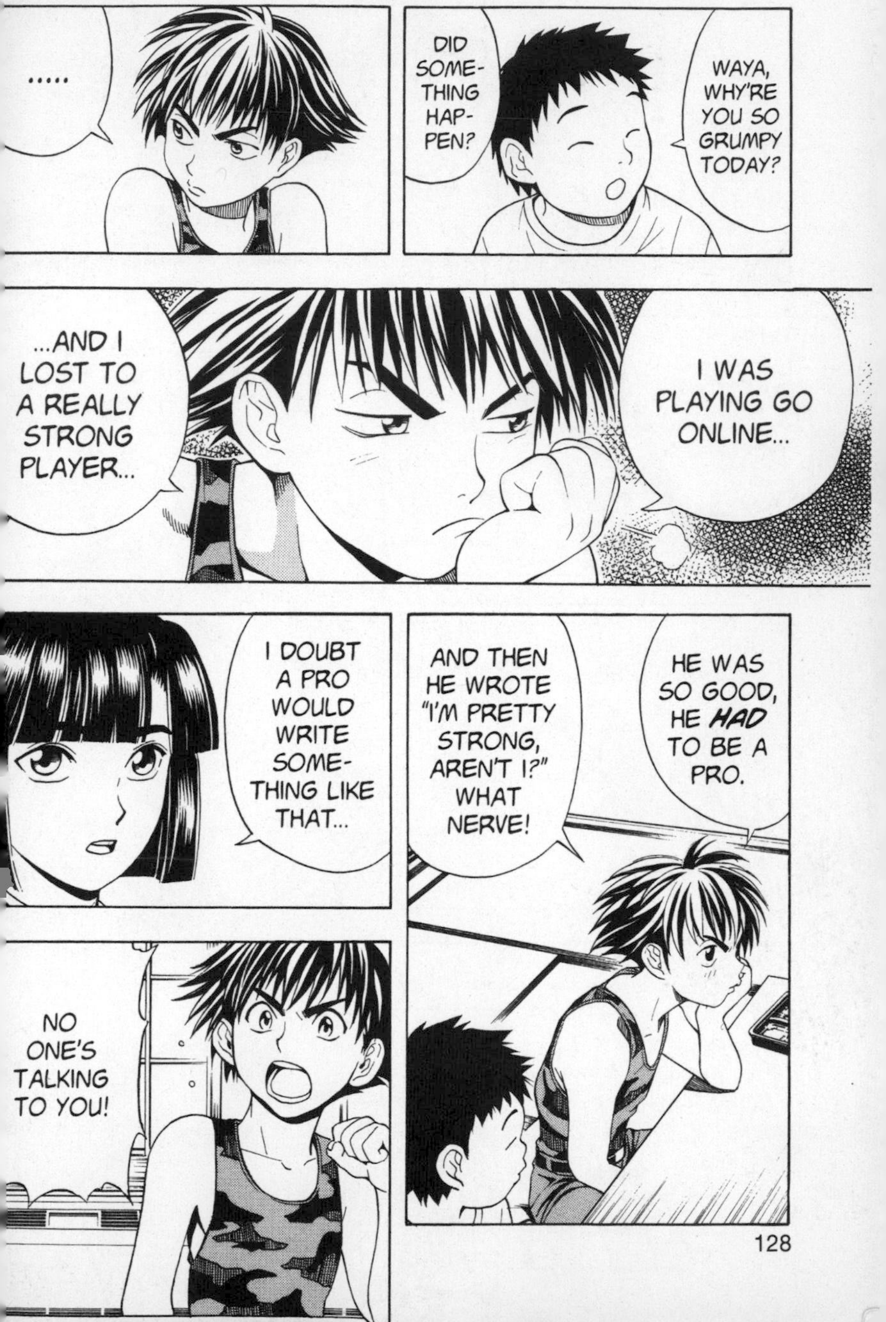
WAYA, WHY'RE YOU SO GRUMPY TODAY?
DID SOME-THING HAP-PEN?
.....
I WAS PLAYING GO ONLINE...
...AND I LOST TO A REALLY STRONG PLAYER...
HE WAS SO GOOD, HE *HAD* TO BE A PRO.
AND THEN HE WROTE "I'M PRETTY STRONG, AREN'T I?" WHAT NERVE!
I DOUBT A PRO WOULD WRITE SOME-THING LIKE THAT...
NO ONE'S TALKING TO YOU!

READ THIS WAY

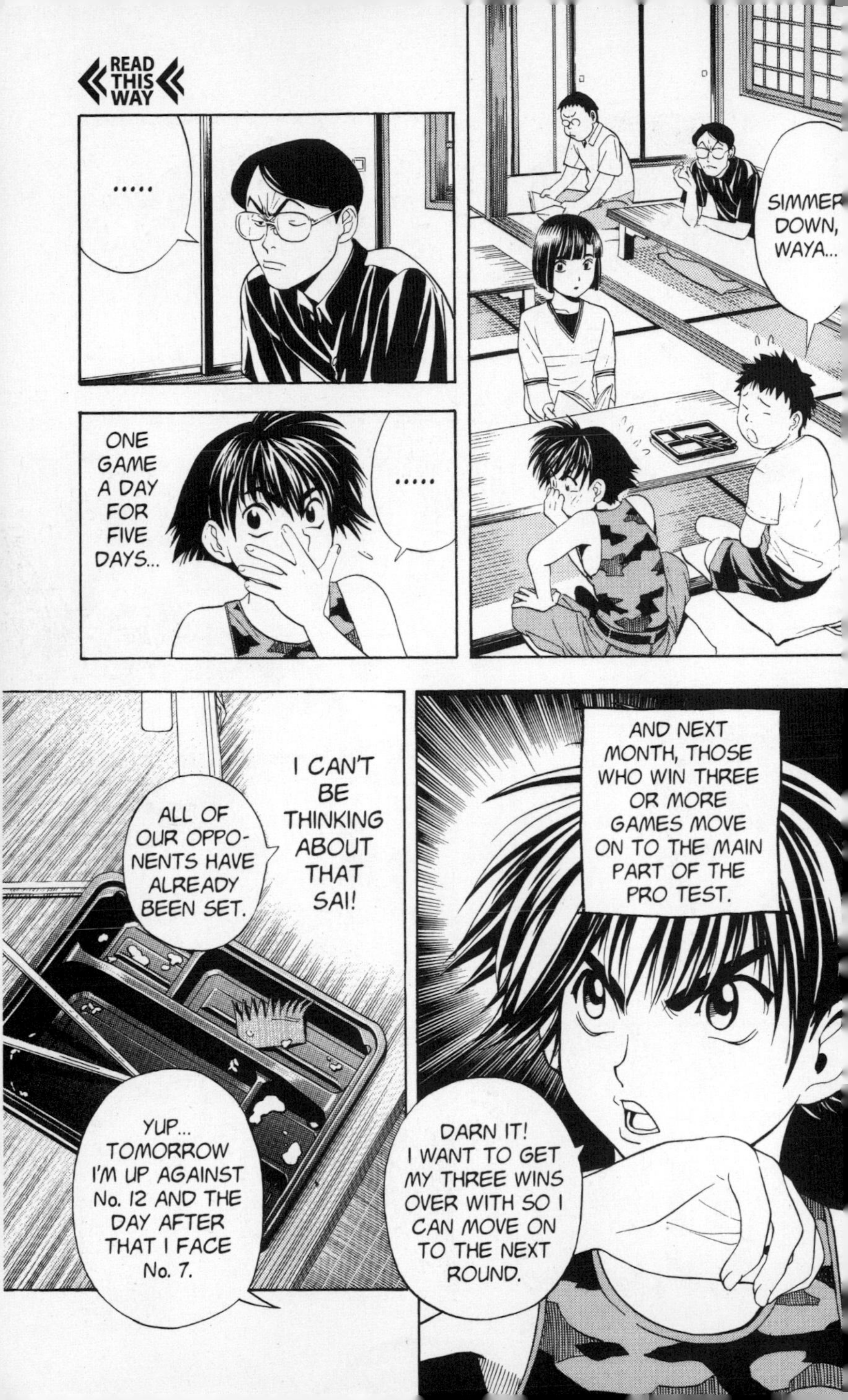

SIMMER DOWN, WAYA...
.....
.....
ONE GAME A DAY FOR FIVE DAYS...
AND NEXT MONTH, THOSE WHO WIN THREE OR MORE GAMES MOVE ON TO THE MAIN PART OF THE PRO TEST.
DARN IT! I WANT TO GET MY THREE WINS OVER WITH SO I CAN MOVE ON TO THE NEXT ROUND.
I CAN'T BE THINKING ABOUT THAT SAI!
ALL OF OUR OPPONENTS HAVE ALREADY BEEN SET.
YUP... TOMORROW I'M UP AGAINST No. 12 AND THE DAY AFTER THAT I FACE No. 7.

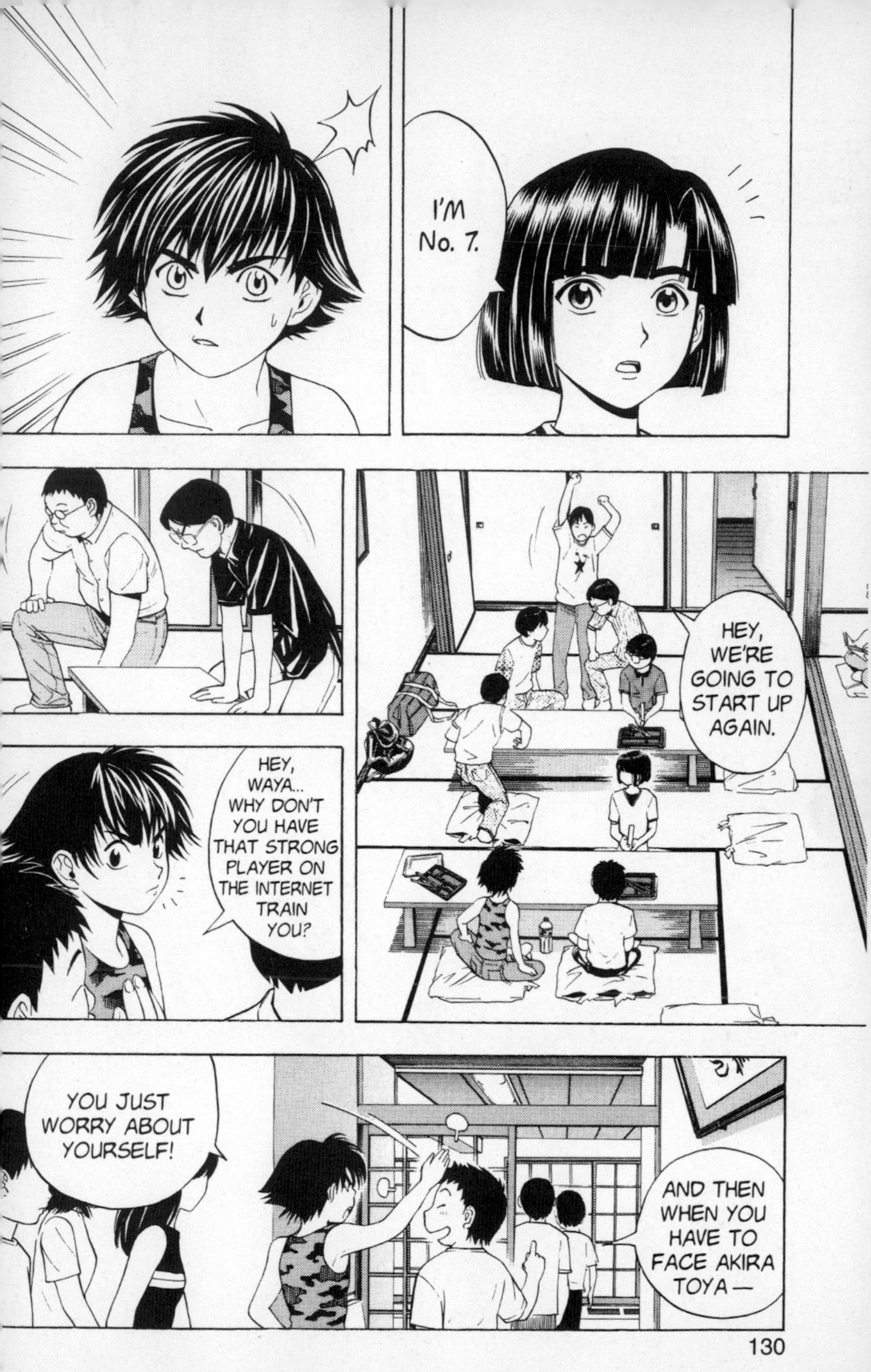
I'M No. 7.
HEY, WE'RE GOING TO START UP AGAIN.
HEY, WAYA... WHY DON'T YOU HAVE THAT STRONG PLAYER ON THE INTERNET TRAIN YOU?
AND THEN WHEN YOU HAVE TO FACE AKIRA TOYA—
YOU JUST WORRY ABOUT YOURSELF!

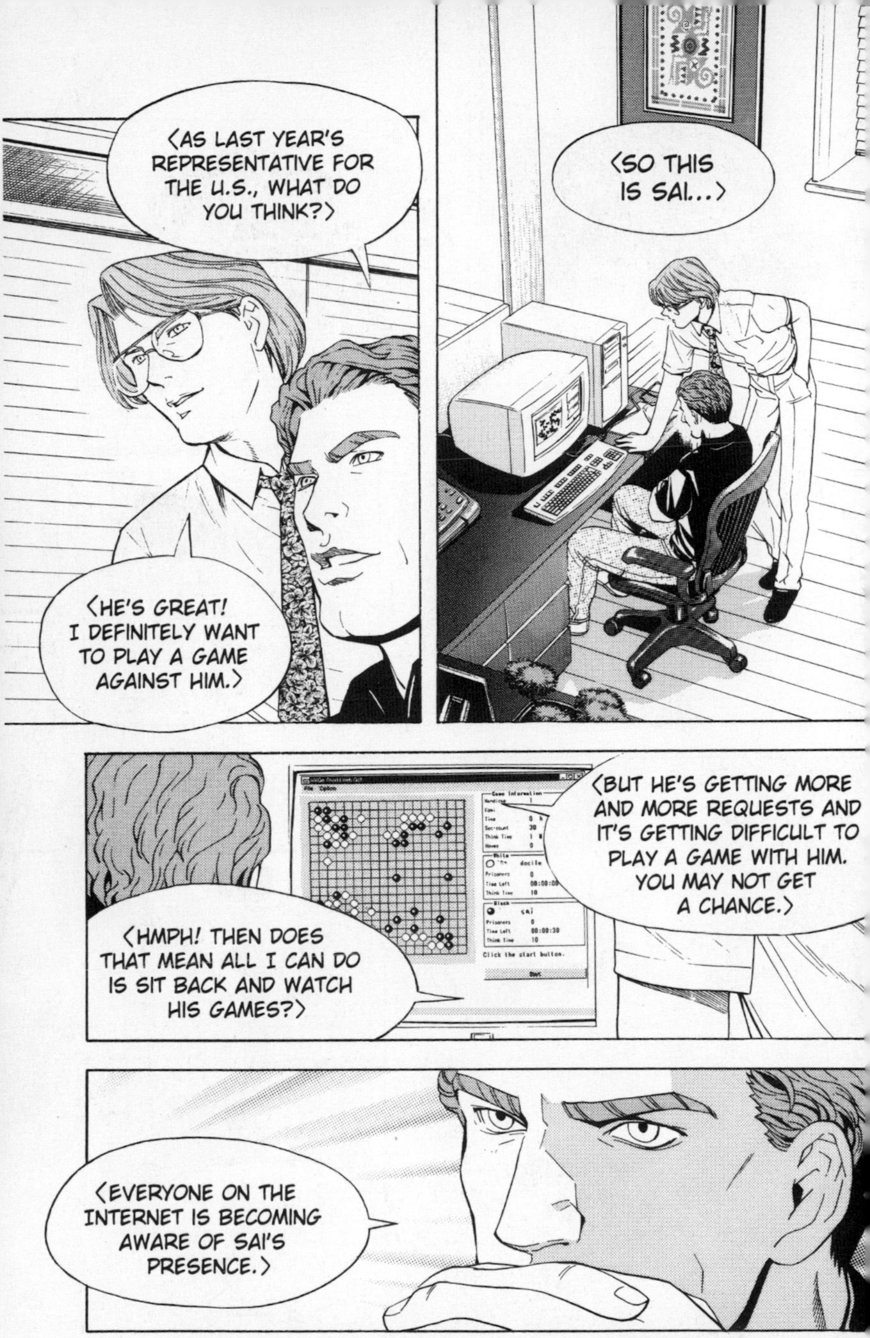
<SO THIS IS SAI...>
<AS LAST YEAR'S REPRESENTATIVE FOR THE U.S., WHAT DO YOU THINK?>
<HE'S GREAT! I DEFINITELY WANT TO PLAY A GAME AGAINST HIM.>
<BUT HE'S GETTING MORE AND MORE REQUESTS AND IT'S GETTING DIFFICULT TO PLAY A GAME WITH HIM. YOU MAY NOT GET A CHANCE.>
<HMPH! THEN DOES THAT MEAN ALL I CAN DO IS SIT BACK AND WATCH HIS GAMES?>
<EVERYONE ON THE INTERNET IS BECOMING AWARE OF SAI'S PRESENCE.>

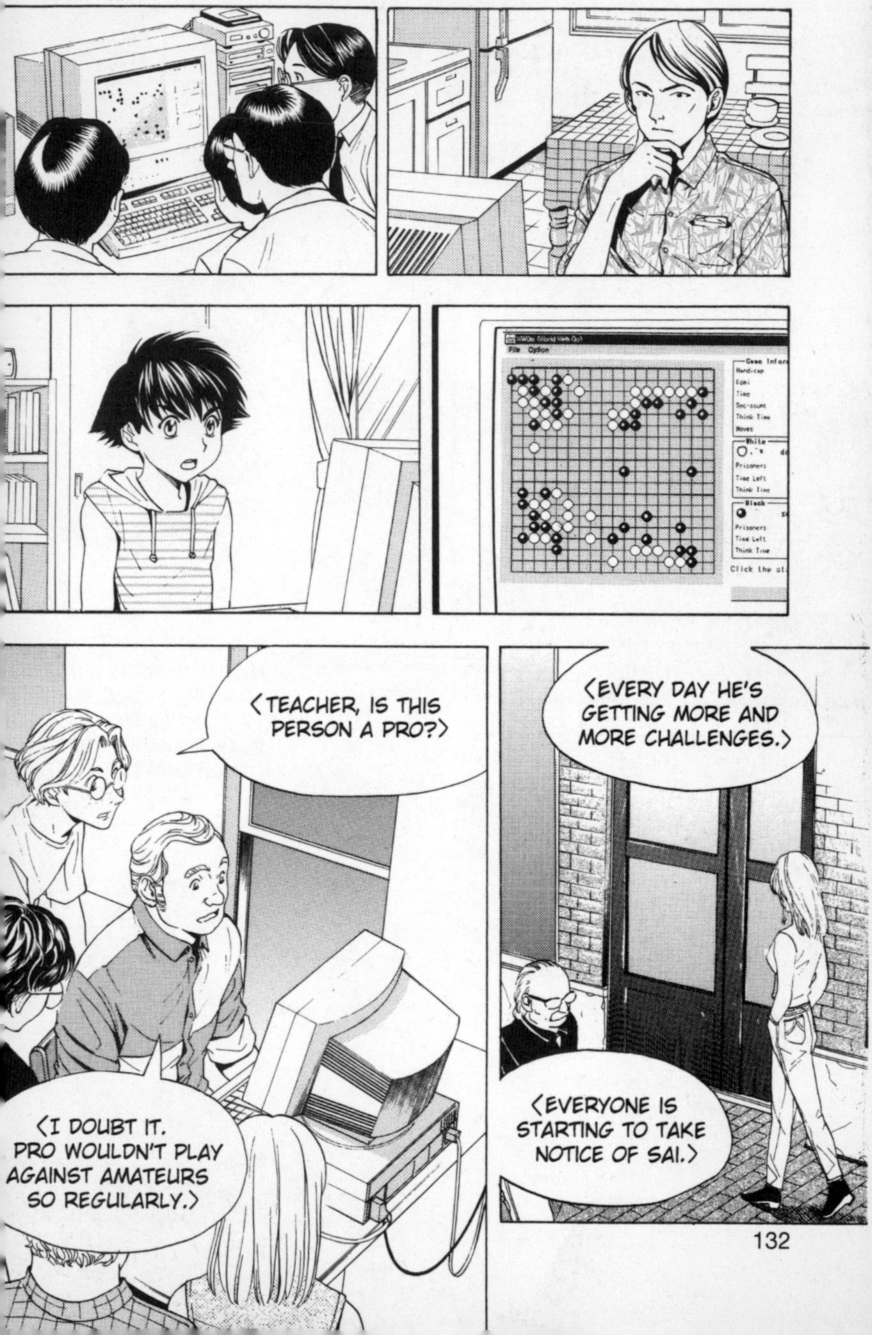
〈EVERY DAY HE'S GETTING MORE AND MORE CHALLENGES.〉
〈EVERYONE IS STARTING TO TAKE NOTICE OF SAI.〉
〈TEACHER, IS THIS PERSON A PRO?〉
〈I DOUBT IT. PRO WOULDN'T PLAY AGAINST AMATEURS SO REGULARLY.〉

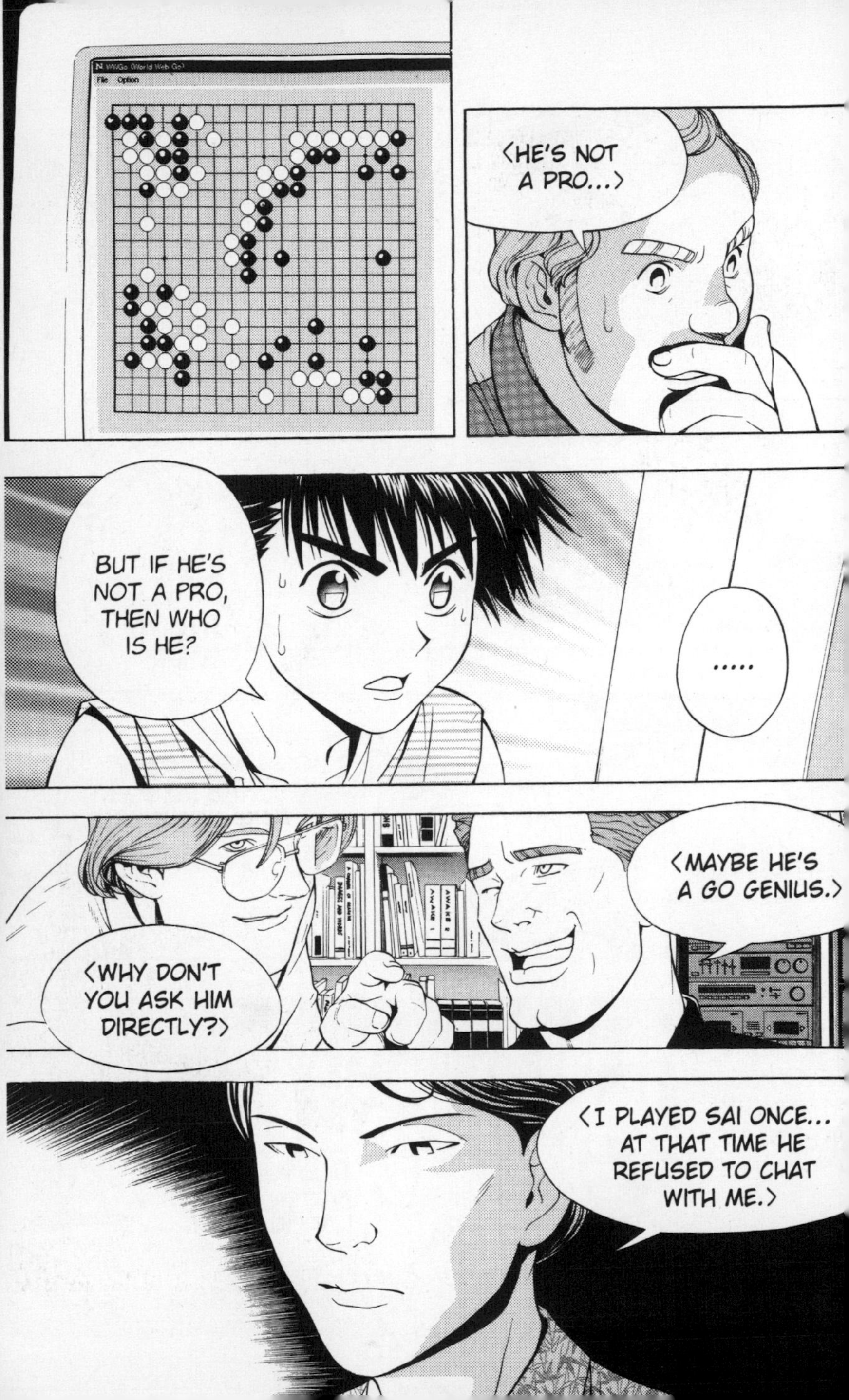
〈HE'S NOT A PRO...〉
WWGo (World Web Go)
File Option
BUT IF HE'S NOT A PRO, THEN WHO IS HE?
.....
〈MAYBE HE'S A GO GENIUS.〉
〈WHY DON'T YOU ASK HIM DIRECTLY?〉
〈I PLAYED SAI ONCE... AT THAT TIME HE REFUSED TO CHAT WITH ME.〉

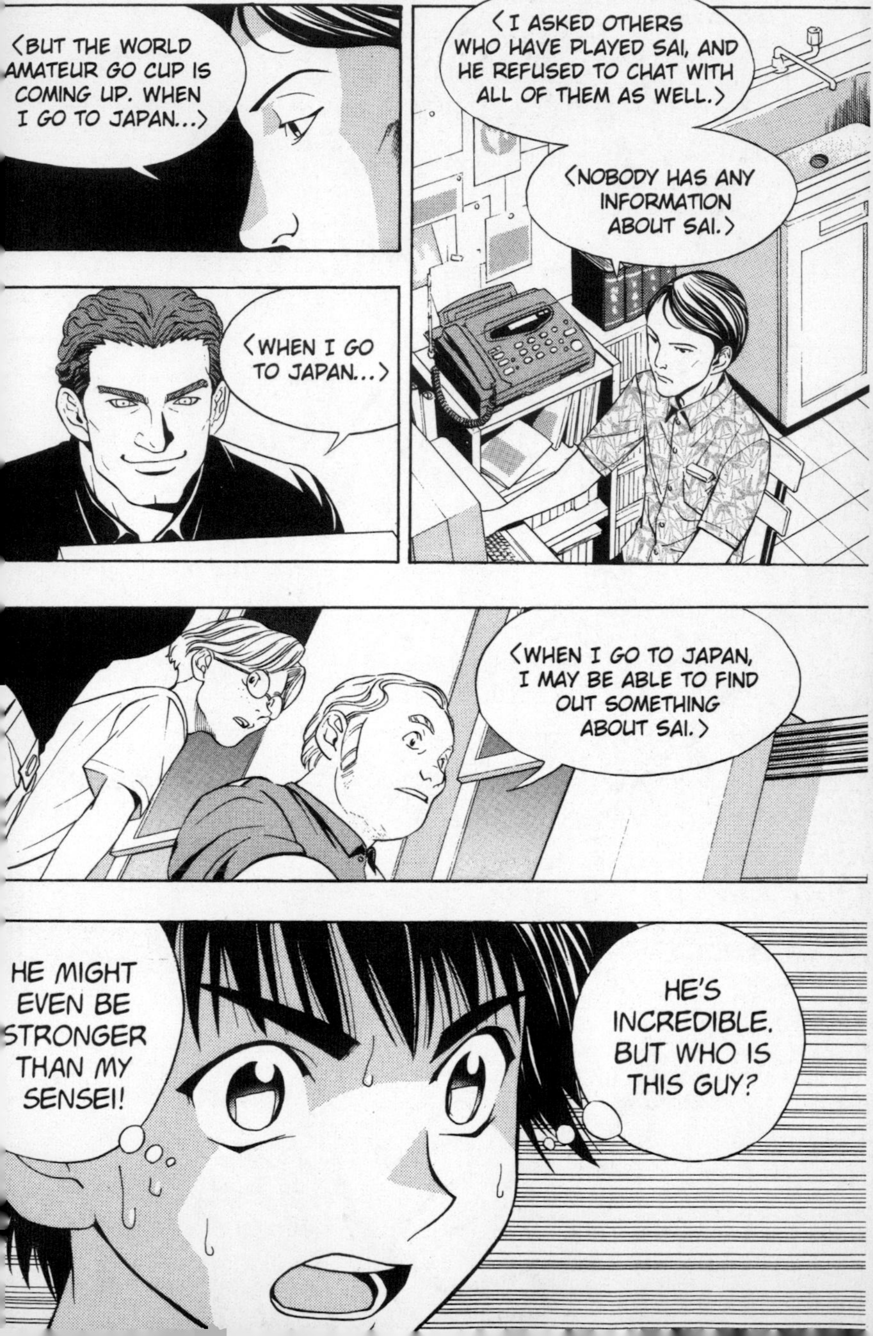
〈I ASKED OTHERS WHO HAVE PLAYED SAI, AND HE REFUSED TO CHAT WITH ALL OF THEM AS WELL.〉
〈NOBODY HAS ANY INFORMATION ABOUT SAI.〉
〈BUT THE WORLD AMATEUR GO CUP IS COMING UP. WHEN I GO TO JAPAN...〉
〈WHEN I GO TO JAPAN...〉
〈WHEN I GO TO JAPAN, I MAY BE ABLE TO FIND OUT SOMETHING ABOUT SAI.〉
HE'S INCREDIBLE. BUT WHO IS THIS GUY?
HE MIGHT EVEN BE STRONGER THAN MY SENSEI!

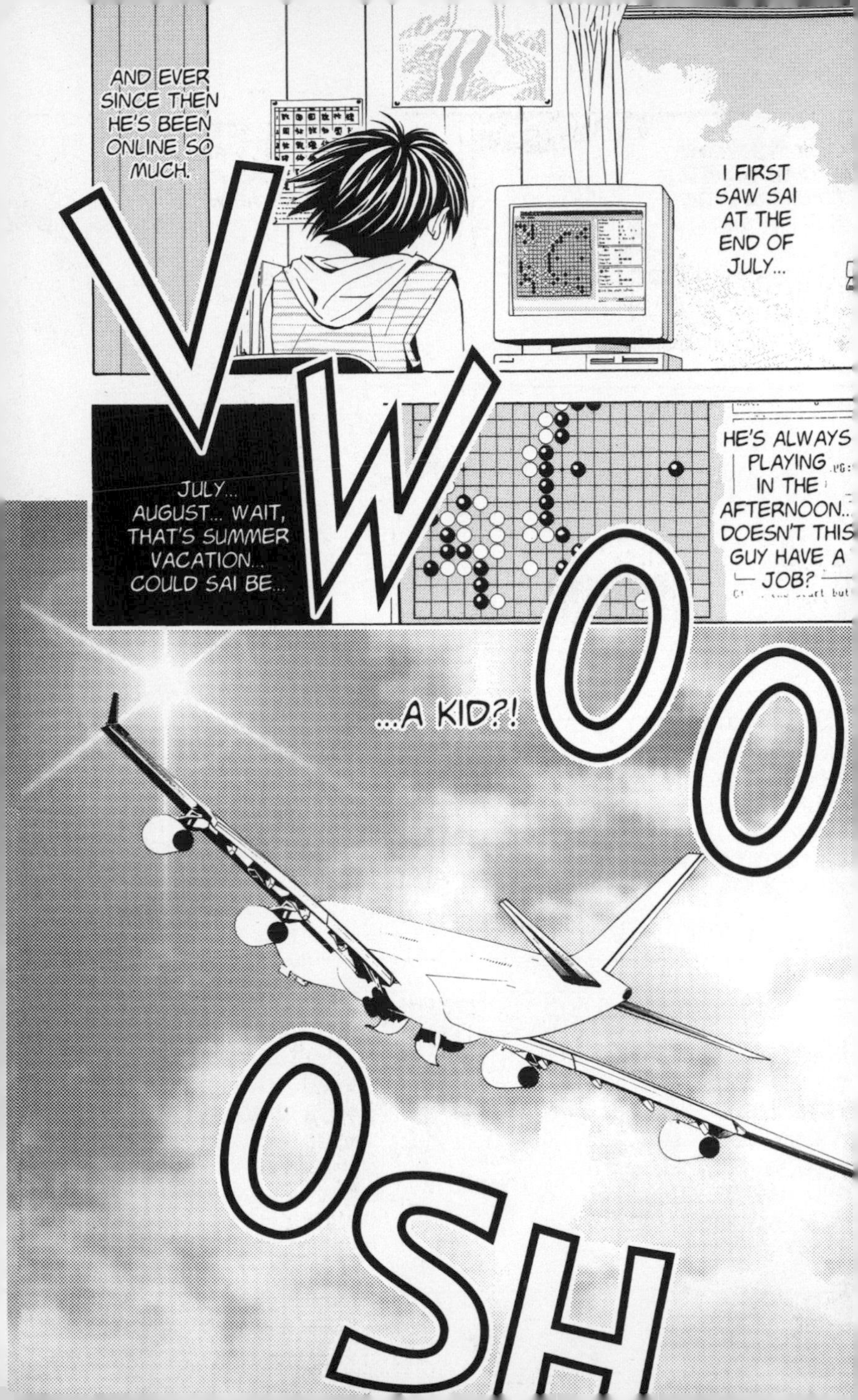
I FIRST SAW SAI AT THE END OF JULY...
AND EVER SINCE THEN HE'S BEEN ONLINE SO MUCH.
HE'S ALWAYS PLAYING IN THE AFTERNOON... DOESN'T THIS GUY HAVE A JOB?
JULY... AUGUST... WAIT, THAT'S SUMMER VACATION... COULD SAI BE...
...A KID?!
VWOOOOSH

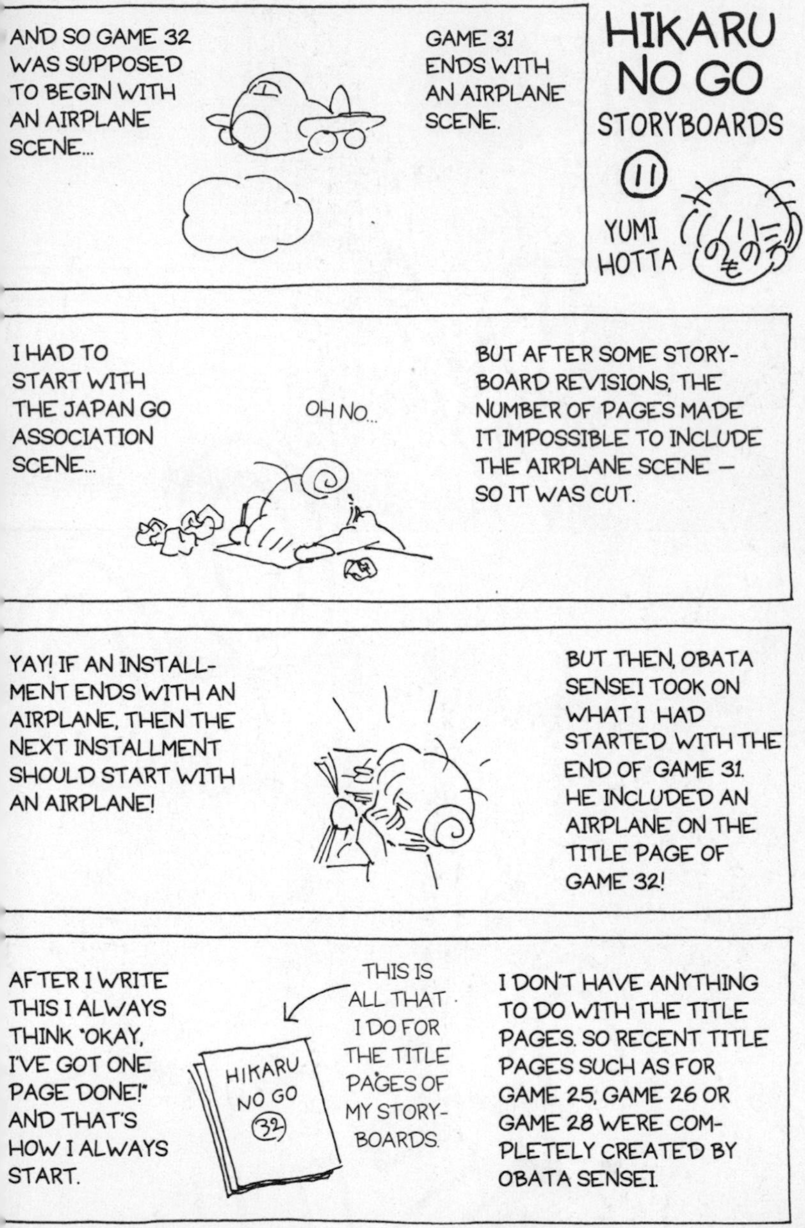
HIKARU NO GO
STORYBOARDS
11
YUMI HOTTA
GAME 31 ENDS WITH AN AIRPLANE SCENE.
AND SO GAME 32 WAS SUPPOSED TO BEGIN WITH AN AIRPLANE SCENE...
BUT AFTER SOME STORY-BOARD REVISIONS, THE NUMBER OF PAGES MADE IT IMPOSSIBLE TO INCLUDE THE AIRPLANE SCENE — SO IT WAS CUT.
I HAD TO START WITH THE JAPAN GO ASSOCIATION SCENE...
OH NO...
BUT THEN, OBATA SENSEI TOOK ON WHAT I HAD STARTED WITH THE END OF GAME 31. HE INCLUDED AN AIRPLANE ON THE TITLE PAGE OF GAME 32!
YAY! IF AN INSTALL-MENT ENDS WITH AN AIRPLANE, THEN THE NEXT INSTALLMENT SHOULD START WITH AN AIRPLANE!
I DON'T HAVE ANYTHING TO DO WITH THE TITLE PAGES. SO RECENT TITLE PAGES SUCH AS FOR GAME 25, GAME 26 OR GAME 28 WERE COM-PLETELY CREATED BY OBATA SENSEI.
THIS IS ALL THAT I DO FOR THE TITLE PAGES OF MY STORY-BOARDS.
HIKARU NO GO 32
AFTER I WRITE THIS I ALWAYS THINK "OKAY, I'VE GOT ONE PAGE DONE!" AND THAT'S HOW I ALWAYS START.

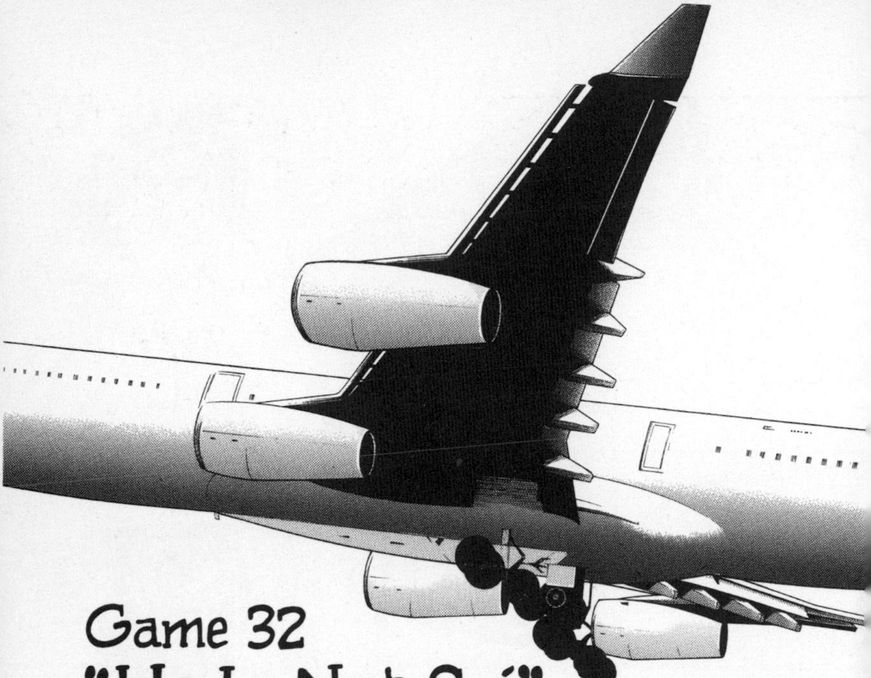

Game 32
"He Is Not Sai"

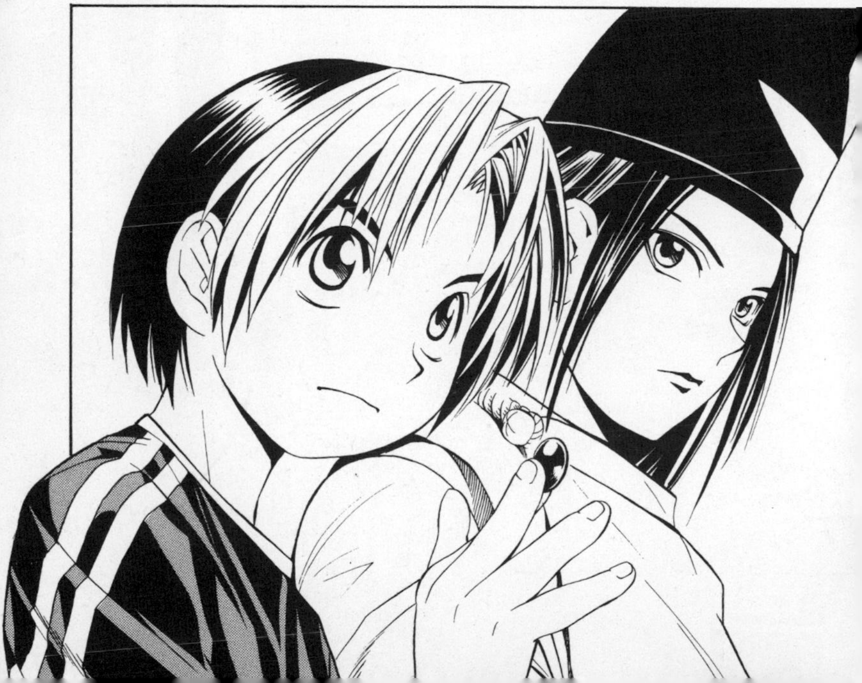

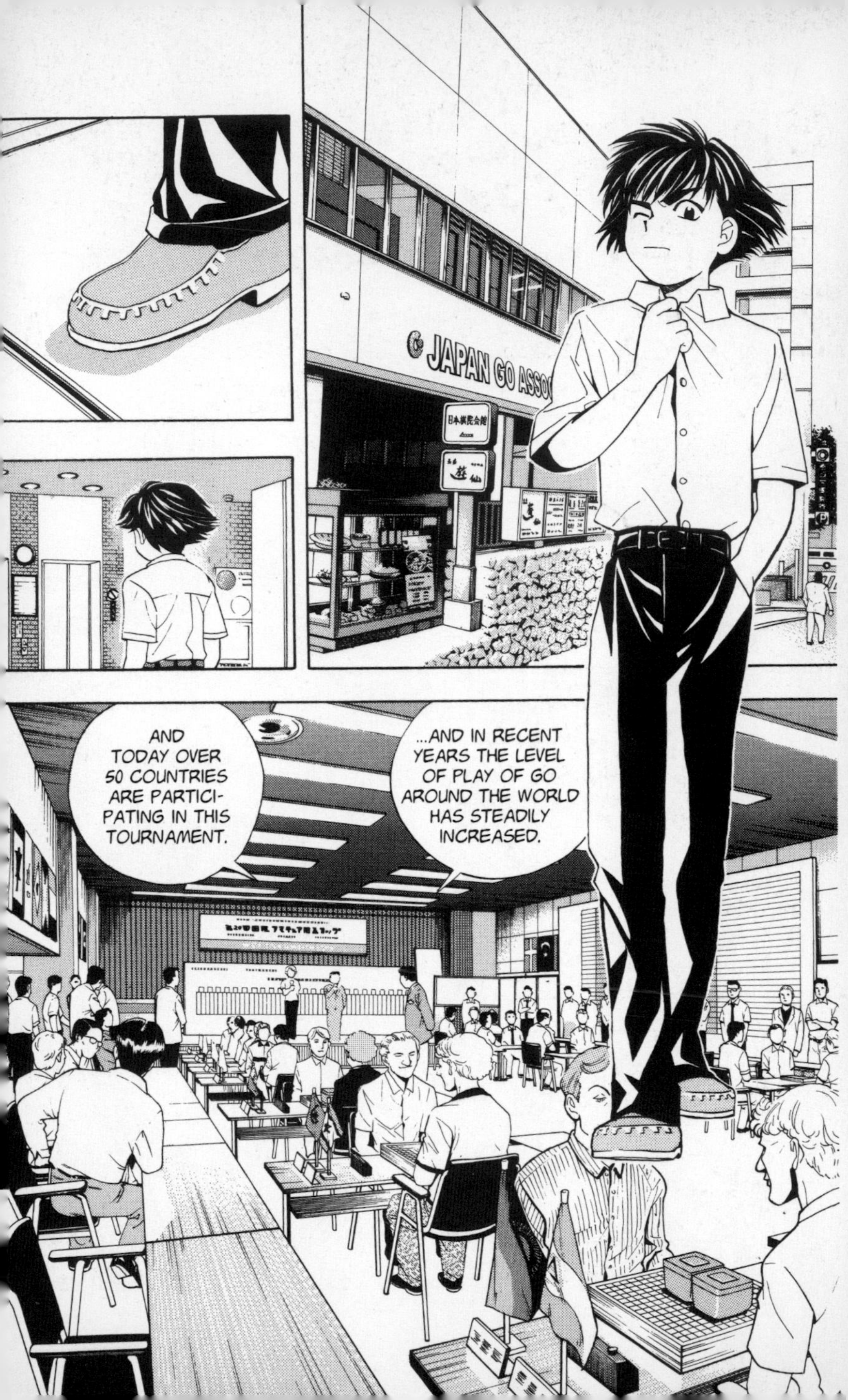
JAPAN GO ASSOC
...AND IN RECENT YEARS THE LEVEL OF PLAY OF GO AROUND THE WORLD HAS STEADILY INCREASED.
AND TODAY OVER 50 COUNTRIES ARE PARTICI-PATING IN THIS TOURNAMENT.

THE 20TH WORLD AMATEUR GO CHAMP

第20回国際アマチュア囲碁カッ

催：日本棋院

STARTING TODAY, YOU WILL PLAY TWO GAMES A DAY FOR FOUR DAYS — THAT'S A TOTAL OF EIGHT GAMES.

DO YOUR BEST AND ENJOY YOUR GAMES!

〈...TWO GAMES A DAY FOR FOUR DAYS — A TOTAL OF EIGHT GAMES.〉

1ST ROUND MATCHUPS

SAI...

THE MYSTERIOUS PLAYER ON THE INTERNET...

〈DO YOUR BEST AND HAVE FUN!〉

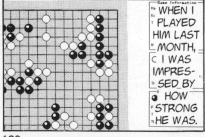

Game Information

WHEN I PLAYED HIM LAST MONTH, I WAS IMPRESSED BY HOW STRONG HE WAS.

139

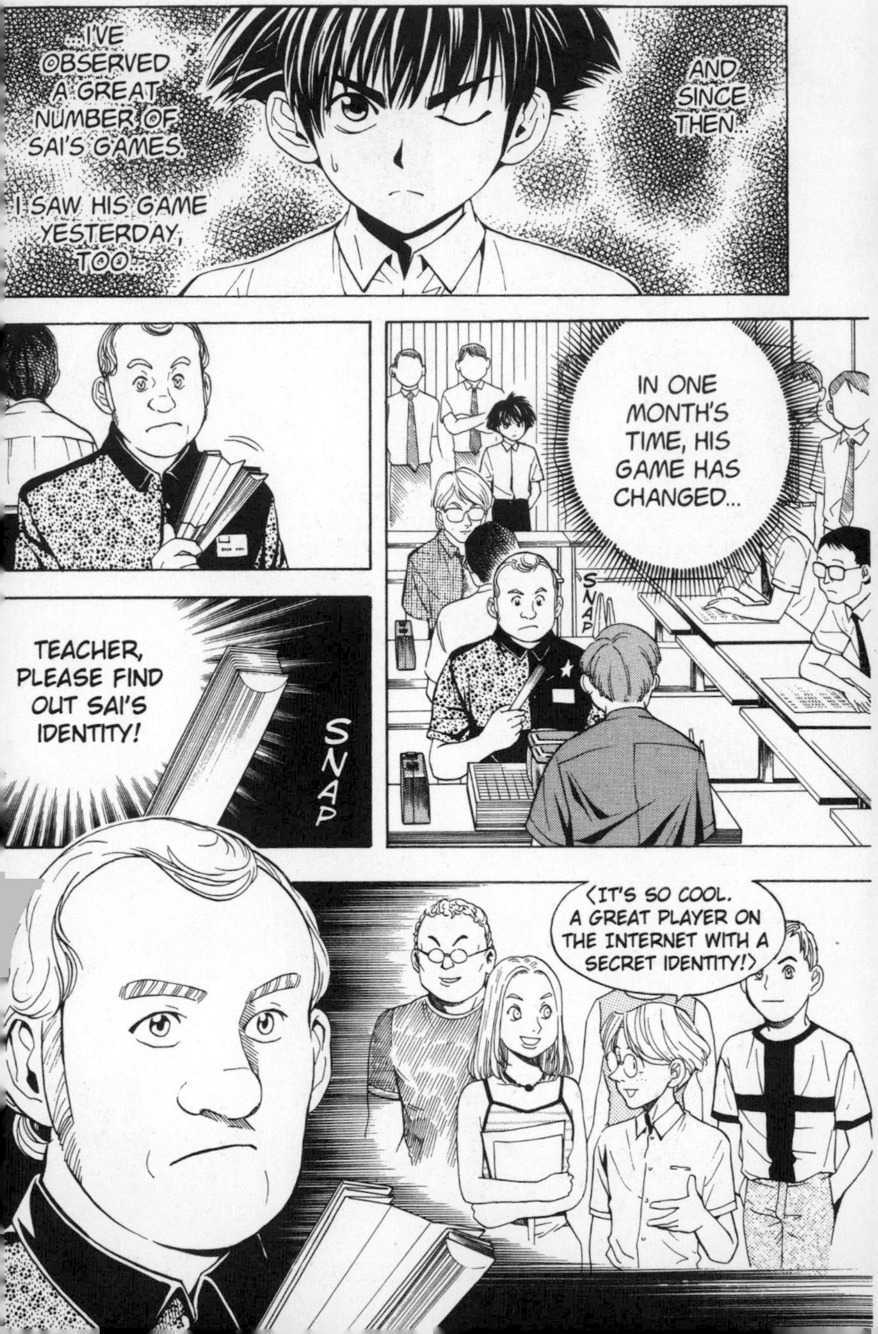
...I'VE OBSERVED A GREAT NUMBER OF SAI'S GAMES.
I SAW HIS GAME YESTERDAY, TOO...
AND SINCE THEN...
IN ONE MONTH'S TIME, HIS GAME HAS CHANGED...
SNAP
TEACHER, PLEASE FIND OUT SAI'S IDENTITY!
SNAP
〈IT'S SO COOL. A GREAT PLAYER ON THE INTERNET WITH A SECRET IDENTITY!〉

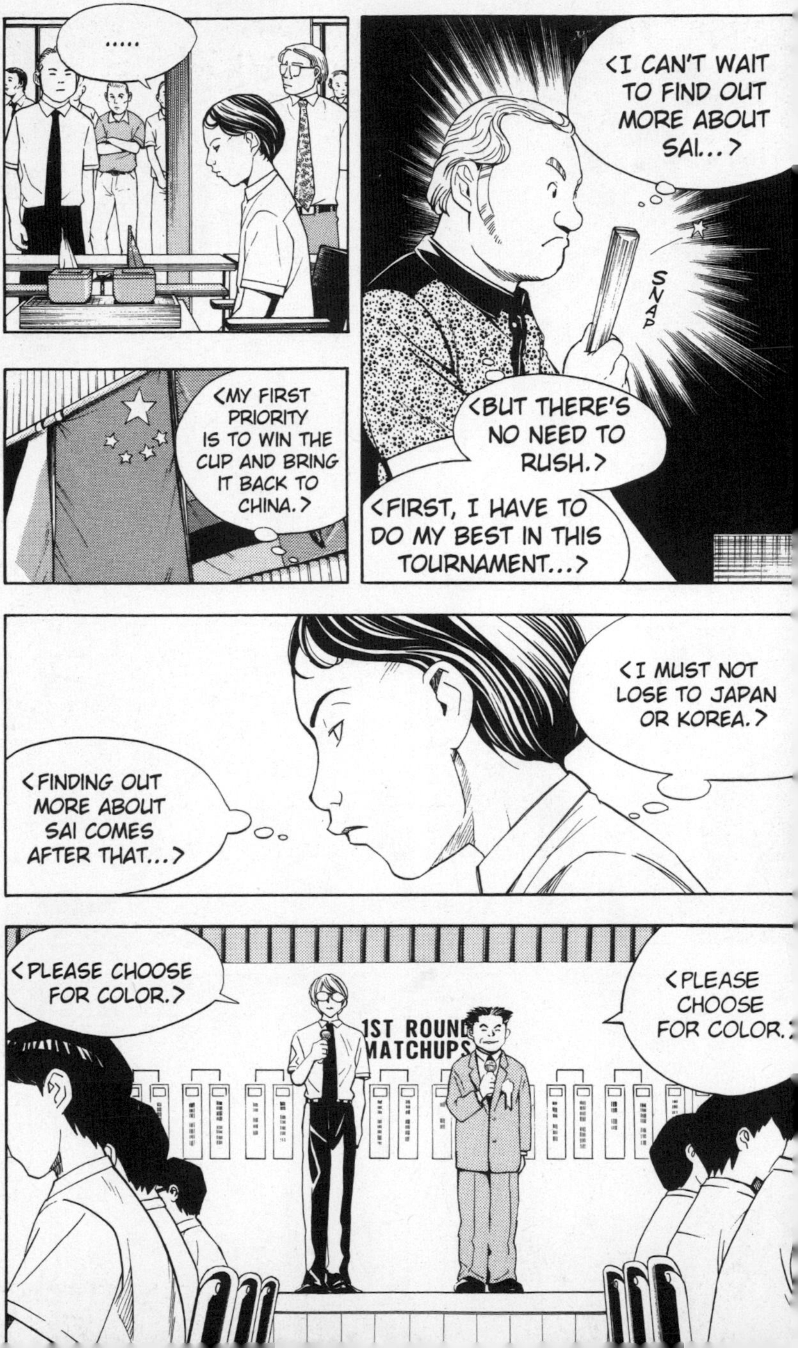
<I CAN'T WAIT TO FIND OUT MORE ABOUT SAI...>
SNAP
<BUT THERE'S NO NEED TO RUSH.>
<FIRST, I HAVE TO DO MY BEST IN THIS TOURNAMENT...>
......
<MY FIRST PRIORITY IS TO WIN THE CUP AND BRING IT BACK TO CHINA.>
<I MUST NOT LOSE TO JAPAN OR KOREA.>
<FINDING OUT MORE ABOUT SAI COMES AFTER THAT...>
<PLEASE CHOOSE FOR COLOR.>
1ST ROUND MATCHUPS
<PLEASE CHOOSE FOR COLOR.>

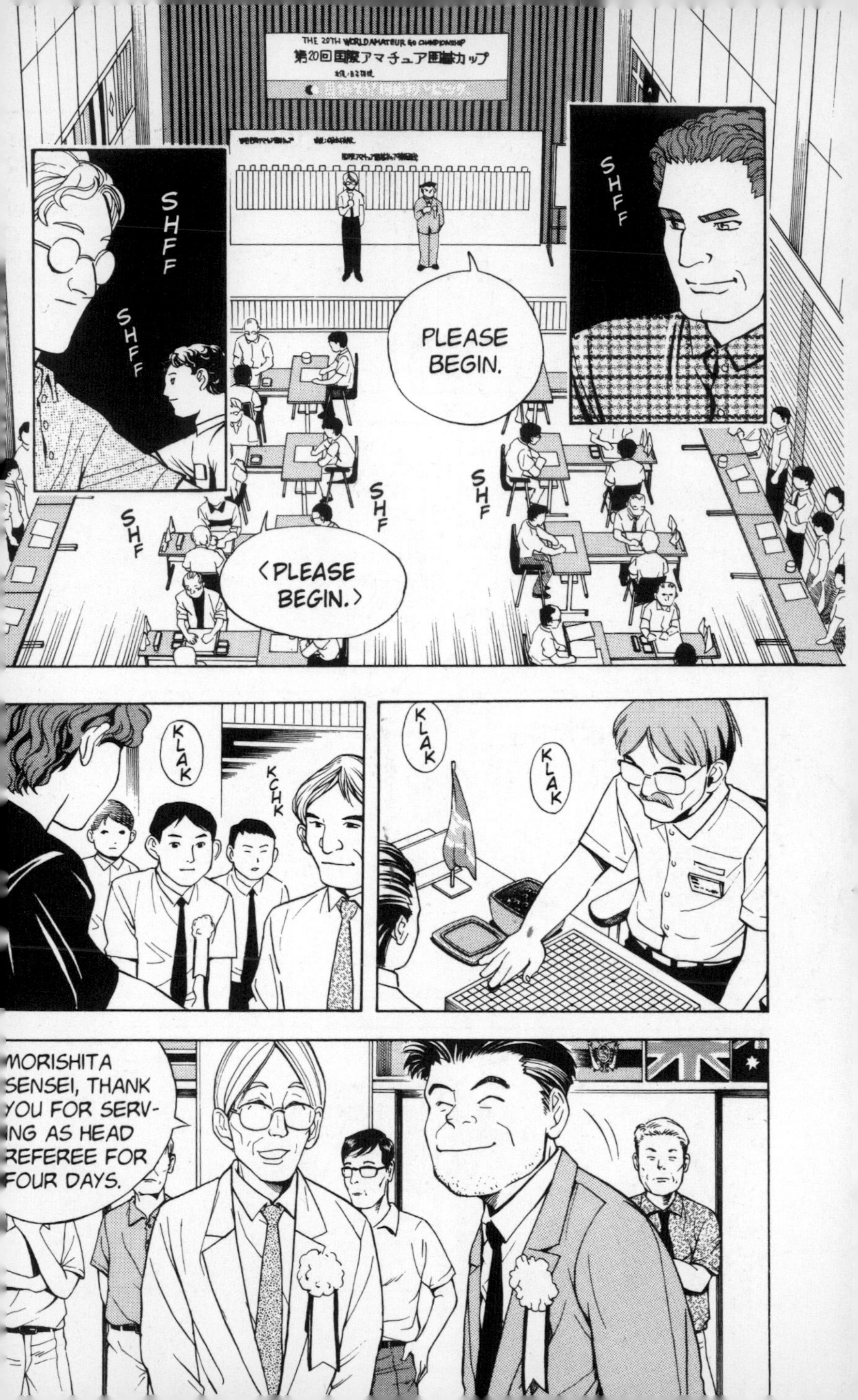
THE 20TH WORLD AMATEUR GO CHAMPIONSHIP
第20回国際アマチュア囲碁カップ
SHFF
PLEASE BEGIN.
SHFF
SHFF
SHF
SHF
SHF
<PLEASE BEGIN.>
KLAK
KLAK
KCHK
KLAK
MORISHITA SENSEI, THANK YOU FOR SERVING AS HEAD REFEREE FOR FOUR DAYS.

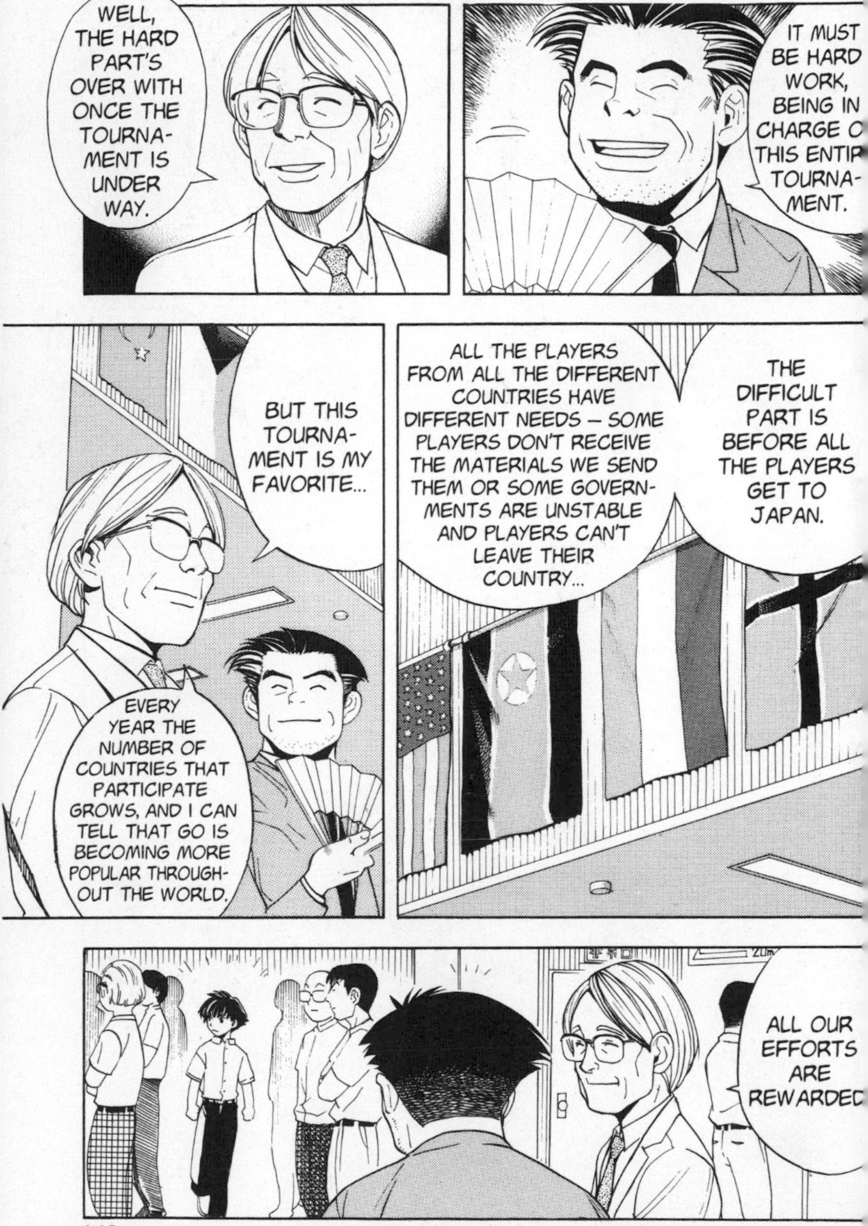
IT MUST BE HARD WORK, BEING IN CHARGE O THIS ENTIR TOURNAMENT.
WELL, THE HARD PART'S OVER WITH ONCE THE TOURNAMENT IS UNDER WAY.
THE DIFFICULT PART IS BEFORE ALL THE PLAYERS GET TO JAPAN.
ALL THE PLAYERS FROM ALL THE DIFFERENT COUNTRIES HAVE DIFFERENT NEEDS – SOME PLAYERS DON'T RECEIVE THE MATERIALS WE SEND THEM OR SOME GOVERNMENTS ARE UNSTABLE AND PLAYERS CAN'T LEAVE THEIR COUNTRY...
BUT THIS TOURNAMENT IS MY FAVORITE...
EVERY YEAR THE NUMBER OF COUNTRIES THAT PARTICIPATE GROWS, AND I CAN TELL THAT GO IS BECOMING MORE POPULAR THROUGHOUT THE WORLD.
ALL OUR EFFORTS ARE REWARDE

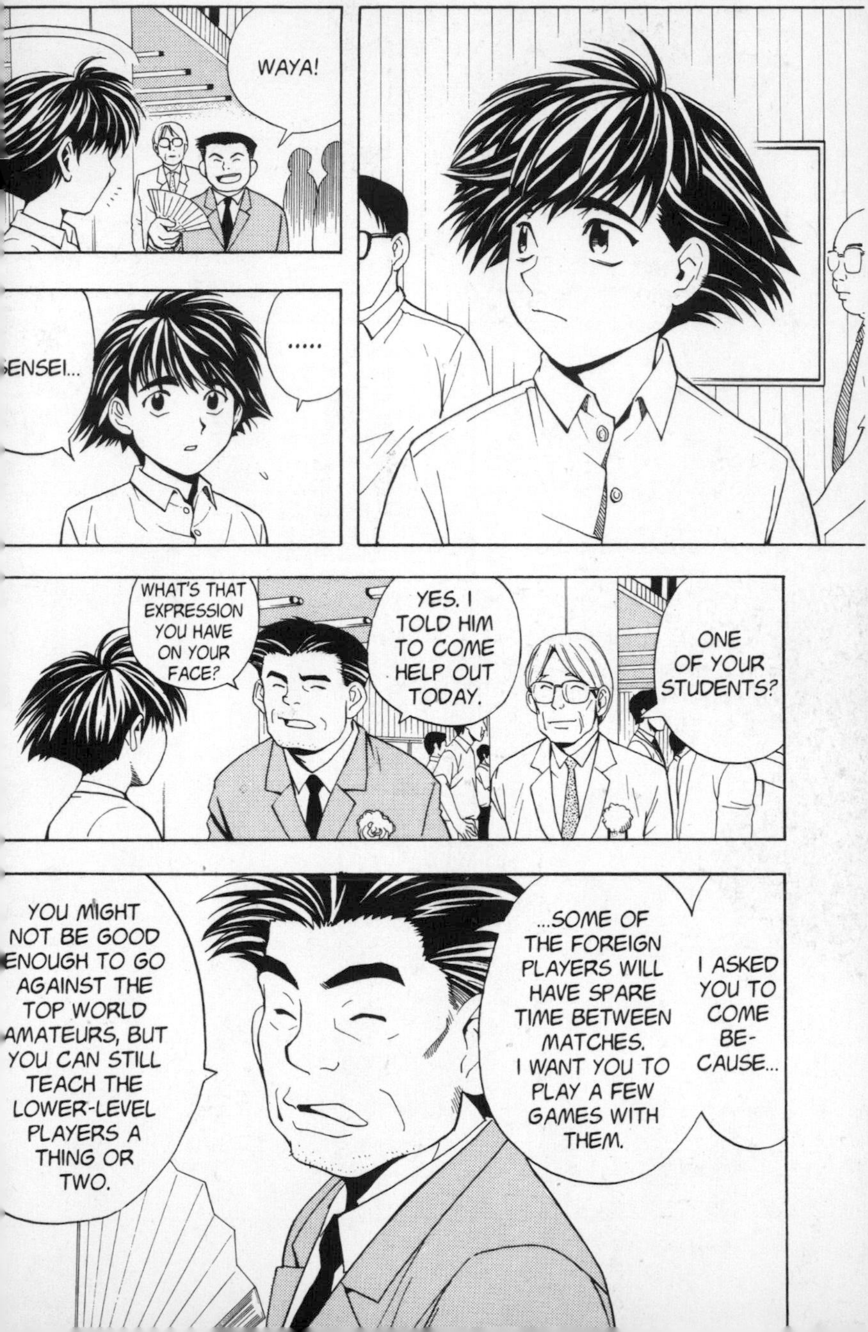
WAYA!
.....
SENSEI...
ONE OF YOUR STUDENTS?
YES. I TOLD HIM TO COME HELP OUT TODAY.
WHAT'S THAT EXPRESSION YOU HAVE ON YOUR FACE?
I ASKED YOU TO COME BE-CAUSE...
...SOME OF THE FOREIGN PLAYERS WILL HAVE SPARE TIME BETWEEN MATCHES. I WANT YOU TO PLAY A FEW GAMES WITH THEM.
YOU MIGHT NOT BE GOOD ENOUGH TO GO AGAINST THE TOP WORLD AMATEURS, BUT YOU CAN STILL TEACH THE LOWER-LEVEL PLAYERS A THING OR TWO.

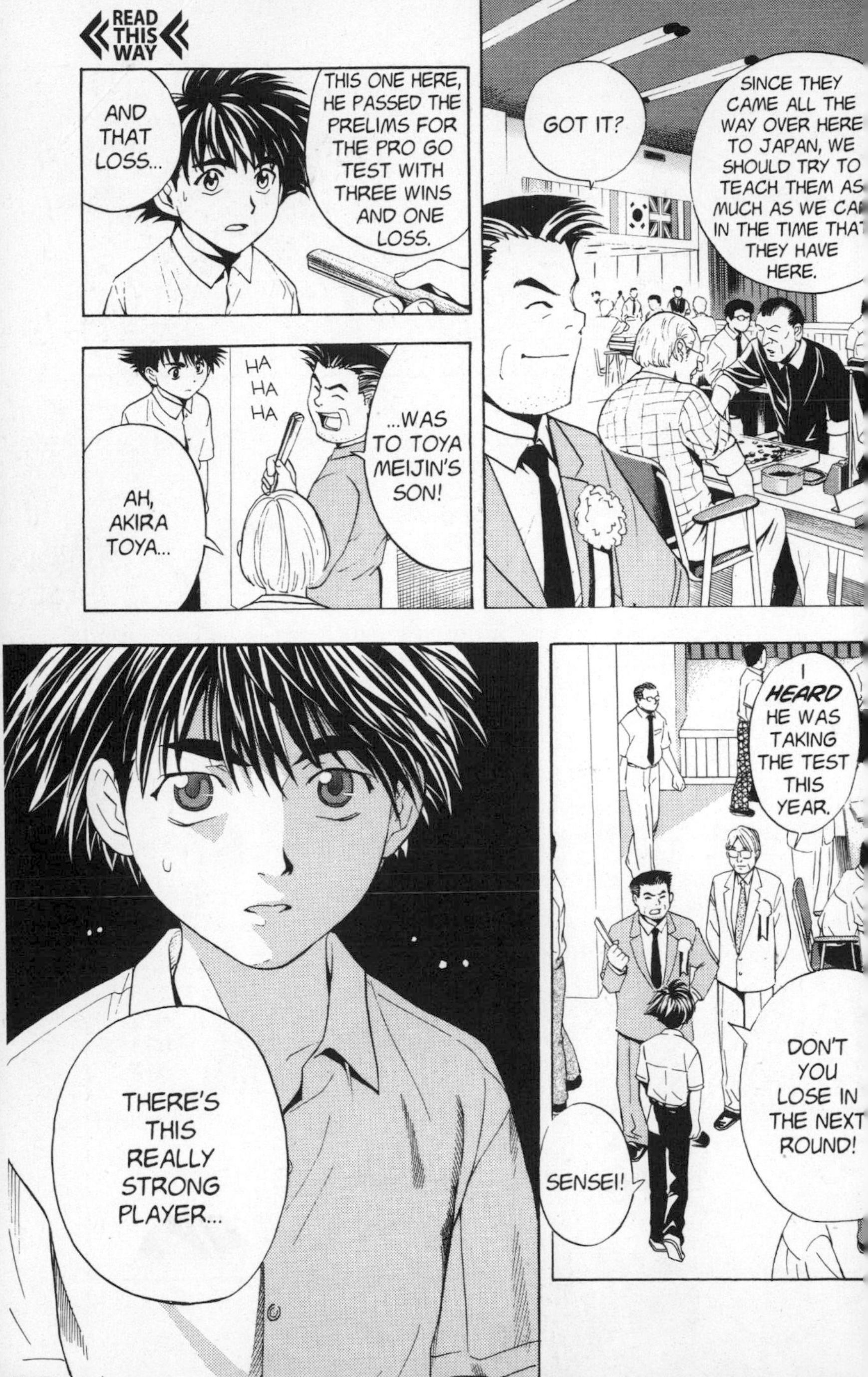
READ THIS WAY
SINCE THEY CAME ALL THE WAY OVER HERE TO JAPAN, WE SHOULD TRY TO TEACH THEM AS MUCH AS WE CA IN THE TIME THA THEY HAVE HERE.
GOT IT?
THIS ONE HERE, HE PASSED THE PRELIMS FOR THE PRO GO TEST WITH THREE WINS AND ONE LOSS.
AND THAT LOSS...
...WAS TO TOYA MEIJIN'S SON!
HA HA HA
AH, AKIRA TOYA...
I HEARD HE WAS TAKING THE TEST THIS YEAR.
DON'T YOU LOSE IN THE NEXT ROUND!
SENSEI!
THERE'S THIS REALLY STRONG PLAYER...

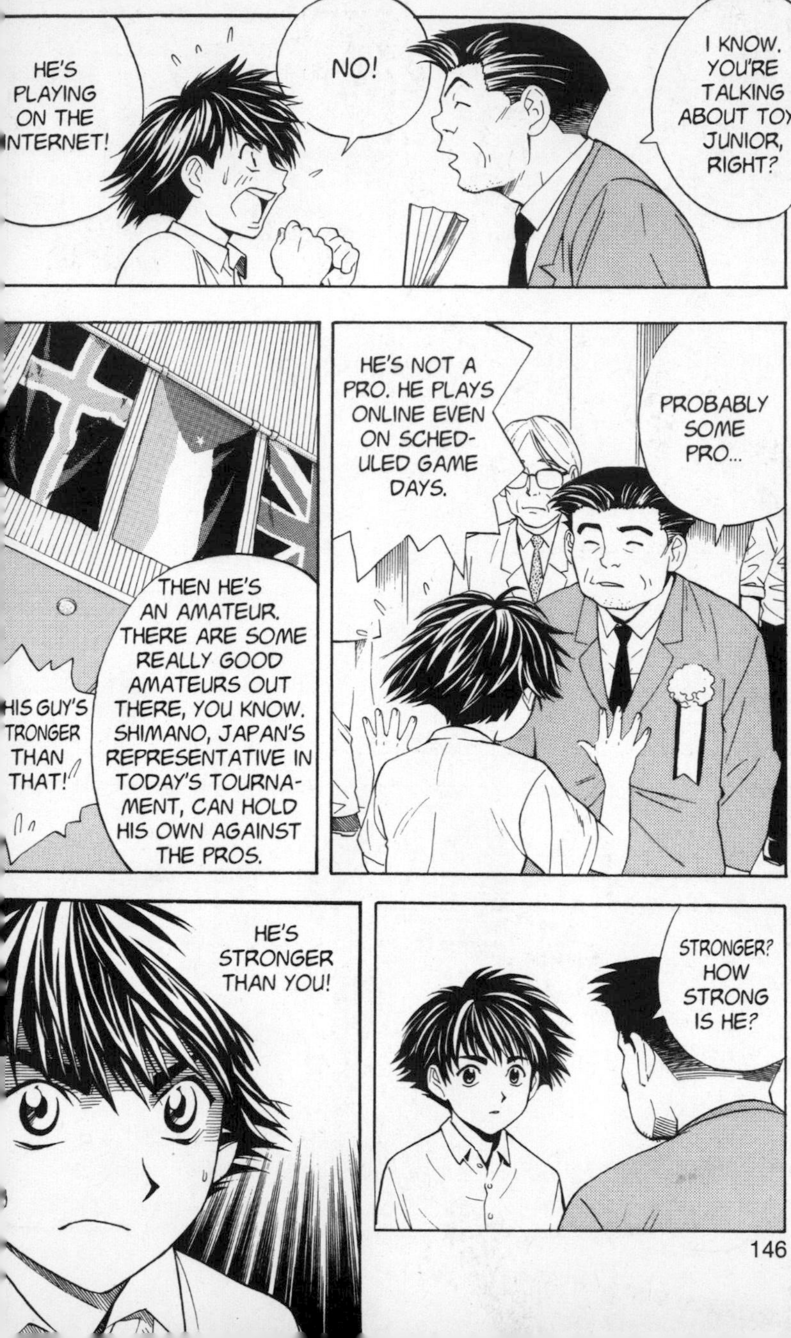
I KNOW. YOU'RE TALKING ABOUT TOYA JUNIOR, RIGHT?
NO!
HE'S PLAYING ON THE INTERNET!
PROBABLY SOME PRO...
HE'S NOT A PRO. HE PLAYS ONLINE EVEN ON SCHED-ULED GAME DAYS.
THEN HE'S AN AMATEUR. THERE ARE SOME REALLY GOOD AMATEURS OUT THERE, YOU KNOW. SHIMANO, JAPAN'S REPRESENTATIVE IN TODAY'S TOURNA-MENT, CAN HOLD HIS OWN AGAINST THE PROS.
HIS GUY'S TRONGER THAN THAT!
STRONGER? HOW STRONG IS HE?
HE'S STRONGER THAN YOU!

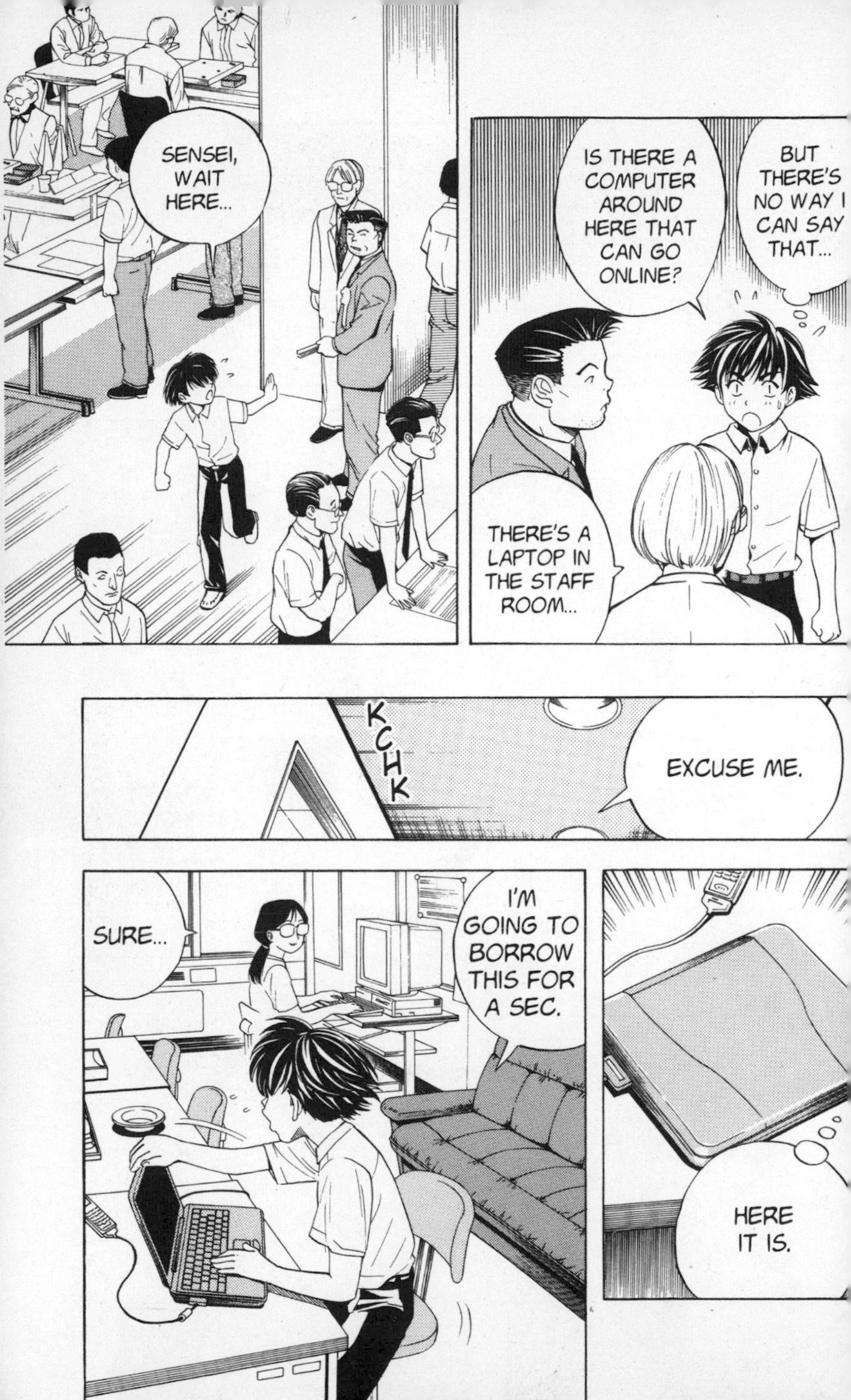

IS THERE A COMPUTER AROUND HERE THAT CAN GO ONLINE?
BUT THERE'S NO WAY I CAN SAY THAT...
THERE'S A LAPTOP IN THE STAFF ROOM...
SENSEI, WAIT HERE...
KCHK
EXCUSE ME.
HERE IT IS.
I'M GOING TO BORROW THIS FOR A SEC.
SURE...

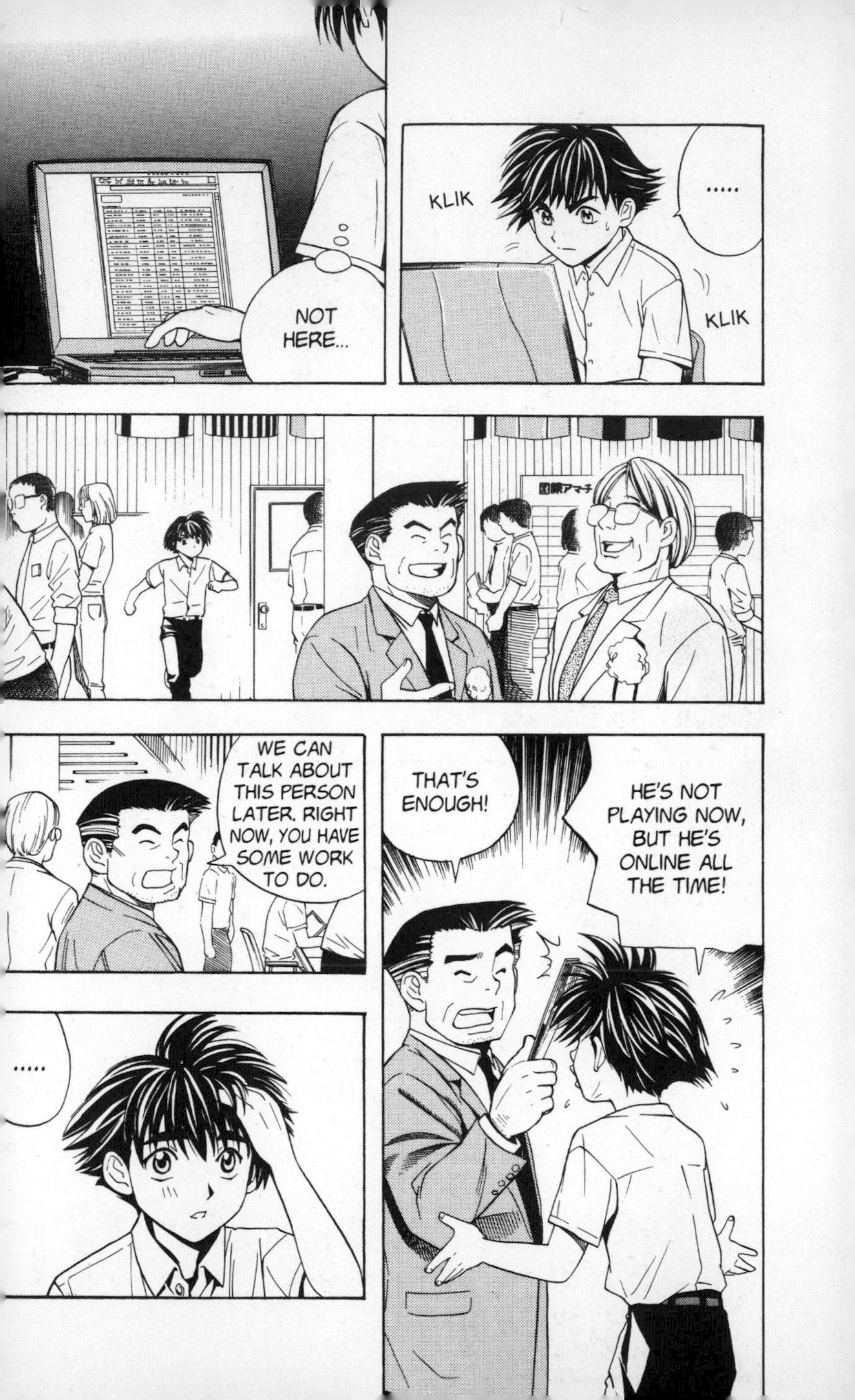
.....
KLIK
KLIK
NOT HERE...
HE'S NOT PLAYING NOW, BUT HE'S ONLINE ALL THE TIME!
THAT'S ENOUGH!
WE CAN TALK ABOUT THIS PERSON LATER. RIGHT NOW, YOU HAVE SOME WORK TO DO.
.....

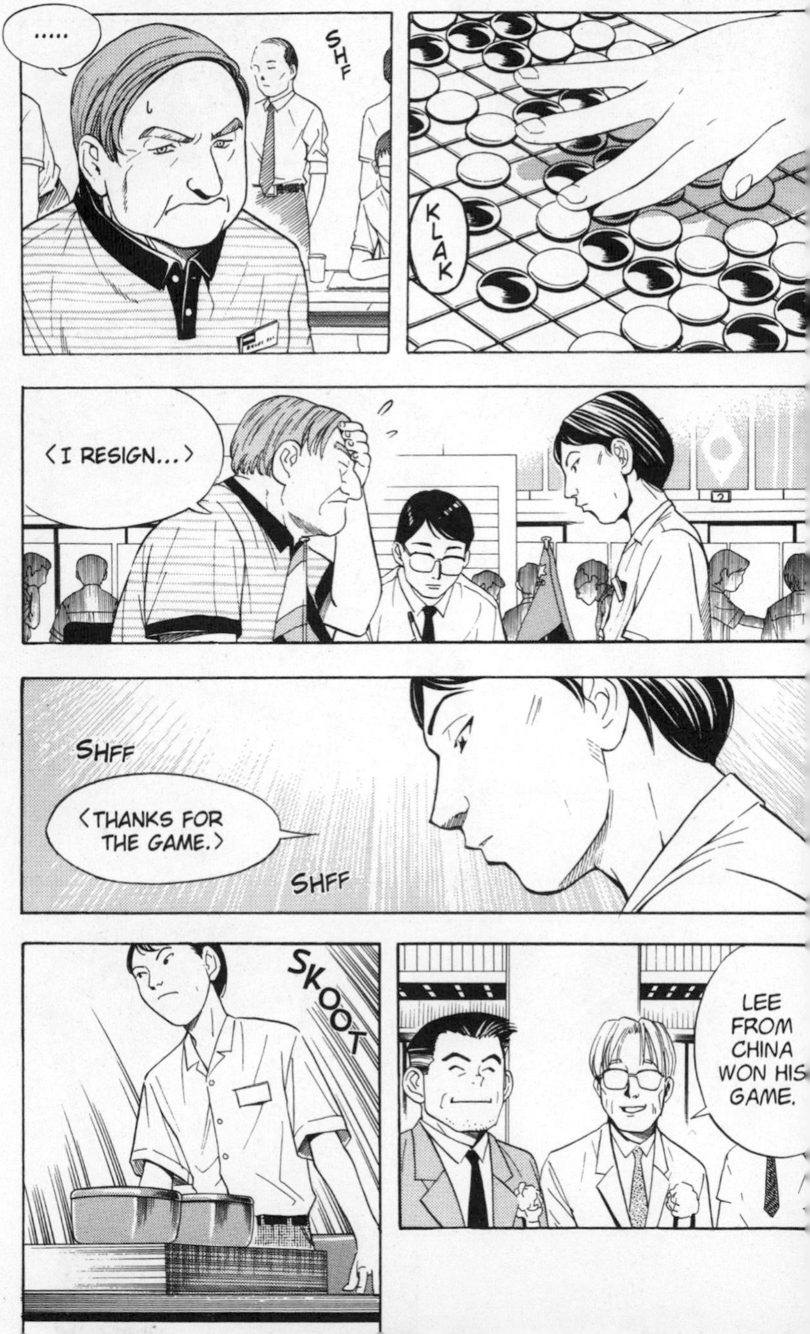
KLAK
.....
SHF
〈I RESIGN...〉
SHFF
〈THANKS FOR THE GAME.〉
SHFF
LEE FROM CHINA WON HIS GAME.
SKOOT

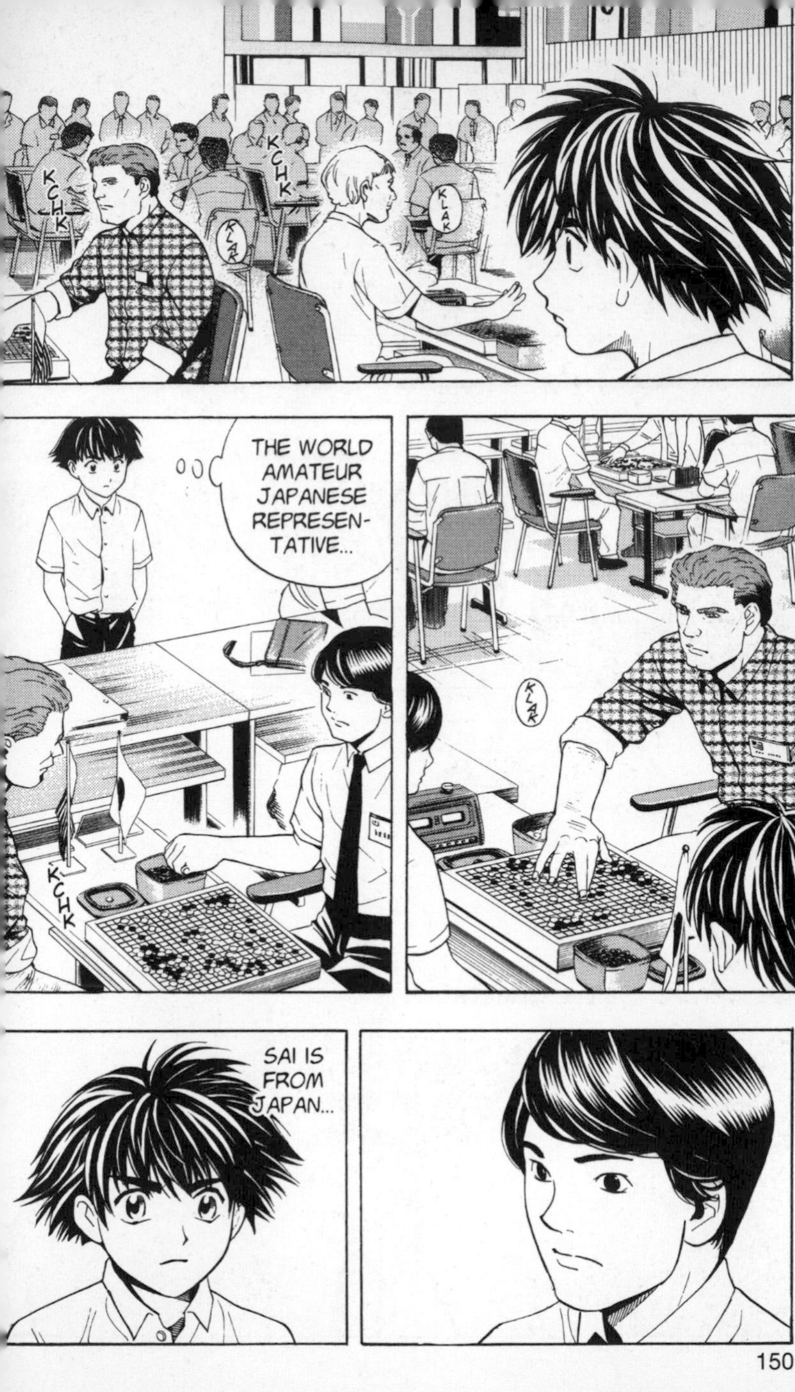
KLAK
KCHK
KLAK
KCHK
KLAK
THE WORLD AMATEUR JAPANESE REPRESENTATIVE...
KCHK
SAI IS FROM JAPAN...

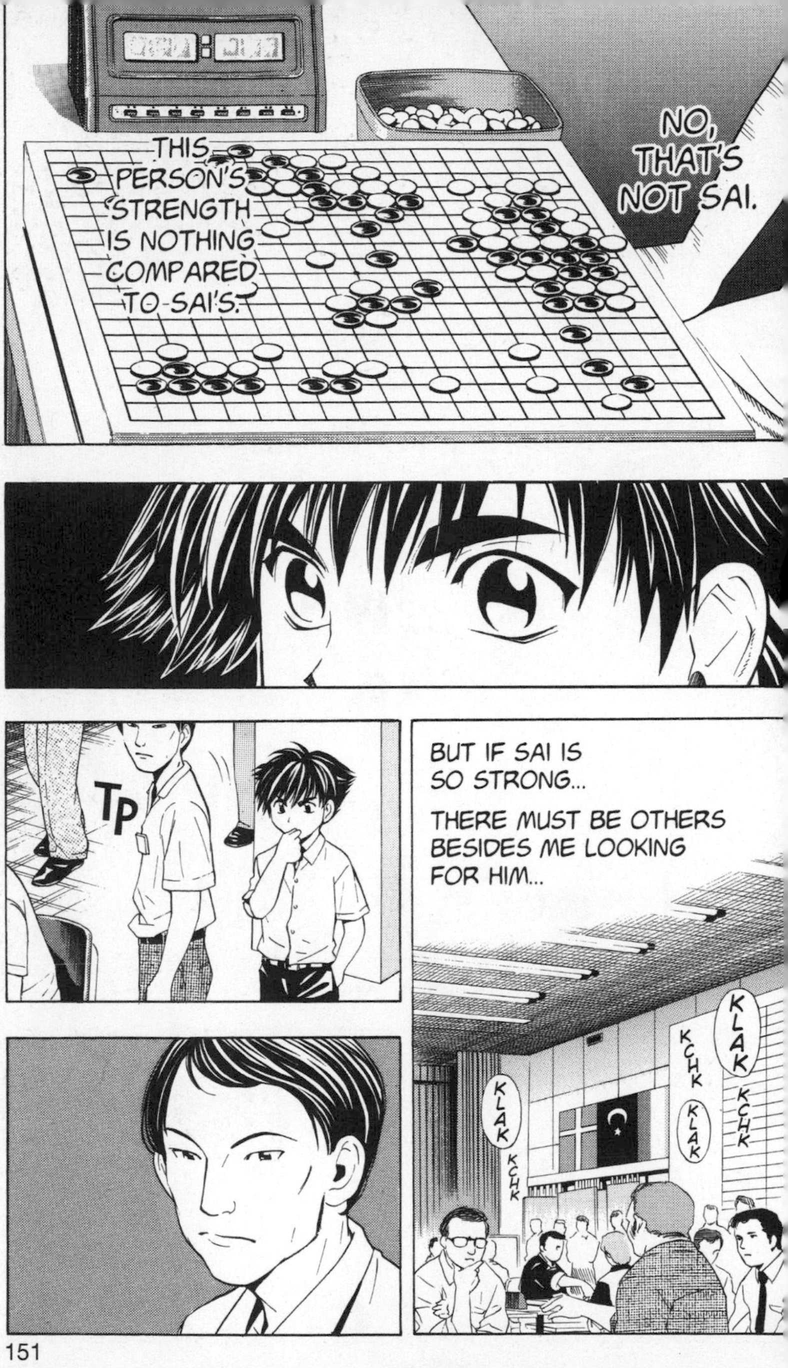
NO, THAT'S NOT SAI.
THIS PERSON'S STRENGTH IS NOTHING COMPARED TO SAI'S.
BUT IF SAI IS SO STRONG...
THERE MUST BE OTHERS BESIDES ME LOOKING FOR HIM...
KLAK
KCHK
KCHK
KLAK
KLAK
KCHK
TP

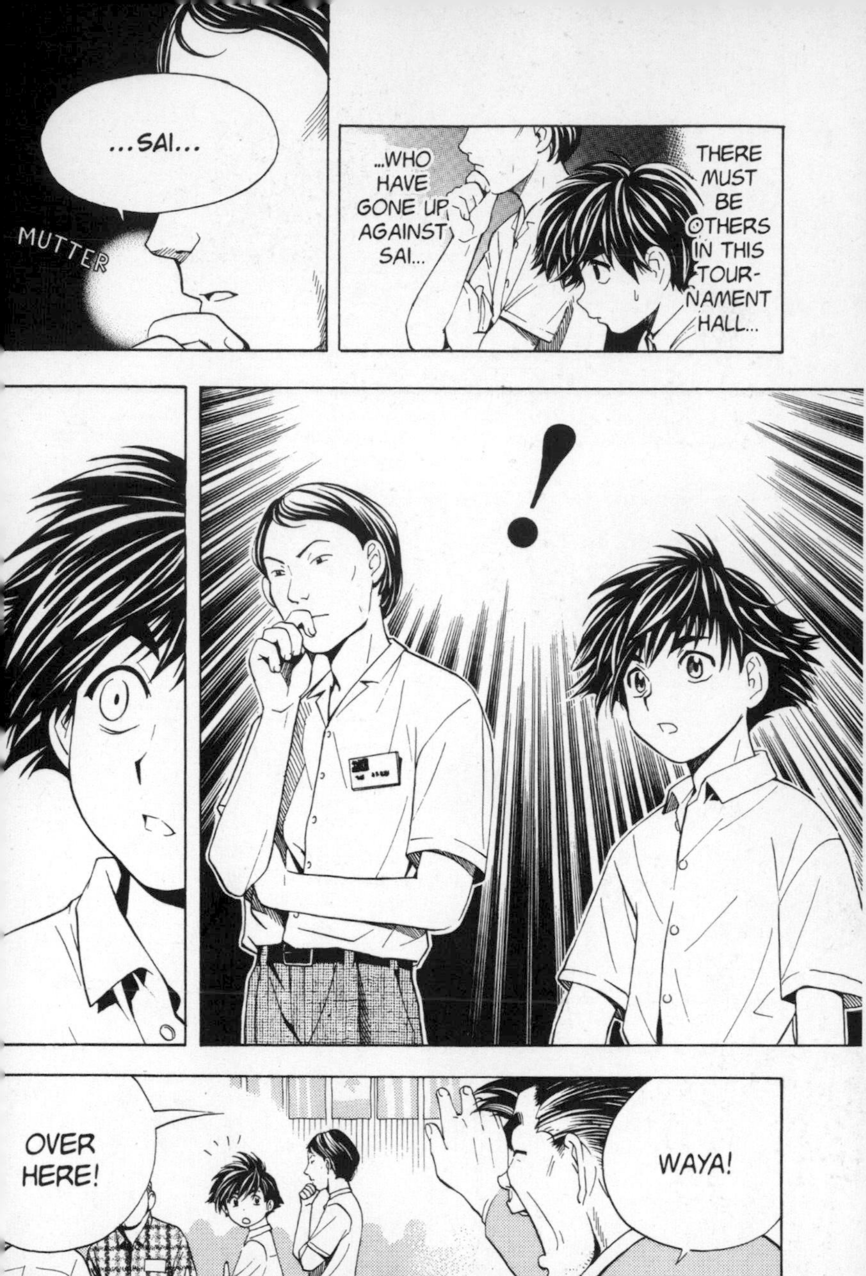
THERE MUST BE OTHERS IN THIS TOUR-NAMENT HALL...
...WHO HAVE GONE UP AGAINST SAI...
...SAI...
MUTTER
!
WAYA!
OVER HERE!

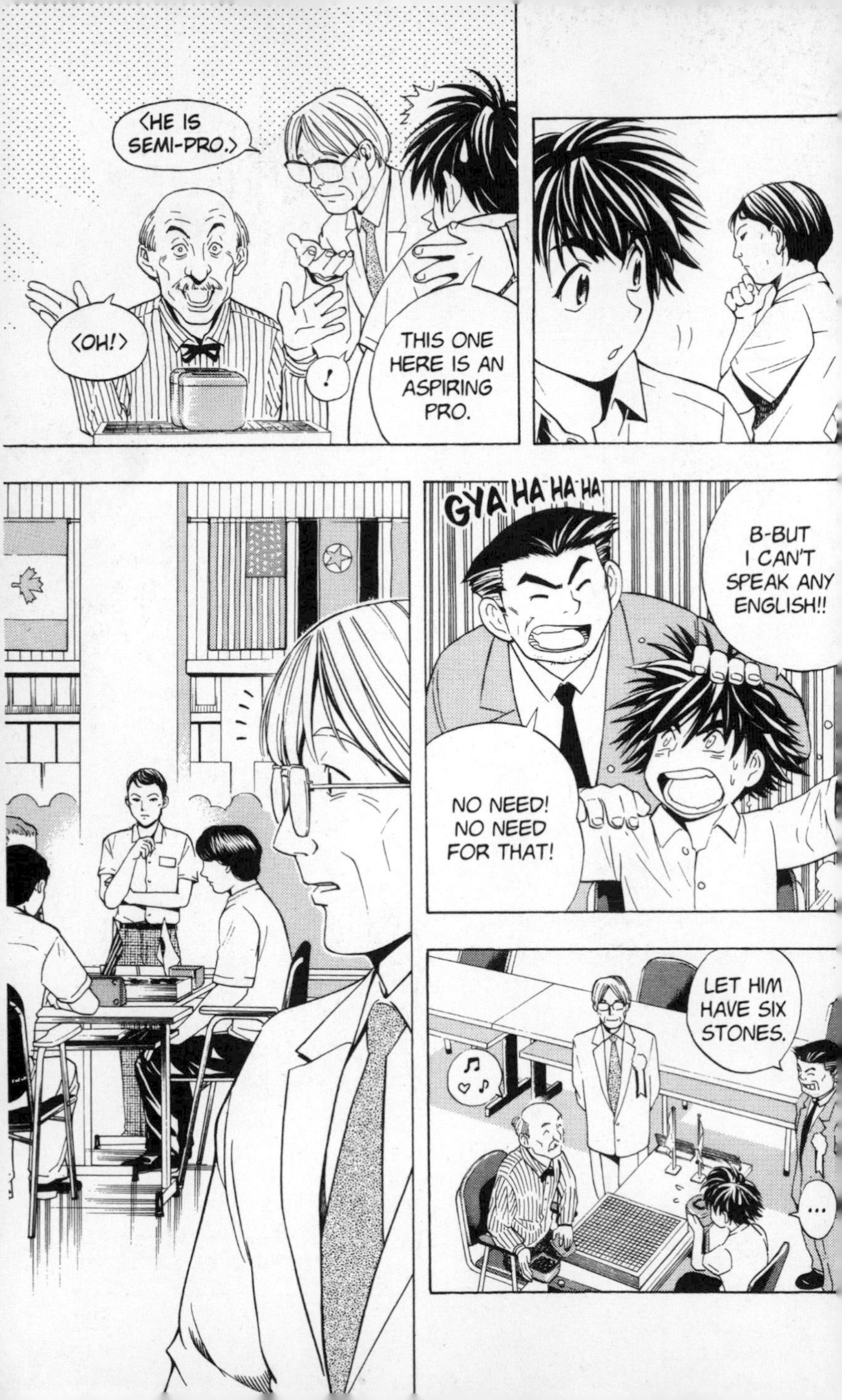
THIS ONE HERE IS AN ASPIRING PRO.
!
<HE IS SEMI-PRO.>
<OH!>
GYA HA HA HA
B-BUT I CAN'T SPEAK ANY ENGLISH!!
NO NEED! NO NEED FOR THAT!
LET HIM HAVE SIX STONES.
...

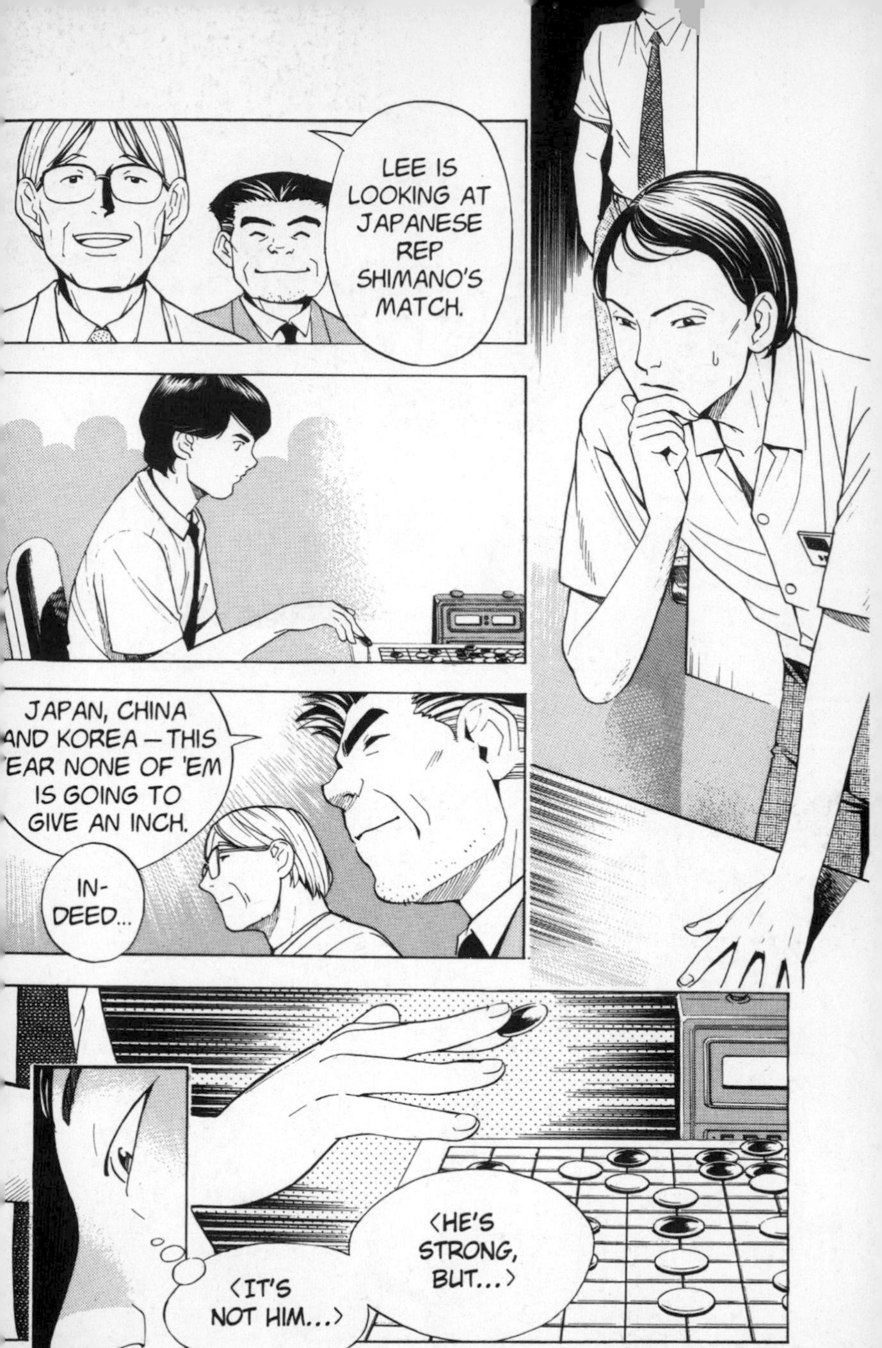
LEE IS LOOKING AT JAPANESE REP SHIMANO'S MATCH.
JAPAN, CHINA AND KOREA — THIS EAR NONE OF 'EM IS GOING TO GIVE AN INCH.
IN-DEED...
‹HE'S STRONG, BUT...›
‹IT'S NOT HIM...›

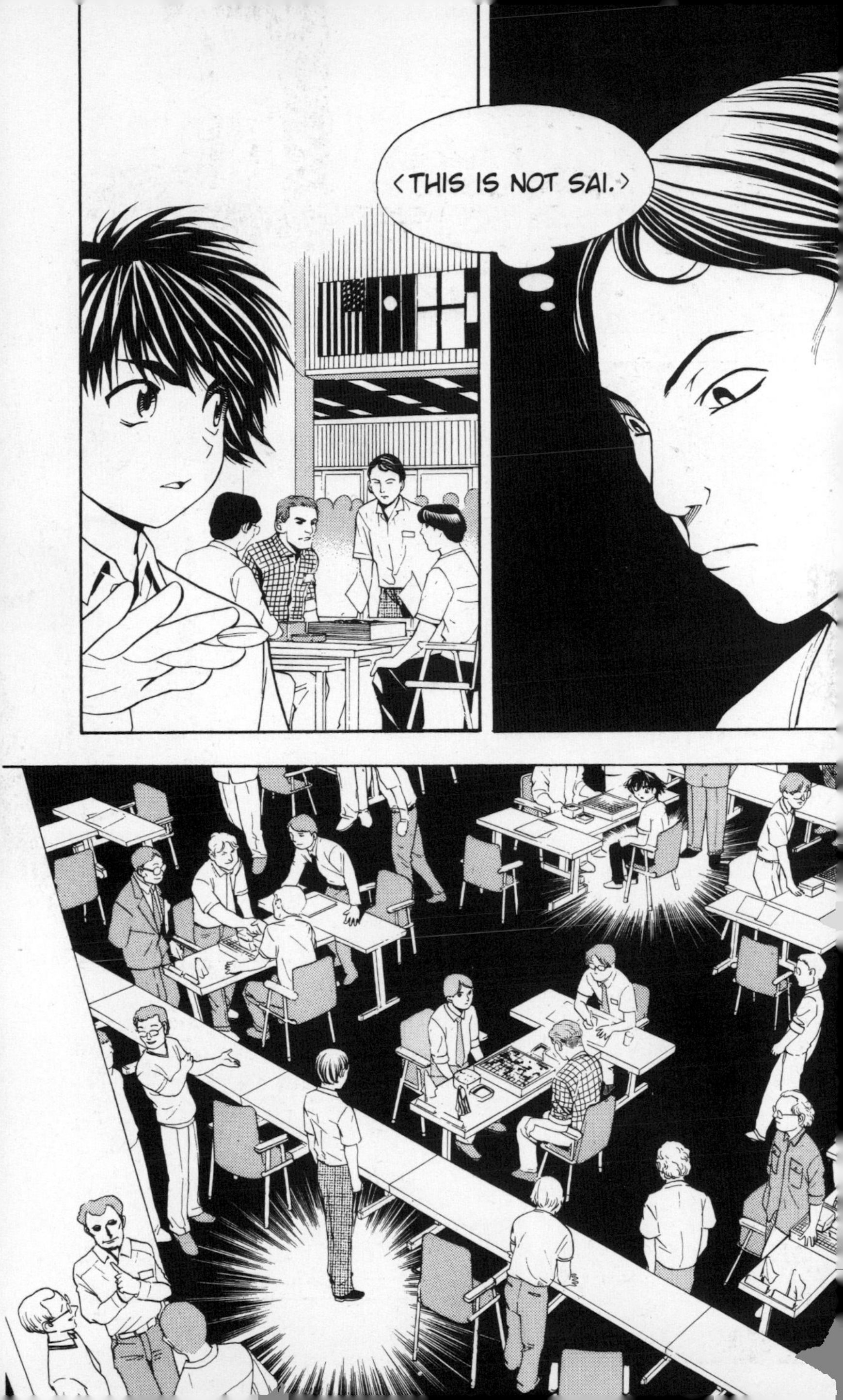
<THIS IS NOT SAI.>

A WORD ABOUT HIKARU NO GO

THE WORLD AMATEUR TOURNAMENT

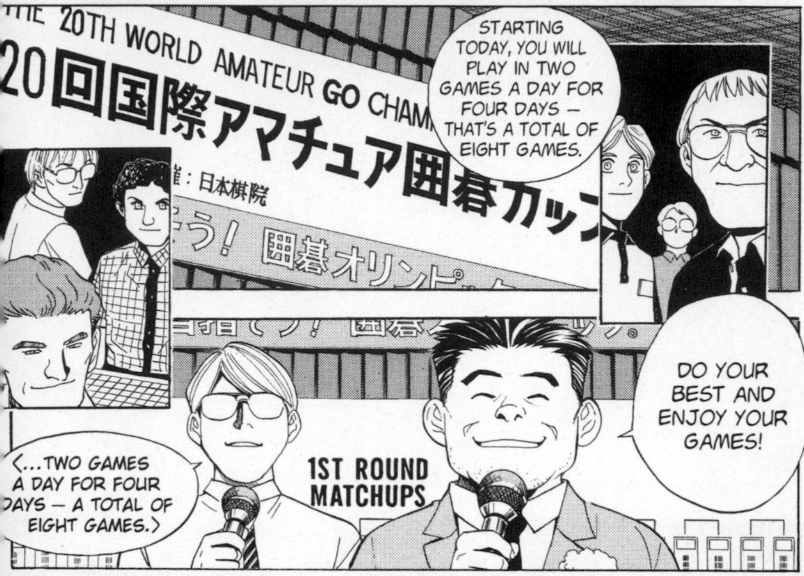
STARTING TODAY, YOU WILL PLAY IN TWO GAMES A DAY FOR FOUR DAYS — THAT'S A TOTAL OF EIGHT GAMES.
DO YOUR BEST AND ENJOY YOUR GAMES!
1ST ROUND MATCHUPS
<...TWO GAMES A DAY FOR FOUR DAYS — A TOTAL OF EIGHT GAMES.>

THE TOURNAMENT IS BASED ON THE WORLD AMATEUR GO CHAMPIONSHIP HELD EVERY YEAR IN JUNE. (THE WORLD AMATEUR TOURNAMENT THAT TAKES PLACE IN *HIKARU NO GO* WAS HELD IN AUGUST.)

JAPAN'S No. 1 AMATEUR (WHO IS ON PAR WITH THE PROS) BATTLES IT OUT THROUGH THE PRELIMINARIES TO PLAY HEATED GAMES AGAINST THE BEST AMATEURS OF MANY DIFFERENT COUNTRIES.
ONE EUROPEAN PLAYER WHO PARTICIPATED IN THIS TOURNAMENT SPENT SOME TIME AS AN INSEI IN JAPAN.

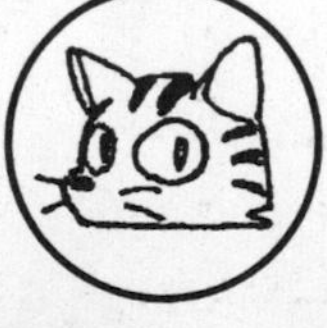

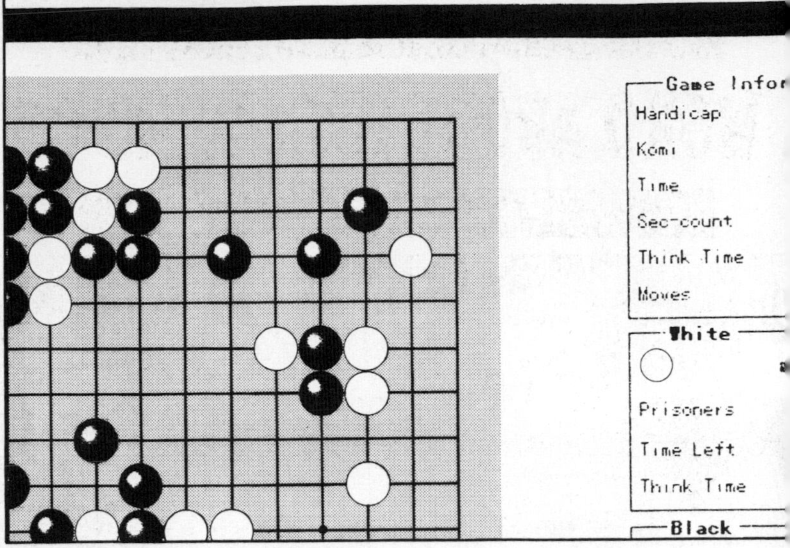
Game Infor
Handicap
Komi
Time
Sec-count
Think Time
Moves
White
Prisoners
Time Left
Think Time
Black

Game 33 "Akira"

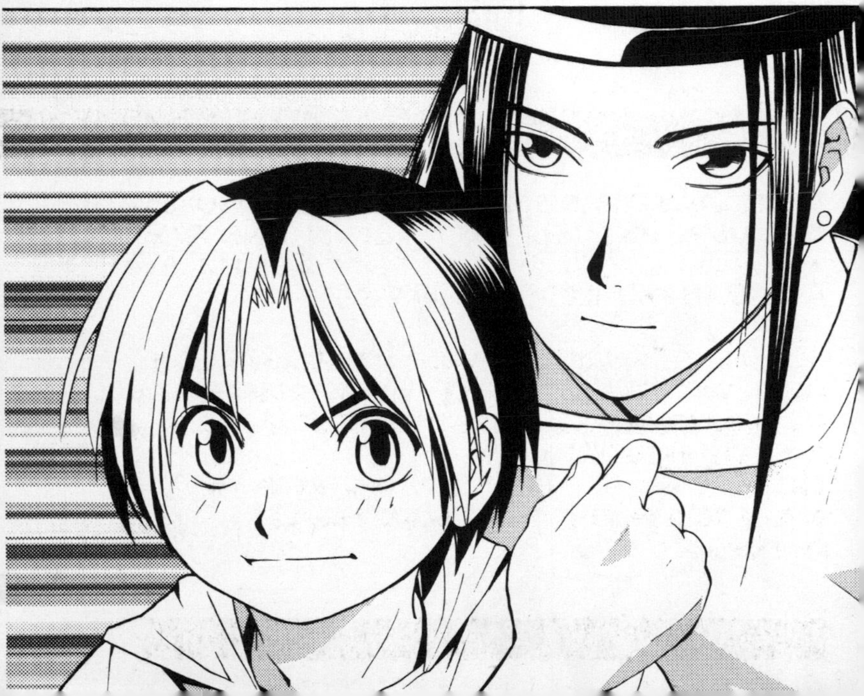

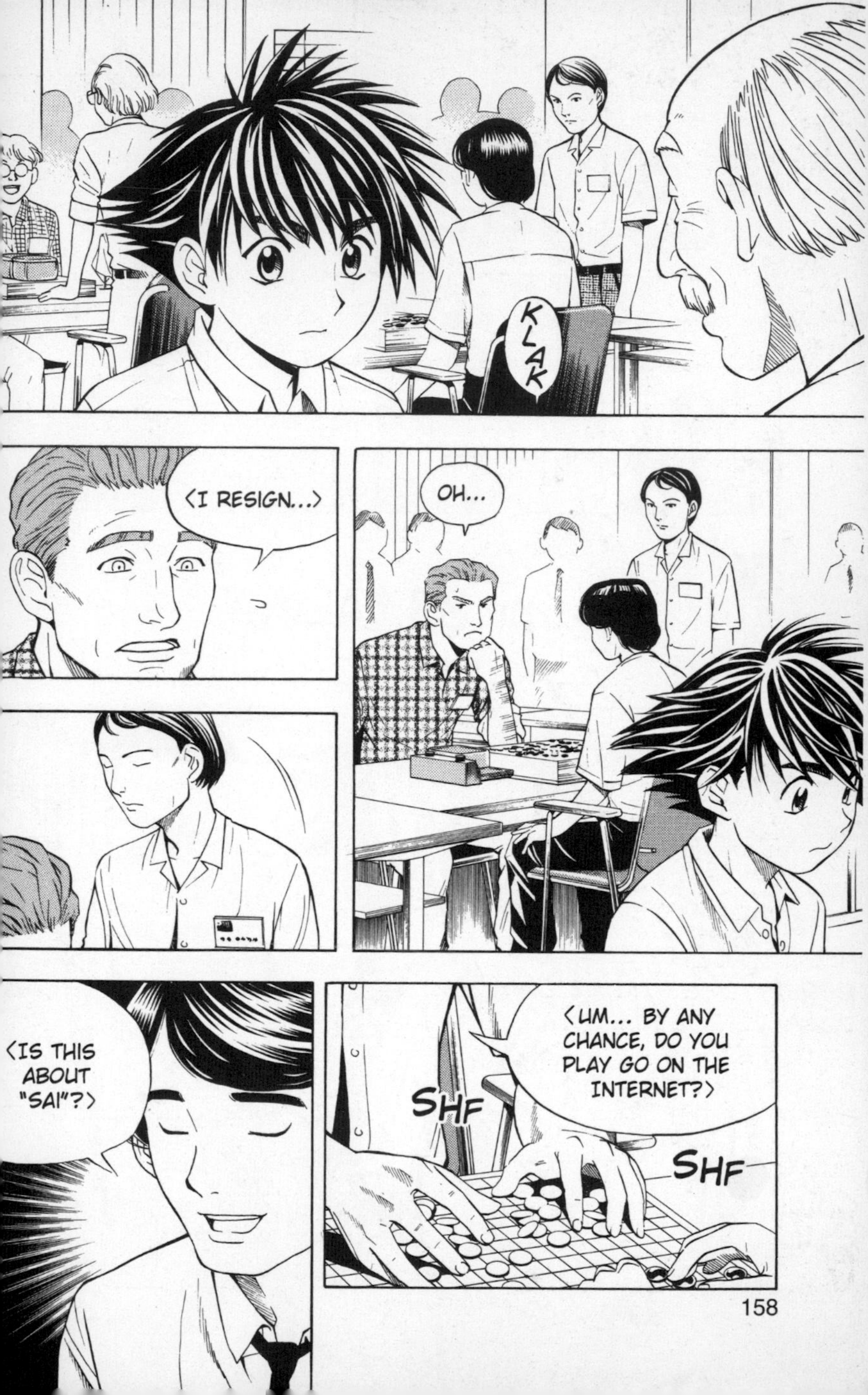
KLAK
OH...
〈I RESIGN...〉
〈UM... BY ANY CHANCE, DO YOU PLAY GO ON THE INTERNET?〉
SHF
SHF
〈IS THIS ABOUT "SAI"?〉

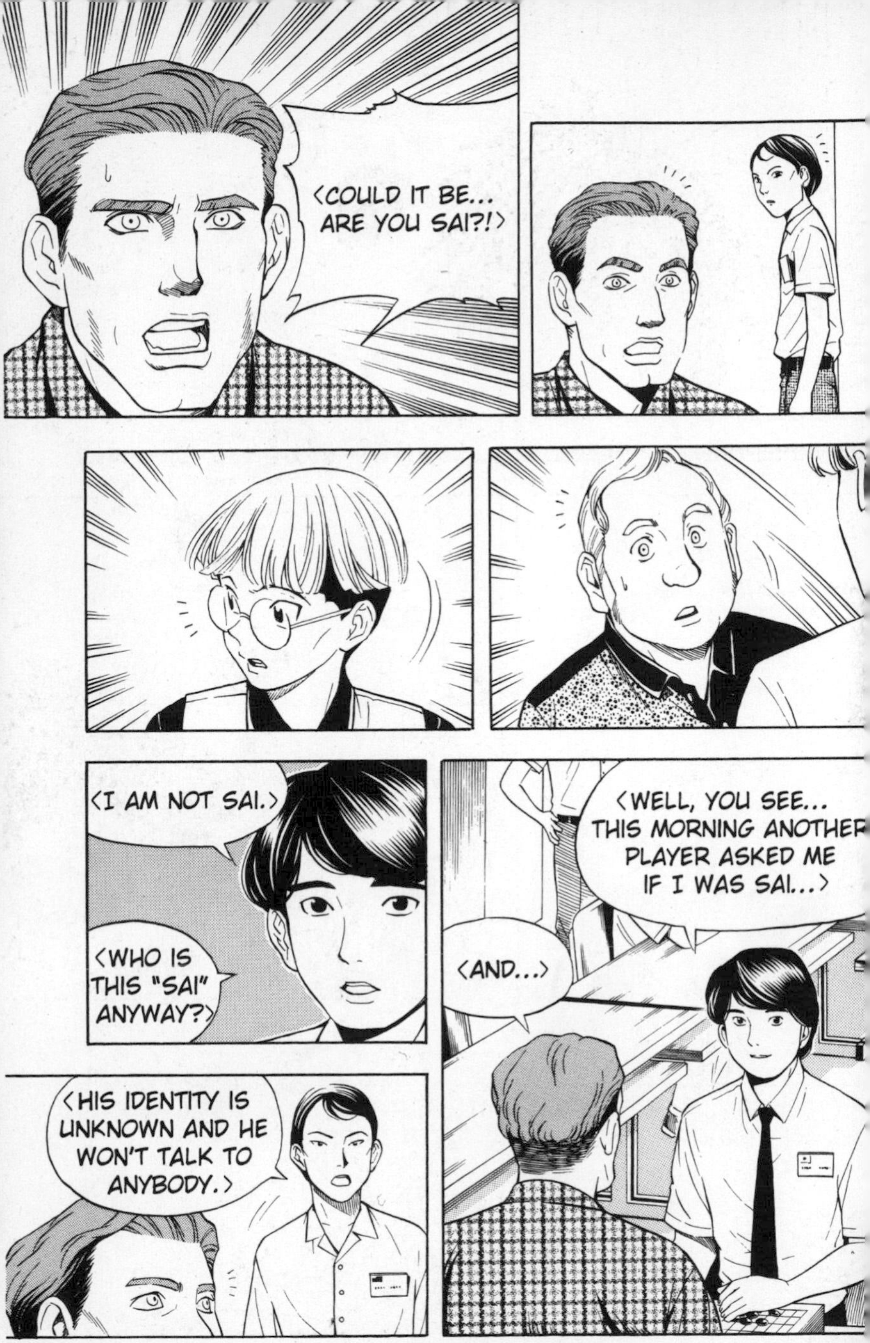
<COULD IT BE... ARE YOU SAI?!>
<WELL, YOU SEE... THIS MORNING ANOTHER PLAYER ASKED ME IF I WAS SAI...>
<AND...>
<I AM NOT SAI.>
<WHO IS THIS "SAI" ANYWAY?>
<HIS IDENTITY IS UNKNOWN AND HE WON'T TALK TO ANYBODY.>

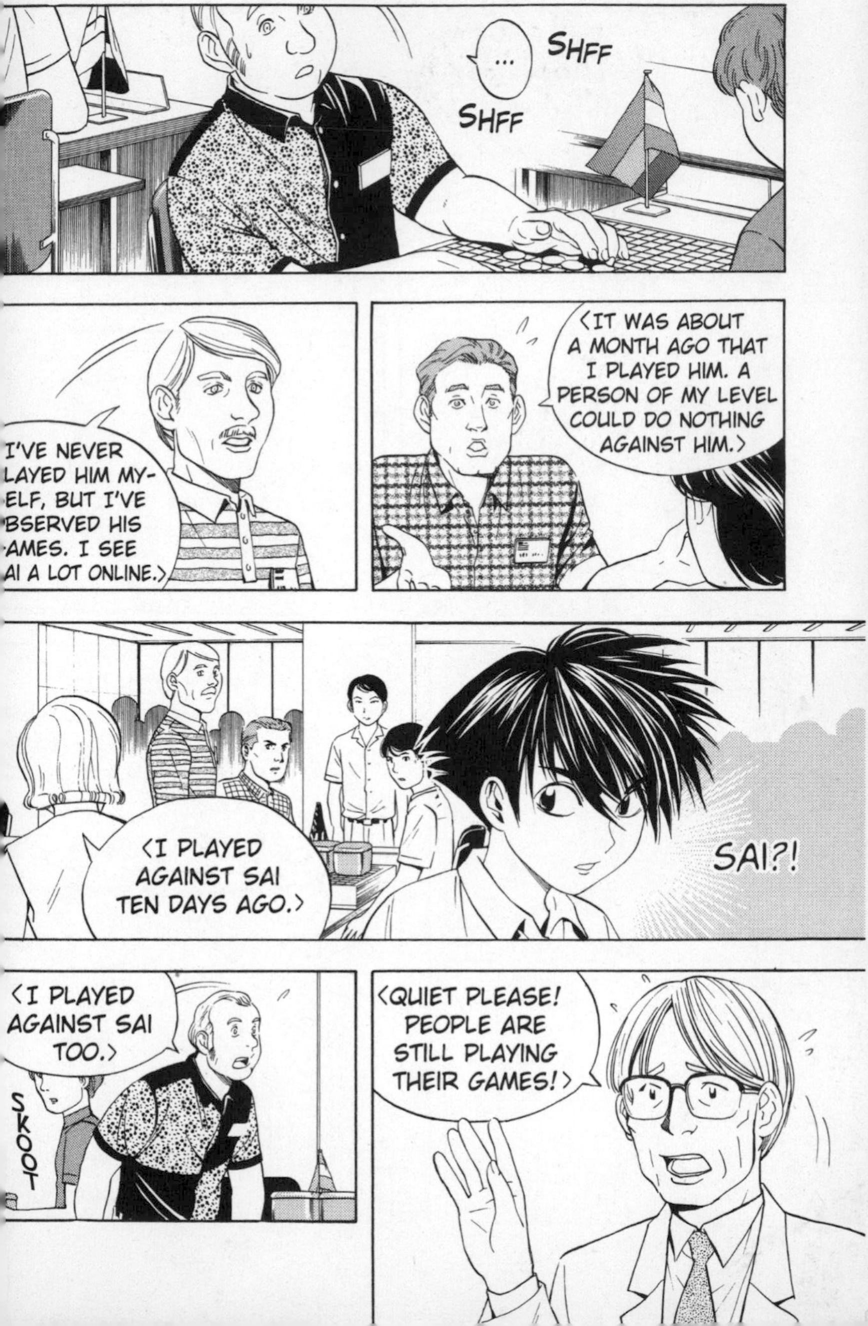
...
SHFF
SHFF
〈IT WAS ABOUT A MONTH AGO THAT I PLAYED HIM. A PERSON OF MY LEVEL COULD DO NOTHING AGAINST HIM.〉
I'VE NEVER LAYED HIM MY-ELF, BUT I'VE BSERVED HIS AMES. I SEE AI A LOT ONLINE.〉
〈I PLAYED AGAINST SAI TEN DAYS AGO.〉
SAI?!
〈QUIET PLEASE! PEOPLE ARE STILL PLAYING THEIR GAMES!〉
〈I PLAYED AGAINST SAI TOO.〉
SKOOT

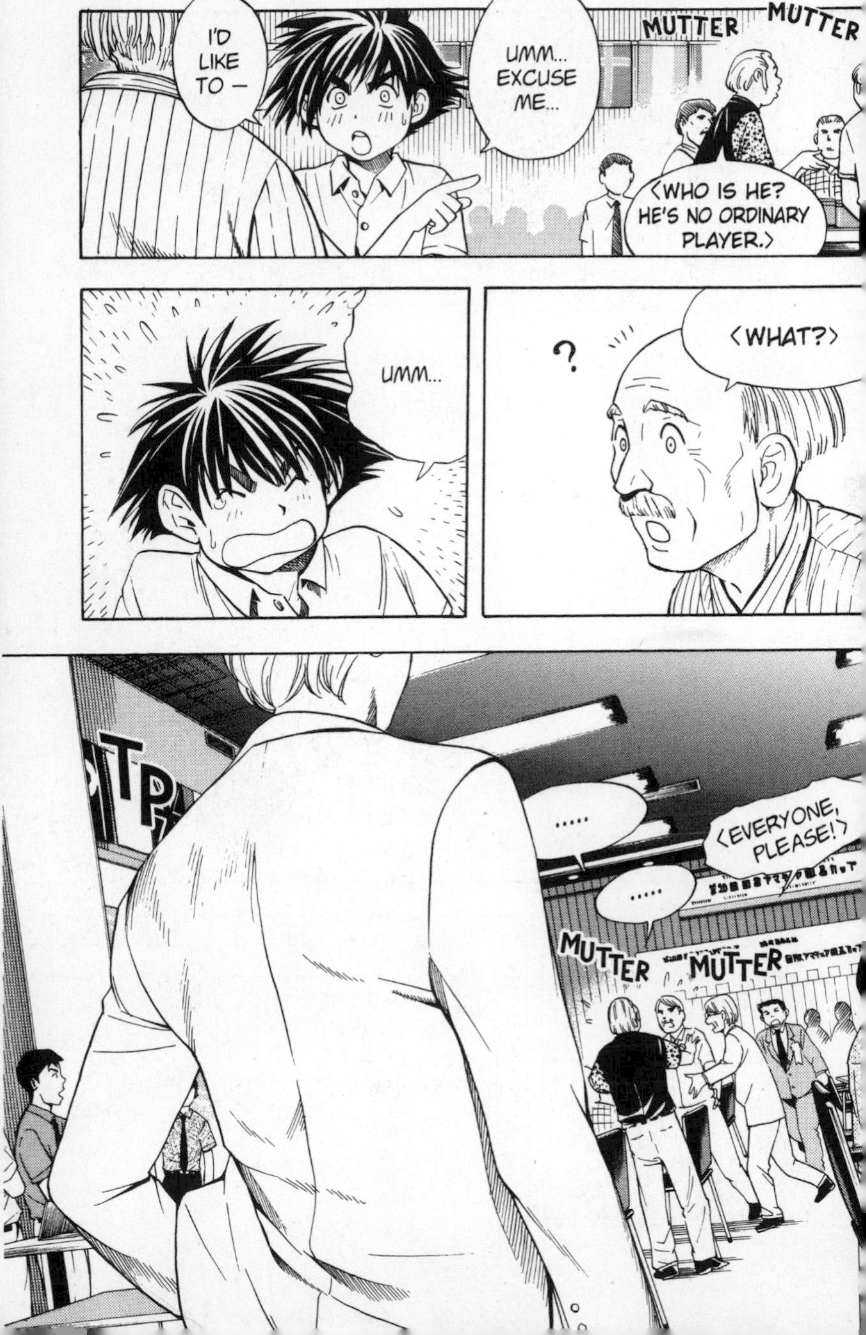
MUTTER MUTTER
<WHO IS HE? HE'S NO ORDINARY PLAYER.>
UMM... EXCUSE ME...
I'D LIKE TO —
?
<WHAT?>
UMM...
<EVERYONE, PLEASE!>
.....
.....
MUTTER MUTTER

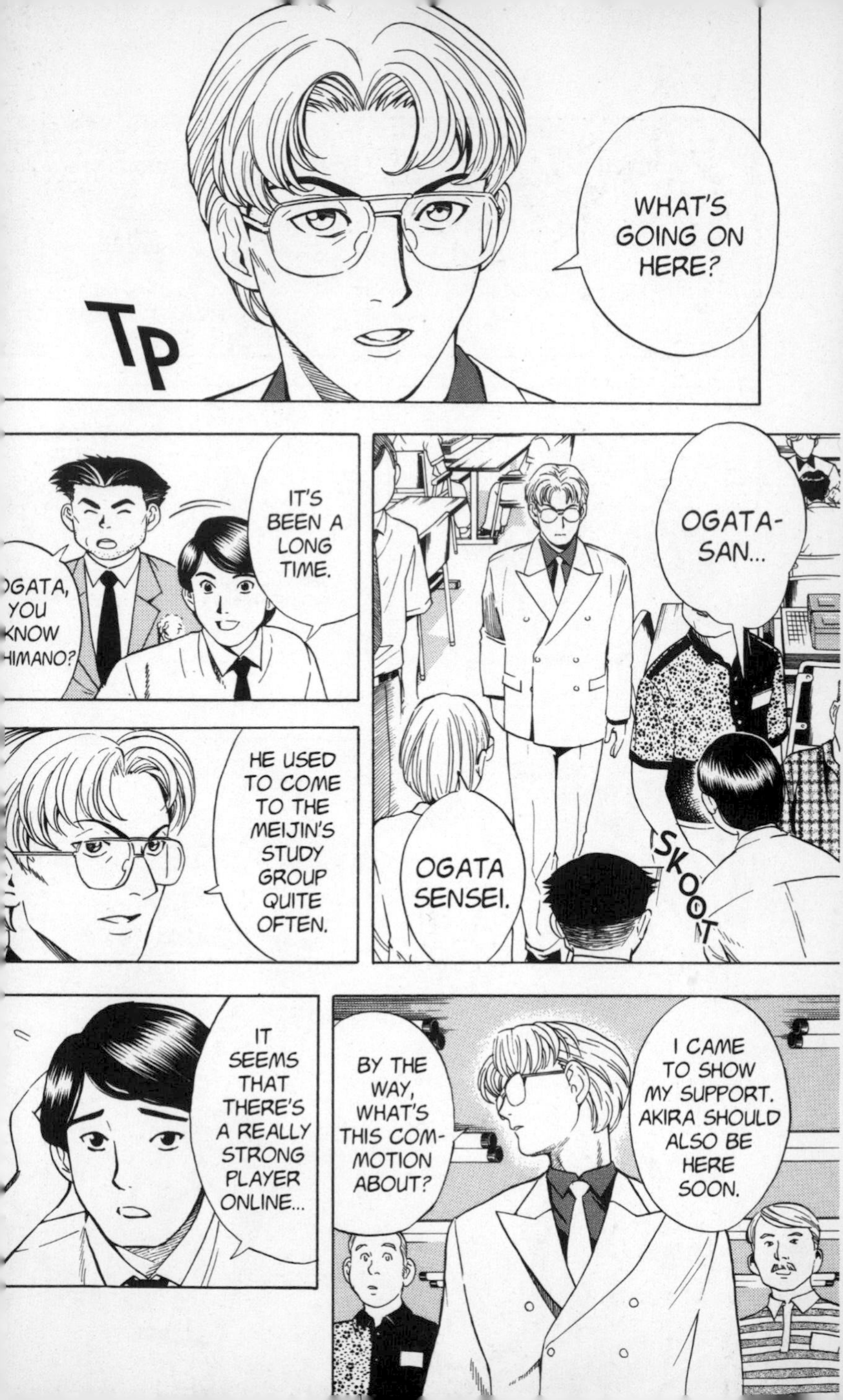
TP
WHAT'S GOING ON HERE?
OGATA-SAN...
SKOOT
OGATA SENSEI.
IT'S BEEN A LONG TIME.
OGATA, YOU KNOW HIMANO?
HE USED TO COME TO THE MEIJIN'S STUDY GROUP QUITE OFTEN.
I CAME TO SHOW MY SUPPORT. AKIRA SHOULD ALSO BE HERE SOON.
BY THE WAY, WHAT'S THIS COMMOTION ABOUT?
IT SEEMS THAT THERE'S A REALLY STRONG PLAYER ONLINE...

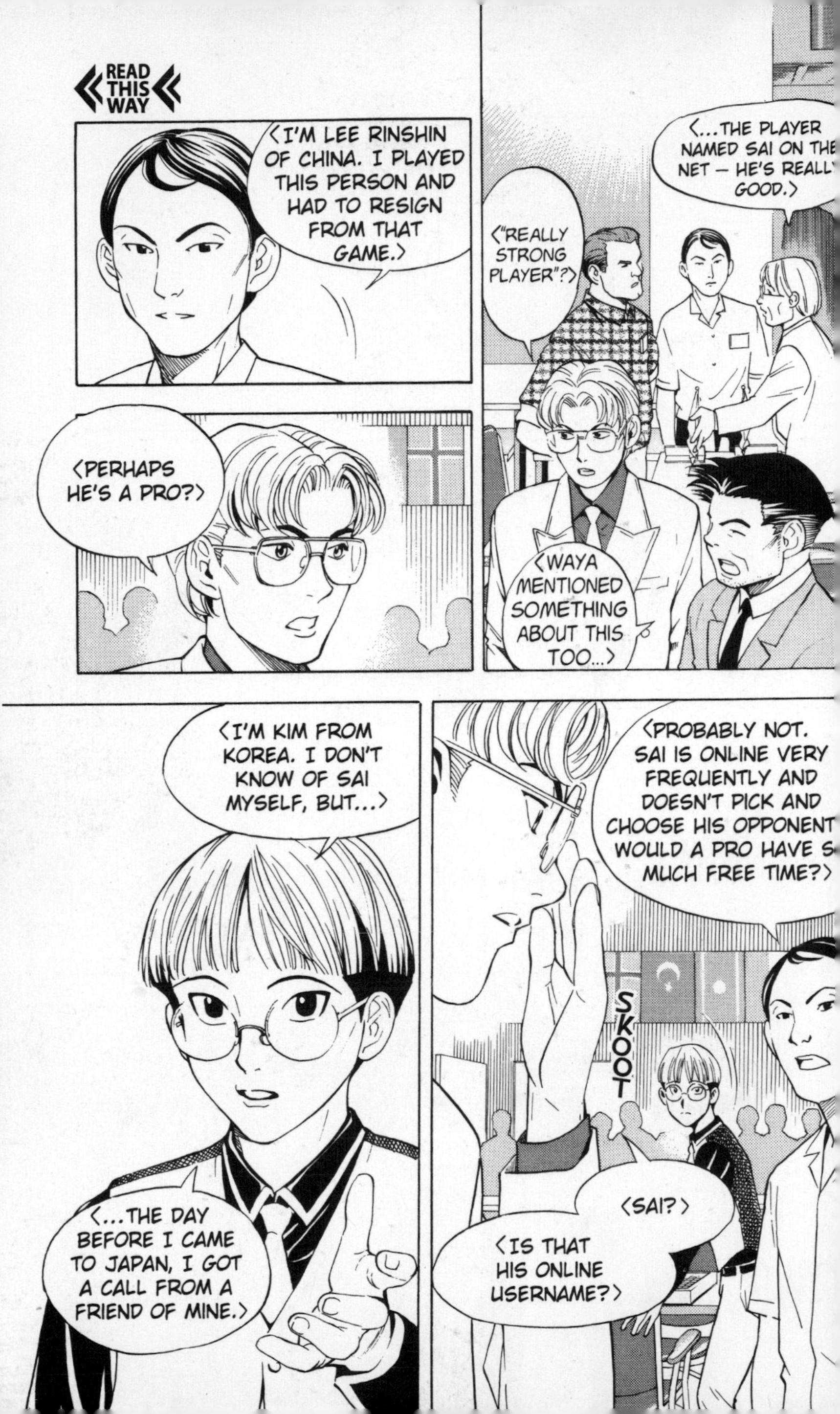
READ THIS WAY
〈...THE PLAYER NAMED SAI ON THE NET — HE'S REALL GOOD.〉
〈"REALLY STRONG PLAYER"?〉
〈WAYA MENTIONED SOMETHING ABOUT THIS TOO...〉
〈I'M LEE RINSHIN OF CHINA. I PLAYED THIS PERSON AND HAD TO RESIGN FROM THAT GAME.〉
〈PERHAPS HE'S A PRO?〉
〈PROBABLY NOT. SAI IS ONLINE VERY FREQUENTLY AND DOESN'T PICK AND CHOOSE HIS OPPONENT WOULD A PRO HAVE S MUCH FREE TIME?〉
SKOOT
〈SAI?〉
〈IS THAT HIS ONLINE USERNAME?〉
〈I'M KIM FROM KOREA. I DON'T KNOW OF SAI MYSELF, BUT...〉
〈...THE DAY BEFORE I CAME TO JAPAN, I GOT A CALL FROM A FRIEND OF MINE.〉

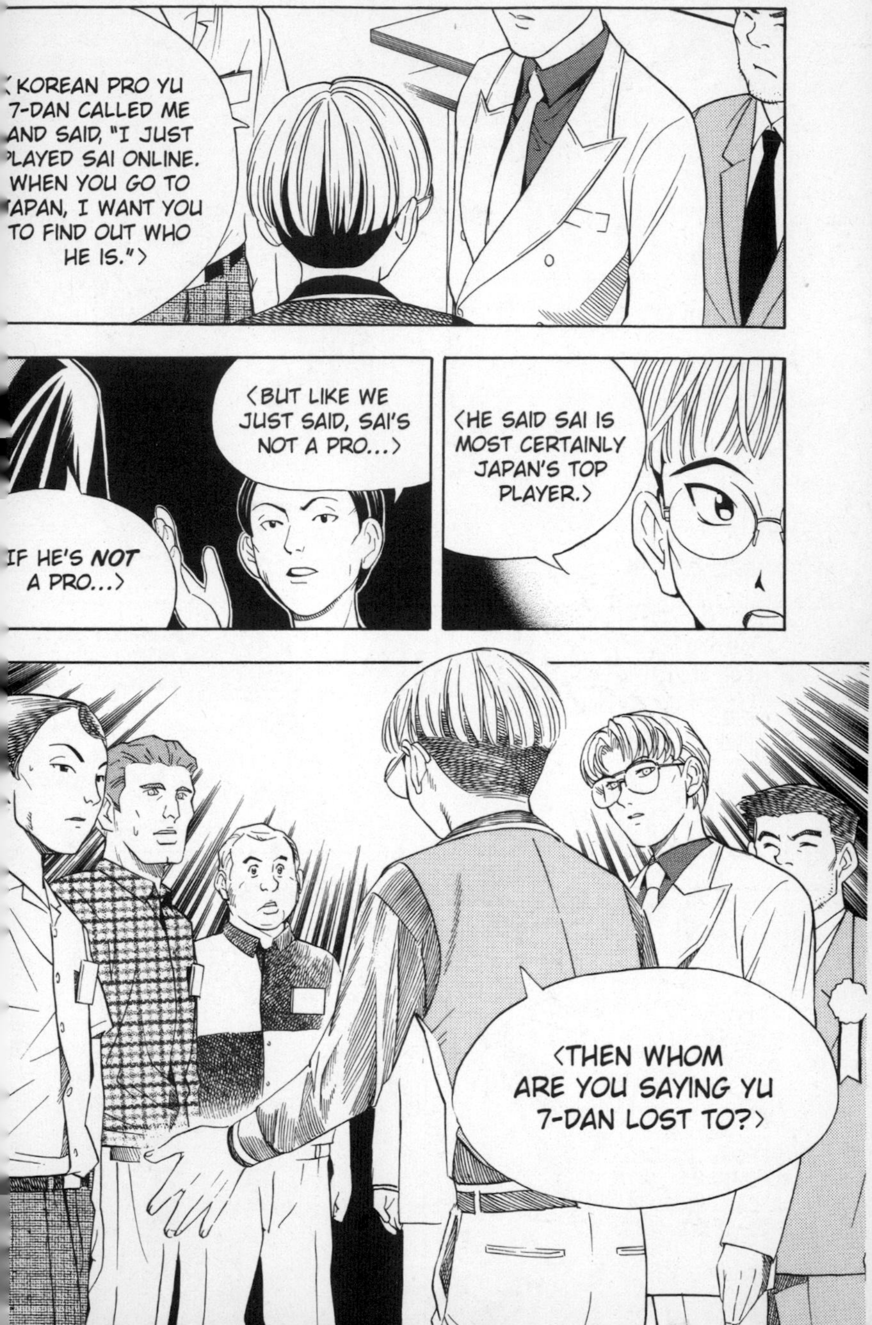
〈KOREAN PRO YU 7-DAN CALLED ME AND SAID, "I JUST PLAYED SAI ONLINE. WHEN YOU GO TO JAPAN, I WANT YOU TO FIND OUT WHO HE IS."〉
〈HE SAID SAI IS MOST CERTAINLY JAPAN'S TOP PLAYER.〉
〈BUT LIKE WE JUST SAID, SAI'S NOT A PRO...〉
〈IF HE'S *NOT* A PRO...〉
〈THEN WHOM ARE YOU SAYING YU 7-DAN LOST TO?〉

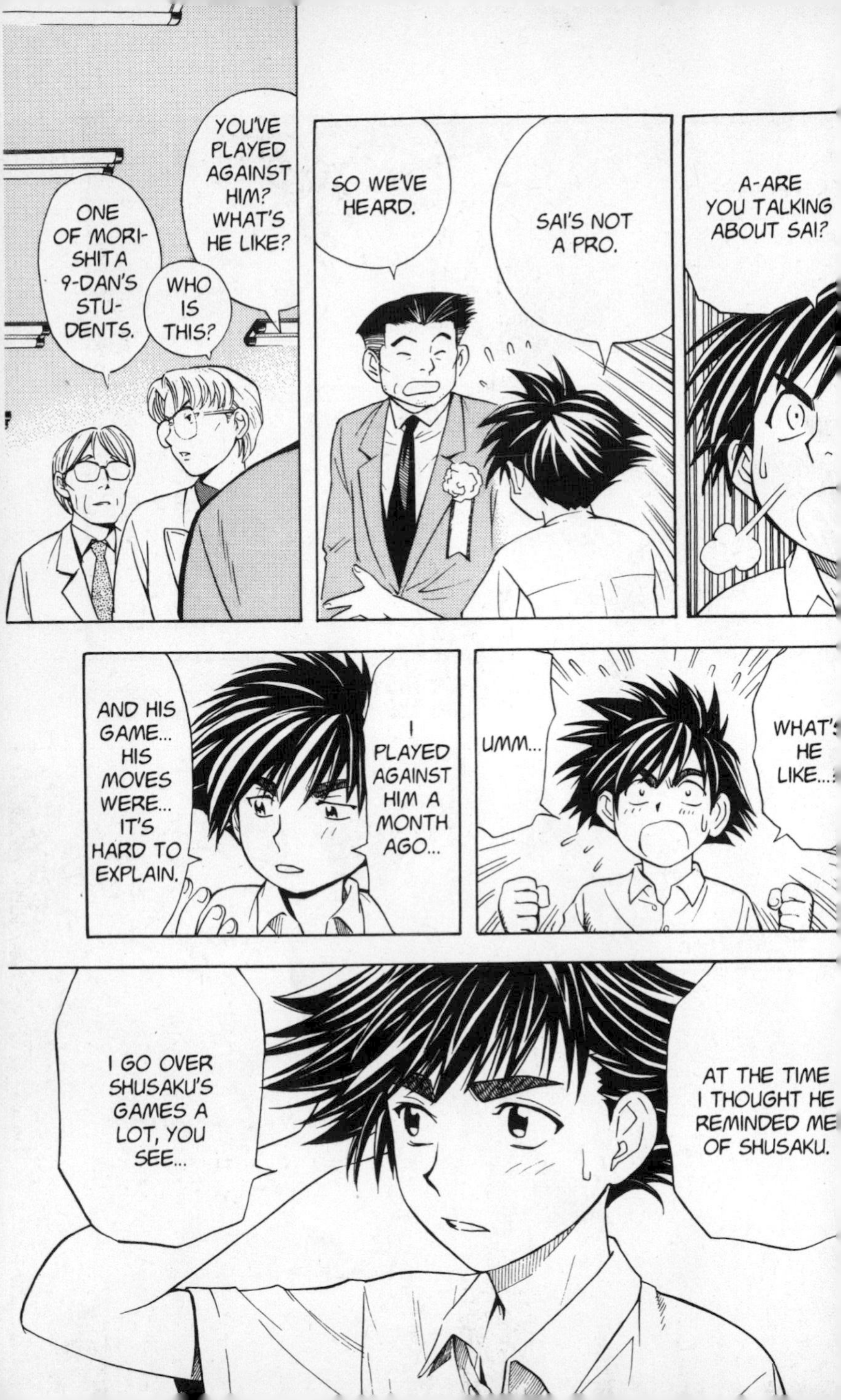
A-ARE YOU TALKING ABOUT SAI?
SAI'S NOT A PRO.
SO WE'VE HEARD.
YOU'VE PLAYED AGAINST HIM? WHAT'S HE LIKE?
WHO IS THIS?
ONE OF MORI-SHITA 9-DAN'S STU-DENTS.
WHAT'S HE LIKE...
UMM...
I PLAYED AGAINST HIM A MONTH AGO...
AND HIS GAME... HIS MOVES WERE... IT'S HARD TO EXPLAIN.
AT THE TIME I THOUGHT HE REMINDED ME OF SHUSAKU.
I GO OVER SHUSAKU'S GAMES A LOT, YOU SEE...

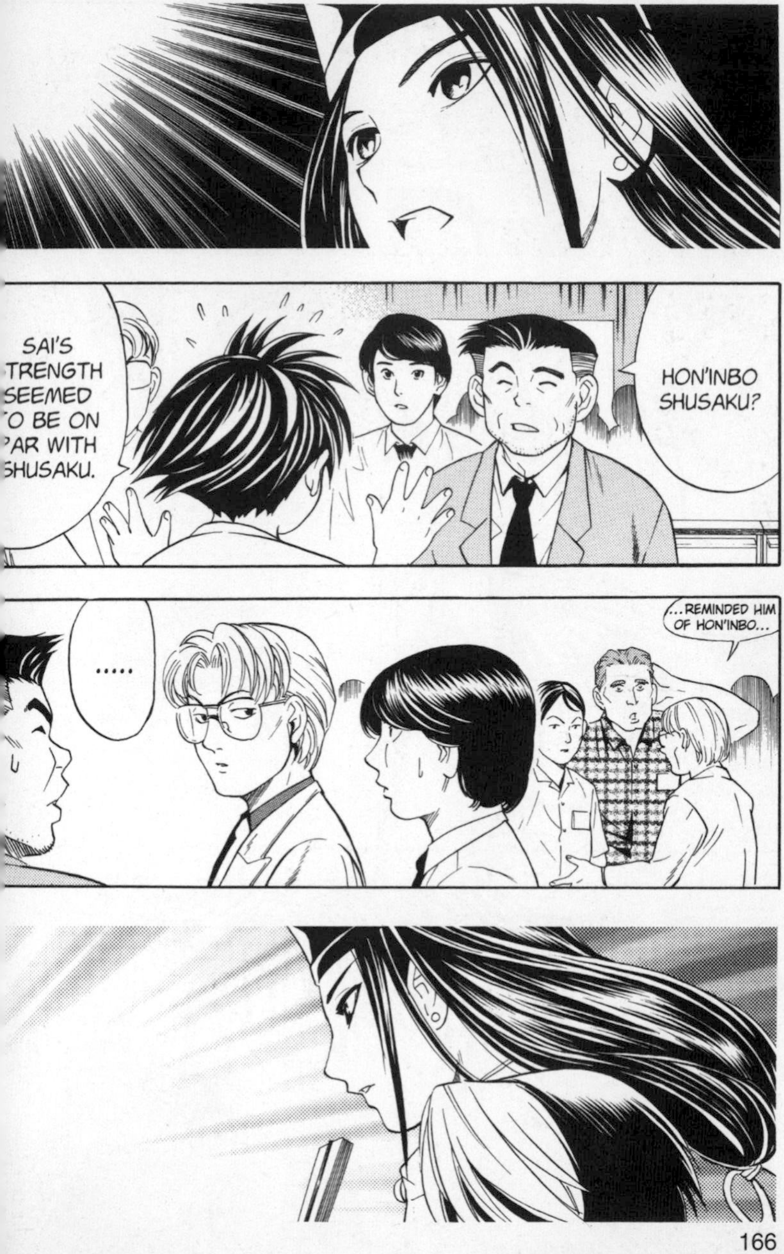
HON'INBO SHUSAKU?
SAI'S TRENGTH SEEMED O BE ON AR WITH HUSAKU.
...REMINDED HIM OF HON'INBO...
.....

READ THIS WAY

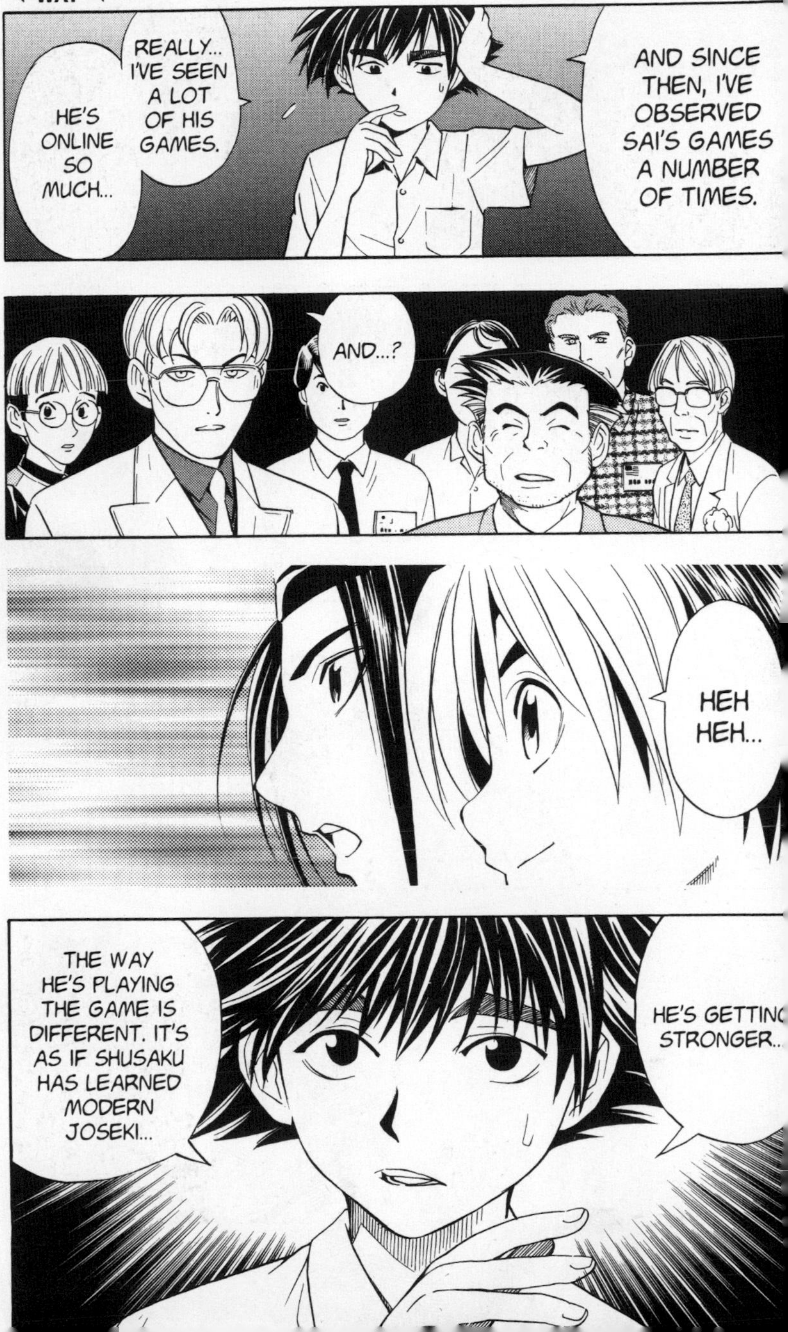
AND SINCE THEN, I'VE OBSERVED SAI'S GAMES A NUMBER OF TIMES.
REALLY... I'VE SEEN A LOT OF HIS GAMES.
HE'S ONLINE SO MUCH...
AND...?
HEH HEH...
HE'S GETTINC STRONGER..
THE WAY HE'S PLAYING THE GAME IS DIFFERENT. IT'S AS IF SHUSAKU HAS LEARNED MODERN JOSEKI...

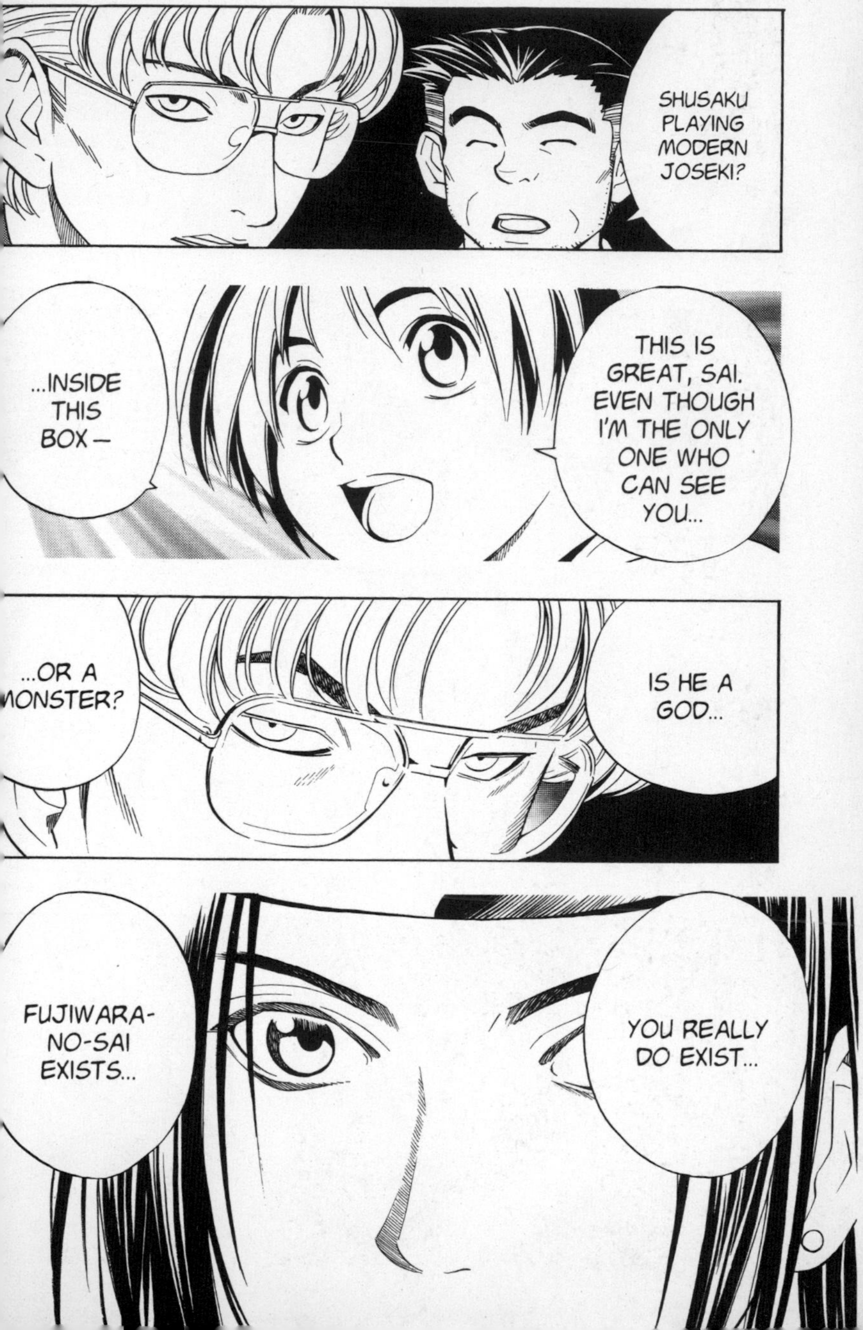
SHUSAKU PLAYING MODERN JOSEKI?
THIS IS GREAT, SAI. EVEN THOUGH I'M THE ONLY ONE WHO CAN SEE YOU...
...INSIDE THIS BOX—
IS HE A GOD...
...OR A MONSTER?
YOU REALLY DO EXIST...
FUJIWARA-NO-SAI EXISTS...

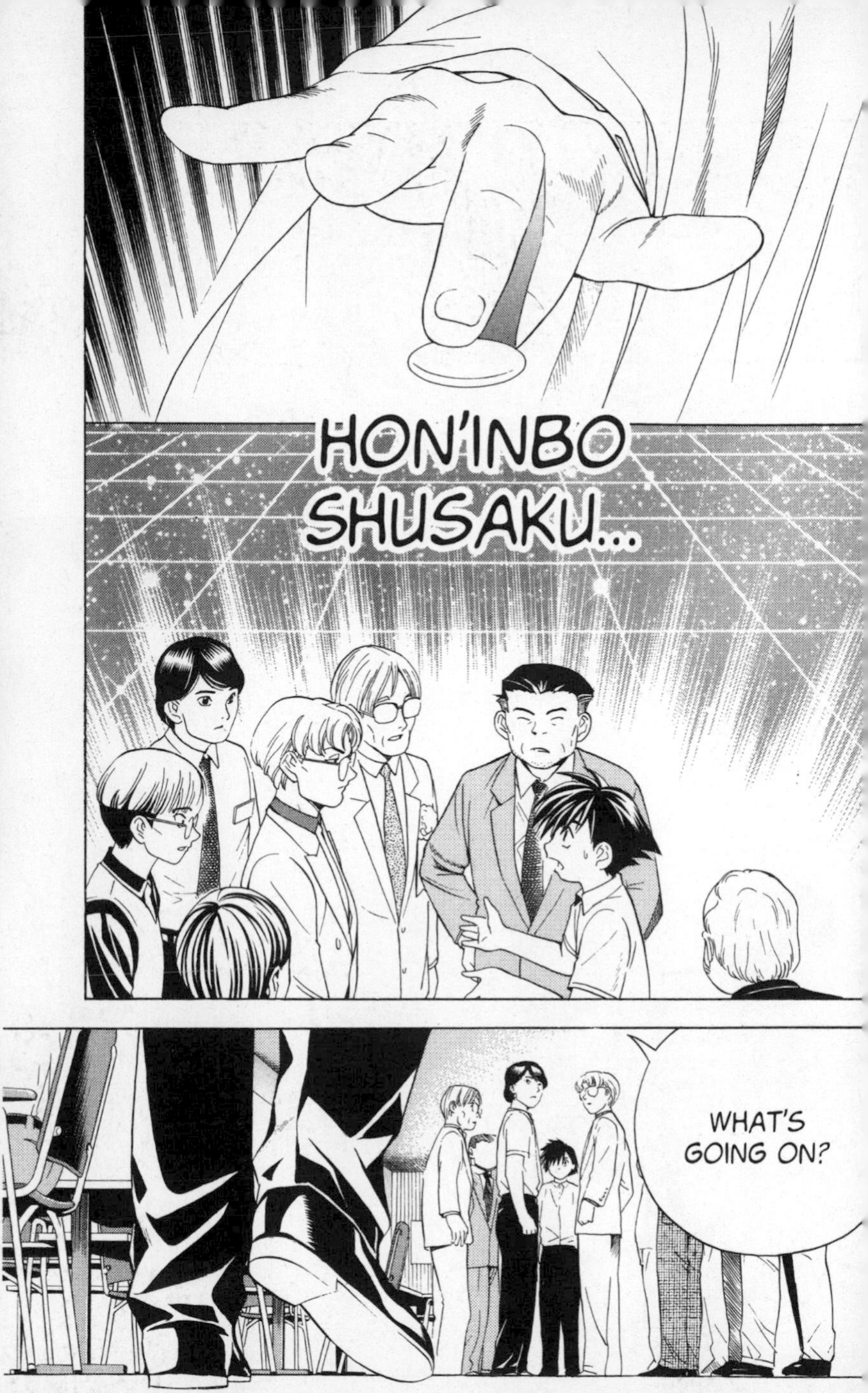
HON'INBO SHUSAKU...
WHAT'S GOING ON?

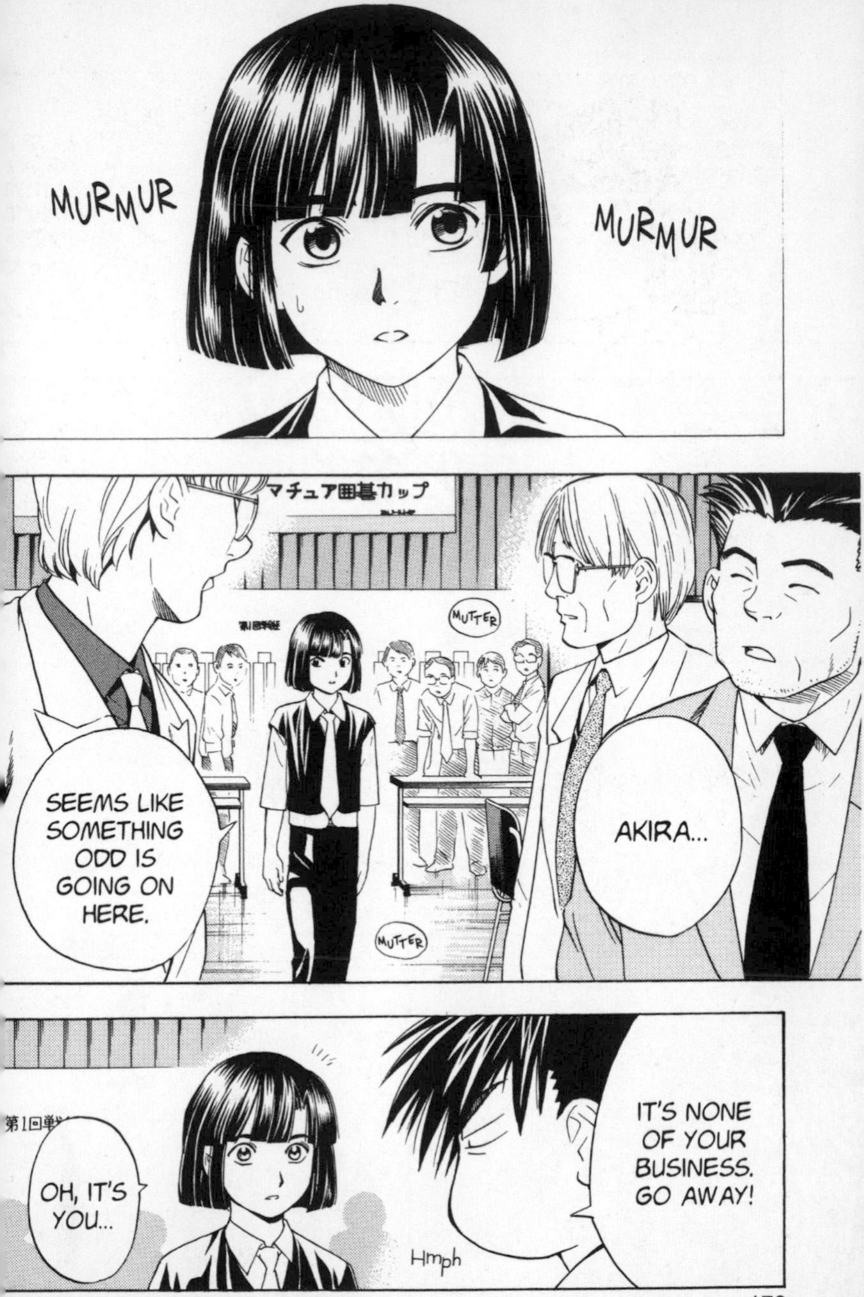
MURMUR
MURMUR
マチュア囲碁カップ
AKIRA...
MUTTER
SEEMS LIKE SOMETHING ODD IS GOING ON HERE.
MUTTER
IT'S NONE OF YOUR BUSINESS. GO AWAY!
Hmph
OH, IT'S YOU...

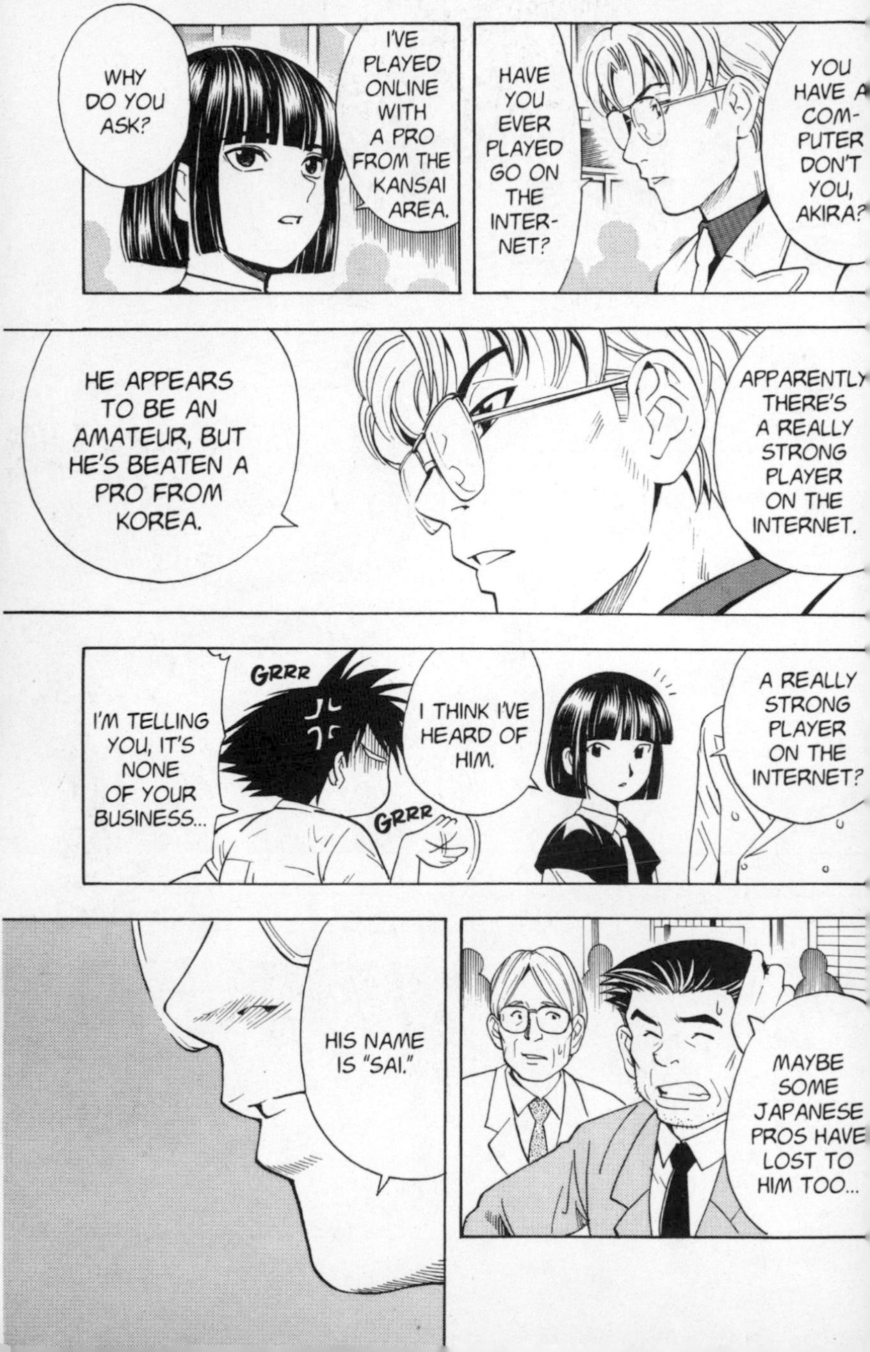
YOU HAVE A COMPUTER DON'T YOU, AKIRA?
HAVE YOU EVER PLAYED GO ON THE INTERNET?
I'VE PLAYED ONLINE WITH A PRO FROM THE KANSAI AREA.
WHY DO YOU ASK?
APPARENTLY THERE'S A REALLY STRONG PLAYER ON THE INTERNET.
HE APPEARS TO BE AN AMATEUR, BUT HE'S BEATEN A PRO FROM KOREA.
A REALLY STRONG PLAYER ON THE INTERNET?
I THINK I'VE HEARD OF HIM.
GRRR
I'M TELLING YOU, IT'S NONE OF YOUR BUSINESS...
GRRR
MAYBE SOME JAPANESE PROS HAVE LOST TO HIM TOO...
HIS NAME IS "SAI."

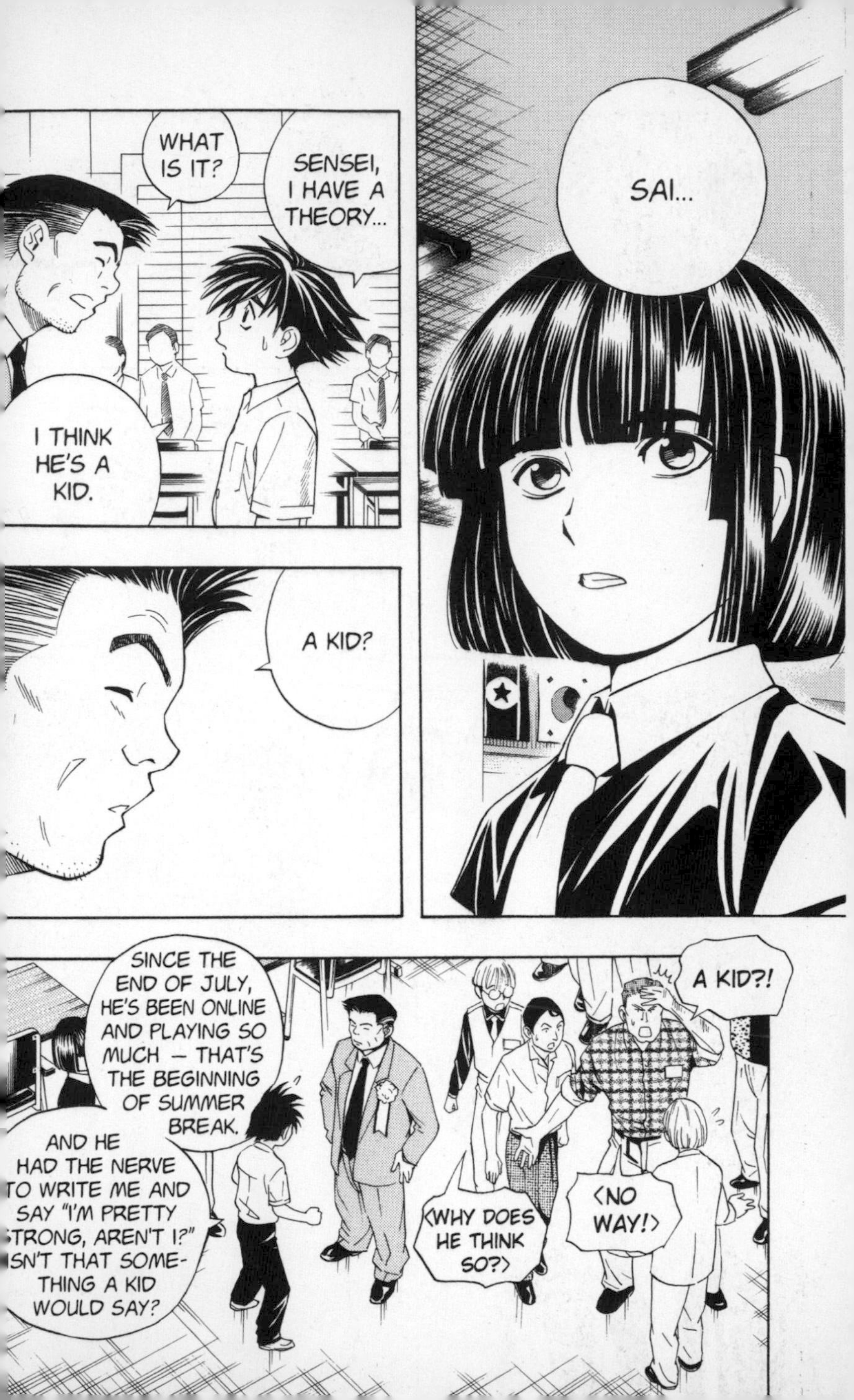
SAI...
SENSEI, I HAVE A THEORY...
WHAT IS IT?
I THINK HE'S A KID.
A KID?
A KID?!
<NO WAY!>
<WHY DOES HE THINK SO?>
SINCE THE END OF JULY, HE'S BEEN ONLINE AND PLAYING SO MUCH – THAT'S THE BEGINNING OF SUMMER BREAK.
AND HE HAD THE NERVE TO WRITE ME AND SAY "I'M PRETTY TRONG, AREN'T I?" SN'T THAT SOME-THING A KID WOULD SAY?

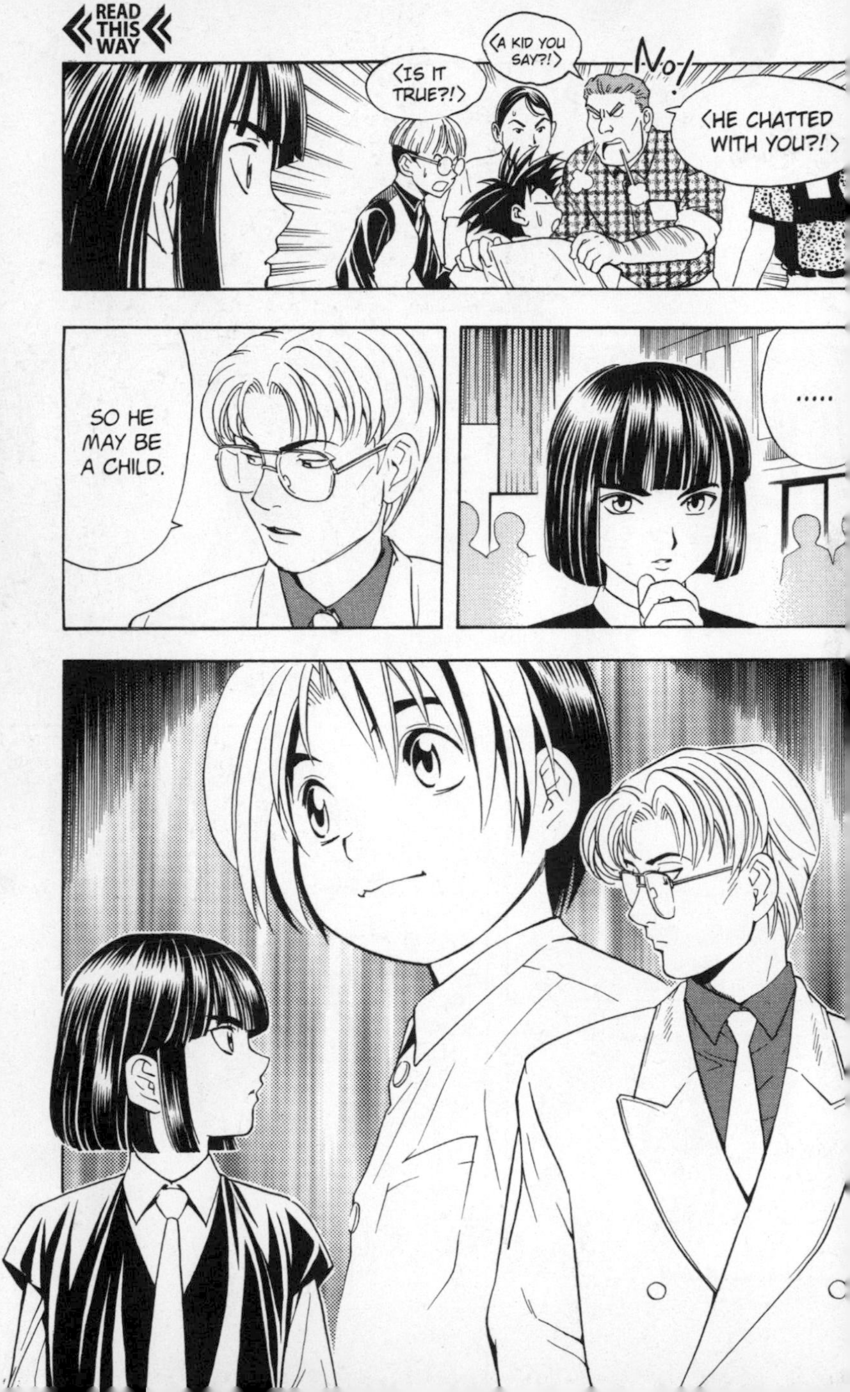
READ THIS WAY
<HE CHATTED WITH YOU?!>
No-!
<A KID YOU SAY?!>
<IS IT TRUE?!>
.....
SO HE MAY BE A CHILD.

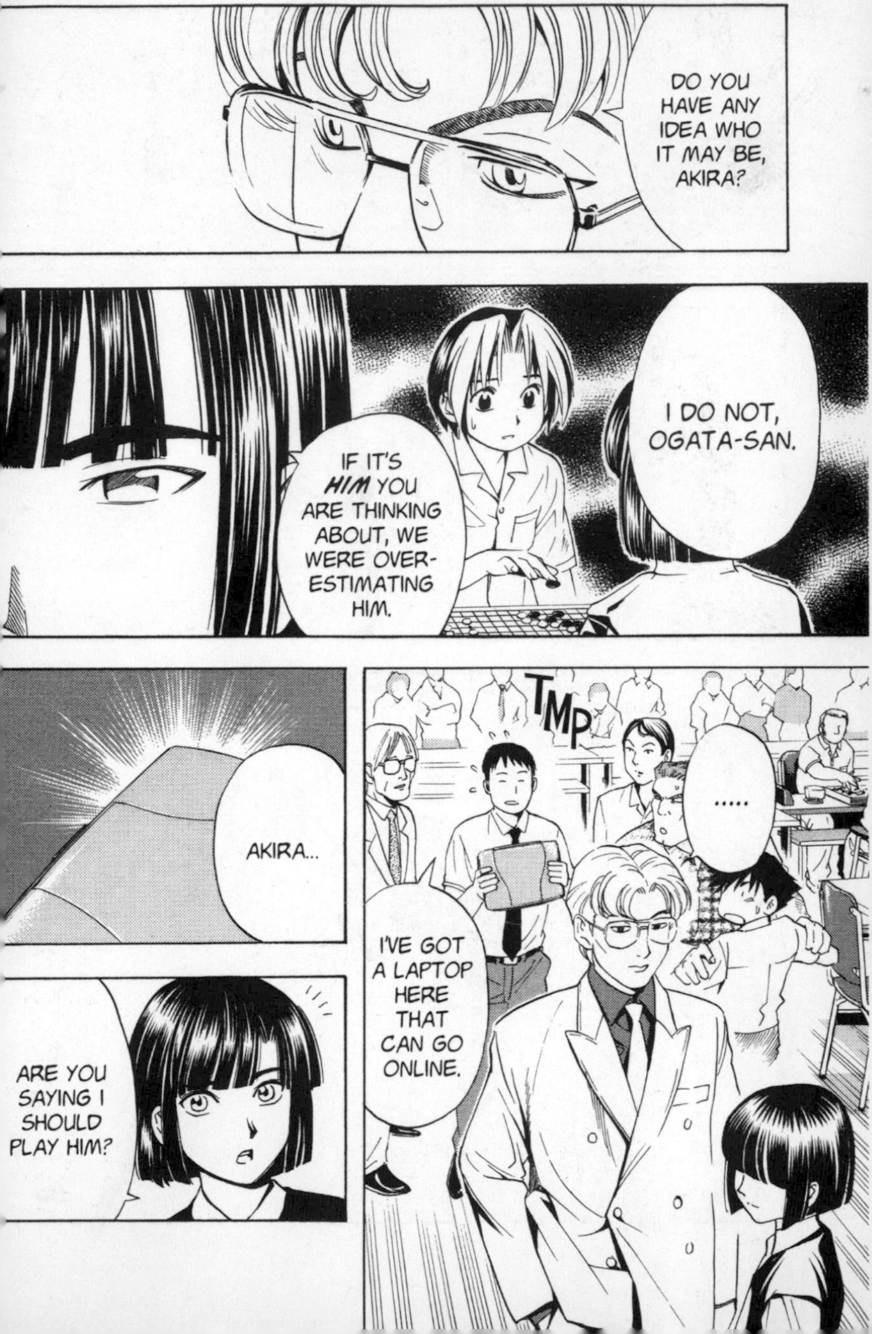
DO YOU HAVE ANY IDEA WHO IT MAY BE, AKIRA?
I DO NOT, OGATA-SAN.
IF IT'S *HIM* YOU ARE THINKING ABOUT, WE WERE OVER-ESTIMATING HIM.
TMP
.....
I'VE GOT A LAPTOP HERE THAT CAN GO ONLINE.
AKIRA...
ARE YOU SAYING I SHOULD PLAY HIM?

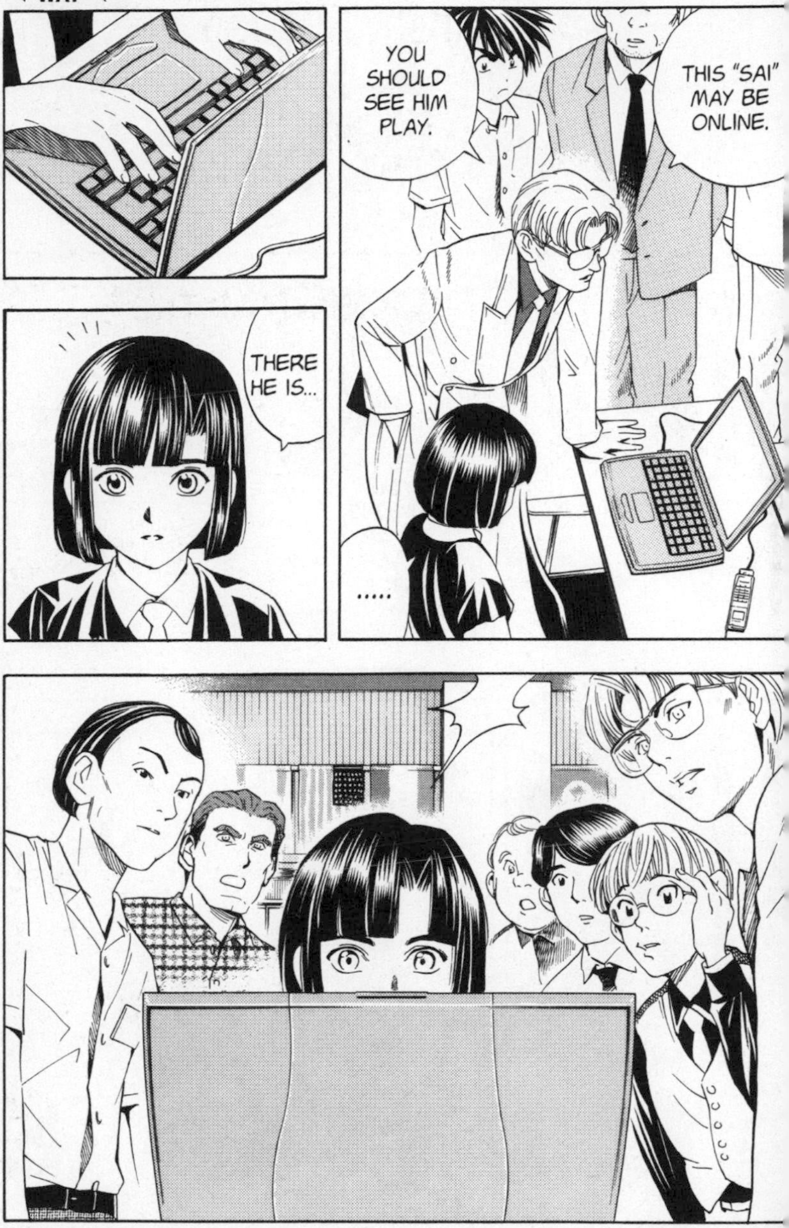
THIS "SAI" MAY BE ONLINE.
YOU SHOULD SEE HIM PLAY.
.....
THERE HE IS...

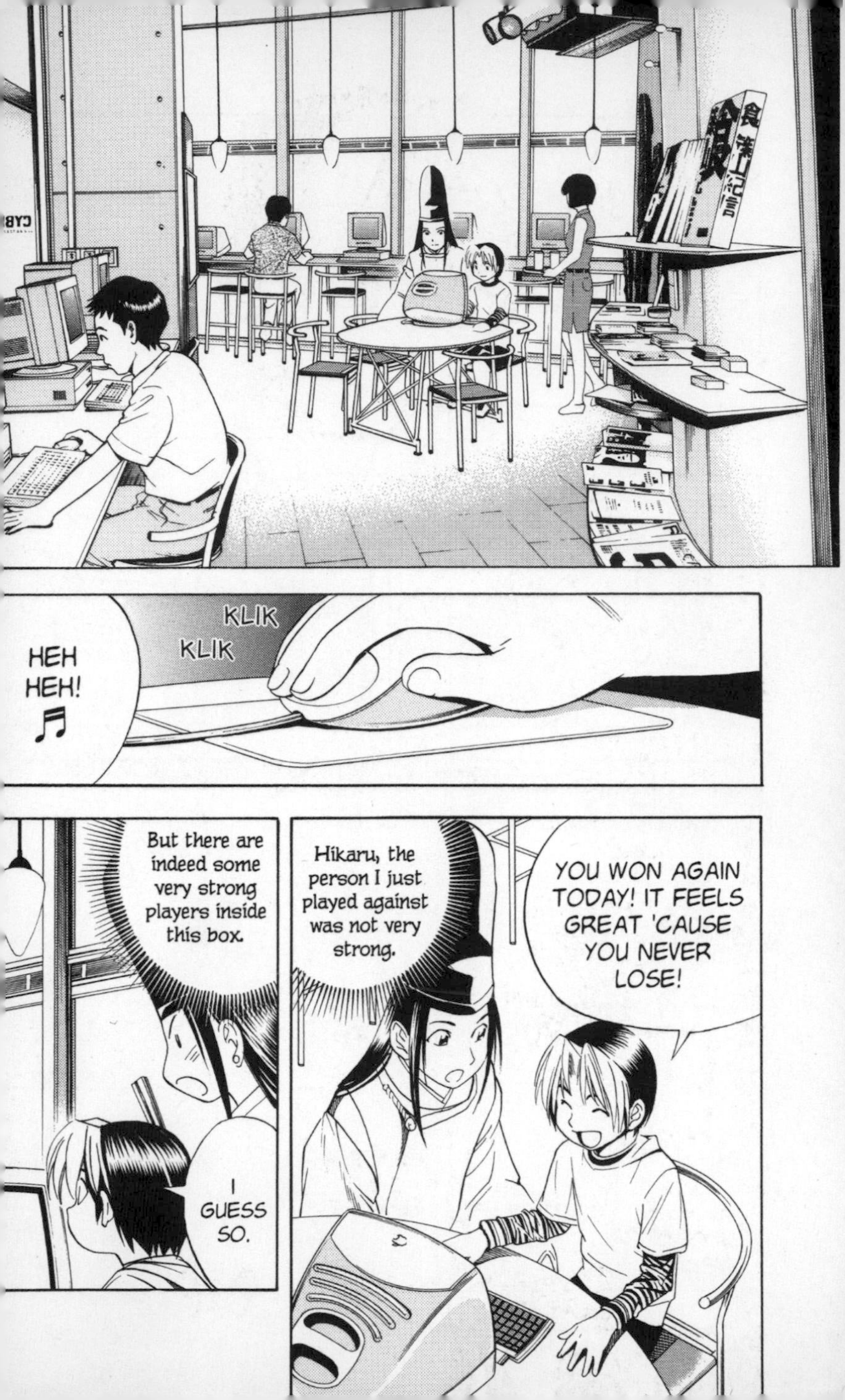
KLIK
KLIK
HEH HEH! ♬
YOU WON AGAIN TODAY! IT FEELS GREAT 'CAUSE YOU NEVER LOSE!
Hikaru, the person I just played against was not very strong.
But there are indeed some very strong players inside this box.
I GUESS SO.

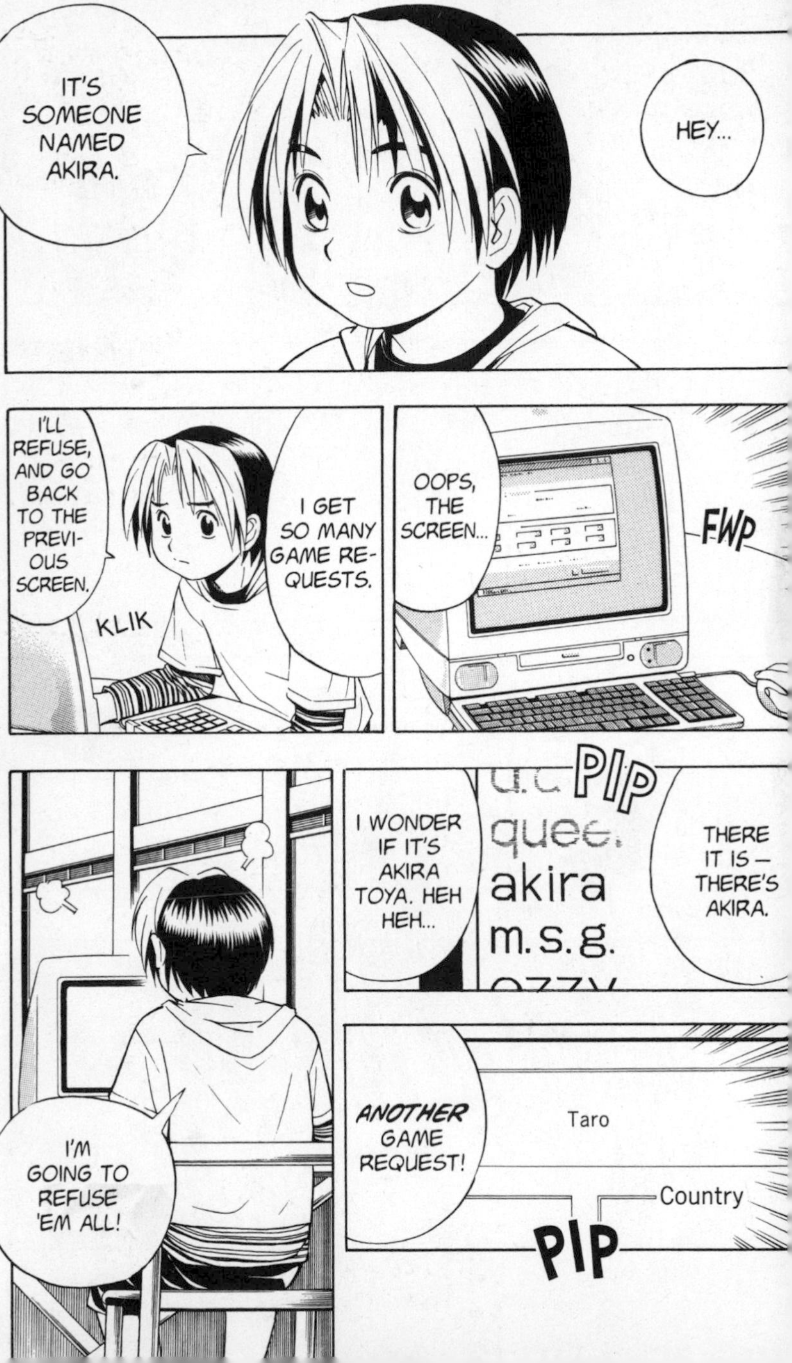
HEY...
IT'S SOMEONE NAMED AKIRA.
FWP
OOPS, THE SCREEN...
I GET SO MANY GAME RE-QUESTS.
I'LL REFUSE, AND GO BACK TO THE PREVI-OUS SCREEN.
KLIK
THERE IT IS — THERE'S AKIRA.
PIP
quee.
akira
m.s.g.
I WONDER IF IT'S AKIRA TOYA. HEH HEH...
Taro
Country
PIP
ANOTHER GAME REQUEST!
I'M GOING TO REFUSE 'EM ALL!

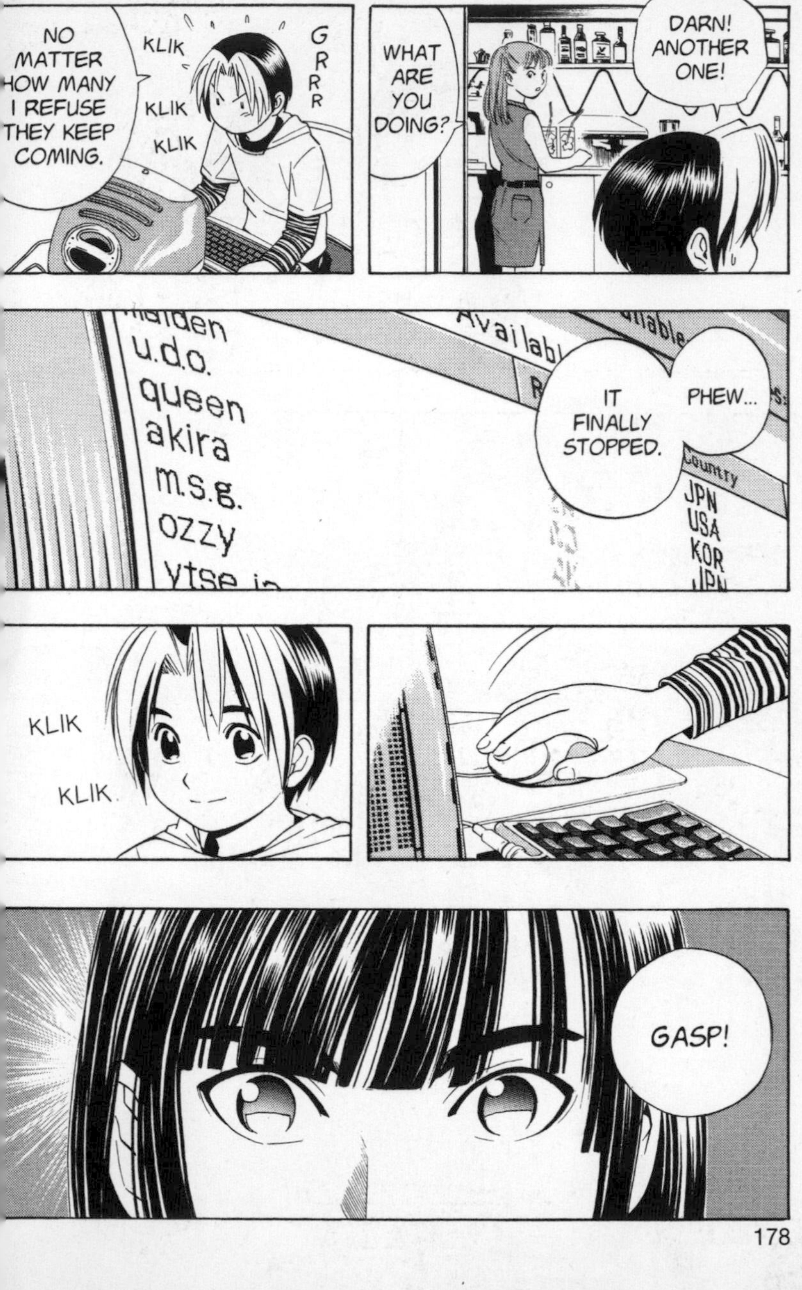
DARN! ANOTHER ONE!
WHAT ARE YOU DOING?
GRRR
KLIK
KLIK
KLIK
NO MATTER HOW MANY I REFUSE THEY KEEP COMING.
Available
Country
JPN
USA
KOR
PHEW...
IT FINALLY STOPPED.
u.d.o.
queen
akira
m.s.g.
ozzy
KLIK
KLIK
GASP!

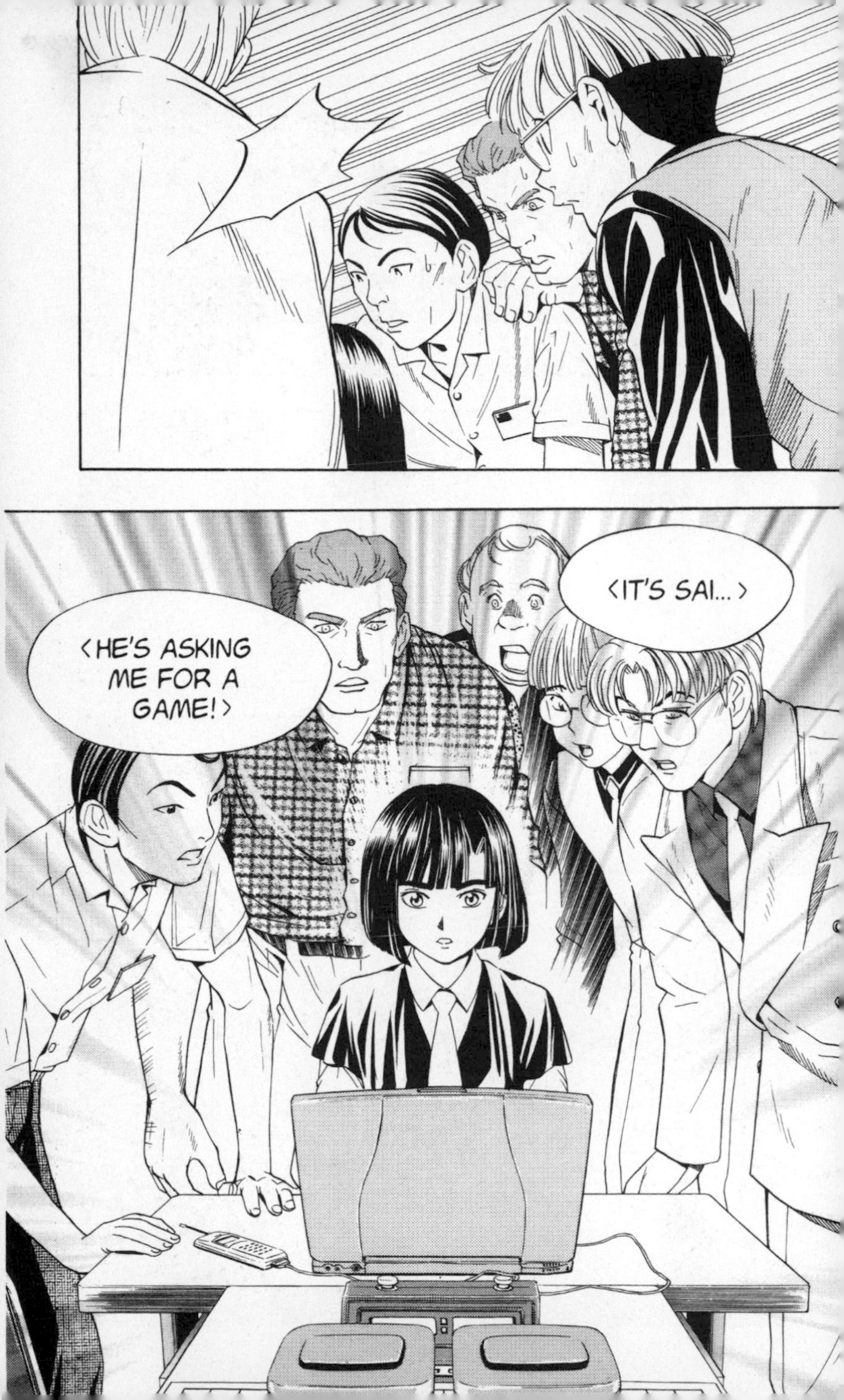
<IT'S SAI...>
<HE'S ASKING ME FOR A GAME!>

A WORD ABOUT HIKARU NO GO

TECHNICAL GO TERMS IN ENGLISH

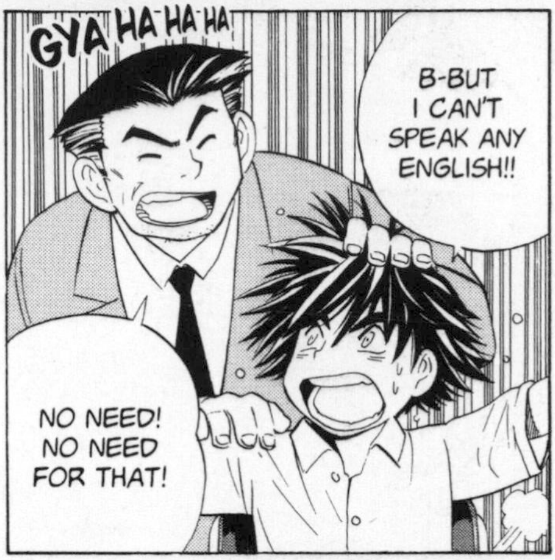
B-BUT I CAN'T SPEAK ANY ENGLISH!!
GYA HA HA HA
NO NEED! NO NEED FOR THAT!

THE BIRTHPLACE OF GO WAS IN CHINA A LONG TIME AGO. BUT IT SPREAD TO THE WORLD FROM JAPAN.

THAT'S WHY A LOT OF GO TERMS IN ENGLISH ARE LEFT IN JAPANESE. FOR EXAMPLE, *SENTE*, *GOTE*, *NIGIRI*, AND *TENUKI* ARE ALL LEFT IN JAPANESE.

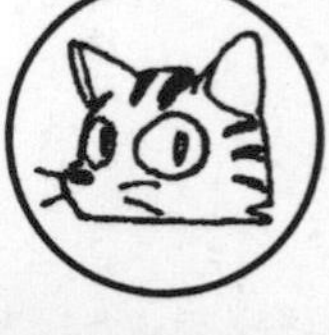

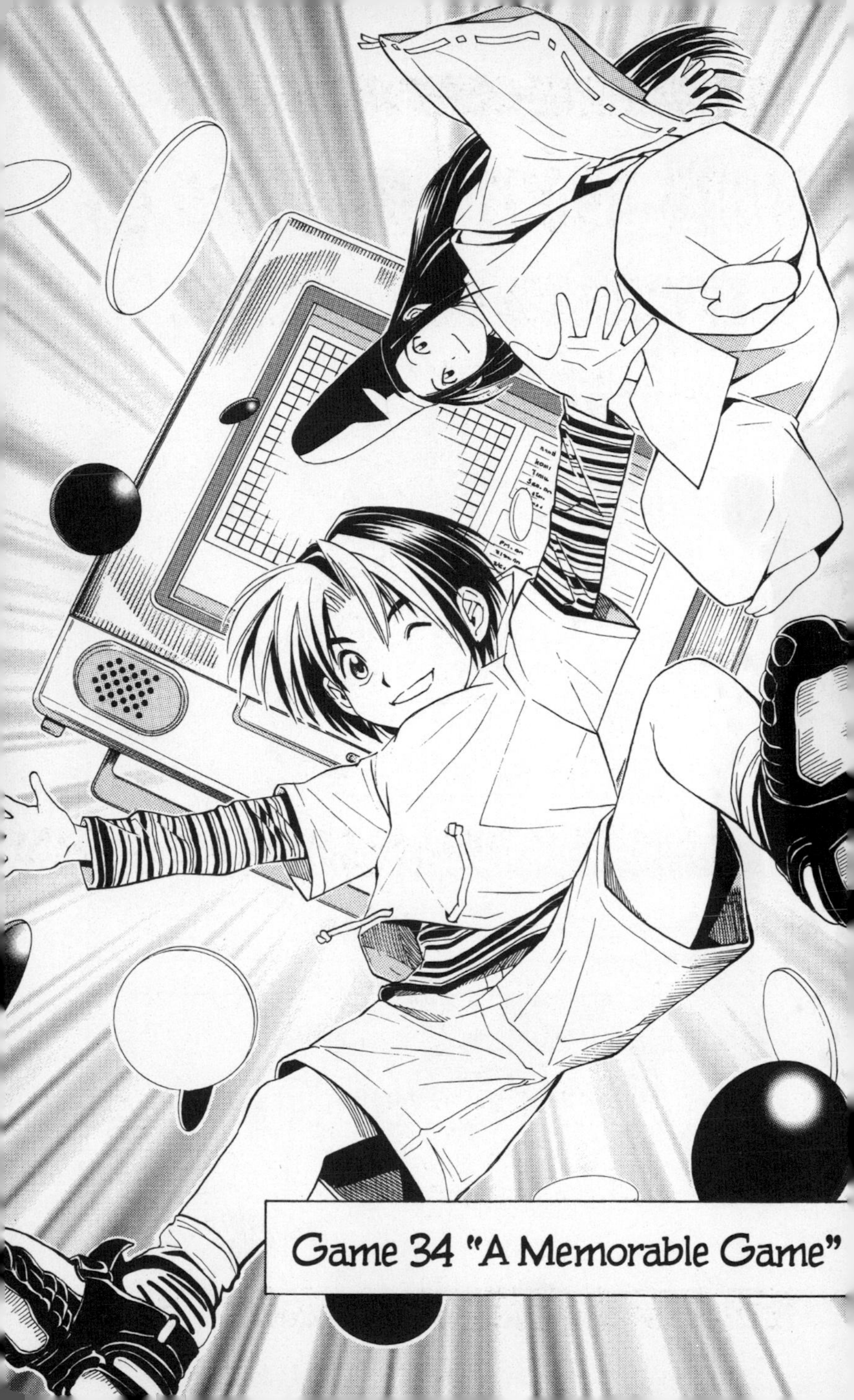
Game 34 "A Memorable Game"

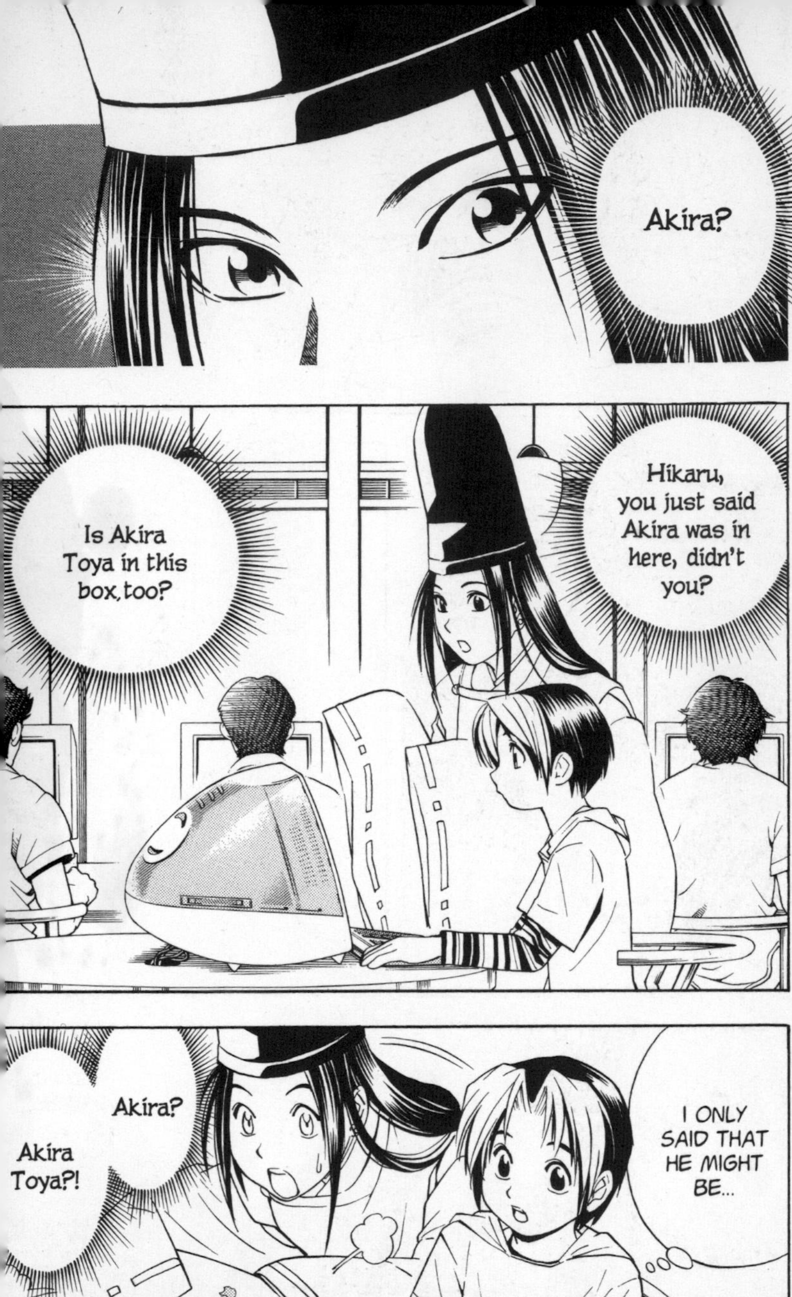
Akira?
Hikaru, you just said Akira was in here, didn't you?
Is Akira Toya in this box, too?
I ONLY SAID THAT HE MIGHT BE...
Akira?
Akira Toya?!

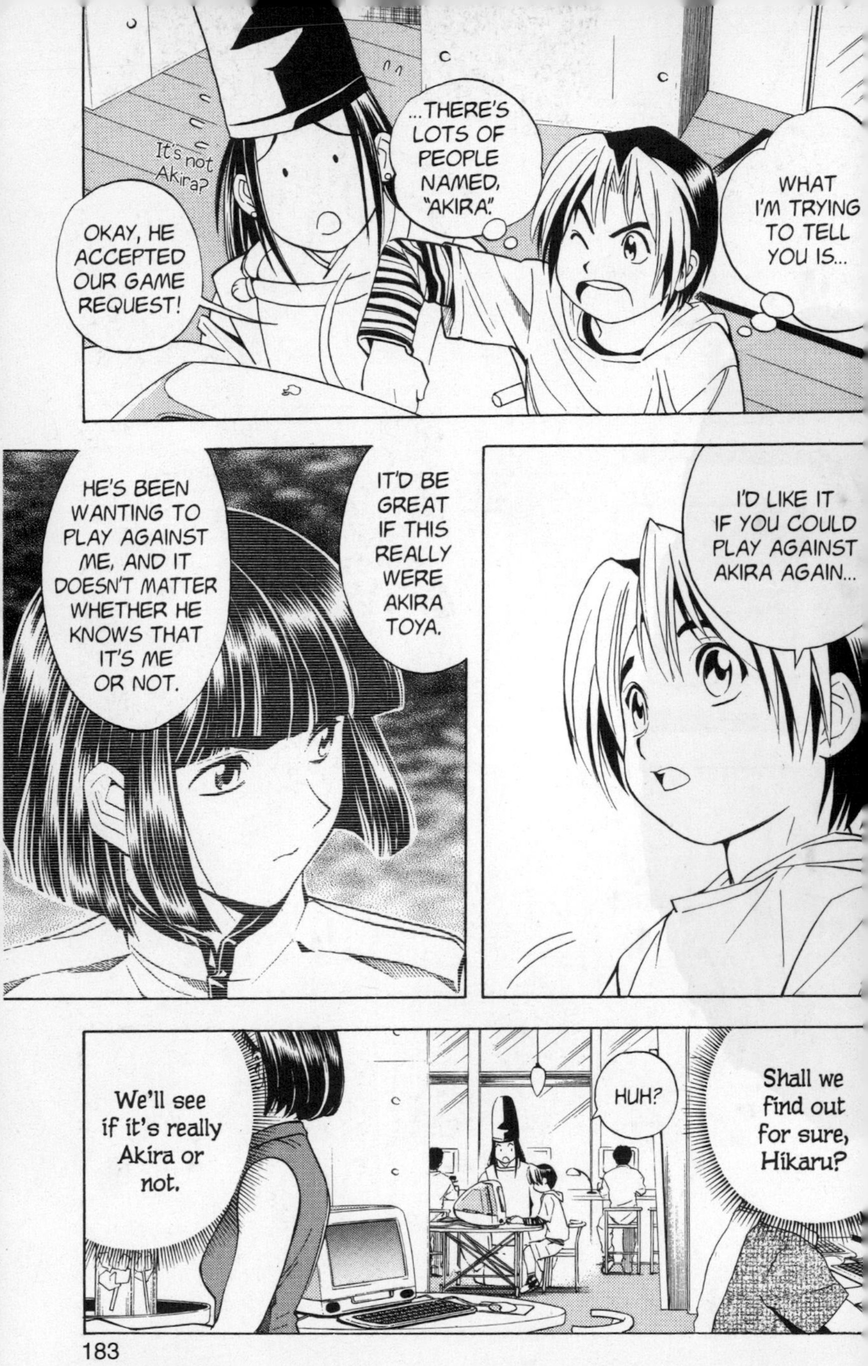
WHAT I'M TRYING TO TELL YOU IS...
...THERE'S LOTS OF PEOPLE NAMED, "AKIRA."
It's not Akira?
OKAY, HE ACCEPTED OUR GAME REQUEST!
I'D LIKE IT IF YOU COULD PLAY AGAINST AKIRA AGAIN...
IT'D BE GREAT IF THIS REALLY WERE AKIRA TOYA.
HE'S BEEN WANTING TO PLAY AGAINST ME, AND IT DOESN'T MATTER WHETHER HE KNOWS THAT IT'S ME OR NOT.
Shall we find out for sure, Hikaru?
HUH?
We'll see if it's really Akira or not.

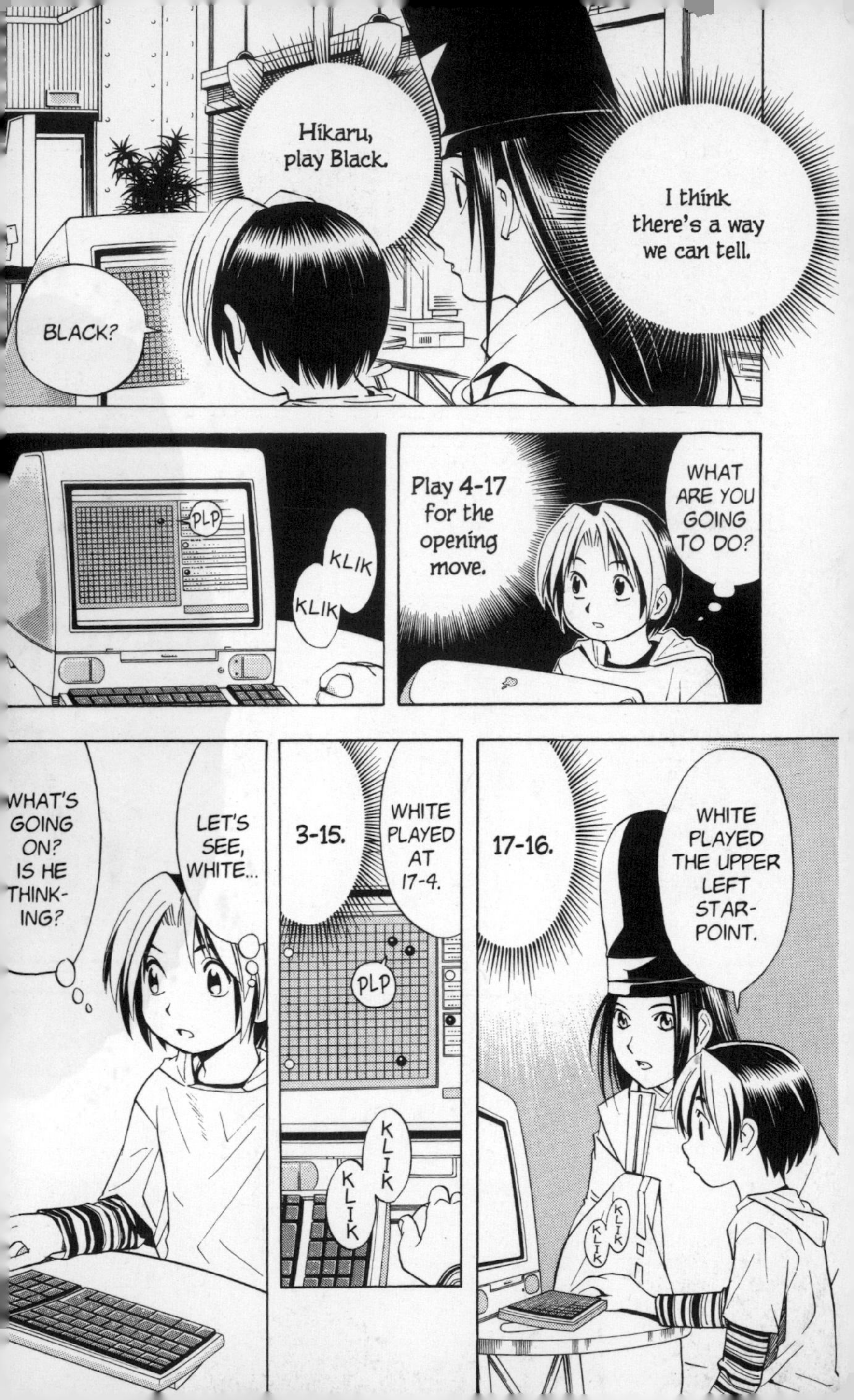
I think there's a way we can tell.
Hikaru, play Black.
BLACK?
WHAT ARE YOU GOING TO DO?
Play 4-17 for the opening move.
KLIK
KLIK
PLP
WHITE PLAYED THE UPPER LEFT STAR-POINT.
17-16.
KLIK
KLIK
WHITE PLAYED AT 17-4.
3-15.
PLP
KLIK
KLIK
LET'S SEE, WHITE...
WHAT'S GOING ON? IS HE THINKING?

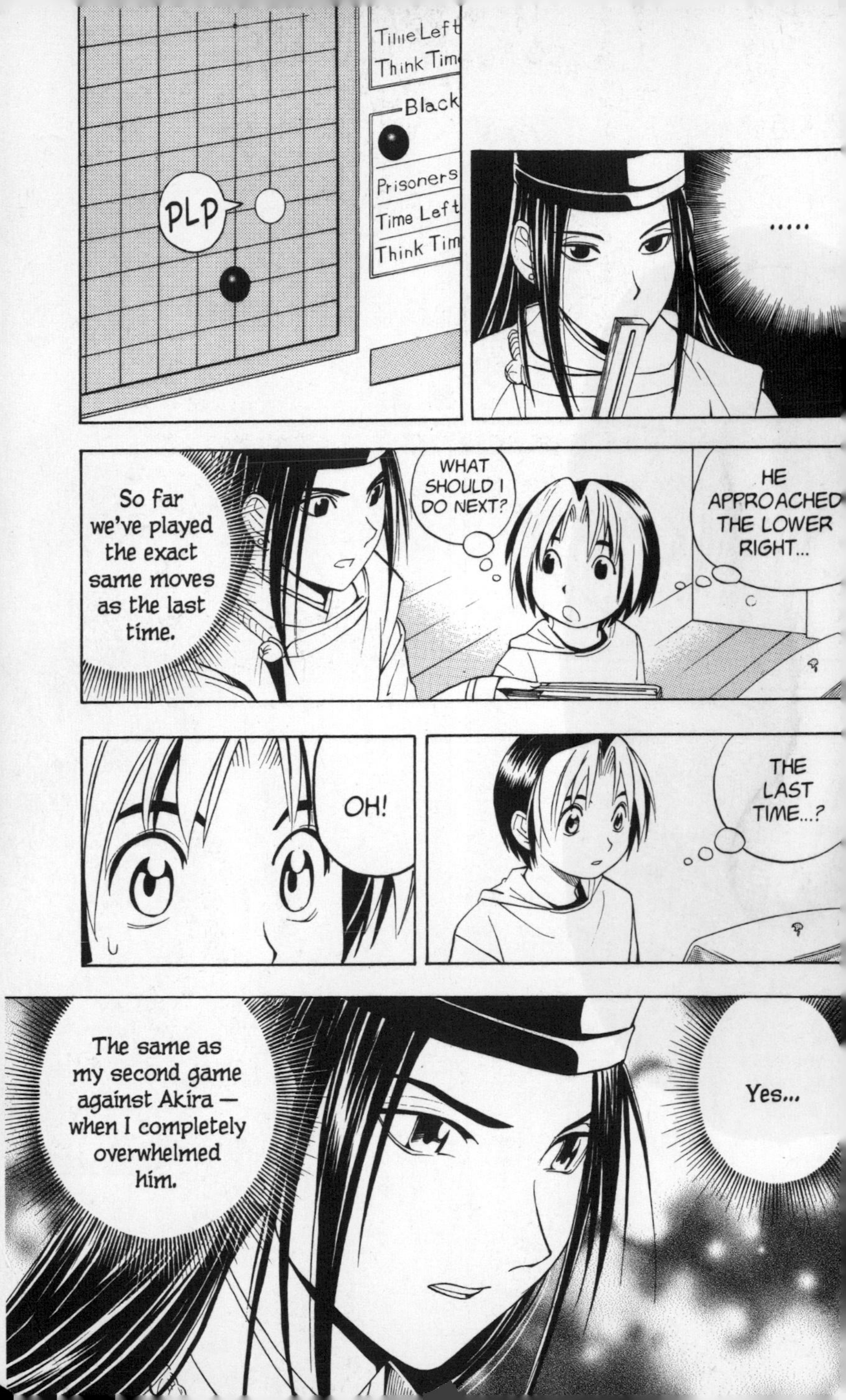
.....
Time Left
Think Tim
Black
Prisoners
Time Left
Think Tim
PLP
HE APPROACHED THE LOWER RIGHT...
WHAT SHOULD I DO NEXT?
So far we've played the exact same moves as the last time.
THE LAST TIME...?
OH!
Yes...
The same as my second game against Akira — when I completely overwhelmed him.

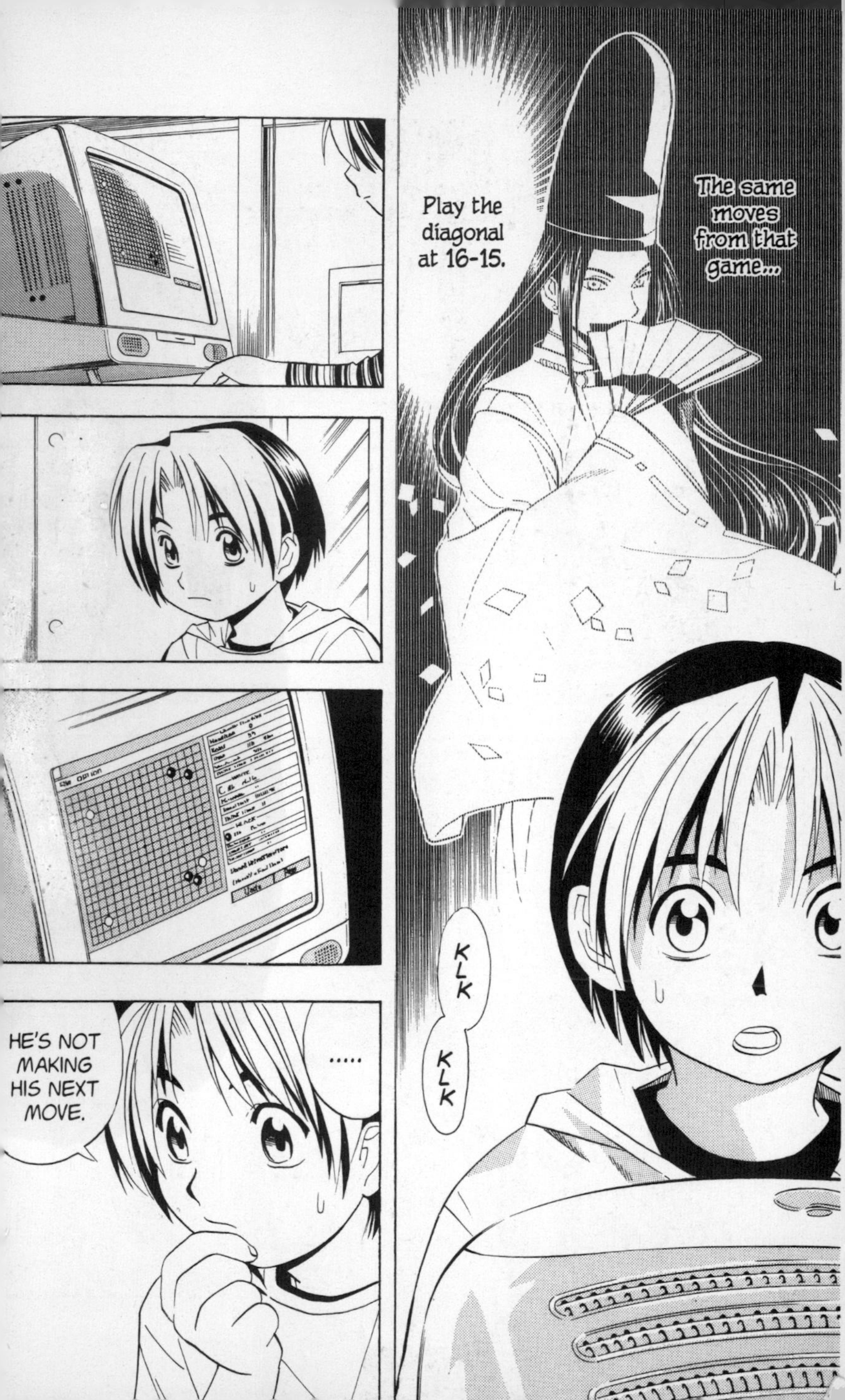
The same moves from that game...
Play the diagonal at 16-15.
KLK
KLK
.....
HE'S NOT MAKING HIS NEXT MOVE.

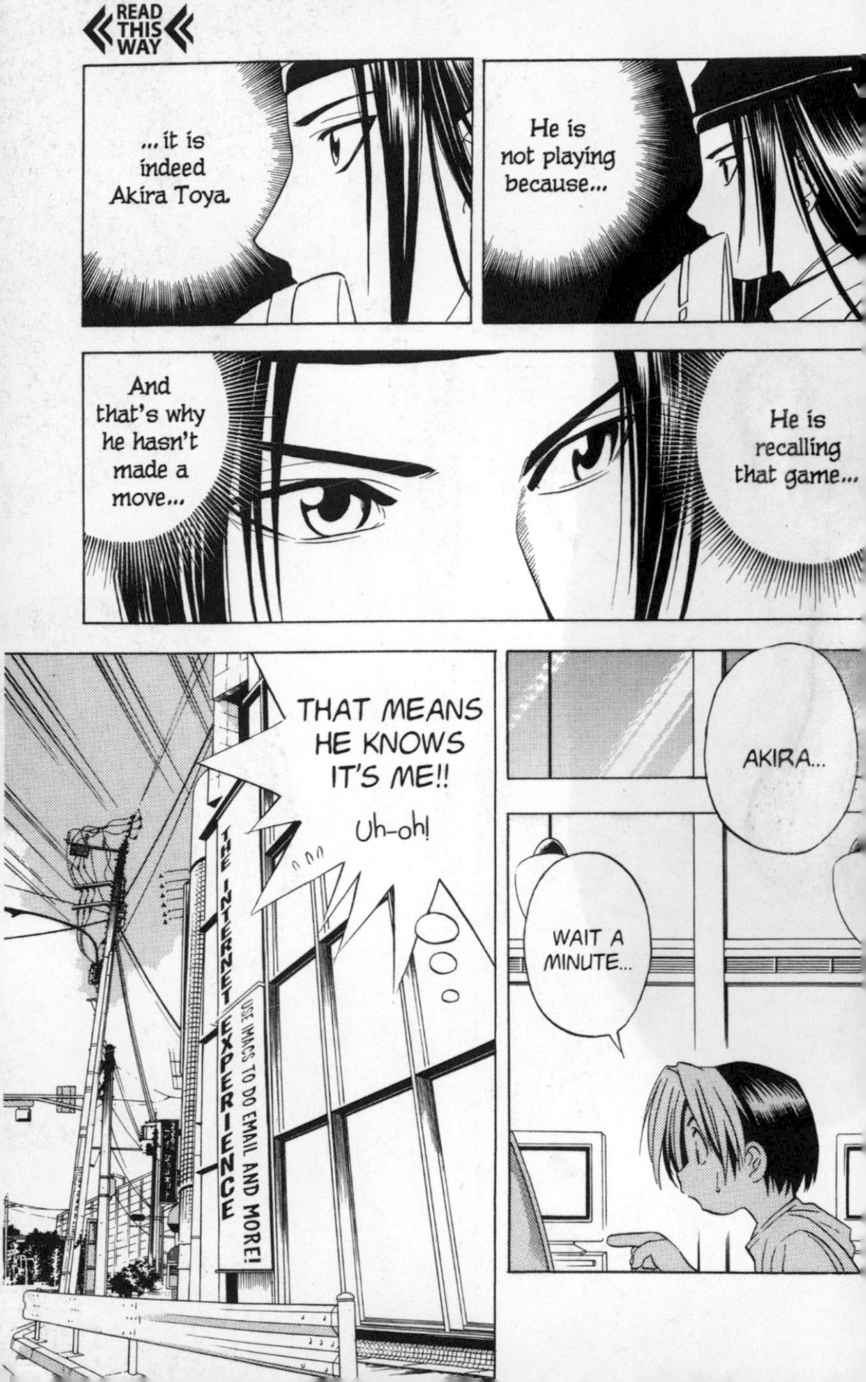
READ THIS WAY
He is not playing because...
...it is indeed Akira Toya.
He is recalling that game...
And that's why he hasn't made a move...
AKIRA...
WAIT A MINUTE...
THAT MEANS HE KNOWS IT'S ME!!
Uh-oh!
THE INTERNET EXPERIENCE
USE IMACS TO DO EMAIL AND MORE!

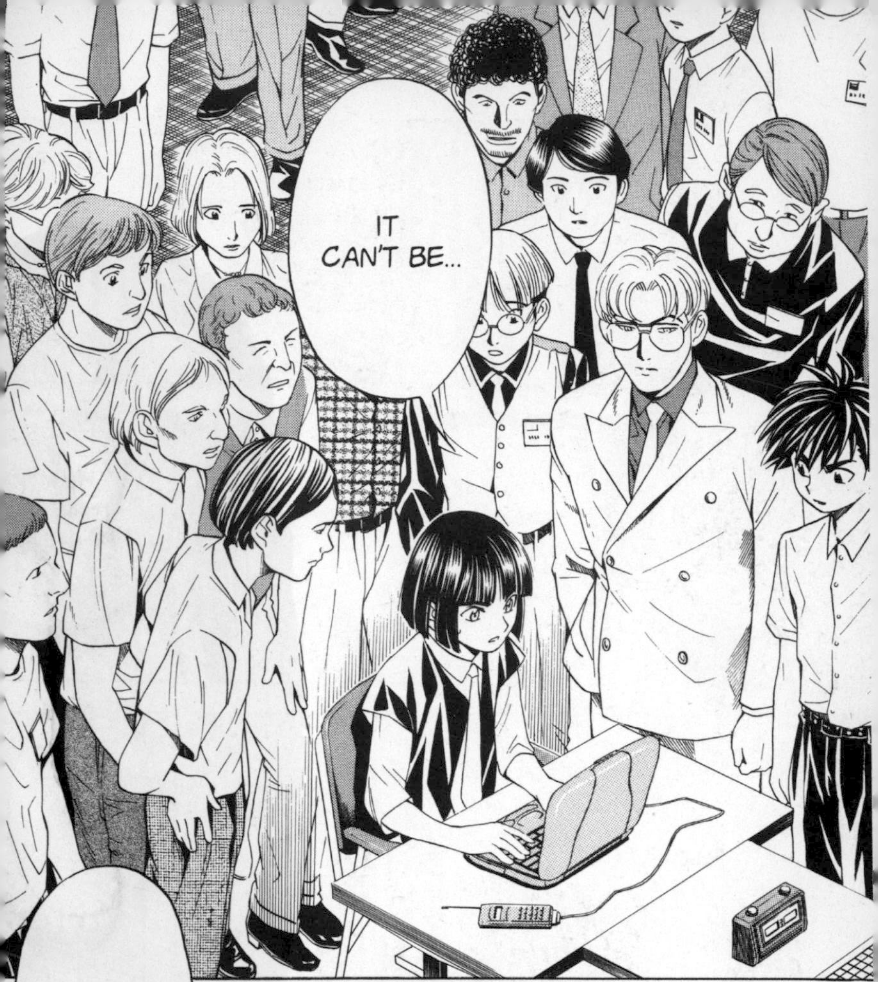
IT CAN'T BE...
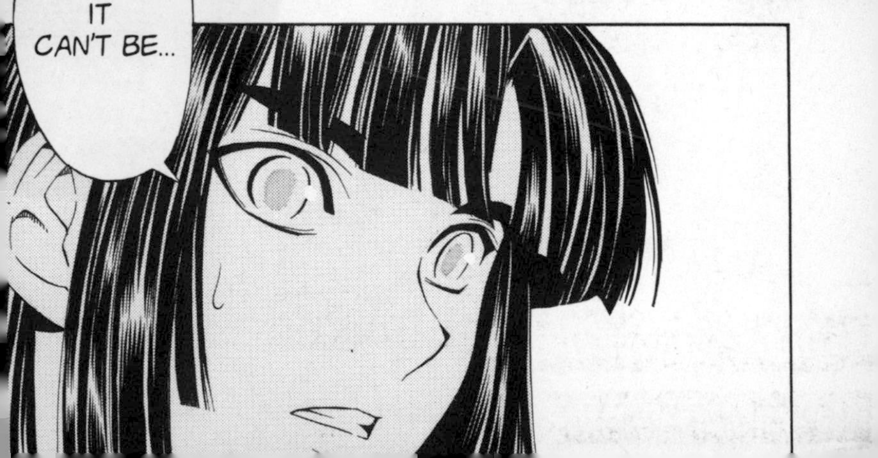
IT CAN'T BE...

READ THIS WAY

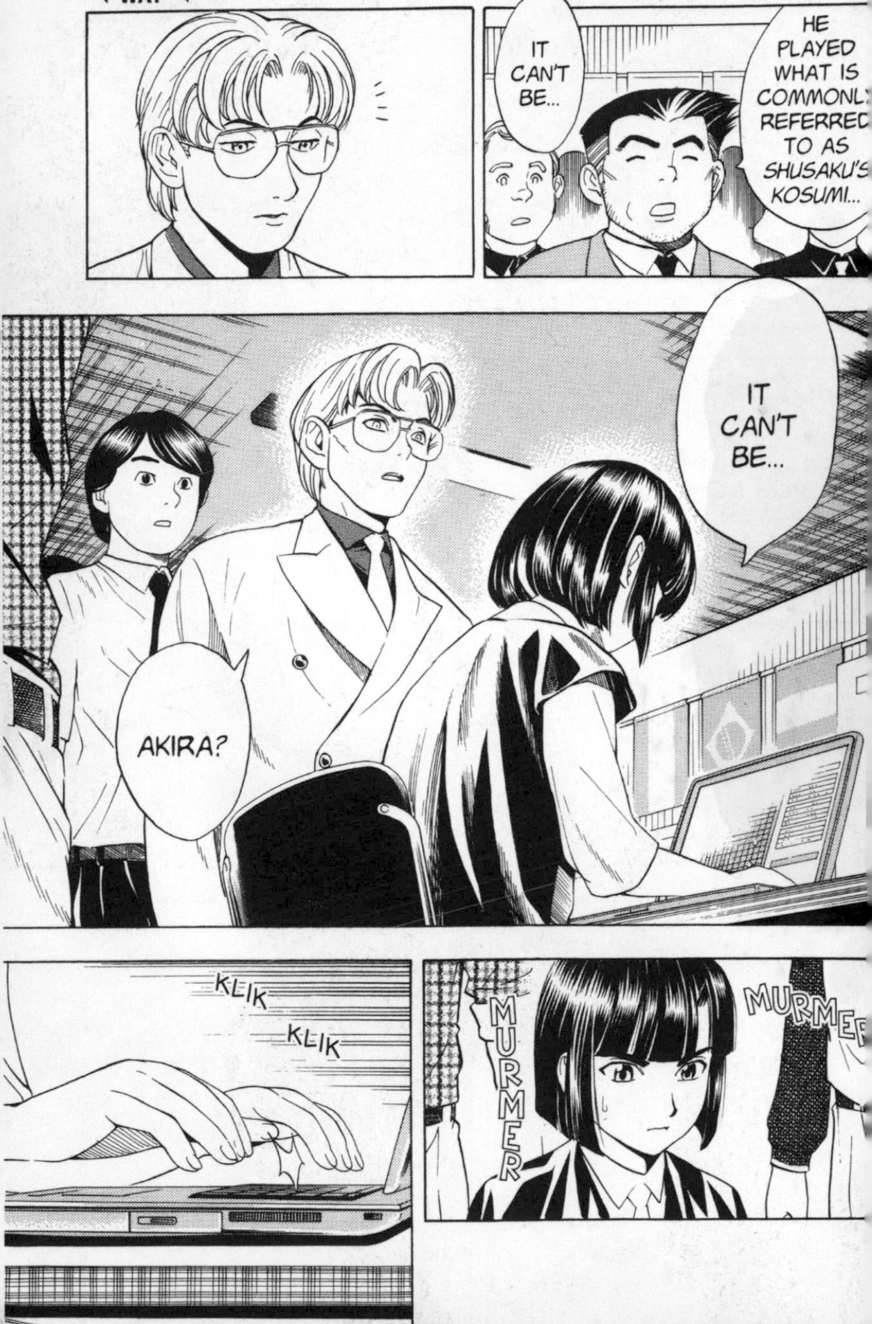

HE PLAYED WHAT IS COMMONLY REFERRED TO AS SHUSAKU'S KOSUMI...
IT CAN'T BE...
IT CAN'T BE...
AKIRA?
MURMER
MURMER
KLIK
KLIK

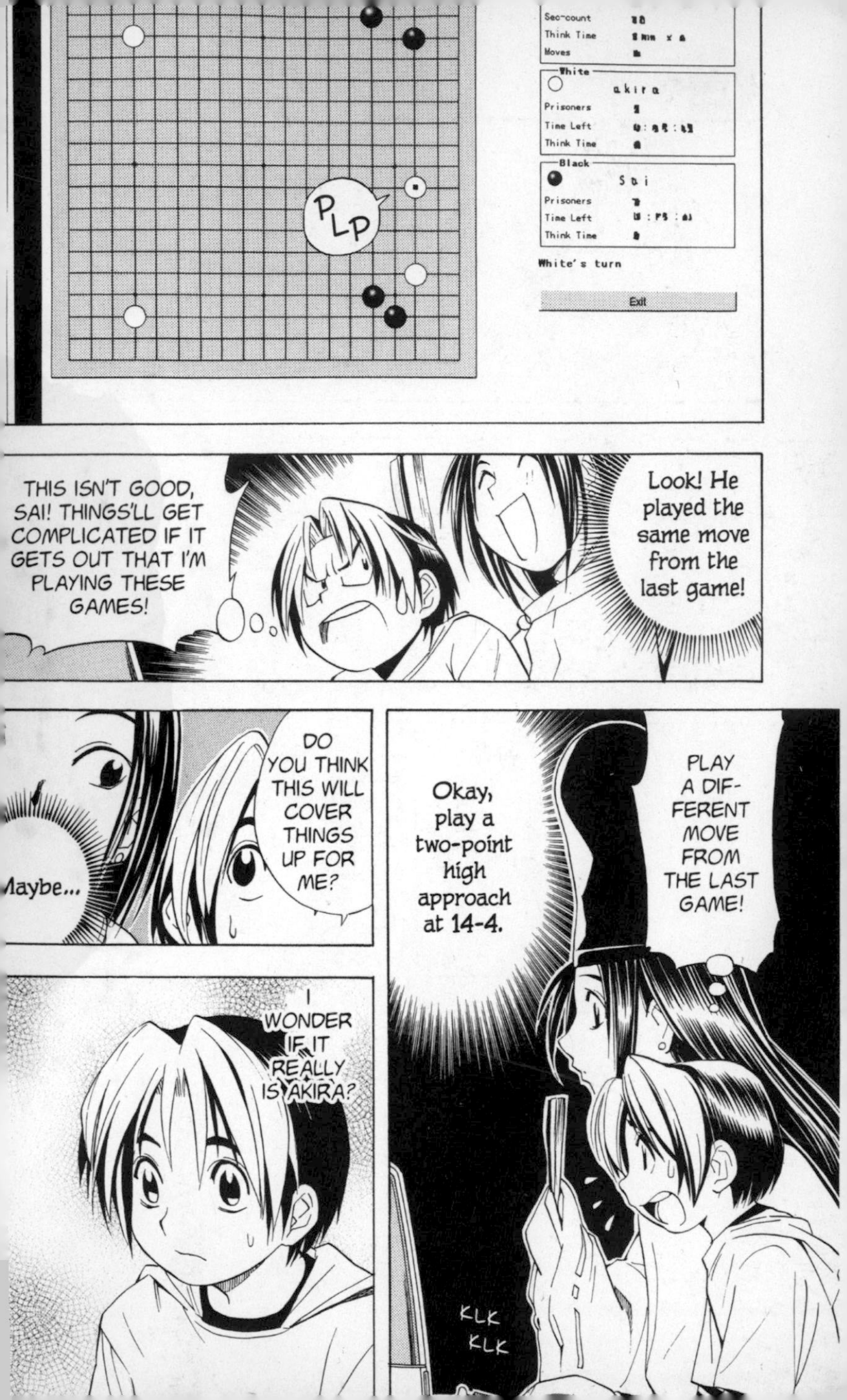
Sec-count
Think Time
Moves
White
akira
Prisoners
Time Left
Think Time
Black
Sai
Prisoners
Time Left
Think Time
White's turn
Exit
PLP
Look! He played the same move from the last game!
THIS ISN'T GOOD, SAI! THINGS'LL GET COMPLICATED IF IT GETS OUT THAT I'M PLAYING THESE GAMES!
PLAY A DIF-FERENT MOVE FROM THE LAST GAME!
Okay, play a two-point high approach at 14-4.
KLK KLK
DO YOU THINK THIS WILL COVER THINGS UP FOR ME?
aybe...
I WONDER IF IT REALLY IS AKIRA?

READ THIS WAY

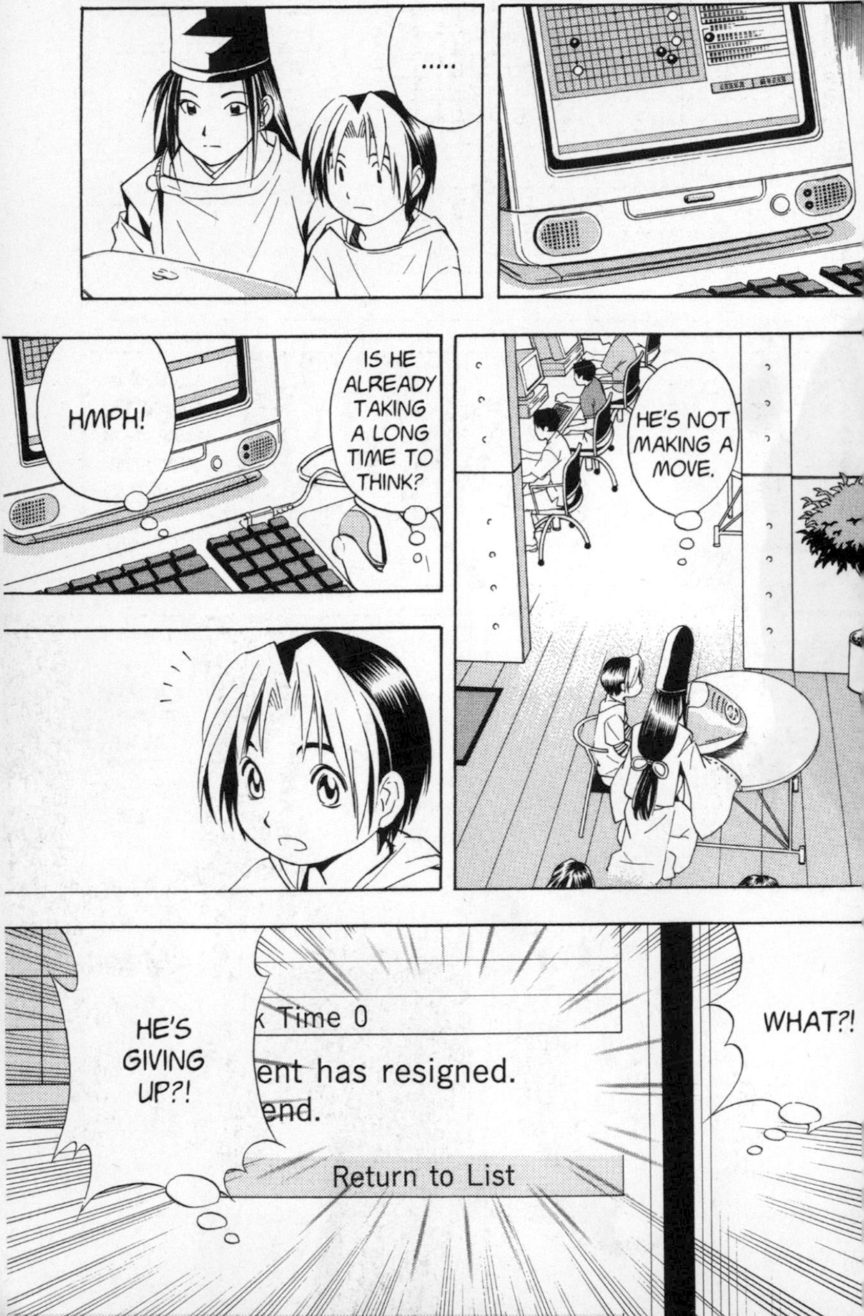

.....
HE'S NOT MAKING A MOVE.
IS HE ALREADY TAKING A LONG TIME TO THINK?
HMPH!
WHAT?!
Time 0
ent has resigned.
end.
Return to List
HE'S GIVING UP?!

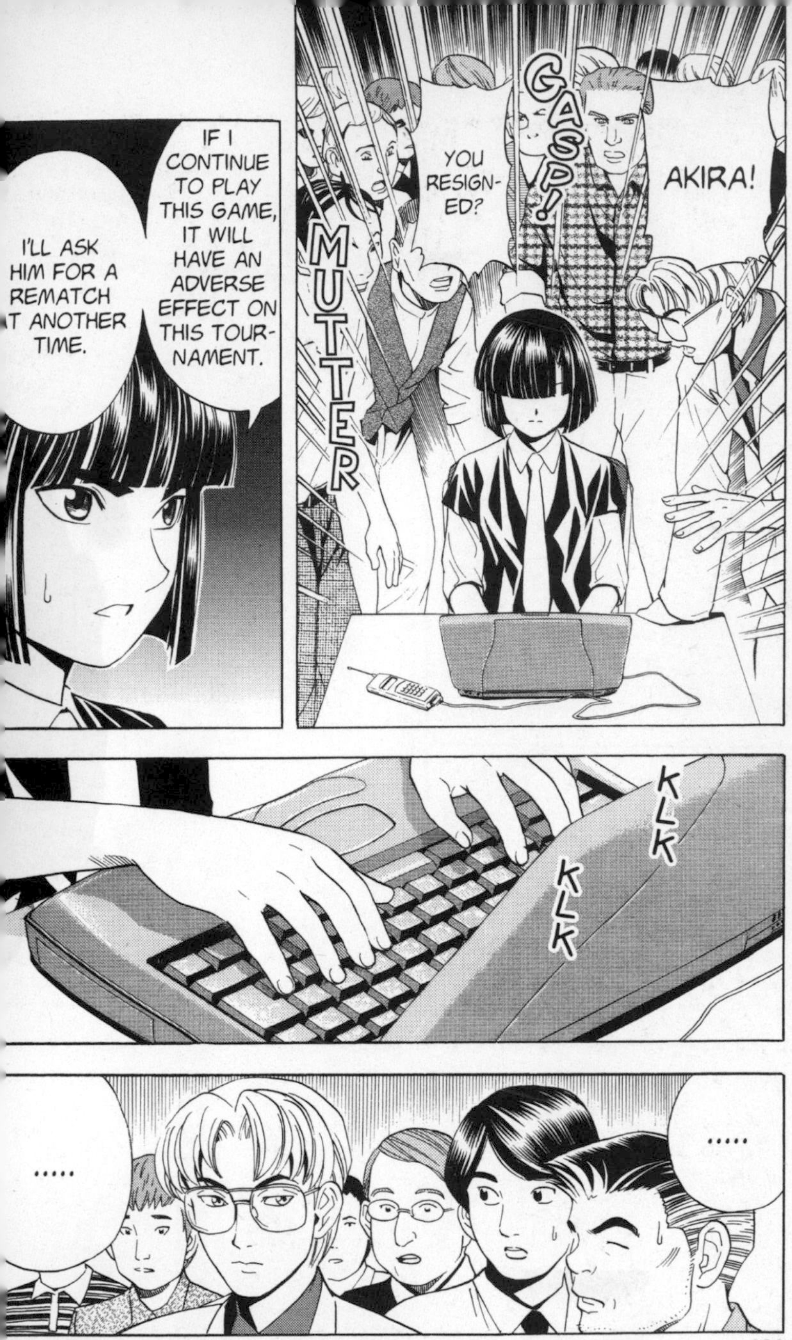
AKIRA!
GASP!
YOU RESIGN-ED?
MUTTER
IF I CONTINUE TO PLAY THIS GAME, IT WILL HAVE AN ADVERSE EFFECT ON THIS TOUR-NAMENT.
I'LL ASK HIM FOR A REMATCH T ANOTHER TIME.
KLK
KLK
.....
.....

READ THIS WAY

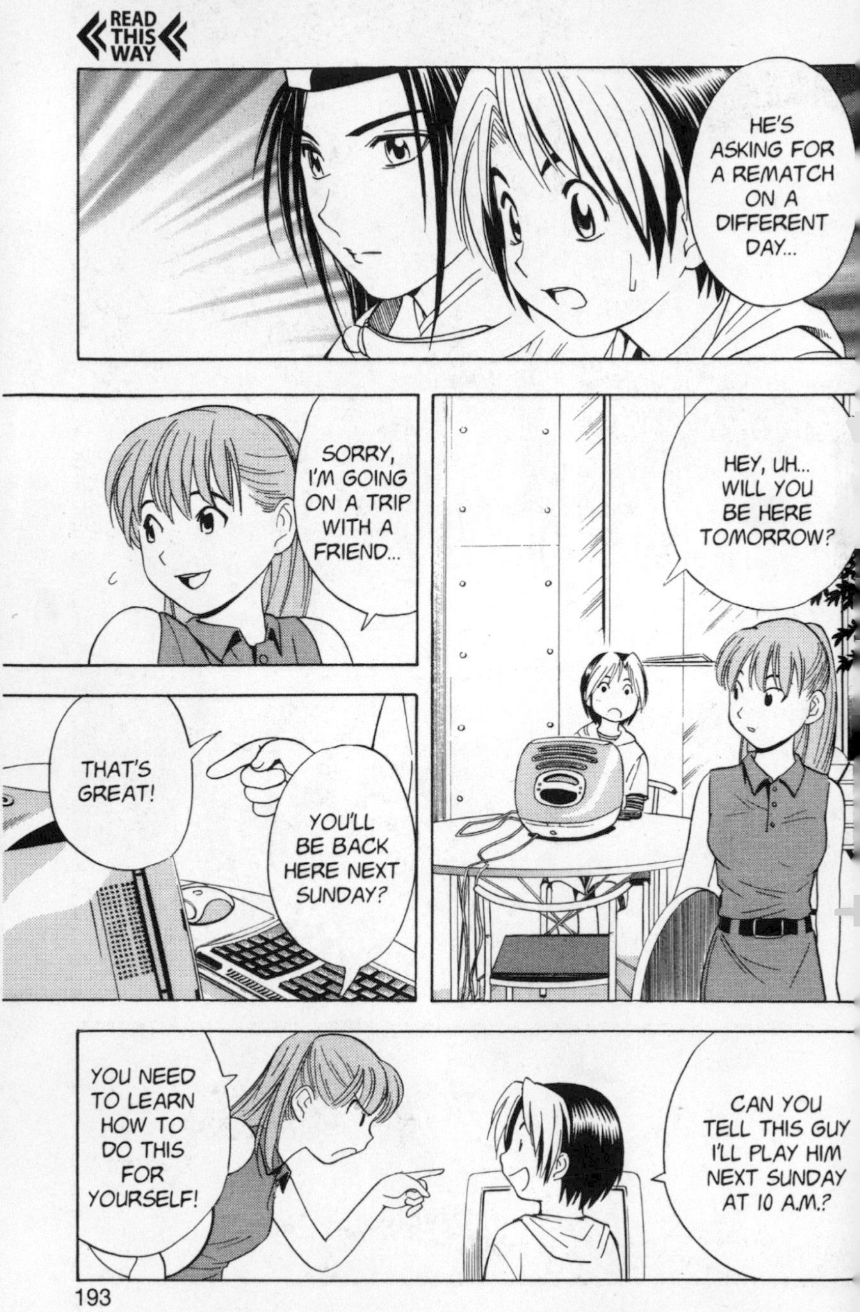

HE'S ASKING FOR A REMATCH ON A DIFFERENT DAY...
HEY, UH... WILL YOU BE HERE TOMORROW?
SORRY, I'M GOING ON A TRIP WITH A FRIEND...
YOU'LL BE BACK HERE NEXT SUNDAY?
THAT'S GREAT!
CAN YOU TELL THIS GUY I'LL PLAY HIM NEXT SUNDAY AT 10 A.M.?
YOU NEED TO LEARN HOW TO DO THIS FOR YOURSELF!

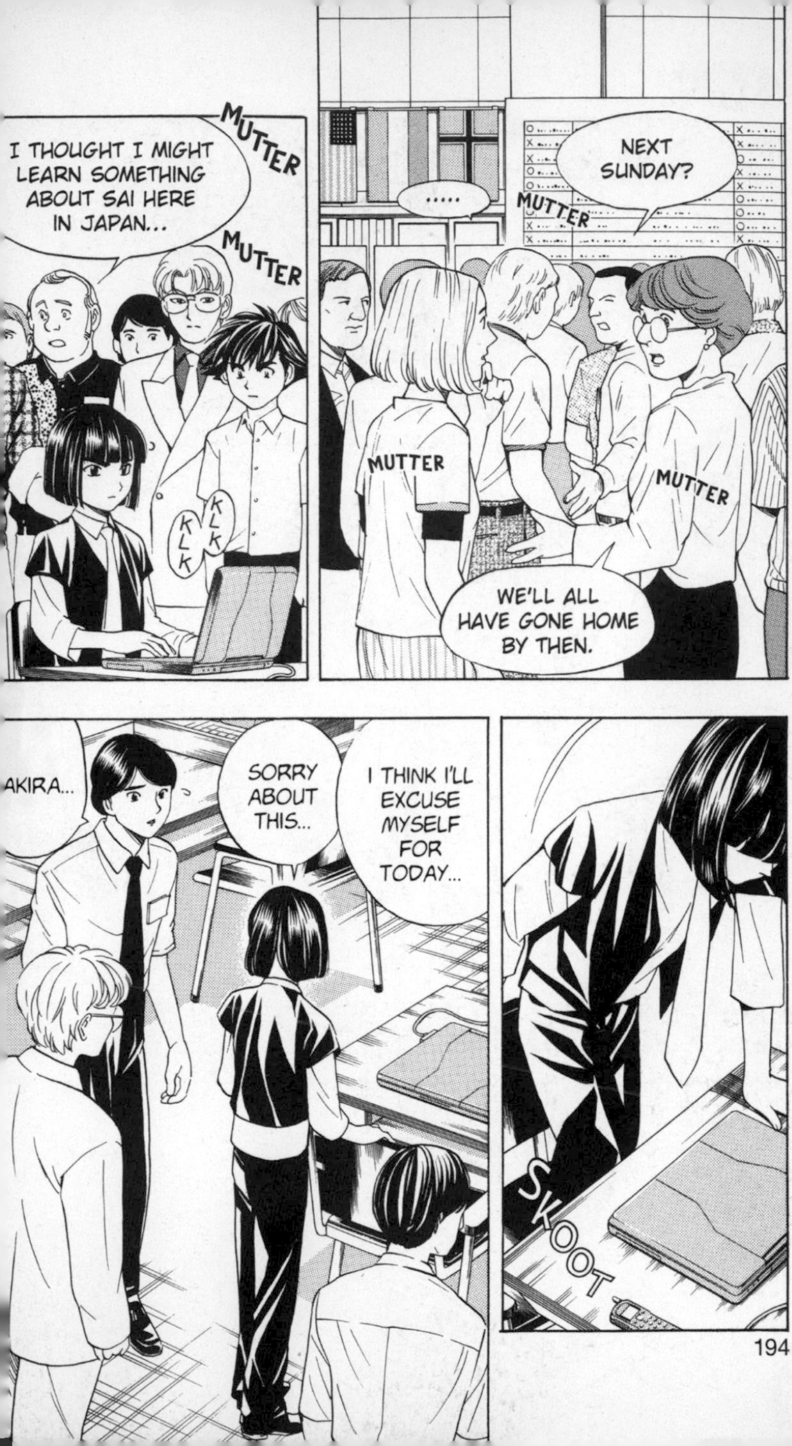
NEXT SUNDAY?
.....
MUTTER
MUTTER
MUTTER
WE'LL ALL HAVE GONE HOME BY THEN.
MUTTER
I THOUGHT I MIGHT LEARN SOMETHING ABOUT SAI HERE IN JAPAN...
MUTTER
KLK
KLK
SKOOT
SORRY ABOUT THIS...
I THINK I'LL EXCUSE MYSELF FOR TODAY...
AKIRA...

READ THIS WAY

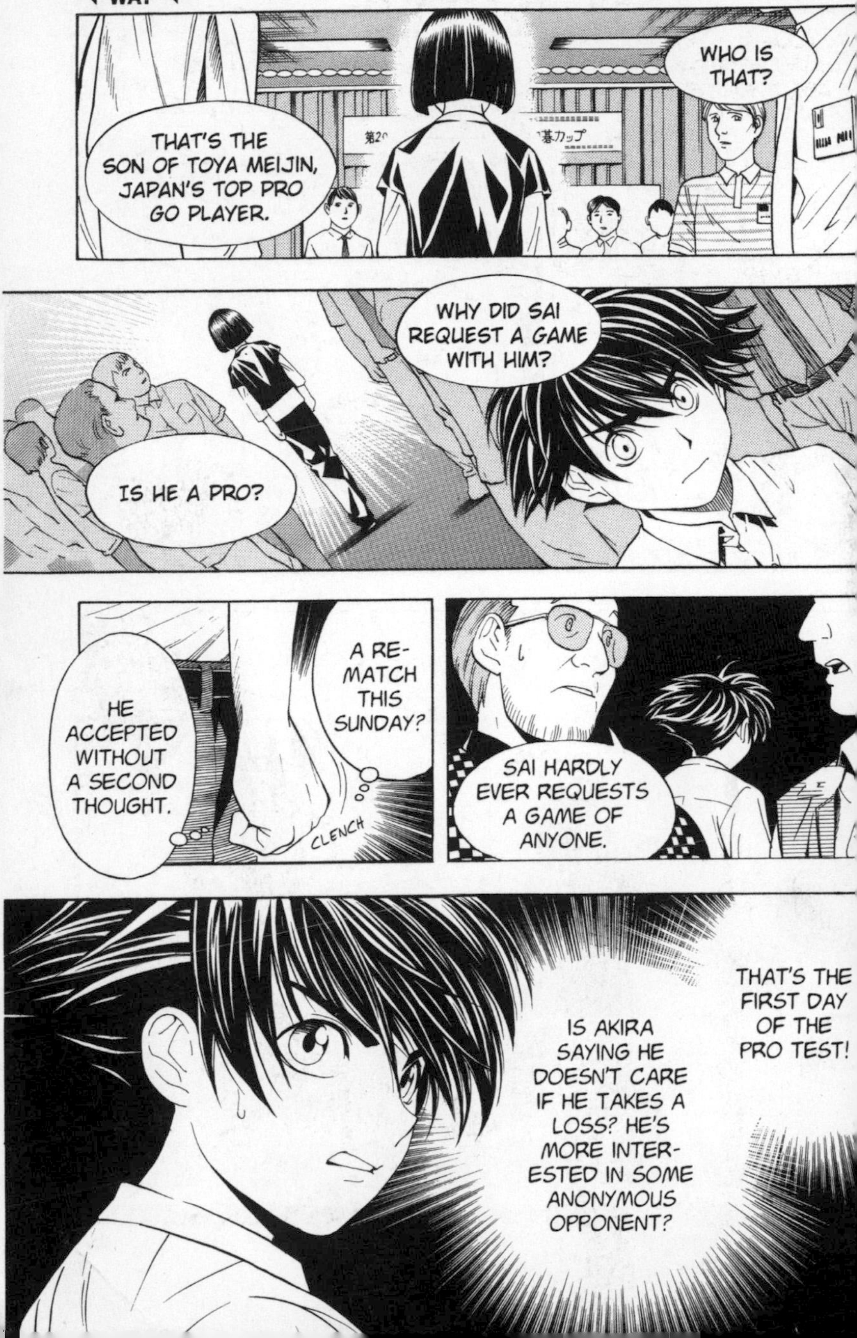
WHO IS THAT?
THAT'S THE SON OF TOYA MEIJIN, JAPAN'S TOP PRO GO PLAYER.
WHY DID SAI REQUEST A GAME WITH HIM?
IS HE A PRO?
SAI HARDLY EVER REQUESTS A GAME OF ANYONE.
A RE-MATCH THIS SUNDAY?
HE ACCEPTED WITHOUT A SECOND THOUGHT.
CLENCH
THAT'S THE FIRST DAY OF THE PRO TEST!
IS AKIRA SAYING HE DOESN'T CARE IF HE TAKES A LOSS? HE'S MORE INTER-ESTED IN SOME ANONYMOUS OPPONENT?

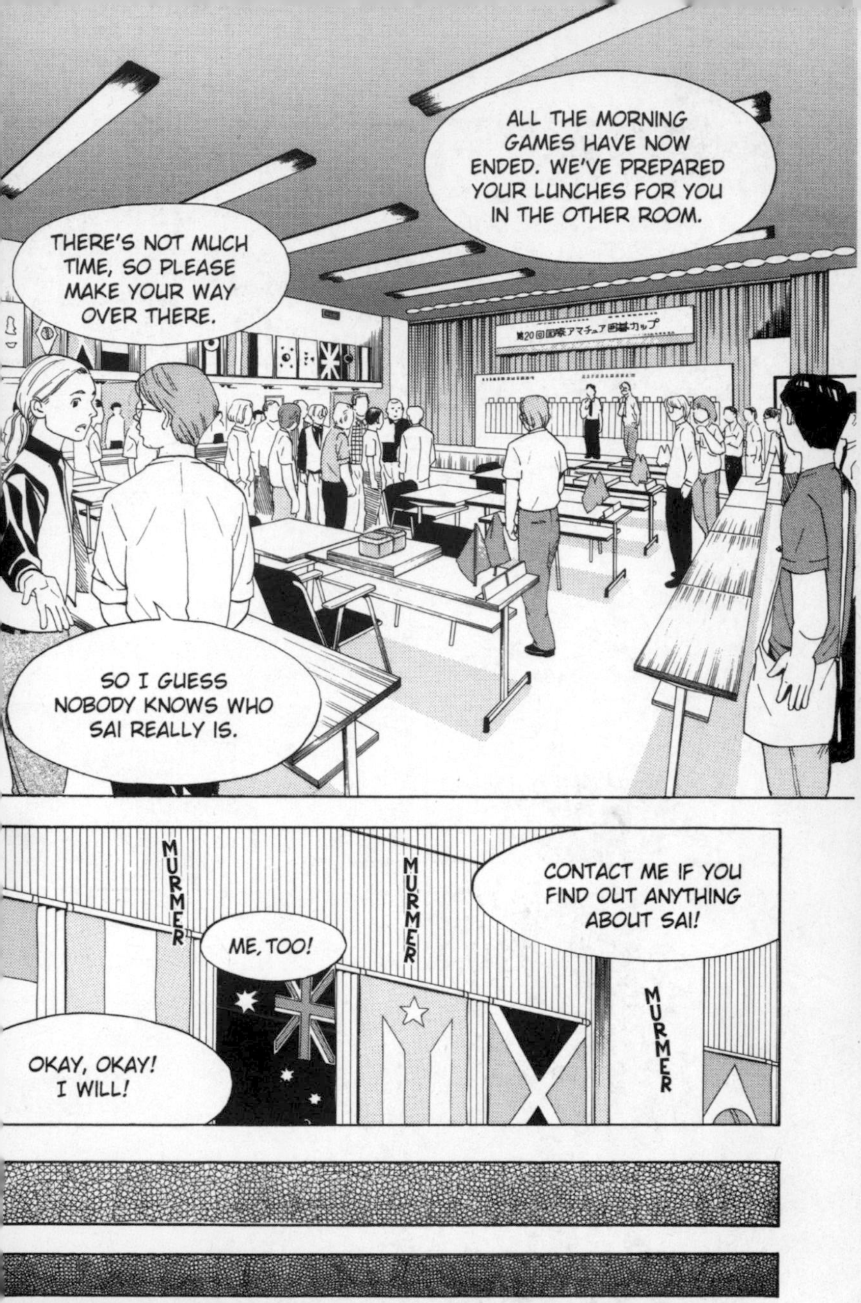
ALL THE MORNING GAMES HAVE NOW ENDED. WE'VE PREPARED YOUR LUNCHES FOR YOU IN THE OTHER ROOM.
第20回国際アマチュア囲碁カップ
THERE'S NOT MUCH TIME, SO PLEASE MAKE YOUR WAY OVER THERE.
SO I GUESS NOBODY KNOWS WHO SAI REALLY IS.
MURMER
CONTACT ME IF YOU FIND OUT ANYTHING ABOUT SAI!
MURMER
ME, TOO!
MURMER
OKAY, OKAY! I WILL!

READ THIS WAY

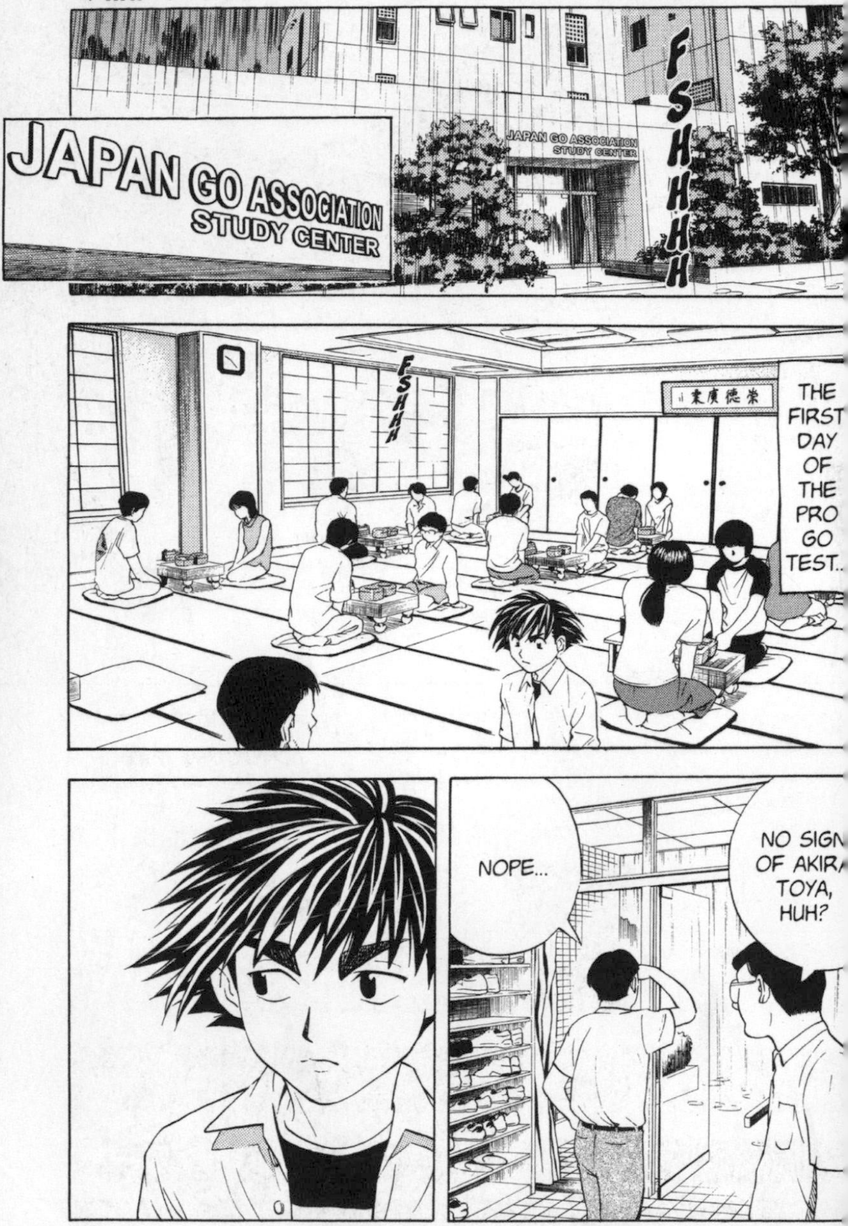
JAPAN GO ASSOCIATION STUDY CENTER
JAPAN GO ASSOCIATION STUDY CENTER
FSHHHH
THE FIRST DAY OF THE PRO GO TEST...
FSHHH
NO SIGN OF AKIRA TOYA, HUH?
NOPE...

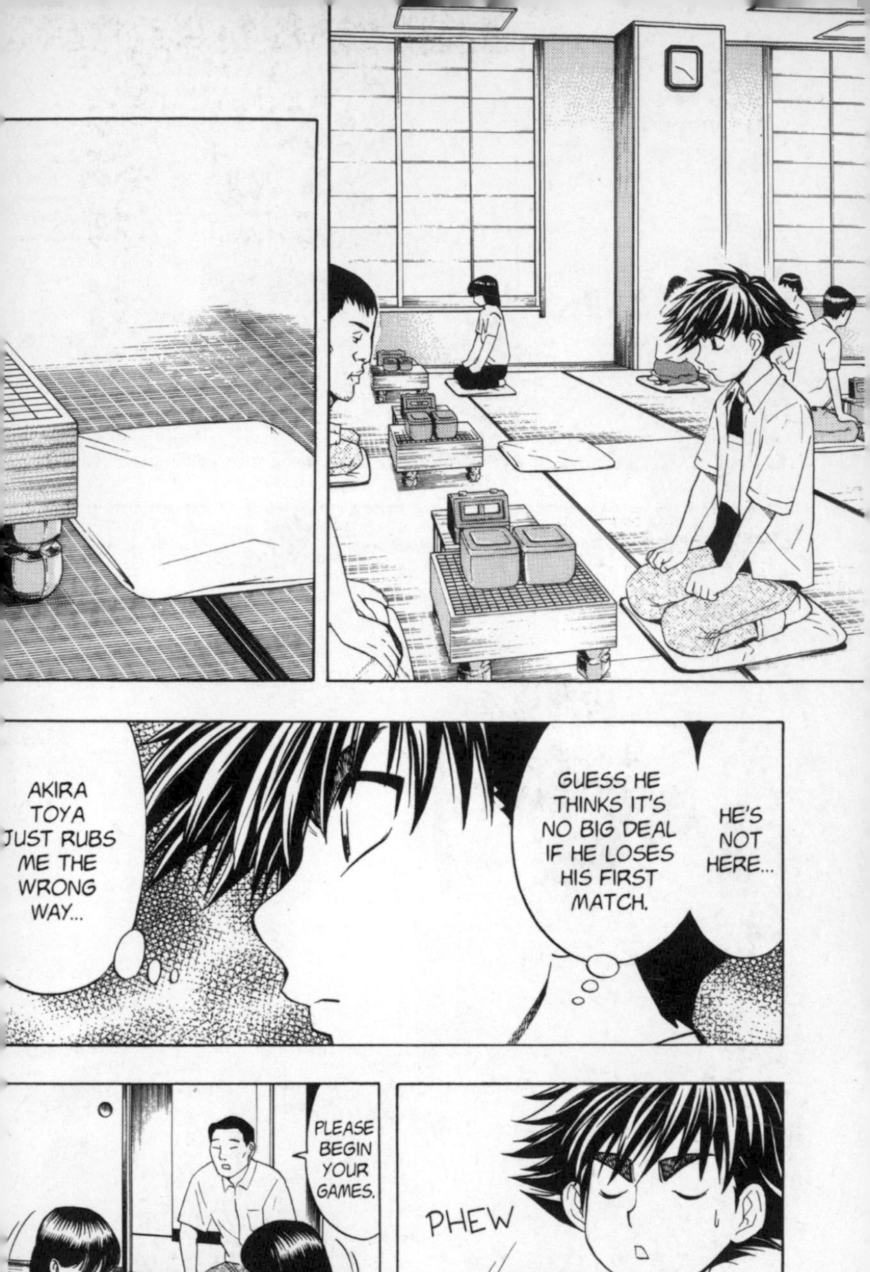
HE'S NOT HERE...
GUESS HE THINKS IT'S NO BIG DEAL IF HE LOSES HIS FIRST MATCH.
AKIRA TOYA JUST RUBS ME THE WRONG WAY...
PHEW
PLEASE BEGIN YOUR GAMES.

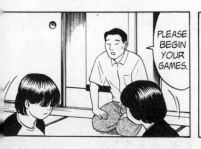

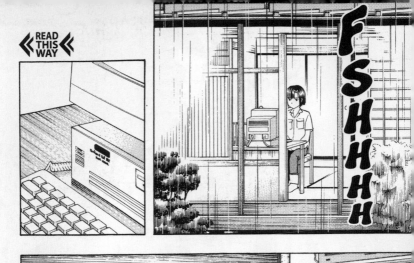

FSHHHH

The End of
Divine
Illusions

Preview

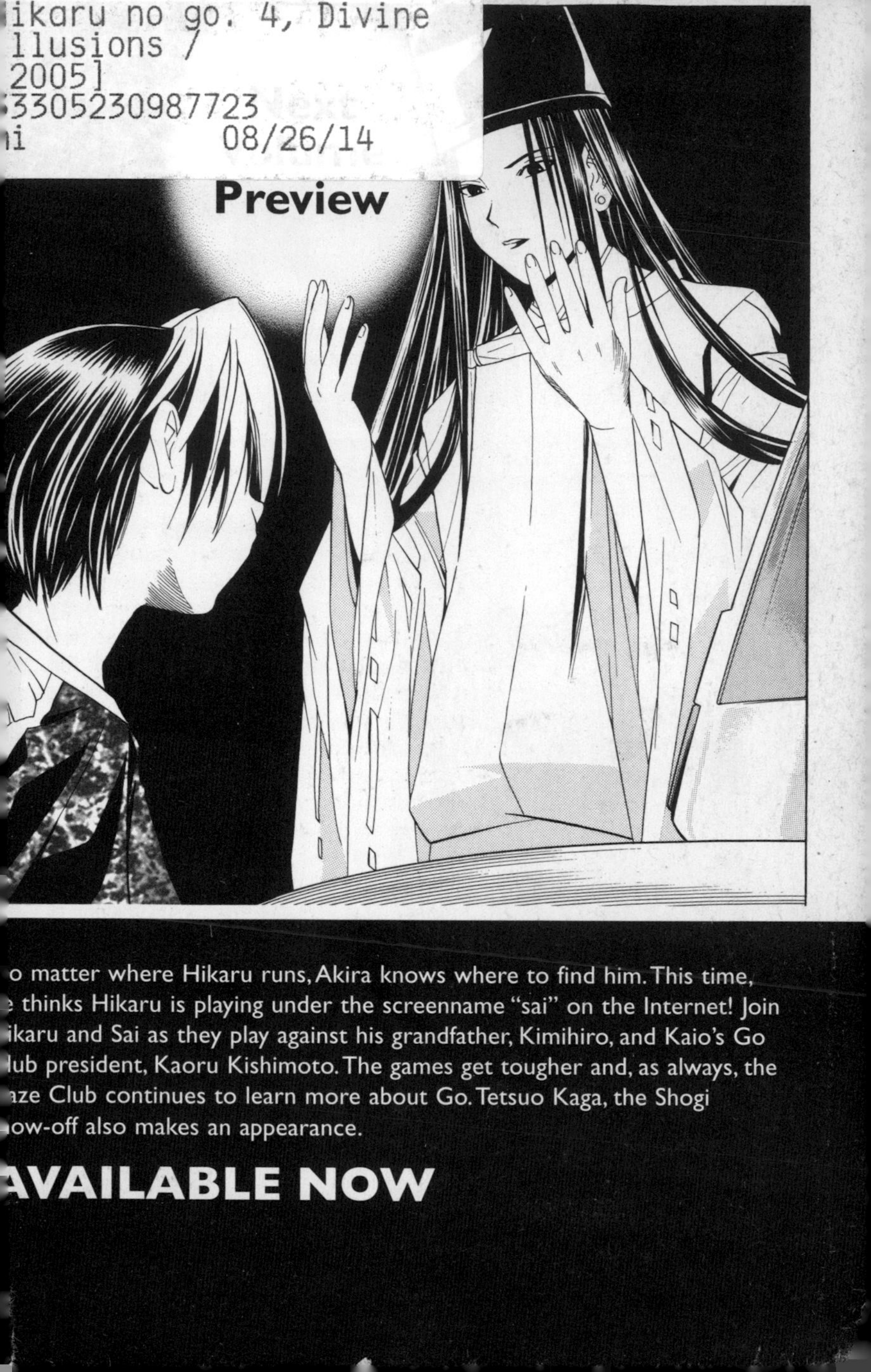

o matter where Hikaru runs, Akira knows where to find him. This time, e thinks Hikaru is playing under the screenname "sai" on the Internet! Join ikaru and Sai as they play against his grandfather, Kimihiro, and Kaio's Go lub president, Kaoru Kishimoto. The games get tougher and, as always, the aze Club continues to learn more about Go. Tetsuo Kaga, the Shogi ow-off also makes an appearance.

AVAILABLE NOW